Placing Internationalism

Histories of Internationalism

Series Editors:
Jessica Reinisch, Birkbeck, University of London, UK
David Brydan, King's College London, UK

Editorial Board:
Tomoko Akami, Australian National University, Australia
Martin Conway, University of Oxford, UK
Adom Getachew, University of Chicago, USA
Sandrine Kott, University of Geneva, Switzerland
Stephen Legg, University of Nottingham, UK
Su Lin Lewis, University of Bristol, UK
Erez Manela, Harvard University, USA
Samuel Moyn, Yale University, USA
Alanna O'Malley, Leiden University, Netherlands
Kiran Patel, Ludwig Maximilian University of Munich, Germany
Tehila Sasson, Emory University, USA
Frank Trentmann, Birkbeck, University of London, UK
Heidi Tworek, University of British Columbia, Canada

This new book series features cutting-edge research on the history of international cooperation and internationalising ambitions in the modern world. Providing an intellectual home for research into the many guises of internationalism, its titles draw on methods and insights from political, social, cultural, economic and intellectual history. It showcases a rapidly expanding scholarship which has begun to transform our understanding of internationalism.

Cutting across established academic fields such as European, World, International and Global History, the series will critically examine historical perceptions of geography, regions, centres, peripheries, borderlands and connections across space in the history of internationalism. It will include both monographs and edited volumes that shed new light on local and global contexts for international projects; the impact of class, race and gender on international aspirations; the roles played by a variety of international organisations and institutions; and the hopes, fears, tensions and conflicts underlying them.

The series is published in association with Birkbeck's Centre for the Study of Internationalism.

Published:
Internationalists in European History: Rethinking the Twentieth Century, Jessica Reinisch and David Brydan (eds)
Organizing the 20th-Century World: International Organizations and the Emergence of International Public Administration, 1920-1960s, Karen Gram-Skjoldager, Haakon Andreas Ikonomou, Torsten Kahlert (eds)
International Cooperation in Cold War Europe: The United Nations Economic Commission for Europe, 1947-64, Daniel Stinsky

Forthcoming:
Relief and Rehabilitation for a Postwar World: Humanitarian Intervention and the UNRRA?, Samantha K. Knapton and Katherine Rossy (eds)
Inventing the Third World: In Search of Freedom for the Postwar Global South, Jeremy Adelman and Gyan Prakash (eds)

Placing Internationalism

International Conferences and the Making of the Modern World

Edited by
Stephen Legg, Mike Heffernan, Jake Hodder and
Benjamin J. Thorpe

BLOOMSBURY ACADEMIC
LONDON • NEW YORK • OXFORD • NEW DELHI • SYDNEY

BLOOMSBURY ACADEMIC
Bloomsbury Publishing Plc
50 Bedford Square, London, WC1B 3DP, UK
1385 Broadway, New York, NY 10018, USA
29 Earlsfort Terrace, Dublin 2, Ireland

BLOOMSBURY, BLOOMSBURY ACADEMIC and the Diana logo are trademarks of Bloomsbury Publishing Plc

First published in Great Britain 2022
This paperback edition published 2023

Copyright ©Stephen Legg, Mike Heffernan, Jake Hodder and Benjamin J. Thorpe, 2022

Stephen Legg, Mike Heffernan, Jake Hodder and Benjamin J. Thorpe have asserted their rights under the Copyright, Designs and Patents Act, 1988, to be identified as Authors of this work.

For legal purposes the Acknowledgements on p. xi constitute an extension of this copyright page.

Cover design: Terry Woodley
Cover image © The Fifth Pan-African Congress, held at Chorlton-upon-Medlock Town Hall in Manchester, 15th - 21st October 1945. Photo by John Deakin/Picture Post/Hulton Archive/Getty Images.

All rights reserved. No part of this publication may be reproduced or transmitted in any form or by any means, electronic or mechanical, including photocopying, recording, or any information storage or retrieval system, without prior permission in writing from the publishers.

Bloomsbury Publishing Plc does not have any control over, or responsibility for, any third-party websites referred to or in this book. All internet addresses given in this book were correct at the time of going to press. The author and publisher regret any inconvenience caused if addresses have changed or sites have ceased to exist, but can accept no responsibility for any such changes.

A catalogue record for this book is available from the British Library.

Library of Congress Cataloging-in-Publication Data
Names: Legg, Stephen, editor.
Title: Placing internationalism: international conferences and the making of the modern world / Edited by Stephen Legg, Mike Heffernan, Jake Hodder and Benjamin Thorpe.
Description: London; New York: Bloomsbury Academic, 2021. | Series: Histories of internationalism | Includes bibliographical references and index.
Identifiers: LCCN 2021025529 (print) | LCCN 2021025530 (ebook) | ISBN 9781350247185 (hardback) | ISBN 9781350247192 (ebook) | ISBN 9781350247208 (epub)
Subjects: LCSH: Internationalism. | Congresses and conventions. | International organization. | World politics.
Classification: LCC JZ1308 .P573 2021 (print) | LCC JZ1308 (ebook) | DDC 320.54/8–dc23
LC record available at https://lccn.loc.gov/2021025529
LC ebook record available at https://lccn.loc.gov/2021025530

ISBN: HB: 978-1-3502-4718-5
PB: 978-1-3502-4721-5
ePDF: 978-1-3502-4719-2
eBook: 978-1-3502-4720-8

Series: Histories of Internationalism

Typeset by Deanta Global Publishing Services, Chennai, India

To find out more about our authors and books visit www.bloomsbury.com and sign up for our newsletters.

Contents

List of figures vii
List of contributors ix
Acknowledgements xi

Introduction *Mike Heffernan, Jake Hodder, Stephen Legg and Benjamin J. Thorpe* 1

1   Towards an historical geography of international conferencing *Mike Heffernan, Jake Hodder, Stephen Legg and Benjamin J. Thorpe* 11

Part I State internationalism

2   Ambassadors, activists and experts: Conferencing and the internationalization of international relations in the nineteenth century *Brian Vick* 39

3   Contesting representations of indigeneity at the First Inter-American Indigenista Congress, 1940 *Joanna Crow* 55

4   Awe and espionage at Lancaster House: The African decolonization conferences of the early 1960s *Peter Docking* 70

Part II Science, civil society and the state

5   Conferencing the aerial future *Martin Mahony* 87

6   Scientific internationalism in a time of crisis: The Month of Intellectual Cooperation at the 1937 Paris World Fair *Jonathan Voges* 104

7   Between camaraderie and rivalry: Geopolitics at the eighteenth International Geographical Congress, Rio de Janeiro, 1956 *Mariana Lamego* 118

Part III Permanent institutions

8   Spectacular peacebuilding: The League of Nations and internationalist visions at interwar World Expos *Wendy Asquith* 137

9   Re-situating Bretton Woods: Site and venue in relation to the United Nations Monetary and Financial Conference, June 1944 *Giles Scott-Smith* 160

10 Countenancing and conferencing Japan at the Institute of Pacific Relations, 1945–54 *Daniel Clayton and Hannah Fitzpatrick*   178

Part IV Political networks

11 Alternative internationalisms in East Asia: The Conferences of the Asian Peoples, Japanese–Chinese rivalry and Japanese imperialism, 1924–43 *Torsten Weber*   199

12 Partnership in/against empire: Pan-African and imperial conferencing after the Second World War *Marc Matera*   216

13 Skies that bind: Air travel in the Bandung era *Su Lin Lewis*   234

Index   253

Figures

1.1	'Die Kongokonferenz in Berlin', 1884, by Adalbert von Rößler	17
1.2	The League of Nations Commission on Opium and Other Narcotic Drugs, in session at the Palais des Nations, Geneva, 15 May 1939	21
1.3	Smt. Vijay Lakshmi Pandit reading out the message that had come from Dr Tai Chi-táo, 'a great Chinese friend', at the Asian Relations Conference, 24 March 1947	26
1.4	U Hla Aung, Genda Sing, U Ba Swe and Soerjomo Koesoemo Wijono presiding at the Second Asian Socialist Conference in Bombay, 1 November 1956	28
2.1	'The Anti-Slavery Society Convention', 1840, by Benjamin Robert Haydon	45
5.1	The empire as a space of aerial flows: Meteorological conditions along the England–India route	92
5.2	The arrangement of the main conference room at the 1929 empire meteorology gathering	97
8.1	'It's them fighting again!' Detail from 'Dessins de A. Dubout: A L'Expo', Candide, 15 Juillet 1937	140
8.2	Carte Postale showing the exterior of the Peace Pavilion captioned 'Cher . . . . Le Pavillon ou la nuit – avec un immense foule d'Ancien Combattants . . .'	141
8.3	Mural depicting youth movements for peace within the 'Grand Salle' of the Peace Pavilion	143
8.4	Artist's impression of the League of Nations' Pavilion, New York World's Fair	146
8.5	'The Good Samaritan', a bas-relief in wood which was displayed among the Health Section's exhibits in Room Two of the League Pavilion at the New York World's Fair	148
8.6	Installation view of Room Six within the League Pavilion at the New York World's Fair, showing lighting and architectural features surrounding central sculpted figures	149
8.7	Installation view of Room Three within the League Pavilion at the New York World's Fair, showing display panel titled 'Wards of Civilization' representing the work of the Permanent Mandates Commission	152
9.1	The scenic location of the Mount Washington Hotel, surrounded by the White Mountains	162
9.2	John Maynard Keynes and Henry Morgenthau confer on the hotel veranda following the opening of the conference, 1 July 1944	168

10.1	Edward Carter and William Holland in China during the Second World War	183
10.2	Round-table discussion (future of Japan), IPR International Conference, Homestead Hotel, Hot Springs, Virginia	184
10.3	Pierre Gourou outside the Homestead Hotel, Hot Springs, with conference delegates	184
11.1	'World Affairs at a Glance', 1926, compiled by Charles Hodges	200
11.2	'Scenes from the site of the Conference of Asian Peoples'	204
12.1	The audience listening to speakers at the Pan-African Congress in Manchester	222
12.2	Oulton Hall, Clacton-on-Sea	228
13.1	Air India route map, October 1958, Detail of Asia-Africa-Europe route	236
13.2	Nasser, U Nu, Nehru and Egyptian minister Salah Salem celebrating the Water Festival in Rangoon en route to the 1955 Bandung conference	239
13.3	Hamid Algadri's personal photo album, featuring his arrival into Tunis in 1958	242

Contributors

Wendy Asquith is a postdoctoral research associate at the University of Liverpool, UK.

Daniel Clayton is Professor of Geography at the University of St Andrews, UK.

Joanna Crow is Senior Lecturer in Latin American Studies at the University of Bristol, UK.

Peter Docking is a visiting researcher in the Department of History at King's College London, UK.

Hannah Fitzpatrick is Lecturer in Human Geography at the University of Edinburgh, UK.

Mike Heffernan is Professor of Historical Geography at the University of Nottingham, UK.

Jake Hodder is Assistant Professor in the School of Geography at the University of Nottingham, UK.

Mariana Lamego is Associate Professor of Cultural Geography at the Universidade do Estado do Rio de Janeiro, Brazil.

Stephen Legg is Professor of Historical Geography at the University of Nottingham, UK.

Su Lin Lewis is Associate Professor in Modern Global History at the University of Bristol, UK.

Martin Mahony is Lecturer in Human Geography at the University of East Anglia, UK.

Marc Matera is Associate Professor of History and Co-director of the Center for Cultural Studies at the University of California, Santa Cruz, USA.

Giles Scott-Smith holds the Roosevelt Chair in New Diplomatic History at Leiden University, and is the academic director of the Roosevelt Institute for American Studies in Middelburg, USA.

Benjamin J. Thorpe is a teaching associate within the School of Geography at the University of Nottingham, UK.

Brian Vick is Professor of History at Emory University, Atlanta, USA.

Jonathan Voges is a research associate at the Leibniz University in Hanover, Germany.

Torsten Weber is a historian of modern East Asia and a principal researcher at the German Institute for Japanese Studies (DIJ), Tokyo, Japan.

Acknowledgements

The co-editors of this volume worked together between 2015 and 2020 on an AHRC-funded (AH/M008142/1) research grant entitled 'Conferencing the International: A Cultural and Historical Geography of the Origins of Internationalism (1919-1939)'. The Royal Geographical Society (with the Institute for British Geographers) supported the application, hosted our month-long exhibition entitled 'Spaces of Internationalism' and helped us organize a two-day conference in December 2018 entitled 'Conferencing the International: Spaces of Modern Internationalism'. We are thankful to them, and Catherine Souch in particular, for their support. At Bloomsbury, we would like to thank Maddie Holder for her editorial enthusiasm for the project and Abigail Lane for helping us see it through production. Thanks also to Jessica Reinisch and David Brydan for welcoming us to this exciting series and the members of the Cultural and Historical Geography research theme at the University of Nottingham for their support throughout.

Most contributors to this volume were participants at our 2018 conference, and we thank all the authors for their commitment and diligence during the most difficult of times. The irony has been lost on none of us that these chapters, focused on international movement and comings together, were written and revised during the Covid-19 pandemic, when international and even local movement was forbidden for many of us. The book is a testament to the ability of international networks and solidarity to endure the harshest of circumstances and policings. The form and contents of this book themselves attest to the conference from which this volume resulted, while the historical case studies presented here emphatically make the case for the vitality of international meetings and the friendships that result.

Stephen Legg, Mike Heffernan, Jake Hodder and Benjamin J. Thorpe
Nottingham, April 2021

Introduction

Mike Heffernan, Jake Hodder, Stephen Legg and Benjamin J. Thorpe

International conferencing as a political practice

When the world's diplomats and politicians arrived in Paris for the Peace Conference in early 1919, there were no recognized conventions on how to organize an international conference of the scale and complexity required. Contemporary witnesses frequently lamented this absence, notably the British diplomat Harold Nicolson, a member of the British delegation, who blamed many of the failings of the agreements reached at Paris on precisely this lack of prior expertise in conference organization.[1] The nearest thing to a handbook of best practice was a report that the British government commissioned in the summer of 1917 from the British Japanologist, former diplomat and foremost scholar of diplomacy Sir Ernest Satow on the history of international congresses.[2]

Satow's handbook provided information on fourteen major international conferences, from the Congress of Vienna in 1814–15 to the Conference of Bucharest in 1913, in the hope that analyses of these precursor events would be useful to British officials so that they could avoid the mistakes of the past as they prepared for the peace negotiations.[3] Nicolson acknowledged this 'admirable monograph', writing that Satow's 'little book was much studied by the junior members of the British Delegation and was by them communicated to their American colleagues, who in their turn read it with interest and respect', though he added that 'It may be questioned whether it was examined with equal diligence by the Plenipotentiaries themselves'.[4] Satow included details on the cities and buildings in which international conferences had taken place, the representation of the nation states and authorities in attendance, the languages used by diplomats and officials, the ordering of proceedings, the arrangement of conference committees, and the protocols of ratification. He argued that international conferencing had grown haphazardly over the years, usually in response to immediate political crises, but implied that a serious study of the history of international conferences offered valuable clues about the norms of conferencing as a political and diplomatic practice.

This book extends this suggestion by considering international conferencing as a distinctive form of political diplomacy. We argue, following Satow, that international conferences require separate analysis to complement the abundant existing historical research on international relations that has tended to view international conferences as 'black-box' events, historical punctuation marks defined by the circumstances that brought them into being, the consequences that flowed from them and the actions of a small number of dominant personalities. While international conferences provide important stages for the politics of the modern world, from climate change summits to world economic forums, constitutive details about the nature, form and organization of these hugely important events have been taken-for-granted and are rarely analysed in detail.

This volume is a history not of conferences but of international conferencing as a political practice. Our inquiries, and those of the authors whose work is presented in the following pages, are shaped by several questions: When, why, how and where did international conferencing emerge? How, and by whom, were international conferences organized and constituted? How did the practices and strategies of international conferencing emerge and develop over time? What were the salient differences, and similarities, between practices of conferencing aimed at addressing political, economic, social and/or scientific questions? And how was conferencing influenced by its places, spaces and environments?

As such, this volume is a collaborative endeavour in *Placing Internationalism* in two senses. First, it looks at conferences as one of, if not the, key locations in which internationalism emerged in the post-war world. Conferences are viewed here not just as locations or material spaces but as lived, sensed and experienced places, buzzing with life, potential futures, hope and despair.[5] Second, the volume pushes us to think about where we place international conferences in terms of disciplines and epistemology. What can we know about these momentous meetings and how? Though with a shared interest in conferences as places of internationalism, we bring together scholars of history, visual and material culture, geography, languages and area studies. What connects us is a shared, spatially attuned methodology, which seeks to address a particular spatial paradox emerging from two fundamental features of modern internationalism. On one hand, this internationalism was premised upon overcoming limitations of location, transcending the nation state in search of the shared interests of humankind. On the other hand, it was geographically contingent on the spaces in which people came together to conceive and enact their internationalist ideas. The primary space in which this paradox played out was that of the international conference.

By taking this perspective, the Paris Peace Conference of 1919–20 becomes significant for histories of internationalism not just for laying the foundations of the League of Nations but for constituting a turning point in the interdependent relationship between international conferencing and internationalism. This shift was widely recognized at the time as a transition from an 'old' to a 'new diplomacy', in which, as Nicolson put it, 'democracy is sovereign of us all'.[6] Following the First World War, travel became easier and faster and societal changes created a new generation for whom internationalism was not a utopia but a living reality. The democratic impulse was clearest in the transition from secret to open diplomacy, a shift that reflected the globalization of American liberalism.[7] Woodrow Wilson had told American pacifists in May 1916, and repeated to the US Congress in January 1917, that 'The peace of the world must henceforth depend upon a new and more wholesome diplomacy'.[8] Accordingly, although cognizant of templates set by nineteenth-century international conferencing, this volume's primary objective is to evaluate how international conferencing evolved beyond the 'Wilsonian moment'.[9] Inspired by diverse interpretations of the potential of internationalism through the middle decades of the twentieth century, the new art of international conferencing paved the way for recent international conferences, from UN climate summits to G7 meetings, that have sought international solutions to global environmental and economic challenges.[10]

The focus of this volume, however, is the half-century following the First World War, when major international conferences convened to address the end of wars and the slow endings of empires. Many twentieth-century international conferences marked the end of periods of violence and warfare occasioned by the collapse of imperial authority. These included empires effaced from the map of Europe and the Middle East at the Paris Peace Conference in 1919–20 and of the European colonial empires whose demise after the Second World War inspired leaders from newly independent states in Asia and Africa to propose an alternative international order at the Bandung conference in 1955.[11] We seek to do justice to the full range of twentieth-century international conferences by considering the global nature of internationalist ambitions that emerged between and beyond Versailles and Bandung. This volume presents a global historical and political geography of international conferencing between 1919 and 1969, drawing on examples from Asia (Bandung, Bombay, Delhi, Kyoto, Lucknow, Nagasaki, Rangoon, Shanghai, Tokyo), Europe (Clacton-on-Sea, London, Manchester, Paris, Vienna), the Pacific (Honolulu) and North, Central and South America (Bretton Woods, NH, Hot Springs, VA, New York, NY, Pátzcuaro, Rio de Janeiro). Our objective is to explore the different sites in which diverse groups grappled with various forms of internationalism through the practice of conferencing and how this practice shaped their political projects.

A broad range of historical sources are considered in the chapters which follow, from the carefully catalogued archives of international organizations such as the League of Nations and the United Nations, through recently declassified files from the UK National Archives on the process of decolonization, to dispersed collections of private correspondence, long-forgotten published texts, articles in obscure scientific manuals, objects and artefacts from dismantled international exhibitions, and personal diaries, memoirs and other documents that record often fleeting international encounters.[12]

In considering this material, the volume widens the scope of international historical scholarship beyond familiar, extensively analysed international organizations and institutions to consider some of the other spaces, sites and venues across the globe where modern internationalism was created and performed. By focusing on international conferences as sites of internationalism, and by emphasizing their internal spaces and external connections, we seek to challenge the dominance of permanent international organizations in the historiography of internationalism and reverse the accepted relationship between international institutions and international conferences. We argue that modern internationalism reflects the ephemeral, messy and unpredictable nature of international conferences rather than the carefully organized bureaucracies of permanent international organizations. International conferences were creative rather than confirmatory events and frequently defined the terms and conditions under which permanent international institutions operated.

Rather than explore how international institutions generated international conferences, we consider how the practices of international conferences shaped the priorities and activities of international organizations, a causal relationship acknowledged by Sir Eric Drummond, the first secretary general of the League of Nations:

> [T]he Secretariat [of the League of Nations] would be nothing more and nothing less than a permanent conference of representatives. . . . Such a system had worked well among the allied powers during the war, and it was therefore thought that it could produce the same admirable results in the League.[13]

By considering different forms of international conference in a single volume, we seek to highlight how multiple, often competing, internationalisms engaged with alternative scales of political affiliation – local, regional, national and imperial. Rather than viewing international conferences as expressions of pre-existing internationalism formulated elsewhere, the chapters that follow *place* twentieth-century internationalisms, showing how they emerged through conference events, reinforcing our central claim that internationalism and the international conference were co-constitutive. While networks of correspondence and publication, generated within and between permanent international organizations, often gave rise to new forms of internationalism at a distance, it was through periodic conferences that internationalism was formalized as both an arena of governance and a scale of investigation.

While acknowledging the importance of the extensive existing literature on international congresses, conferences and summits, this volume makes three distinctively geographical interventions. First, we emphasize the constitutive significance of the physical locations, infrastructures and internal spaces of international conferences on the forms of internationalism generated at these events.[14] Second, we move from spaces to places, considering the cultural and social content of international conferences, with particular reference to the role of speech and rhetoric, sound and music, and food and drink in shaping international exchanges.[15] Third, we examine international conferences as nodes in emerging global networks through which people, objects and ideas circulated – as meeting places where global, regional and local actors came together to articulate international claims to establish international solidarity.[16] This approach involves serious consideration of the technologies that supported international meetings, such as the printing presses used by national delegates at the Paris Peace Conference or the transport systems deployed for the World Pacifist Meeting of 1949.[17] By focusing on the material and cultural histories of international conferences, this volume offers a new and more open approach to internationalism, considered as a putative form of governance defined by geographically specific conduct and embodied practice.[18]

Structure

Conferencing has been a key political technology across various strains of internationalism. In the present volume, however, we aim to move on from this typological approach by developing a new way of looking at conferences. The structure of this volume is informed by the following question: What would happen to our view of international conferences if we started not from the type of internationalism that they were associated with, but rather from the conference itself as a political event? Such a perspective allows us to make creative juxtapositions, revealing commonalities in conferencing that would otherwise be obscured. In this spirit, the categories proposed below ought to be thought of not as a watertight typology but a porous and overlapping set of ways in which conferences intersected with internationalism of all stripes.

The first part of the book is devoted to conferences related to what we might think of as 'state internationalism'. Most expressions of internationalism were aligned with – and indeed grew out of – forms of interstate diplomacy and were practised through state-sponsored international conferences. Brian Vick's chapter begins with the 1814–15 Congress of Vienna and looks at how a system of conferencing emerged that 'established precursors and set templates' for international conferences to follow. He shifts our view of conferencing in this age from high-level congresses to lower-level events involving 'second-tier diplomats, campaigners for international reforms or scientific experts in academic and professional gatherings', thus drawing links between state internationalism and what would come to be known as 'international civil society'. This is followed by two examples of states using international conferences to negotiate or manage challenges to their sovereignty. Joanna Crow looks at the 1940 Inter-American Indigenista Congress in Pátzcuaro, Mexico, as a state-led and state-sponsored event, yet one in which non-state indigeneity was an active presence, both in the subject of discussions and in the persons of the two Mapuche delegates at the conference. Peter Docking takes as his focus the decolonization conferences of the early 1960s, in which British and African actors each sought to use the conference for their own advantage while negotiating African states' independence from the British Empire.

In the second part, we move on to international conferences oriented around science, civil society and the state. Though state-level politics retained an active role in these conferences, and in many ways guided how they played out, they aimed for the nominally apolitical goal of scientific and intellectual cooperation across national borders. Martin Mahony's chapter analyses the technical production of a domesticated 'airspace' at the 1926 and 1930 Imperial Conferences and the 1929 Conference of Empire Meteorologists. Meteorological concerns meshed with imperial ambition, and airships and conferences formed the mutually sustaining double-pivot through which connections between the dominions and the metropole could be strengthened. Jonathan Voges meanwhile focuses on the conferences organized during the Month of Intellectual Cooperation at the 1937 Paris Exposition (which Asquith also explores from the perspective of the League of Nations), exploring how Nazi Germany tried to steer the tiller of internationalism towards a more technical conception, pushing for a more 'modest' version of scientific internationalism. Lastly, Mariana Lamego turns the focus of analysis on the press coverage of one such international scientific conference: the 1956 International Geographical Congress in Rio de Janeiro. While the conference proceedings are self-consciously inert, by interrogating the contemporary media coverage Lamego shows how the conference was suffused with both a sense of camaraderie and Cold War geopolitical tensions.

In the third part, we turn to the permanent international institutions that held conferencing close to the heart of how they functioned. These institutions were the primary actors negotiating the conduct of politics at a new, 'international' scale, albeit forging this new path with constant reference to extant national and imperial scales of politics. One of the most significant of these was of course the 'permanent conference' of the League of Nations, which Wendy Asquith's chapter approaches by way of the League's exhibits at the 1937 Paris Exposition and the 1939 New York World's Fair. By focusing on the material culture of these exhibits, and the ways in which they used art and architecture, she reveals the conscious development of a visual vocabulary of internationalism. Giles Scott-Smith carries the historical thread forwards in his chapter on the 1944 United Nations Monetary and Financial Conference, as the League was being reshaped into the United Nations. The location of this conference, Bretton Woods, has become a metonym for the financial apparatus it birthed, but Scott-Smith takes us back to the conference itself, embedding it in the all-too-human context in which it took place. Finally, Daniel Clayton and Hannah Fitzpatrick take the Institute of Pacific Relations (IPR) as their subject, looking at how Japan was brought into focus in both its absence and its presence at four consecutive international conferences of the IPR between 1945 and 1954, as the IPR was itself having to adapt to decolonization, the Cold War and the new post-war world.

Finally, the fourth part of the book turns to the less well-resourced and often more radical international political networks that also operated primarily through conferencing. These were the plethora of political networks that operated tangential to, outside of or in outright opposition to the 'establishment internationalism' of permanent institutions like the League or United Nations. One such example was pan-Asianism, which Torsten Weber examines by focusing on Conferences of the Asian Peoples in Nagasaki (1926) and Shanghai (1927), and the 1943 Greater East Asia Conference in Tokyo, at which familiar tensions between nationalist and internationalist motives were complicated by conflicts over the nature of East Asian internationalism and its relationship with (anti-)imperialism. Marc Matera's chapter juxtaposes two avowedly anti-colonial, socialist conferences – the 1945 Pan-African Congress organized by the Pan-African Federation in Manchester and the 1946 Conference on the Relationship between the British and Colonial Peoples organized by the Fabian Colonial Bureau in Clacton-on-Sea – and explores how the tensions between these conferences highlighted the rifts between their respective visions of international partnership. Finally, Su Lin Lewis steps back to look at the practices of air travel that both enabled conferencing to become so central to the functioning of political networks and shaped the way that it did so, with particular reference to the Bandung-era conferences of the 1950s that forged bonds of solidarity and collective purpose among Asians and Africans across the decolonizing world.

Approaches

Cross-cutting this thematic structure, this volume embraces a range of innovative methodological approaches that bring a vibrant and diverse array of methods to bear on the study of internationalism. Drawing from a range of disciplines, including from new diplomatic history and cultural studies, we see international conferences as polyvalent events that can and ought to be approached from multiple directions. Throughout the volume, threads of methodological commonality run through and connect the sections. These might be broken down into four broad strands, each of which tap into contemporary concerns that cut across the humanities and social sciences.

The first such methodological strand is a concern for the material factors necessary for conference spaces to function: the logistics, networks and infrastructures required. The common starting point that conferences ought to be taken seriously as events (rather than merely as sets of outcomes) means that factors such as where conferences take place and how participants get there take on a new level of importance. For instance, Crow looks at the choice to hold the First Inter-American Indigenista Congress at Pátzcuaro, Docking analyses the choice of London venues in which the decolonization conferences were held and Scott-Smith explores the story behind the choice of Bretton Woods as the location for the United Nations Monetary and Financial Conference. In all cases, these choices were freighted with practical, political and symbolic significance. The importance of the infrastructure needed for international travel is addressed by Mahony in relation to airships in the 1920s and Lewis in relation to the expansion of aeroplane travel in the 1950s, while Docking also notes the importance of the tarmac greeting afforded African delegates returning from London. They analyse how conferences were both enabled by and productive of a new form of mobility, and that our view of conference space ought therefore to be stretched to include the sites that enabled this mobility.

The second methodological thread running through the volume is an attentiveness to questions of subalternity and adoption of decentred perspectives to tell new stories. This includes a concern for the ways in which questions of imperial-colonial relations were both subjects of and shot throughout international conferencing. Crow and Mahony's chapters look at imperial conferences to solve the 'problems' of Indigenous peoples and colonial distance and weather, though in neither case was the subject passive. Docking looks directly at the place of conferencing in the negotiation of decolonization, while Matera discusses how conferencing operated as a 'mainstay of transregional political networking among anti-colonial intellectuals, liberation movements, and, after decolonization, representatives of postcolonial states'. Eurocentric understandings of internationalism and imperialism are complicated in Lewis's analysis of the broad arc of conferences of the Bandung era, and Weber and Crow's analyses of the development of alternative forms of internationalism in East Asia and Latin America. Methodologically, a de-centred or off-kilter perspective is adopted by looking beyond the keynote addresses and focusing instead on minor delegates and lesser-known figures, from Vick's second-tier diplomats to the Mapuche political figures Venancio Coñuepán and César Colima (Crow), to the French geographer Pierre Gourou (Clayton and Fitzpatrick), anto the German bibliographical expert Hugo Andres Krüss (Voges).

The third thread is a regard for the art, culture and theatricality of conferences as living places. We have embraced illustration as a means to convey conference life, not least in the following chapter, where we use images that demonstrate the centrality of cartography to conferencing. The connection to artistic depictions of conference life is exemplified by John Deakin's October 1945 photograph of the Fifth Pan-African Congress in Manchester (see the book cover and Matera's chapter in this volume, where the image is contextualized and discussed). The photograph presents a brilliant play on perspective, in two senses. As with Velazquez's much discussed painting *Las Meninas* (1656) the object of the event is hidden from view. What we observe is the gaze of people enthralled by something out of sight. Here the audience is the subject of this conference art, just as the aim of modern conferencing more broadly was to produce both an audience and a broader public. Second, the central aisle directs our eye down the perspective line to the impressive interior of Chorlton-on-Medlock Town Hall. This is a curated space, geometrically orchestrated by the benches, chairs and colonnaded walls. Yet as the image blurs in the distance, so does its tidy ordering, with chairs nudged askew and delegates spread out in the un-cramped back rows. The scene speaks to the spatial ambitions of conference organizers and the vital unravelling that occurs in the placing of internationalism.

Such officially sanctioned conference photos typically presented a male-dominated scene that disguised a reality in which, as Scott-Smith notes, wives as well as 'small army of secretaries and stenographers' were also present. Nor were representations of conferences limited to photography or even the visual. Matera, for instance, analyses the representation of the Clacton-on-Sea conference in both Louise Bennett's poetry and Peter Abrahams's prose. At the conferences themselves, attentiveness to these cultural facets reveals the story told by the art and architecture of the venues (Asquith), as well as the geopolitically coded use of music, dance and food at social events (Lamego). Indeed, conferences were often carefully choreographed, with sites of performance stretching from the dais to the airport tarmac (Docking and Lewis). Clayton and Fitzpatrick extend this perspective by reading post-war conferencing through Erving Goffman's contemporaneous theorization of theatricality.

The fourth thread is an attunement to the emotions and atmospheres that permeated these international conference places. Such a perspective encourages a widening of focus from the 'business' sessions of international conferences to the receptions and social programme that invariably accompanied them, and the gamut of para-conference spaces in which delegates moved while at the conference but not *at* the conference. As Vick shows, these social programmes developed out of the intersection of salon society with emergent forms of international conferencing. Forms of conference sociability were complex and often conflicting: Lamego looks at the coexistence of camaraderie and tension, and Scott-Smith at bonhomie and fatigue. Lewis highlights how long journeys and the multiple stopovers they entailed encouraged sociability and granted important opportunities for personal connection. Atmospherics was not merely a social matter but a meteorological one too, and both Mahony and Scott-Smith discuss the mercurial role of weather in the planning and execution of conferences.

Taken collectively, the chapters that comprise this collection unpack international conferences and show that by treating them not as black-box events but as a political technology embedded in specific historical and geographical contexts, a whole host of interesting questions open out. These include a number of larger questions about the nature of conferencing, probably too large to be answered in full, but which the chapters that follow touch on in different ways. A far-from-exhaustive list might include the following: Does the conference method prescribe or favour particular kinds of political outcomes? That is, what is the relationship between the politics of conferencing and the ideologies at play? Does it reify those with the authority to codify its norms? That is, what is the nature of the power wielded by those in a position to define how conferences are to play out? Is conferencing a failure? That is, what is the nature of the afterlife of the theatrics and performance of conferences, and how exactly does a more rounded appreciation of the conference-as-event help us think about its patterns of influence? What kinds of empirical traces do conferences leave behind? That is, how can we set about reconstructing conference life from the evidence that is left to us?

Notes

1 Harold Nicolson, *Peacemaking 1919: Being Reminiscences of the Paris Peace Conference* (Boston & New York: Houghton Mifflin Company, 1933).
2 G. W. Prothero to Ernest Satow, 2 June 1917, in *List of Sir Ernest Satow's General Correspondence from 1906 to 1927*, ed. Ian Ruxton (Lulu.com, 2018), 39. See also Erik Goldstein, 'Historians Outside the Academy: G. W. Prothero and the Experience of the Foreign Office Historical Section 1917-20', *Historical Research*, 63, no. 151 (1990): 195–211; and, more generally, Erik Goldstein, *Winning the Peace: British Diplomatic Strategy, Peace Planning, and the Paris Peace Conference, 1916–1920* (Oxford: Clarendon, 1991).
3 Ernest Satow, *Handbooks Prepared Under the Direction of the Historical Section of the Foreign Office – No. 151: International Congresses* (London: HMSO, 1920).
4 Nicolson, *Peacemaking 1919*, 80.
5 Tim Cresswell, *Place: An Introduction* (London: John Wiley & Sons, 2014).
6 Nicolson, *Peacemaking 1919*, 5.
7 Sasson Sofer, 'Old and New Diplomacy: A Debate Revisited', *Review of International Studies* 14, no. 3 (1988): 195–211, 198; Felix Gilbert, 'The "New Diplomacy" of the Eighteenth Century', *World Politics* 4, no. 1 (1951): 1–38.
8 Thomas J. Knock, *To End All Wars: Woodrow Wilson and the Quest for a New World Order* (New York: Oxford University Press, 1992), 77.
9 Erez Manela, *The Wilsonian Moment: Self-Determination and the International Origins of Anticolonial Nationalism* (Oxford: Oxford University Press, 2007). For a brilliant analysis of a pre-twentieth-century international conferences, see Brian E. Vick, *The Congress of Vienna: Power and Politics after Napoleon* (Cambridge, MA: Harvard University Press, 2014); also see Maartje Abbenhuis, Christopher Ernest Barber & Annalise R. Higgins (eds), *War, Peace and International Order? The Legacies of the Hague Conferences of 1899 and 1907* (Abingdon: Routledge, 2017).
10 Margaret Macmillan, *Peacemakers: The Paris Conference of 1919 and Its Attempt to End War* (London: John Murray, 2001); Mark Mazower, *Governing the World: The History of an Idea* (London: Penguin, 2012); David Reynolds, *Summits: Six Meetings that Shaped the Twentieth Century* (London: Allen Lane, 2007); Emmanuel Mourlon-Druol & Federico Romero (eds), *International Summitry and Global Governance: The Rise of the G7 and the European Council, 1974–1991* (Abingdon: Routledge, 2014); and Chris Tudda, *Cold War Summits: A History, from Potsdam to Malta* (London: Bloomsbury Academic, 2015).

11 Christopher J. Lee (ed.), *Making a World After Empire: The Bandung Moment and Its Political Afterlives* (Athens, OH: Ohio University Press, 2010); Adom Getachew, *Worldmaking After Empire: The Rise and Fall of Self-Determination* (Princeton, NJ: Princeton University Press, 2019).
12 Afro-Asian Networks Research Collective, 'Manifesto: Networks of Decolonization in Asia and Africa', *Radical History Review* 131 (2018): 176–82; Jake Hodder, Michael Heffernan & Stephen Legg, 'The Archival Geographies of Twentieth Century Internationalism: Nation, Empire, Race', *Journal of Historical Geography* 71 (2021): 1–11.
13 Eric Drummond, 'The Secretariat of the League of Nations', *Public Administration* 9, no. 2 (1931): 228–35, 228–9.
14 For related studies, see Jason Dittmer & Fiona McConnell (eds), *Diplomatic Cultures and International Politics: Translations, Spaces and Alternatives* (Abingdon: Routledge, 2016) and Iver B. Neumann, *Diplomatic Sites: A Critical Enquiry* (Oxford: Oxford University Press, 2013). For an alternative approach to 'situating' internationalism in the League of Nations, see Benjamin Auberer, Timo Holste & Carolin Liebisch, 'Editors' Note: Situating Internationalism 1919–1940s', *New Global Studies* 10, no. 3 (2016): 201–16. For the regional and national situating of international actors, see Antje Dietze & Katja Naumann, 'Revisiting Transnational Actors from a Spatial Perspective', *European Review of History: Revue européenne d'histoire* 25, no. 3–4 (2018): 415–30.
15 For related studies, see Daniel Laqua, 'Exhibiting, Encountering and Studying Music in Interwar Europe: Between National and International Community', *European Studies* 32 (2014): 207–23; Stephen Legg, '"Political Atmospherics": The India Round Table Conference's Atmospheric Environments, Bodies and Representations, London 1930–1932', *Annals of the American Association of Geographers* 110, no. 3 (2020): 774–92; Marc Matera, *Black London: The Imperial Metropolis and Decolonization in the Twentieth Century* (Oakland, CA: University of California Press, 2015); Su Lin Lewis, *Cities in Motion: Urban Life and Cosmopolitanism in Southeast Asia, 1920–1940* (Cambridge: Cambridge University Press, 2016).
16 Giles Scott-Smith & J. Simon Rofe (eds), *Global Perspectives on the Bretton Woods Conference and the Post-War World Order* (Basingstoke: Palgrave Macmillan, 2017); Naoko Shimazu, 'Diplomacy as Theatre: Staging the Bandung Conference of 1955', *Modern Asian Studies* 48, no. 1 (2014): 225–2.
17 Sally Marks, 'Behind the Scenes at the Paris Peace Conference of 1919', *Journal of British Studies* 9, no. 2 (1970): 154–80; Jake Hodder, 'Conferencing the International at the World Pacifist Meeting, 1949', *Political Geography* 49 (2015), 40–50.
18 Jake Hodder, Stephen Legg & Mike Heffernan, 'Introduction: Historical Geographies of Internationalism, 1900–1950', *Political Geography* 49 (2015): 1–6. See also Thomas J. Biersteker & Cynthia Weber, *State Sovereignty as Social Construct* (Cambridge: Cambridge University Press, 1996).

1

Towards an historical geography of international conferencing

Mike Heffernan, Jake Hodder, Stephen Legg and Benjamin J. Thorpe

Introduction

Historians of international conferencing confront some thorny definitional challenges. It is by no means obvious what constitutes an 'international conference' given that both words – 'international' and 'conference' – are equally ambiguous. Should the category include bilateral conferences involving representatives from just two nation states? If not, how many nation states need to be represented for a conference to qualify as an 'international' event? And are conferences that involve delegates from different countries who explicitly reject national affiliations 'international' in any meaningful sense?

These problems are compounded by the complexities of the term 'conference'. This word is often used interchangeably with traditional political and ecclesiastical alternatives such as 'congress', 'assembly', 'senate', 'diet' or 'synod' and has recently jostled alongside intriguing examples of semantic change such as 'summit' and 'retreat'. This imprecision, and the attempts to bring clarity by applying strict definitions, has had important political consequences. Harold Nicolson argued that the reason Germany was excluded from the negotiations at Paris in 1919 lay in the initial tacit understanding that a 'conference' comprising representatives of the Allied forces would be followed by a larger 'congress' of all belligerents as well as neutral parties. As the conference progressed, this distinction gradually collapsed, along with the prospect of any second stage being organized that would include German involvement. Whether through cynicism or, as Nicolson argued, convenience and bureaucratic momentum, the conference had simply become the congress.[1]

In thinking of conferencing as a process, we adopt an inclusive approach that does not seek to impose any divisions between conferences, congresses and so on. Rather, this approach pays close attention to the production of knowledge about conferences. Journal papers, monographs and newspaper articles worked to invent, reproduce and subvert distinctions between types of international meetings while also contributing towards histories of conferencing itself. In this chapter, we provide a critical commentary which incorporates the canonical version of conference history while also pushing out in two directions. First, we reflect on the context in which conference histories were written and the ways in which they were coloured by the intentions of the author. And second, we seek to encompass recent literature that expands our understanding of what and who conferencing involved. We thus provide both a history and a blueprint for the study of international conferencing.

This chapter proceeds in two sections. The first traces two different histories of the modern international conference: an older tradition of diplomatic conferences organized to settle territorial disputes and a newer form of periodic conferencing, emerging in the mid-nineteenth century and initially associated with scientific, technical and commercial conferences. This latter model sought to cultivate a wider international public sphere within which the process of internationalization might be managed. As the frequency and scale of both these forms of conferencing increased through the later decades of the nineteenth century, so the distinction between them began to blur.

The second section examines how these earlier forms of international conference converged during the Paris Peace Conference in 1919–20. Although the novelty of the Paris Peace Conference has often been overstated, it nonetheless inspired a period of prodigious conferencing in the years which followed. In the twentieth century the international conference matured into the pre-eminent political instrument of global governance. Conference rules and procedures became codified in the emerging discipline of international relations, and conferences involved an increasingly diverse range of actors, such as non-governmental organizations. Conferences became important forums for defining the terms of internationalism and agreeing the rules and conventions by which it would be governed. What emerged was a distinctive understanding of internationalism as simultaneously a scientific and a political practice, a fusion enabled by conference spaces themselves which brought together politicians, diplomats, academics and activists. Whereas pre-existing national and imperial systems of governance were legitimated by scientific analysis conducted at one remove from their implementation, internationalism involved ambitious programmes that combined scientific analysis, large-scale educational reform and the establishment of new rules and conventions by which international governance could be operationalized. The international conference became, we argue, the defining arena of modern internationalism precisely because it was simultaneously a space of scientific analysis and a forum for political action, a place where internationalism was both studied and implemented.

The scale, frequency and focus of international conferences expanded dramatically during the 1920s just as political theorists, pioneering scholars of international relations and historians of diplomacy began to study how international organizations, notably the League of Nations, might codify conferencing rules and procedures as the basis for international governance. However, the rapid growth of conferences also spoke to a broader range of internationalist projects, especially outside of Europe, where the geopolitical orthodoxies of League and empire were being challenged from multiple directions. We show how the conference method was not restricted to liberal advocates of the League of Nations who considered internationalism in terms of the interactions between pre-existing, ideally democratic nation states or as a means of securing free trade within and between colonial empires. The international conference was also the preferred method for social and political movements which sought to develop and implement alternative forms of internationalism – anti-colonialist, feminist, socialist, anarchist and even fascist. For each of these constituencies, the international conference became a key mechanism to seek publicity and legitimacy.

Pre-histories of the modern conference

As the scale and frequency of international conferences grew dramatically in the twentieth century, contemporary writers sought to identify a longer history from which modern conferencing had emerged. Nicolson, for instance, claimed diplomacy, which he defined as the 'management of international relations by negotiation', was first formulated as a political practice in the ancient world. The semi-annual ancient Greek councils of the Amphictyonic League provided the original template for the modern international conference, Nicolson claimed, and were still being invoked well into the nineteenth century. Simón Bolívar's doomed attempt to forge a permanent alliance of new Latin American republics at the 1826 Congress of Panama was described at the time, and is still sometimes known, as the Amphictyonic Congress.[2]

International diplomacy collapsed in the medieval period, argued Nicolson, but re-emerged in Renaissance Italy when something approaching a modern system of embassies and ambassadors developed to facilitate the kinds of international exchange famously described in the early sixteenth century by Niccolò Macchiavelli.[3] What might now be defined as international conferences waxed and waned in a similar sequence, claimed Nicolson, until periodic meetings of emperors, kings and courtly advisers finally became important instruments of statecraft in the early modern era. Nicolson's contemporaries, better attuned to ecclesiastical interactions, traced the origins of the international conference to the medieval era that he had dismissed. Norman L. Hill described the pre-Tridentine ecumenical councils of the Roman Catholic Church as foundational 'international congresses working toward the establishment of a uniform law for the civilized world', while Alfred Zimmern cited the 'account given by an ecclesiastical historian of the manoeuvring between the parties at the Congress of Arras in 1435 [which] reads almost like a description of contemporary happenings'.[4]

Later generations of historians have added to these early histories of international conferences, emphasizing their symbolic propaganda value in promoting new relationships between rival monarchs, usually for the benefit of fractious and scheming courts. The extraordinary events of the Field of Cloth of Gold, a three-week festival in June 1520 in Balinghem in what was then the English Pale of Calais, are often described in these terms. As an international conference it was part pageant, part political summit and featured dozens of English and French nobles desperately seeking to out-spend one another on food, clothing and music in hundreds of richly decorated tents. These were ostensibly to celebrate the new bond of friendship between Henry VIII of England and Francis I of France, established by the Anglo-French Treaty of 1514, but also served to reinforce the domestic authority of both monarchs.[5]

A key event identified in virtually all histories of international conferences, however, was the 1648 Congress of Westphalia, convened in the two neighbouring cities of Münster and Osnabrück to negotiate peace terms at the end of the Thirty Years' War. It was held to be the first major international conference that possessed characteristics resonant of contemporary conferencing, most notably its apparent formalization of state sovereignty as the political grid through which such conferences operated.[6] Even by 1919, the Congress of Westphalia was still seen by some to offer a useful template for how to manage diplomatic protocol and procedure at a major international gathering.[7]

Post-Westphalia, peace conferences displayed increasing complexity and sophistication in their proceedings, often venturing into topics that laid outside of post-conflict territorial negotiation. The locations of such conferences often became metonyms for the political regimes they ushered in. Hill's list of the 'most important' post-Westphalian peace conferences is typical:[8]

1648 – Westphalia	1772 – Fokchany; Bucharest
1659 – Pyrenees	1779 – Teschen
1668 – Aix-la-Chapelle	1797 – Rastadt
1679 – Nijmegen	1802 – Amiens
1697 – Ryswick	1815 – Vienna
1699 – Carlowitz	1856 – Paris
1719 – Utrecht	1878 – Berlin
1721 – Chambray	1905 – Portsmouth
1728 – Soissons	1912–13 – London
1748 – Breda; Aix-la-Chapelle	1919 – Paris

These early international conferences shared several common themes. They were elite gatherings of monarchs, aristocrats and statesmen with limited reach to wider publics. As the American scholar of international relations Frederick Sherwood Dunn noted, 'Political life was organized, not horizontally, but vertically, and the various political units that grew out of the ruins of the feudal system touched each other only at the top.'[9] As such, most early international conferences were a mixture of formalized discussions, resolutions and treaties with much ceremonial pomp and display. They were also reactive events, convened in response to crises and limited, in most cases, to issues of war and peace that reflected the restricted domain of international affairs. The ever-changing location and cast of actors prevented experience in the techniques of conferencing from being passed on; as Zimmern lamented, 'to read the proceedings of a pre-[WWI] Conference of the usual improvised type is to discover that its members were moving about in "worlds unrealised", encountering obstacle after obstacle and circumventing them as best they could with little help either from general rules or, in most cases, from particular experience.'[10] The penetration of internationalism into daily life changed significantly during the nineteenth century, a consequence of increasingly integrated modern capitalist economies, a growing middle class and the emergence of mass media serving a predominantly literate public. The new internationalism also reflected technological innovations in travel and communication, notably the invention of the steamship in 1807, the steam locomotive in 1825 and the development of the electric telegraph by Gauss, Weber and Morse between 1830 and 1850. As people and states became increasingly interconnected, the international conference emerged as a key and less overtly geopolitical mechanism through which ongoing processes of internationalization might be managed. Conferencing did not develop, therefore, from an abstract political science or a fundamental law of international integration. It emerged in a spontaneous and haphazard manner driven by economic and political needs and the growing demands of international life.[11]

International conferences that sought to improve interactions in science, commerce and technology, domains deemed to be driven by inherently global forces beyond the control of nation states, were at the forefront of the new wave of nineteenth-century internationalism. Delegates to scientific or commercial conferences often represented their academic disciplines and fields of technical expertise rather than their nation states, and their deliberations provided an ostensibly apolitical, scientific model of enlightened international governance.[12] Internationalization was embraced with particular ease and enthusiasm by representatives of mathematical sciences, including physics and statistics, whose common language of numbers and symbols, rather than national languages, seemed ideally suited to international exchange.[13] Such internationalization was a process facilitated almost entirely by regular international conferences organized in major cities around the world, even by those disciplines, such as geography, that were strongly associated with the national and imperial aspirations of the great powers.[14]

In many cases, international scientific agreements were urgently required for commercial reasons, including establishing global standards in the measurement of time and space. For example, long-standing disputes about the prime meridian were finally reconciled (more or less) at the 1884 International Meridian Conference in Washington DC.[15] Global standards in other spheres were also agreed at late nineteenth-century international conferences to ease global commercial exchange. The Universal Postal Union (UPU), established at the Treaty of Bern of 1874, provided an early model for international governance facilitated by periodic conferences. The UPU eventually became a single, centrally organized international association that welcomed delegates from the great powers alongside representatives of non-European and colonial states, including British India, a signatory to the foundational conference of the International Telegraphic Union (ITC) in Vienna in 1868.[16] By 1891, there were fifty-eight UPU member states, eight classed as colonies and fifteen as semi-sovereign members. Scientific-technical international conferences were, therefore, innovative spaces in which colonial and non-state groups could participate and gain a measure of official recognition: as Ellen Ravndal argues, '[by] joining IOs [International Organisations] and implementing their agreements on postal services, telegraphs, customs tariffs, patents and sanitary measures, a state could prove to the world (and its domestic constituency) that it was doing what "modern" states were supposed to do.'[17]

Unknown before the 1850s, scientific-cum-political international conferences rapidly outnumbered diplomatic conferences that continued the earlier Westphalian tradition. For Dunn, the new international conferences, by seeking to engage technical and scientific topics of direct relevance to the lives of ordinary people, were more important – and democratic – than traditional diplomatic conferences because they promoted the international sphere as the realm of science and expertise. That version of internationalism constituted an application of international government to daily life, continuously, at the instant moment, and directly in contact with the ultimate units of international life, the citizens and subjects of the nations engaged in international intercourse of one sort or another. Other forms of international government, notably arbitration, operate upon international life intermittently, retrospectively, and indirectly, through the national units. The former, it need hardly be said, is much more useful where it is feasible.[18]

Similarly, the historian Mark Mazower argues that international institutions, and the conferencing method they embraced, arose from

scientific visions of an internationally organized world. Across a range of new professions – statistics, engineering, geography, bibliography, public health – men [sic] emerged who did not want to do away with the state but to take it over, to replace aristocracy with a professionalized meritocracy, to push aside the well-connected amateurs and bring in new cadres of educated and rational elites.[19]

As such, the later decades of the nineteenth century witnessed the coexistence of two distinct forms of international conferencing. The first was a continuation of traditional forms of international political diplomacy based on the Westphalian system, while the second promoted a newer and less obviously political version of internationalism within which regular scientific and technical conferences functioned as legislative governing bodies implementing policies of global governance. This highlights how nationalism and internationalism were mutually sustaining ideologies in this period, both dominated by an emergent industrial class whose values and interests were expressed by an expanding mass media and who could travel internationally ever more quickly and cheaply. Across much of *fin de siècle* Europe, North America and the 'settler' colonies, a new public sphere emerged, perhaps best described by the German word *Öffentlichkeit*, that was simultaneously national, imperial and international.[20]

The distinction between these two forms of pre-twentieth-century international conferences fed the popular idea that internationalization was a predominantly natural, rather than political, process. However, these distinctions often blurred in practice. Large diplomatic conferences not only attempted to resolve political tensions following periods of warfare but also sought to regulate international affairs and establish ground rules for international governance. For example, representatives at the Congress of Vienna in 1814–15 grappled with the territorial disputes arising from the Revolutionary and Napoleonic wars through the creation of a permanent 'Concert of Europe', a 'congress system' of regular diplomatic summits between representatives of the five great European powers: Prussia, Russia, Britain, France and Austria.[21] But resolutions were also passed in Vienna on the free navigation of 'international' rivers, notably the Rhine and the Danube; on the new rules governing who could claim diplomatic status; and on the Atlantic slave trade, all of which were based on general principles for the governance of the international community at large. The Congress of Vienna, therefore, marked a key moment on the gradual transition from a Westphalian model of the international conference, dominated by representatives of rival royal

Figure 1.1 'Die Kongokonferenz in Berlin', 1884, by Adalbert von Rößler. From *Über Land und Meer: Allgemeine illustrirte Zeitung* 53, no. 14 (October 1884–5), 308.

courts seeking to protect their interests, and the modern international conference as a system of ongoing international governance. The Congress can be viewed, in Dunn's phrase, as 'a kind of universal parliamentary assembly acting on behalf of Europe as a single community'.[22] The 1884 Congress of Berlin, which sought to resolve tensions between Russia and the Ottoman Empire and to seek international agreement on how best to divide the land resources of the African continent (see the visual interplay of cartography and diplomacy in Figure 1.1), involved a similar fusion of traditional territorial geopolitics and modern international governance.[23]

Modern international conferences

The 1919–20 Paris Peace Conference was another key moment in the emergence of modern conferencing. It was a product of the convergent traditions of diplomatic conferencing and scientific-technical conferencing outlined earlier but involved an unprecedented complexity of organization. Twenty-seven states participated; the British delegation alone comprised around 400 people and the American contingent was almost as large. Unlike previous gatherings, most of those who attended were not professional diplomats but prime ministers and foreign ministers assisted by an unusually large number of scientific advisors and technical experts in a way which, as

Hill argues, 'put the technician in a far more conspicuous place than he had attained before'.[24] Many at the time viewed the event as marking the dawn of a new era of international cooperation and governance, exemplified by the creation of the League of Nations in 1920, which took the modern international conference as its modus operandi. Contemporaries wrote of the Paris Peace Conference as the culmination of a long history of diplomatic conferences, paying particular note to the Congresses of Westphalia and Vienna as models for what was now being undertaken in the French capital.

The focus on the distant past lent an air of tradition to what were, in some cases, radically new forms of politics while paradoxically also underplaying its continuities with events of the more immediate past. With the horrors of war so fresh, it suited all those participating to see 1919 as a historical break that would make a reality of H. G. Wells's prophecy that the First World War would be 'the war to end all wars'. Accordingly, contemporary commentators were reluctant to acknowledge the more recent history of international conferences from which the Paris Peace Conference emerged. Reflections on the practical insights drawn from the Congresses of Westphalia or Vienna should be met with some degree of caution. Comparisons to the great diplomatic conferences of the past reflected organizers' hopes that Paris would also come to be understood as an event which gave rise to a period of post-war prosperity and calm, rather than its more immediate precursors which had failed to quell rising tensions, most notably the Hague Peace Conferences (1899 and 1907).

Besides its size and complexity, the Paris Peace Conference was not the radical break its organizers anticipated. As recent research has shown, the Hague Peace Conferences of 1899 and 1907 foreshadowed many of the debates and decisions often associated with the Paris Peace Conference, and it is likely that the third Hague conference, scheduled for 1915 but cancelled after the outbreak of the First World War, would have provided additional political inspiration. Certainly the articles, clauses and declarations of the Hague Conventions profoundly shaped the ideas of international governance and international law promoted in Paris in 1919–20 and furthermore the conferences themselves provided an organizational template for the Paris negotiations. As Maartje Abbenhuis argues, 'the 1907 Hague Peace Conference constituted the first time almost all of the world's governments negotiated their concerns in a multilateral setting. In so doing, they initiated a revolutionary trend in global organisation and transnational interaction.'[25] While appreciation of these conferences is often overshadowed by the war which followed, they played a critical role in establishing the 'international sphere' as a political and judicial scale of governance. The Hague system of global governance was a model for those meeting in Paris in 1919 and the League of Nations system which they created. Moreover, several aspects which emerged as part of the Hague system, such as the Permanent Court of Arbitration, continued to play a role in the new international order.[26]

Notwithstanding these points, the Paris Peace Conference was a key moment in the development of international conferencing in at least three respects. First, as we have already seen, 1919 marked a significant shift in how conferencing was approached as an object of study in its own right, closely tied to the establishment of the new field of international relations. Starting with Satow's *Handbook* on conferencing prepared for the Paris Peace Conference and continuing in works by the likes of Dunn, Hill, Nicolson and Zimmern in the interwar period, as well as post-war authors such as the French jurist Georges Scelle and the American anthropologist Margaret Mead, conferencing became not just a pragmatic means of preserving peace but an instrument to unlock a new, international future.[27] As another analyst of conference method, the British civil servant Maurice Hankey, said in 1920, the best hope of averting future war lay in 'the judicious development of diplomacy by conference'.[28]

Second was the Paris Peace Conference's establishment of the League of Nations as the primary piece of political architecture around which a new scale of political action could be built. From its foundation, the central aim of the League of Nations was to change the way in which diplomacy was conducted, ridding it of the self-interest and secrecy that was blamed for the outbreak of war, and ushering in a new age of enlightened global governance. While it is important not to overstate the extent to which the League's methods were entirely new, it is equally important to appreciate the extent to which they *felt* new and therefore were approached with an imagination and vigour that was different to that which had preceded it. International conferences became emblematic of the 'new diplomacy' and quantitatively mushroomed in number while qualitatively becoming more self-consciously professional and 'modern' than had previously been the case.

Third were the reverberations that carried international conferencing beyond the bounds of the League. The Paris Peace Conference offered remarkable access to non-state groups, from peace and women's groups to anti-colonial activists.[29] More international non-governmental organizations were founded in 1919 than in any previous year, and over the course of the 1920s twice as many were founded as in the entire nineteenth century.[30] This emergent international public sphere produced important advocates of the international conference, but it was by no means limited to the brand of internationalism embodied by the League of Nations or United Nations. For international relations scholar Fred Halliday, internationalism had at least three major competing forms.[31] League-style 'liberal internationalism' assumed that societies and individuals cooperate across borders on equal terms. 'Hegemonic internationalism' represented world integration on asymmetric, unequal terms, such as forms of empire and imperialism. 'Radical or revolutionary internationalism', meanwhile, encompassed a diverse range of ideologies from Marx's proletarian internationalism to radical republican, anarchistic, revolutionary and Islamic internationalism. These forms of internationalism were differentiated by not only their political ideologies but also their degree of formality and structure. In this section, we consider modern international conferences successively according to Halliday's three modes of internationalism.

Liberal international conferencing

Alfred Zimmern opened his 1936 account of the political history of the League of Nations by suggesting that the best way of approaching the study of the League was to think of it as a *method* rather than an institution.[32] By this, he meant the way in which it put into practice the tenets of the so-called new diplomacy, prioritizing transparency over secrecy, participation over exclusion and scientific cooperation over military alliances.³³ It was hoped that these foundational principles would entrench a new way of enacting relations between states, which would make it less likely that disagreements would result in war. This was perhaps best exemplified by the League's great set pieces: the Council meetings that would respond to developments in world politics and the annual General Assembly at Geneva, a highly public event to which the world's press was invited to report on the League's activities. These activities all took place in Geneva, where the League was housed first in the Palais Wilson (which had been hastily converted from its previous existence as the Hôtel National), and then from 1937 in the purpose-built Palais des Nations. The new presence of the League, combined with a local internationalist tradition embodied by the Salle de la Réformation, the large conference hall built in 1866 which hosted the League's General Assemblies throughout the 1920s, led to the popularization of the notion of *l'esprit de Genève*, by which Geneva became firmly associated with the new era of internationalism.³⁴

However, these very public set pieces were dwarfed in number by the myriad smaller conferences and meetings held with increasing regularity, predominantly in Geneva but also elsewhere, in established conference cities (Paris, London), in cities located in small or comparatively neutral states (Brussels, Warsaw) or on occasion beyond Europe (Lima, Bangkok).³⁵ There was a steady increase in meetings held under the auspices of the League from 23 in 1920 to over 100 in 1926, a rise that pointed to the increasing size and responsibilities of the League's Secretariat and its various advisory bodies.³⁶ As the League insider William Rappard put it, the progressive multiplication and specialization of these committees and conferences were the 'structural expression of a world need': that of a 'great administrative agency' able to administer non-partisan expertise, primarily through the convocation of conferences.³⁷ The League's founding principles were becoming interpreted more broadly, as tenets not just for avoiding war but for guiding cooperation in peacetime. This made possible the re-routing into the international sphere of all sort of affairs, many of which were less overtly political and more 'technical' in character. These included regulating communication and transit through agreements on postal, telegraph, submarine, cable and radio services; restricting railway, car and air traffic; and controlling navigation on international rivers, sounds, straits and international waters. In commerce and industry, conferences were held on patents and trademarks, copyrights, tariffs, customs arrangements, commercial arbitration, imports, exports and unfair business practices. Issues of public health figured prominently in international conferences, including those on the control of plagues, quarantine procedures, notification of epidemics, standardization of drug formulae and relief from disasters. Regarding labour, conferences were held on questions of hours, night work, unemployment, child labour, sickness insurance and workers' compensation; in terms of agriculture, on the preservation of birds, containment of agricultural disease (such as phylloxera) and standardized agricultural statistics; and taking in welfare, the traffic of obscene publications, liquor, drugs, arms, women and children and slavery were all discussed, operating under the sign of a newly internationalist cartography (see Figure 1.2).³⁸ In short, nearly every branch of government activity had been internationalized.

The cast of characters involved with international conferences changed too. While prime and foreign ministers increasingly came to Geneva for Council sessions and

Figure 1.2 The League of Nations Commission on Opium and Other Narcotic Drugs, in session at the Palais des Nations, Geneva, 15 May 1939. Source: United Nations Archives at Geneva, LN/279.

the General Assembly, the majority of conferences and committees were filled with technical experts trained in the emerging 'science' of international relations.[39] Nor were they quite so male-dominated: Article 7 of the League of Nations Covenant had pointedly specified that 'All positions under or in connection with the League, including the Secretariat, shall be open equally to men and women'.[40] The League's secretary general for its first thirteen years, Eric Drummond, believed women to be 'very successful at such [international] conferences', and the presence of women was certainly seen as indicative of the modernity of the organization's new political practice.[41] To be sure, gender equality was imperfectly implemented, with women overrepresented among secretaries and in 'central services' and underrepresented in the higher grades, but this situation nevertheless contrasted starkly with most Foreign Offices' simple refusal to countenance the idea of women occupying high positions.[42] The League also professed a commitment to having a representative staff in terms of nationality, though the Eurocentric criteria by which appointments were made tended to render non-Europeans less qualified and filtered them into positions in which they were valued for their regional knowledge or language skills.[43] Those from colonial dependencies, aside from the special case of India, were entirely absent.[44]

Meanwhile, there was a parallel growth of international conferences affiliated with the ever-increasing assortment of international and non-governmental organizations, many of whom transferred their seats to Geneva during the 1920s to be closer to the League.[45] Indeed, upon the League's move to the new Palais des Nations in 1937, their old premises at the Palais Wilson were rapidly filled by thirty different international organizations, from the Carnegie Endowment for International Peace, the International

Council of Women and the International Labour Organization to the World Alliance for International Friendship Through the Churches, the World Association for Reform of the Calendar and the Universal Esperantist Association.[46] This move from the homes of their secretaries to a non-residential office building constituted a major step towards towards the professionalization of international organizations.[47] Their meetings tended to be nimbler in decision-making and more tightly defined in their topic of study. They gained legitimacy through close observation of increasingly formalized conferencing procedures and, often, through their affiliation with the League of Nations.

With the rapid growth of conferencing, concerns surrounding codification and rules became increasingly pronounced. Here, the League also played a key role. As one of the most prolific conference organizing bodies, the League offered both a template for international conference procedure and a forum to formalize the norms and procedures of international conferences in international law. Like conference analysts from Satow on, the League's experts sought to identify common characteristics from the haphazard growth of international conferencing over the preceding century. In 1925 the League's Committee of Experts, concerned with the codification of international law, listed conference procedure as a desirable field of international regulation. A questionnaire produced in 1926 identified 'A certain number of practices [which] have grown up and these reappear at each conference and are handed on from one to the other'.[48]

Yet the League's members were divided on the issue of codification. The importance of conferencing as a mode of international governance suggested the need for codification, and yet the success of conferencing historically could be partly explained by its flexibility as a method which was largely unencumbered by formal rules and procedures. While fourteen members were in favour, and a further five with reservations, seven opposed efforts to create a conferencing code, including Germany, Japan, the United States, India and 'the British Empire'.[49] The latter felt that procedure should be left to delegates, with historical precedent offered as an example or model rather than code. This reflected a familiar experience of the League's work, where education and normalization work often succeeded while law and codification failed.[50] While the British Empire was shaping League policy, the conference method and imperialism were also reshaping each other in a host of forms and spaces.

Colonial, imperial and Commonwealth conferencing

Exhibitions and world fairs tracked and complemented the emergence of international conferences.[51] While prioritizing commerce and trade, these events celebrated internationalism as a cultural and political aspiration, beginning with the triumphant 1851 Great Exhibition in London, and were especially significant in bringing together the imperial and international imaginations. The *Exposition Coloniale Internationale*, originally planned to commemorate the 1930 centenary of the French conquest of the Ottoman Regency of Algiers, attracted nine million visitors to newly created pavilions and exhibition spaces in the Bois de Vincennes, to the east of central Paris, in the summer and autumn of 1931. This was a forum for international debates about the future of European colonial empires, and more than 3,000 reports were published by the French government before and during the Exposition on every conceivable aspect of colonial management. More than 100 congresses were organized in the French capital to coincide with the Exposition, including the thirteenth International Geographical Congress, many of which made use of the salons and amphitheatres in the exotically frescoed Palais de la Porte Dorée, today the home of the *Cité nationale de l'histoire de l'immigration*. The racism and self-importance of the Palais and its decoration were mocked at the time by a surrealist counter exhibition, backed by the Comintern-funded *Ligue anti-impérialiste* and featuring works by André Breton and Louis Aragon.[52]

The *Exposition Coloniale* featured meticulously re-created buildings, landscapes and environments from across the French Empire, including a replica of Angkor Wat, and had a lasting impact on the city's cultural and intellectual environment, inspiring new fashions in music, the arts and cuisine.[53] Inspired by British debates about the possibilities of imperial reform, the Exposition hosted a colonial economic conference from December 1934 to April 1935 in an ultimately futile attempt to convert the grand cultural and intellectual ideals invoked in 1931 into concrete commercial realities.[54]

The British themselves had a long tradition of using conferences to orchestrate the empire and negotiate evolving demands for constitutional reform. From the mid-nineteenth century, imperialism was transformed by the emerging norms of internationalism and international conferences. Following the 'Sepoy Mutiny' of 1857–8 in India and the 'Morant Bay Rebellion' of 1865 in Jamaica, theories of racial difference hardened across British colonies while in majority-white 'settler colonies' progress was made towards self-government.[55] Canada, South Africa, Australia and New Zealand were the largest of the 'dominions' and demanded a voice in the conduct of imperial politics which, in turn, was reimagined as a form of international confederation.[56] For Daniel Gorman this began a process of 'imperial internationalism', defined as the international life of the dominions *within* the British Empire.[57] The progress of this internationalization centred on 'colonial', and later 'imperial', conferences. The 1887 Colonial Conference in London was the first of twelve such conferences by 1937, nearly all of which were convened in London.[58]

By the interwar years the British Empire was remade in the image of internationalism, and what Alfred Zimmern dubbed the 'Third British Empire' was forged.[59] In under ten years the UK was reordered and an Irish dominion established, a new Middle Eastern empire amassed, free trade ideology questioned, the Government of India restructured and the constitutional status of the white dominions redefined.[60] The dominions and India secured international recognition (through the League of Nations and elsewhere) but without settling the question of their sovereign status.[61] Like the broader domain of internationalism, conferencing was a key mechanism in managing the ongoing process of the internationalization of empire. The periodic Imperial Conferences from 1923 were modelled as consultative forums, with foreign policy set by dominion governments themselves. The position was affirmed at the 1926 conference, which produced the Balfour Declaration, whereby dominions were defined as autonomous communities united as 'members of the British Commonwealth of Nations'.[62] At the 1930 Imperial Conference the dominions were granted legislative equality, which was formalized in the Statute of Westminster the following year. The Commonwealth had no permanent parliament or chamber in London but was organized through the practice of conferencing. As the Canadian multi-term prime minister William Lyon Mackenzie King put it in 1941:

> It is true we have not, sitting in London continuously, a visible Imperial War Cabinet or Council. But we have, what is much more important, though invisible, a continuing conference of the Cabinets of Commonwealth.[63]

India had been represented at the Imperial Conferences since 1921 but only by the secretary of state for India and, later, a few selected delegates.[64] Dozens of Indian delegates were, however, invited to London for the Round Table Conference, which sat in three sittings between 1930 and 1932.[65] Neither a traditional 'imperial' nor an 'international' conference, the meeting sought to determine the constitutional future of India within the empire.[66] The conference format presented benefits to the hosts, especially because the British and colonial Indian governments had selected the delegates. When Gandhi himself proved unable to resolve the impasse between Hindu and Muslim delegates at the second conference session (he suggested that they had been selected so as to be incompatible), the British could absolve themselves of blame. Likewise, they could claim to be respecting demands by Indian feminists for representation when selecting two conservative women, one Hindu and one Muslim, who didn't back Indian nationalist claims for full adult franchise.[67] Indian women's groups, meanwhile, were campaigning for a wider female franchise at both national congresses (such as the All India Women's Congress) and international conferences (such as the 1931 All-Asian Women's Conference in Lahore).[68]

During the Second World War colonial and imperial conferences were refashioned into British Commonwealth Conferences. While meetings in 1944 and 1945 remained dominated by dominion representatives, the independence and accession to the Commonwealth of India, Pakistan and Ceylon between 1947 and 1948 forced a negotiation of the terms of membership of both the association and its conferences.[69] The London Declaration of 1949 allowed members to have their own head of state, and to be a republic, facilitating an ever expanding membership as other colonies won their freedom, rising from eight in 1949, to twenty-one in 1965, thirty-three in 1977 and fifty in 1990.

The Commonwealth Heads of Government Meetings (CHOGMs) increased in size correspondingly, from eleven representatives at London in 1960 to twenty-one in 1965, thirty-one at Singapore in 1971, forty-two in Melbourne in 1981 and forty-seven in Harare in 1991.[70] As Ruth Craggs has shown, these events offered a prominent platform for post-colonial voices. The Singaporean premier Lee Kuan Yew used the 1971 CHOGM, for example, to mark out the developmental vision of his fledgling and vulnerable state, while the British prime minister Edward Heath was rounded upon for his determination to sell arms to South Africa.[71] Margaret Thatcher fared little better at Lusaka in 1979, dancing to the tune (literally) of the seasoned Zambian president Kenneth Kaunda.[72] These meetings were a product not just of imperial conferencing but of a tradition that emerged from spaces designed exactly to challenge imperial sovereignty.

Anti-colonial, non-aligned and activist conferencing

A plethora of international blueprints for remaking the world in the aftermath of the First World War lay beyond the boundaries of liberal or imperial forms of internationalism. Among those Raza, Roy and Zachariah list were pacifist, pan-Islamist and pan-Africanist, Aryanist, anti-imperialist, suffragist, romanticist, feminist, temperance, eugenic and fascist internationalisms: 'Their divergent ends and objectives were held together, if temporarily, by a euphoria for the vastness and integratedness of the world and the desire and optimism to remake it and shape the future of humanity.'[73] Likewise, Glenda Sluga and Patricia Clavin stress the diversity of voices in twentieth-century internationalism, drawing attention to the 'uneasy alliances and unlikely fellow travellers across the conceptual borders of nationalism and internationalism, and a broader spectrum of international thought and action'.[74] Their edited collection features chapters on religious, socialist, feminist, capitalist, fascist and indigenous internationalisms. These approaches emphasize the rich diversity of movements, governments and conditions that lay claim to the title 'international'. Prompted by Halliday, here we trace 'radical internationalism' through anti-colonial, non-aligned and activist conferencing, acknowledging that these radical politics expressed themselves through a conference format forged in the liberal tradition.

From the outset, anti-colonial activists used conferences to coordinate international networks and legitimize political claims. As Hakim Adi has shown in the case of pan-Africanism, periodic conferences became key feature of anti-colonial politics from the start of the twentieth century.[75] Progressive race reformers organized the 1900 Pan-African Conference, 1911 Universal Races Congress and 1919–27 Pan-African Congresses;[76] more radical pan-Africanists such as Marcus Garvey became associated with the spectacular UNIA conventions in the 1920s; and some of the most powerful anti-colonial voices emerged out of the Communist International ('Comintern'). At the Comintern's foundational First Congress in 1919, the Nikolai Bukharin-drafted congress 'Platform' declared its support for 'exploited colonial peoples in their struggles against imperialism'.[77] This translated into covert financing of movements such as the League Against Imperialism, itself established at a conference in Brussels in 1927.[78] These conferences connected wider anti-imperialist networks. For example, Jawaharlal Nehru, the rising star of the Indian National Congress, attended the founding congress of the League Against Imperialism in Brussels, drawn by its aim to forge a 'real' (i.e. racially inclusive and progressive) League of Nations.[79] Solidarity between proletarian and anti-colonial struggles was called for, with particular emphasis on delegates from China, India and Mexico. These conferences took on a new role in the postwar period as anti-imperial sentiment solidified into a concrete political programme of decolonization. The Fifth Pan-African Congress in Manchester in 1945 is widely hailed for its role in spurring liberation movements across the continent and served as one the most important crucibles for training many of the future leaders of post-colonial Africa.[80] Meanwhile at the 1956 First Meeting of Black Writers and Artists in Paris, Francophone intellectuals met to examine the relationship between negritude and pan-Africanism.

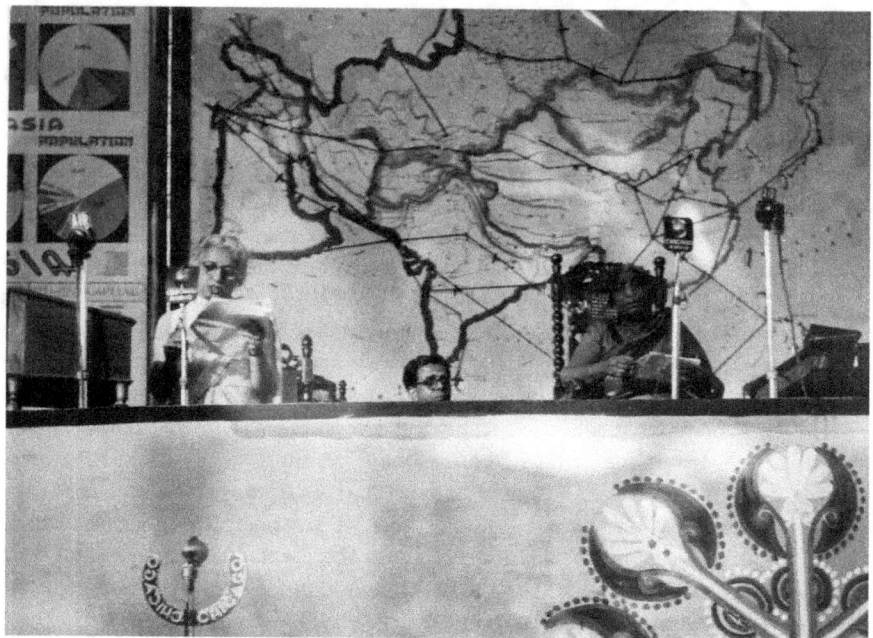

Figure 1.3 Smt. Vijay Lakshmi Pandit reading out the message that had come from Dr Tai Chi-táo, 'a great Chinese friend', at the Asian Relations Conference, 24 March 1947. Source: Nehru Memorial Museum and Library.

Regional conferences became a favoured means of anti-colonial and new post-colonial leaders to meet. For example, the Asian Relations Conference (ARC), which took place in Delhi in April 1947 just four months before India's independence, is being reconsidered as an important space of anti-imperial integration and unity which has long been overshadowed by the more famous Afro-Asian Conference in Bandung in 1955.[81] The meeting marked the emergence of the non-alignment movement, at which the term 'third world' entered political discourse.[82] Unlike the focus of later conferences on heads of state, the ARC included delegations from organizations and institutions as well as national representatives; as Vineet Thakur has argued, 'the text and texture of the Conference needs to be situated in the liminal moment between the "internationalist" and "inter-national" eras'.[83] The opening conference sessions were conducted in front of a map of Asia, showing its infrastructural unity, which was flanked by continental and regional statistics relating to areas and populations (Figure 1.3).

The ARC also incorporated a 'Status of Women and Women's Movement' group, which voted in favour of reviving the All-Asian Women's Conference, which had last met in Lahore in 1931.[84] It came to be held in Beijing in 1949, under the auspices of the Women's International Democratic Foundation, and was followed by further feminist conferences which expanded the remit to include more African delegates, taking place in Colombo in 1958 and Cairo in 1961. Unlike the forms of feminist internationalism of the early 1930s described by Sumita Mukherjee, these organizations resisted the imperial feminist tones of Western women's organizations.[85] Instead they strove for Global South–South union and drew together leftist feminists who had been radicalized by anti-colonial, antifascist and cross-class social reform movements.

Elisabeth Armstrong has shown that international women's anti-imperialist meetings pre-dated Bandung by some years.[86] A growing body of work has charted the rich diversity of meetings and ideologies that were emerging across territories as they negotiated decolonization, just as post-war powers attempted to bifurcate the world into capitalist and communist blocs. These works resist both the Cold War narrative of the 1940s to 1960s and the idea that the Bandung conference stood alone in its refutation of Cold War politics. This literature draws attention to other conferences across the Afro-Asiatic world, to a broader range of activists, intellectuals, cultural figures, and political leaders and to the changing social dynamics and material realities of internationalism.[87]

This work involves engaging with minor and dispersed archives to tell the stories of forgotten conferences.[88] Rachel Leow has studied the events of the 1952 Beijing Asia-Pacific Peace Conference, which was organized by the China Peace Council in response to ongoing military activity and hostility in the region.[89] Despite drawing 470 peace activists from nearly 50 countries, the gathering is absent from histories of world peace movements in part because it was held outside the West and in part due to presumptions that it was a front for Soviet foreign policy. Leow shows that the conference ought instead to be viewed as part of a diverse set of reactions to the Cold War in a decolonial context, facilitating new forms of mobility, interaction between state and non-state actors, and experiments with the urban as a stage for international conferencing. Similarly, Su Lin Lewis has recounted how the Asian Socialist Conference, at its meetings in Rangoon (1953) and Bombay (1956) (see Figure 1.4 for the stage of the opening session, conducted before a map of Asia including regional icons), drafted plans for the post-colonial state that would cater for the welfare of all while protecting individual freedoms, the press and the existence of political parties.[90] This vision ultimately floundered in the years that followed as the nation state became the dominant political form driven by a regional turn to military dictatorship. These events also explain why such conference meetings are absent from the historiography of international conferences.

Even large, state-organized conferences of Asian-African representatives have faded from view, including the 'Conference of Asian Countries for the Relaxation of International Tension' which took place in New Delhi eleven days before the Bandung meeting.[91] In contrast to tightly stage-managed theatrical summits, this was a public event, attended by large crowds, as part of an effort to build bottom-up mass support for decolonization and nuclear disarmament. The Indian prime minister Jawaharlal Nehru as a co-convenor of the Bandung conference, could not be seen to publicly support a rival conference, but nevertheless entertained leaders from Egypt and Vietnam privately.

These conferences have been overshadowed by the Afro-Asian Conference held in Bandung in 1955. The conference was a landmark gathering of twenty-nine African and Asian states, many newly independent, who met in order to promote economic and cultural cooperation. It was at Bandung that the principles for the eventual creation of

Figure 1.4 U Hla Aung, Genda Sing, U Ba Swe and Soerjomo Koesoemo Wijono presiding at the Second Asian Socialist Conference in Bombay, 1 November 1956. Photographer: Arno Scholz. Source: International Institute of Social History (Amsterdam), IISG BG B5/348-9.

the non-aligned movement were first laid out.[92] Yet the appeal of Bandung reflects the conference's symbolism, as expressive of a moment of rising post-colonial confidence; a shared refutation of colonialism in the Global South; and a rejection of Cold War geopolitical narratives, encapsulated in what became known as the 'Bandung Spirit', a term popularized by Roeslan Abdulgani, the secretary general of the conference.[93] For scholars, therefore, Bandung has become a central point of orientation which cuts across Cold War history, decolonization, international relations and post-colonial studies. As Christopher J. Lee has argued, the 'attraction of Bandung as an event is its capacity to bring these subjects into conversation with one another, presenting a historical moment and site generative of intersecting vantage points and their storied outcomes'.[94] Like Vienna or Versailles before it, Bandung has become shorthand for both a discrete diplomatic conference and long-standing historical processes.

Early accounts of the Congress, including the African-American writer Richard Wright's famous first-hand account, read Bandung through a metropole-colony lens, focusing on the realignment of colonial relations in the 1950s.[95] More recent work, however, has emphasized connections within the Global South and the difficulties they faced as anti-colonialism confronted the political realities of nation-building. As Lee argues, 'Bandung contained both the residual romance of revolution, as well as the *realpolitik* of a new world order in the making.'[96] Recent scholarship has sought to challenge the mythology of Bandung. Scholars such as Su Lin Lewis and Carolien

Stolte have decentred the conference by situating it within the wider constellation of Afro-Asian internationalisms which were a key feature of the early Cold War years.[97] Others offer a closer, critical reading of the conference itself. Naoko Shimazu examines the conference as a theatrical performance wherein both the cast and stage were scripted in very particular ways, and a recent edited volume has shown how the political possibilities of Bandung were less certain than the state-centrism of both the event and its later readings suggest.[98] Its editors argue that as Bandung grappled with the uncertainties of the modern world order, these debates were mixed with a heady 'utopian dimension of peoples across the world actively reimaging, changing and prefiguring' that order.[99] The significance of Bandung was hotly contested at the time and since, and its ambiguous status reflects that of the conferencing method itself. For some, the conference marked the arrival of African and Asian states as powerful actors on the world stage, whereas for others the liberal conferencing form visibly symbolized the ongoing legacies of European imperialism.

Conclusion

The flow of the narrative that we have drawn reflects something of the trajectory of how international conferences have been treated in the historical scholarship. Interwar scholars collated a history in which conferencing happened through, and thereby reinforced, a Westphalian system of sovereign states. However, this major-key conservatism had a minor-key radical edge: conferences were where new systems were formalized and therefore held worldmaking potential. This was explicitly linked to the new realities of the interwar years, in which conferencing would be foregrounded and accelerated as the means through which a new internationalism could be implemented, whether liberal, imperial or radical at heart. Over the years, underlying tendencies in the historiography towards presentism and Eurocentrism filtered out conferences held outside the 'West', conferences held in the name of causes that had ended in failure, or conferences that did not fit with overarching narratives about the past. The present current, with which we swim, seeks to redress this filtering by de-privileging interstate conferences as the quintessential form of conferencing and instead opening out the scope of enquiry to a wider range of conferences, refocusing on what was previously held to be historical marginalia.

This is not just a matter of what we look at but the methodologies employed. As the Afro-Asian Networks Research Collective have proposed, in order to ask new questions researchers need to adopt new practices, including collaborative and collective research, working across multiple archives (including those in the Global South). By doing so, they argue, we can move from seeing Bandung as a single event to seeing a broader 'Bandung moment' formed by a multiplicity of networks and actors.[100] They draw upon a broader turn in the study of international history from interstate relations, analysed by way of documents found in national diplomatic archives, to a self-consciously transnational approach.[101] In this book, we apply these imperatives to the study of international conferencing, arguing that there is a broader need to move from analyses of conferences as momentous events to conferencing as a process comprised of a constellation of people and events, ideas and ideologies. We therefore present the historical geography of international conferencing between and beyond Versailles and Bandung by turning away from these twin pillars and looking instead to what less well-known events can tell us about the practice of conferencing, and what studies of conferencing can tell us about more geographically and politically diffuse forms of internationalism.

Notes

1 Harold Nicolson, *Peacemaking 1919: Being Reminiscences of the Paris Peace Conference* (Boston & New York: Houghton Mifflin Company, 1933), 97–9.
2 See, for an excellent commentary, Simon Collier, 'Nationality, Nationalism, and Supranationalism in the Writings of Simón Bolívar', *Hispanic American Historical Review* 63, no. 1 (1983): 37–64.
3 Harold Nicolson, *Diplomacy* (London: Butterworth, 1939), 15, 26. See also J. G. A. Pocock, *The Machiavellian Moment: Florentine Political Thought and the Atlantic Republican Tradition* (Princeton: Princeton University Press, 2003 [1975]); J. G. A. Pocock, 'The Machiavellian Moment Revisited: A Study in History and Ideology', *Journal of Modern History* 53, no. 1 (1981): 49–72; and Quentin Skinner, *The Foundations of Modern Political Thought. Vol. 1: The Renaissance* (Cambridge: Cambridge University Press, 1998 [1978]).
4 Norman L. Hill, *The Public International Conference, Its Function, Organization, and Procedure* (Stanford, CA: Stanford University Press, 1929), 1; Alfred Zimmern, *The League of Nations and the Rule of Law, 1918–1935* (London: Macmillan and Co., 1936), 33, citing M. Creighton, *A History of the Papacy from the Great Schism to the Sack of Rome*, vol. II (London: Longmans, Green & Co.; 1897), 293.
5 For a brilliant account, see Glenn Richardson, *The Field of Cloth of Gold* (New Haven: Yale University Press, 2014).
6 See, for important discussions of an enormous literature, Andreas Osiander, 'Sovereignty, International Relations and the Westphalian Myth', *International Organization* 55, no. 2 (2001): 251–87; and Derek Croxton, *Westphalia: The Last Christian Peace* (London: Palgrave, 2013).
7 Kenneth Colegrove, 'Diplomatic Procedure Preliminary to the Congress of Westphalia', *The American Journal of International Law* 13, no. 3 (1919): 450–82.
8 Hill, *The Public International Conference*, 4.
9 Frederick Sherwood Dunn, *The Practice and Procedure of International Conferences* (Baltimore: The Johns Hopkins University Press, 1929), 7.
10 Zimmern, *The League of Nations and the Rule of Law*, 37.
11 On this, see Dunn, *The Practice and Procedure of International Conferences*, 6.
12 See the essays in a theme issue by Wolf Feuerhahn & Pascale Rabault-Feuerhahn (eds), 'La fabrique international de la science: les congrès scientifiques de 1865 à 1945', *Revue Germanique Internationale* 12 (2010); and Anne Rasmussen, 'Jalons pour une histoire des congrès internationaux au XIXe siècle: régulation scientifique et propaganda intellectuelle', *Relations Internationales* 62 (1990): 115–33. For related context, see Martin H. Geyer & Johannes Paulmann (eds), *The Mechanics of Internationalism: Culture, Society, and Politics from the 1840s to the First World War* (Oxford: Oxford University Press, 2001); M. Herren, *Hintertüren zur Macht: Internationalismus und modernisierungsorientierte Außenpolitik in Belgien, der*

Schweiz und den USA 1865–1914 (Munich: Oldenbourg, 2000); Geert J. Somsen, 'A History of Universalism: Conceptions of the Internationality of Science from the Enlightenment to the Cold War', *Minerva* 46 (2008): 361–79; and, especially, Robert Fox, *Science Without Frontiers: Cosmopolitanism and National Interests in the World of Learning, 1870–1940* (Corvallis, OR: Oregon State University Press, 2016).

13 See Nico Randeraad, 'The International Statistical Congress (1853–1876): Knowledge Transfers and Their Limits', *European History Quarterly* 41, no. 1 (2011): 50–65. On language and science, see Michael D. Gordin, *Scientific Babel: The Language of Science from the Fall of Latin to the Rise of English* (London: Profile Books, 2015).

14 See Marie-Claire Robic, A.-M. Briend & Mechtild Rössler (eds), *Géographes Face au Monde: l'Union Géographique Internationale et les Congrès Internationaux de Géographie/Geographers and the World: The International Geographical Union and the International Geographical Congresses* (Paris: L'Harmattan, 1996).

15 Charles W. J. Withers, *Zero Degrees: Geographies of the Prime Meridian* (Harvard: Harvard University Press, 2017).

16 See Dunn, *The Practice and Procedure of International Conferences*, 152–3; and, for more detail, Francis Lyall, *International Communications: The International Telecommunication Union and the Universal Postal Union* (London: Routledge, 2016 [2011]). On colonial India and the ITU, see Ellen Ravndal, 'From an Inclusive to an Exclusive International Order: Membership of International Organisations from the 19th to the 20th Century', *STANCE Working Paper Series* 8 (2016): 11. For more on the role of international conferences in this area, see Richard R. John, 'Projecting Power Overseas: U.S. Postal Policy and International Standard-Setting at the 1863 Paris Postal Conference', *Journal of Policy History* 27, no. 3 (2015): 416–38.

17 Ellen Ravndal, 'Acting Like a State: Non-European Membership of International Organizations in the Nineteenth Century', in *De-Centering State Making: Comparative and International Perspectives*, eds. Jens Bartelson, Martin Hall & Jan Teorell (Cheltenham: Edward Elgar, 2018), 175–96, 176.

18 Dunn, *The Practice and Procedure of International Conferences*, 139, quoting Pitman B. Potter, a specialist in international law from the University of Wisconsin-Madison.

19 Mark Mazower, *Governing the World: The History of an Idea* (London: Penguin, 2012), 95.

20 Jürgen Habermas, *The Structural Transformation of the Public Sphere: An Inquiry into a Category of Bourgeois Society*, trans. Thomas Burger with Frederick Lawrence (Cambridge: Polity, 1989 [1962]); Valeska Huber & Jürgen Osterhammel (eds), *Global Publics: Their Power and Their Limits, 1870–1990* (Oxford: Oxford University Press, 2020).

21 The pervasive influence of the Congress of Vienna on later international conferences and geopolitical strategists is evident in pages of C. K. Webster, *The Congress of Vienna, 1814–1815* (London: HMSO, 1919), which, like Satow's report, was commissioned by Prothero's Historical Section in the British Foreign Office during the First World War; Harold Nicolson, *The Congress of Vienna: A Study of Allied Unity 1812–1822* (London: Constable, 1946), in which the Congress formed the basis for a commentary on the post-1945 world order envisaged by the author; and Henry Kissinger, *A World Restored: Metternich, Castlereagh and the Problems of Peace, 1812–1822* (London: Weidenfeld & Nicolson, 1957). On the Congress itself, see Brian E. Vick, *The Congress of Vienna: Power and Politics after Napoleon* (Cambridge, MA: Harvard University Press, 2014). On the pioneering use of Prussian statistical expertise at the Congress, see Beatrice de Graaf, 'Second-tier Diplomacy: Hans von Gagern and William I in Their Quest for an Alternative European Order, 1813–1818', *Journal of Modern European History* 12, no. 4 (2014): 546–65, especially 558.

22 Dunn, *The Practice and Procedure of International Conferences*, 55. For a thoughtful analysis of the impact on these early attempts to internationalize the natural world, specifically Europe's great rivers, see Joanne Yao, '"Conquest of Barbarism": The Danube Commission, International Order and the Control of Nature as a Standard of Civilisation', *European Journal of International Relations* 25, no. 2 (2019): 335–59.

23 See Stig Förster, Wolfgang J. Mommsen & Ronald Robinson (eds), *Bismarck, Europe and Africa: The Berlin Africa Conference 1884–1885 and the Onset of Partition* (Oxford: Oxford University Press, 1988); John M. MacKenzie, *The Partition of Africa, 1880–1900 and European Imperialism in the Nineteenth Century* (London: Methuen, 1983). For commentaries on specific aspects of this event, see Patrick Brantlinger, 'Victorians and Africans: The Genealogy of the Myth of the Dark Continent', *Critical Inquiry* 12, no. 1 (1985): 166–203; John Darwin, 'Imperialism and the Victorians: The Dynamics of Territorial Expansion', *English Historical Review* 112, no. 447 (1997): 614–42. On the legal consequences, see Anthony Anghie, *Imperialism, Sovereignty and the Making of International Law* (Cambridge: Cambridge University Press 2004), 90–100; Matthew Craven, 'Between Law and History: The Berlin Conference of 1884–1885 and the Logic and Free Trade', *London Review of International Law* 3, no. 1 (2015): 31–59; and for comments on the influence of the United States and the recognition of new sovereign bodies, see Carl Schmitt, *The Nomos of the Earth in the International Law of the Jus Publicum Europaeum* (New York: Telos Press Ltd, 2003 [1950]), 214–26.

24 Hill, *The Public International Conference*, 40; c.f. also 104–5.

25 Maartje Abbenhuis, 'Introduction: Unbridled Promise? The Hague's Peace Conferences and Their Legacies', in *War, Peace and International Order? The Legacies of the Hague Conferences of 1899 and 1907*, eds. Maartje Abbenhuis, Christopher Ernest Barber & Annalise R. Higgins (London: Routledge, 2017), 1–11, 2.

26 For more on the Hague Peace Conferences, see Maartje Abbenhuis, Christopher Ernest Barber & Annalise R. Higgins (eds), *War, Peace and International Order? The Legacies of the Hague Conferences of 1899 and 1907* (London: Routledge, 2017); Maartje Abbenhuis, *The Hague Conferences and International Politics, 1898–1915* (London: Bloomsbury, 2018); Ian Clark, *International Legitimacy and World Society* (Oxford: Oxford University Press, 2007).

27 Georges Scelle, 'The Evolution of International Conferences', *International Social Science Bulletin* 5 (1953), 241–57, in a theme issue on 'The Technique of International Conferences'; Margaret Mead, 'A Meta-Conference: Eastbourne, 1956', *ETC: A Review of General Semantics* 15, no. 2 (1957-1958): 148–51; Mary Capes, in collaboration with A. T. M. Wilson (eds) *Communication or Conflict: Conferences, Their Nature, Dynamics and Planning* (London: Tavistock, 1960); Margaret Mead & Paul Byers, *The Small Conference: An Innovation in Communication* (Paris & The Hague: Mouton & Co., 1968). See also Karl Franz Schweig, *Wie Organisiere ich einen Kongress? Handbuch über die Organisation internationaler Kongresse und Tagungen* (Düsseldorf: Droste, 1957); Karl Franz Schweig, *The Organization of an International Congress*, trans. Jules Cortell & Henry Marx (New York: Atpac Tours, 1966); Johan Kaufmann, *Conference Diplomacy: An Introductory Analysis* (Leyden: A.W. Sijthoff/ Dobbs Ferry, NY: Oceana Publications, 1968).

28 Maurice Hankey, 'Diplomacy by Conference', paper read at the British Institute of International Affairs on 2 November 1920, printed in *The Round Table: A Quarterly Review of the Politics of the British Empire* 11 (1920–1921), 287–311, 310.

29 For example, see Jake Hodder, 'The Elusive History of the Pan-African Congress, 1919–1929', *History Workshop Journal* 91 (2021), 113–131; Erika Kuhlman

'The "Women's International League for Peace and Freedom" and Reconciliation after the Great War', in *The Women's Movement in Wartime: International Perspectives, 1914–19*, eds. Alison S. Fell & Ingrid Sharp (Basingstoke: Palgrave Macmillan, 2007), 227–43.

30 Thomas Davies, *NGOs: A New History of Transnational Civil Society* (London: Hurst and Company, 2013), 77–106.

31 Fred Halliday, 'Three Concepts of Internationalism', *International Affairs* 64, no. 2 (1988): 187–98.

32 Zimmern, *The League of Nations and the Rule of Law*, 1.

33 Mazower, *Governing the World: The History of an Idea*, 116.

34 Robert de Traz, *L'esprit de Genève* (Paris: B. Grasset, 1929); Madeleine Herren, 'Geneva, 1919–1945: The Spatialities of Public Internationalism and Global Networks', in *Mobilities of Knowledge*, eds. Heike Jöns, Peter Meusburger & Michael Heffernan (Cham: Springer, 2017), 211–26.

35 Data formerly available via the League of Nations Photo Archives at Indiana University, http://www.indiana.edu/~league/conferencedata.htm; much of the same data is now available through the still-active LONSEA database at the University of Heidelberg, http://www.lonsea.de/.

36 William E. Rappard, 'The Evolution of the League of Nations', *The American Political Science Review* 21, no. 4 (1927): 792–826, 817.

37 Rappard, 'Evolution of the League of Nations', 818.

38 Dunn, *The Practice and Procedure of International Conferences*, 142–3.

39 Rappard, 'Evolution of the League of Nations', 805.

40 Covenant of the League of Nations, Article 7, http://avalon.law.yale.edu/20th_century/leagcov.asp; see Madeleine Herren, 'Gender and International Relations through the Lens of the League of Nations (1919–1945)', in *Women, Diplomacy and International Politics Since 1500*, eds. Glenda Sluga & Carolyn James (Abingdon: Routledge, 2016), 182–201.

41 Minutes of the Fifth Meeting of the Appointments Committee held on 8 May 1926, 9, in LNA, Box S955, Appointment Committee, file 2; quoted in Klaas Dykmann, 'How International Was the Secretariat of the League of Nations?' *The International History Review* 37, no. 4 (2015): 721–44, 734.

42 Herren, 'Gender and International Relations through the Lens of the League of Nations'; Myriam Piguet, 'Gender Distribution in the League of Nations: The Start of a Revolution?' *The Invention of International Bureaucracy* blog (16 March 2017): https://projects.au.dk/inventingbureaucracy/blog/show/artikel/gender-distribution-in-the-league-of-nations-the-start-of-a-revolution/.

43 Dykmann, 'How International Was the Secretariat of the League of Nations?'

44 Susan Pedersen, *The Guardians: The League of Nations and the Crisis of Empire* (Oxford: Oxford University Press, 2015); Stephen Legg, 'An International Anomaly? Sovereignty, the League of Nations and India's Princely Geographies', *Journal of Historical Geography* 43 (2014): 96–110.

45 Benjamin Auberer, Timo Holste & Carolin Liebisch, 'Situating Internationalism 1919–1940s', *New Global Studies* 10, no. 3 (2016): 201–16; Glenda Sluga, 'Remembering 1919: International Organizations and the Future of International Order', *International Affairs* 95, no. 1 (2019): 25–43.

46 Quinn Slobodian, *Globalists: The End of Empire and the Birth of Neoliberalism* (Cambridge, MA: Harvard University Press, 2018), 56–7.

47 Herren, 'Geneva, 1919–1945', 217.

48 'Questionnaire no. 5. – Procedure of International Conferences and Procedure for the Conclusion and Drafting of Treaties', *American Journal of International Law* 20, Special Supplement (1926): 204–21, 207.
49 'Annex III: Analyses of Replies Received from Governments to Questionnaires nos. 1 to 7 Submitted by Members of the Committee', *American Journal of International Law* 22, Special Supplement (1928): 5–38, 21–5.
50 Stephen Legg, '"The Life of Individuals as Well as of Nations": International Law and the League of Nations' Anti-Trafficking Governmentalities', *Leiden Journal of International Law* 25, no. 3 (2012): 647–64.
51 Wouter Van Acker & Christophe Verbruggen, 'World's Fairs in Perspectives: The Aggregation of Modern Times and Spaces at the Beginning of the Twentieth Century (Ghent 1913)', in *A Taste of Progress: Food at International and World Exhibitions in the Nineteenth and Twentieth Centuries*, eds. Nelleke Teughels & Peter Scholliers (London: Routledge, 2016), 11–33; Daniel Laqua, *The Age of Internationalism and Belgium, 1880–1930: Peace, Progress and Prestige* (Manchester: Manchester University Press, 2013).
52 Patricia A. Morton, *Hybrid Modernities: Architecture and Representation at the 1931 Colonial Exposition, Paris* (Cambridge, MA: MIT Press, 2000); Catherine Hodeir & Michel Pierre, *1931: L'Exposition Coloniale* (Bruxelles: Éditions Complexe, 1991); Herman Lebovics, *True France: The Wars over Cultural Identity, 1900–1945* (Ithaca, NY: Cornell University Press, 1992); Alexander C. T. Geppert, *Fleeting Cities: Imperial Expositions in Fin-de-Siècle Europe* (Basingstoke: Palgrave Macmillan, 2010), 179–200, including a fascinating map on p. 197 showing the origins of school groups that visited the exposition. On the 1931 IGC, see Hugh Clout, 'Geographers in Their Ivory Tower: Academic Geography and Popular Geography in Paris 1931', *Geografiska Annaler B: Human Geography* 87, no. 1 (2005): 15–29; and Hugh Clout, 'French Geographers under International Gaze: Regional Excursions for the XIIIth International Geographical Congress, 1931', *Belgeo*, 1–2 (2012): 1–15.
53 See, for example, Lauren Janes, *Colonial Food in Interwar Paris: The Taste of Empire* (London: Bloomsbury, 2016), 127–60.
54 Samir Saul, 'Les pouvoirs publics métropolitains face à la Depression: La Conférence économique de la France métropolitaine et d'Outre-Mer (1934–1935)', *French Colonial History* 12 (2011): 167–91; Jacques Marseille, *Empire Colonial et Capitalisme Français: Histoire d'un Divorce* (Paris: Albin Michel, 2005).
55 Thomas R. Metcalf, *Ideologies of the Raj* (Cambridge: Cambridge University Press, 1994); Catherine Hall, *Civilising Subjects: Metropole and Colony in the English Imagination, 1830–1867* (Oxford: Polity, 2002).
56 Lanka Sundaram, 'India and the Imperial Conference – I: A Retrospective', *The Asiatic Review* 26 (1930): 369–73.
57 Daniel Gorman, *The Emergence of International Society in the 1920s* (Cambridge: Cambridge University Press, 2012).
58 John Edward Kendle, *The Colonial and Imperial Conferences, 1887–1911: A Study in Imperial Organization* (London: Longmans, 1967).
59 Alfred Zimmern, *The Third British Empire: Being a Course of Lectures Delivered at Columbia University, New York* (2nd ed., rev.) (London: Humphrey Milford/Oxford University Press, 1927).
60 John Darwin, 'A Third British Empire? The Dominion Idea in Imperial Politics', in *The Oxford History of the British Empire: Volume: IV: The Twentieth Century*, eds. Judith Brown & Wm Roger Louis (Oxford: Oxford University Press, 1999), 64–87.

61 Nicholas Mansergh, *The Commonwealth Experience: Volume Two: From British to Multiracial Commonwealth* (London: Macmillan, 1982), 5.
62 Mansergh, *From British to Multiracial Commonwealth*, 27.
63 Quoted in Mansergh, *From British to Multiracial Commonwealth*, 2.
64 Sundaram, 'India and the Imperial Conference – I: A Retrospective'.
65 R. J. Moore, *The Crisis of Indian Unity, 1917–1940* (Oxford: Clarendon Press, 1974); Carl Bridge, *Holding India to the Empire: The British Conservative Party and the 1935 Constitution* (New Delhi: Sterling Publishers, 1986).
66 Stephen Legg, 'Imperial Internationalism: The Round Table Conference and the Making of India in London, 1930–32', *Humanity: An International Journal of Human Rights, Humanitarianism, and Development* 11, no. 1 (2020): 32–53.
67 Sumita Mukherjee, *Indian Suffragettes: Female Identities and Transnational Networks* (Oxford: Oxford University Press, 2018), 211.
68 Sumita Mukherjee, 'The All-Asian Women's Conference 1931: Indian Women and Their Leadership of a Pan-Asian Feminist Organisation', *Women's History Review* 26, no. 3 (2017): 363–81.
69 Stuart Mole, '"Seminars for Statesmen": The Evolution of the Commonwealth Summit', *The Round Table: The Commonwealth Journal of International Affairs* 93, no. 376 (2004): 533–46.
70 Mole, 'Seminars for Statesmen', 535.
71 Ruth Craggs, 'Postcolonial Geographies, Decolonization, and the Performance of Geopolitics at Commonwealth Conferences', *Singapore Journal of Tropical Geography* 35, no. 1 (2014): 39–55.
72 Ruth Craggs, 'Hospitality in Geopolitics and the Making of Commonwealth International Relations', *Geoforum* 52 (2014): 90–100.
73 Ali Raza, Franziska Roy & Benjamin Zachariah, 'Preface', in *The Internationalist Moment: South Asia, Worlds, and World Views, 1917–39*, eds. Ali Raza, Franziska Roy & Benjamin Zachariah (London; New Delhi: SAGE, 2015), vii.
74 Glenda Sluga & Patricia Clavin, 'Rethinking the History of Internationalism', in *Internationalisms: A Twentieth-Century History*, eds. Glenda Sluga & Patricia Clavin (Cambridge: Cambridge University Press, 2016), 11.
75 Hakim Adi, *Pan-Africanism: A History* (London: Bloomsbury, 2018); Hakim Adi, 'Pan-Africanism and Communism: The Comintern, the "Negro Question" and the First International Conference of Negro Workers, Hamburg 1930', *African and Black Diaspora: An International Journal* 1, no. 2 (2008): 237–54.
76 Sarah Claire Dunstan, 'Conflicts of Interest: The 1919 Pan-African Congress and the Wilsonian Moment', *Callaloo* 39, no. 1 (2016): 133–50.
77 'Platform of the Communist International Adopted by the First Congress', in *The Communist International 1919–1943: Documents, vol. 1: 1919–1922*, ed. Jane Degras (London: Oxford University Press, 1956), 17–24, 23.
78 Vijay Prashad, *The Darker Nations: A People's History of the Third World* (New York & London: The New Press, 2007), 16–30.
79 Michele L. Louro, *Comrades Against Imperialism: Nehru, India, and Interwar Internationalism* (Cambridge: Cambridge University Press, 2018). On the difficulties the League faced in sustaining itself, and the role of Berlin as an organizational hub, see Fredrik Petersson, 'Hub of the Anti-Imperialist Movement: The League Against Imperialism and Berlin, 1927–1933', *Interventions* 16, no. 1 (2014): 49–71.
80 Hakim Adi & Marika Sherwood, *The 1945 Manchester Pan-African Congress Revisited* (London: New Beacon Books, 1995).

81 Carolien Stolte, '"The Asiatic Hour": New Perspectives on the Asian Relations Conference, New Delhi, 1947', in *The Non-Aligned Movement and the Cold War*, eds. Natasa Miskovic, Harald Fischer-Tiné & Nada Boskovska (London: Routledge, 2014), 75–93.
82 Vineet Thakur, 'An Asian Drama: The Asian Relations Conference, 1947', *The International History Review* 41, no. 3 (2019): 673–95.
83 Thakur, 'An Asian Drama', 17.
84 Elisabeth Armstrong, 'Before Bandung: The Anti-Imperialist Women's Movement in Asia and the Women's International Democratic Federation', *Signs: Journal of Women in Culture and Society* 41, no. 2 (2016): 305–31.
85 Mukherjee, 'The All-Asian Women's Conference 1931'.
86 Armstrong, 'Before Bandung', 307.
87 Su Lin Lewis & Carolien Stolte, 'Other Bandungs: Afro-Asian Internationalisms in the Early Cold War', *Journal of World History* 30, no. 1–2 (2019): 1–19.
88 Jake Hodder, Michael Heffernan & Stephen Legg, 'The Archival Geographies of Twentieth Century Internationalism: Nation, Empire, Race', *Journal of Historical Geography* 71 (2021): 1–11.
89 Rachel Leow, 'A Missing Peace: The Asia-Pacific Peace Conference in Beijing, 1952 and the Emotional Making of Third World Internationalism', *Journal of World History* 30, no. 1–2 (2019): 21–53.
90 Su Lin Lewis, 'Asian Socialism and the Forgotten Architects of Post-Colonial Freedom, 1952–1956', *Journal of World History* 30, no. 1–2 (2019): 55–88.
91 Carolien Stolte, '"The People's Bandung": Local Anti-Imperialists on an Afro-Asian Stage', *Journal of World History* 30, no. 1–2 (2019): 125–56.
92 Natasa Miskovic, Harald Fischer-Tiné & Nada Boskovska (eds), *The Non-Aligned Movement and the Cold War: Delhi-Bandung-Belgrade* (London: Routledge, 2014); See Seng Tan & Amitav Acharya (eds), *Bandung Revisited: The Legacy of the 1955 Asian-African Conference for International Order* (Singapore: National University of Singapore Press, 2008).
93 Roeslan Abdulgani, *Bandung Spirit: Moving on the Tide of History* (Djakarta, Prapantja, 1964).
94 Christopher J. Lee, 'Introduction', in *Making a World After Empire: Bandung and Its Political Afterlives*, ed. Christopher J. Lee (Athens, OH: Ohio University Press, 2010), 3.
95 Richard Wright, *The Colour Curtain: A Report on the Bandung Conference* (London: Dennis Dobson, 1956).
96 Lee, 'Introduction', 3.
97 Lewis & Stolte, 'Other Bandungs'.
98 Naoko Shimazu, 'Diplomacy as Theatre: Staging the Bandung Conference of 1955', *Modern Asian Studies* 48, no. 1 (2014): 225–252.
99 Luis Eslava, Michael Fakhri & Vasuki Nesiah, 'The Spirit of Bandung', in *Bandung, Global History and International Law: Critical Pasts and Pending Futures*, eds. Luis Eslava, Michael Fakhri & Vasuki Nesiah (Cambridge: Cambridge University Press, 2017), 3.
100 Afro-Asian Networks Research Collective, 'Manifesto: Networks of Decolonization in Asia and Africa', *Radical History Review* 131 (2018): 176–82.
101 Hodder et al., 'The Archival Geographies of Twentieth Century Internationalism'.

Part I

State internationalism

2

Ambassadors, activists and experts

Conferencing and the internationalization of international relations in the nineteenth century

Brian Vick

Analyses of nineteenth-century international relations typically emphasize the Congress of Vienna as the origin of a new kind of cooperative summit diplomacy. This chapter aims to show some ways in which the Congress of Vienna and the system of international relations that emerged from it established precursors and set templates for even wider developments in conferencing and international governance as interconnected processes through the nineteenth century and beyond. Doing so can offer new perspectives on twentieth-century trends, the primary focus of this volume. The chapter thereby also shifts the focus from congresses as such, that is, the highest-level summit meetings of rulers and ministers, to networks of actors and institutions one or two levels lower on the diplomatic scale, including beyond the halls of government. Conferencing was just as central to international politics when it involved second-tier diplomats, campaigners for international reforms or scientific experts in academic and professional gatherings. That the classic age of internationalization in the sense of the dramatic expansion of international civil society and international organizations came later, after the 1850s, or even the 1870s, I have no intention to dispute. But while most depictions stress the novelty of these later developments, I argue that they represent more a growth in scale and numbers, and that they built on existing trends whose roots often lay in the early decades of the nineteenth century.[1] The interrelationships and involvement of activists and experts – and, as I shall emphasize, increasingly professional ambassadors – began already with the Vienna Congress and its immediate successor bodies. As the chapter also highlights, despite continued structural exclusion, women and people of colour too created opportunities for engagement within this wider framework of international relations in the first half of the nineteenth century.

Beginning with my book on the Vienna Congress, I have presented a more expansive view of diplomacy, based on broader conceptions of power and of politics. Rather than thinking only in terms of power politics as in the realist school of IR theory, I suggest that we should also analyse diplomacy and international relations in terms of what

I call 'influence politics'. One can even still call it power politics so long as the more complex, diffuse and contested nature of power behind this term is recognized and the fact that international relations involves more than simply the relations of state to state. I thus also emphasize the role of transnational salon society, festive culture, court culture, governmental institutions, intellectual and cultural trends, and the press and publics in the praxis of politics, and hence of a wider range of actors, including non-governmental actors and women as well as men. Such an analytical shift incorporates the persuasive force of spoken and written words, of ideas, of symbols and rituals and of social practice, all as elements that fed into what actors then already referred to as public opinion. As we shall see in this chapter, politically engaged women and men attempted to sway public opinion at various levels, or to lobby rulers, officials and their advisors, through the power of print, speech, associations and public meetings. They too leveraged the advantages of face-to-face negotiation, integrative socialization, public-facing demonstrative persuasion and geographic and social scope to be found in international conferencing. I want to underscore that making the analytical shift to influence politics does not anachronistically apply later concepts to earlier developments; the actors at the time, the Metternichs, Castlereaghs and Talleyrands, and rulers such as Tsar Alexander I and Emperor Franz I of Austria, also thought of politics and diplomacy in such ways, and tried in their turn to sway public opinion or elite opinion in salon society, often in official or unofficial cooperation with writers, artists and salonnières. Moreover, the Great Powers' concern with public opinion held true not just in the case of abolition of the slave trade, where one might have expected it, but also in the highest stakes and allegedly most secret negotiations of all, those over the fates of the Saxon and Polish lands.[2]

Expanding the analysis of power and politics in this way also means investigating a wider set of modes and venues of politics and diplomacy, and, of particular concern in this volume and among historical geographers generally, a wider set of spaces, whether thought of solely as geographic and architectural spaces or also as institutional spaces or social fields of the Bourdieuan sort. Here it is important to note that institutional spaces can themselves be conceptualized in both ways, as the networked links between individuals and the organizational structures in which they fit, and as the physical spaces in which institutions operate, from the office buildings and localities that house them to the geographies that they attempt to map onto, know and control. The institutions fit into the physical spaces, but not perfectly, and while the latter may sometimes be chosen or designed to match the institution, they also mould its operation and relationships. Such considerations apply to salons and academic conferences as to diplomatic venues and foreign ministries.

From multiple perspectives, then, the Vienna Congress represents a particularly rich and generative moment in international history, in part revealing the existing nature of European international relations and in part changing its nature and moving it further in that direction of lobbying, persuasion and publicity. The Congress of Vienna also laid down institutional innovations that provided models for multilateral diplomacy in the future, where the drive to cooperative multilateral relations comprised an important part of internationalization in the nineteenth century. For one, the Congress experimented with smaller commissions of mixed mid-level diplomats and experts to tackle specific and often thorny problems that were resistant to traditional negotiations. For example, the Swiss Commission and the Statistical Commission (to assess population figures and territorial boundaries) both consisted of mid-level diplomatic personnel knowledgeable in those areas, who then worked through controversial material under higher-level instruction to arrive at compromise solutions.[3] The Statistical Commission in particular gave extra clout to the Prussians, despite being the smallest Great Power, since they were able to appoint Johann Gottfried Hoffmann, a Foreign Ministry official more noted as a professor of political science and founder of the Royal Statistical Bureau in Berlin. The Prussian statistics and interpretations ultimately carried the most weight and helped to secure extra territory for Prussia in the final settlement, even if it did not yield them all of Saxony or a larger portion of Poland as they had hoped. The British and Hanoverians for their part called Georg Friedrich von Martens to the committee, Martens being a renowned scholar of international law from the University of Göttingen who became committee secretary. These examples at least foreshadow the role of academic experts and technocratic governance in later decades. The small commissions of Russian, Prussian and Austrian delegates who prepared the final treaties for the disposition of the Polish territories and the constitution for the new Duchy of Cracow also serve as precursors, most obviously for the ambassadorial conferences of the late 1820s that drafted plans for Greek autonomy and independence within or outside the Ottoman Empire, including a Greek constitution. Those conferences were held partly in London, as is generally known, but also on the island of Poros near Athens, involving the ambassadors to Istanbul, as is often forgotten.[4]

Of the institutional innovations, I highlight the role of ambassadors, not in their traditional guise as rulers' representatives to foreign courts but rather as experienced and increasingly professional diplomats who could be called on to join with their ambassadorial colleagues to manage crisis situations or difficult negotiations, in the form of multilateral ambassadorial conferences. In describing the Vienna system of international relations, diplomatic historians often make the distinction between the actual congress system, which ended in 1822 with the Congress of Verona, and the succeeding phase of the Concert of Europe, which endured until the Crimean War in the 1850s or even until the First World War (depending on how one defines it or whether one finds the era of Italian and German unifications a true caesura). Ambassadorial conferences link the two phases and help to explain the system of multilateral cooperation's longevity past 1822, as these gatherings extended the role of face-to-face diplomacy beyond the summit meetings of leading statesmen and rulers at the congresses. As much as the congresses, ambassadorial conferences afforded central venues for the action of what international relations scholar Jennifer Mitzen terms 'forum talk'. Conversing together with increasingly familiar peers, in a semi-public forum that carried weight and responsibility, the ambassadors could more readily come to compromise agreements and feel committed to the final decisions. Such conferences also promoted cooperation through transparency and information sharing. Institutionally ambassadorial conferences point as well to the origins of international agencies and multilateral commissions to address specific international problems.[5] I would add that the fact that the diplomats and often their wives and daughters had already built up some familiarity in the course of salon and court sociability involving the diplomatic corps allowed the conferences to function all the more smoothly when needed.

The new ambassadorial conferences were products of the Vienna Congress. The Allied Council in Paris to supervise the occupation of France after Waterloo is the better known of the successor ambassadorial conferences, and the first convened, but the first to be conceived were those in London to oversee efforts to extend abolition of the African slave trade internationally, following Britain's unilateral abolition in 1807 and the Congress declaration against the slave trade in February 1815. British foreign secretary Lord Castlereagh proposed that meetings of the Great Power ambassadors in London to discuss the progress and problems in achieving this goal would make practical action more effective while simultaneously heading off potential conflicts that might arise in pursuit of the great aim, as, for instance, in the requisite maritime policing of possible slave ships. As he put it, the conferences would constitute 'a sort of permanent European congress'.[6] Tsar Alexander, Austrian foreign minister Prince Metternich and the other assembled rulers and statesmen agreed that these forums could provide effective means of promoting further negotiation and enforcement as well as addressing conflicts before they escalated to crises. After Napoleon's return and defeat at Waterloo in 1815, the Allied Council in Paris was convened on this model and met over three hundred times to handle the day-to-day running of the occupation of France and the various negotiations among the occupying powers that were also often quite contentious.[7]

When the London conferences on abolition finally convened in 1816, they had by then acquired the added task of finding an international solution to the problem of renewed raids by the Barbary corsairs of North Africa. This addition to their mission was in part the result of pressure from smaller states and lobbying and press activity in civil society, similar to the public campaign for abolition if on a smaller scale. Moreover, much of the information and statistics that the London conferences worked with were supplied by activists in abolition networks and organizations, particularly the African Institution, an organization in civil society aiming to replace the slave trade with a profitable commerce in goods. These connections point to the interlocking of governmental and non-governmental actors and organizations in the development of new modes of international governance.[8] In this respect and others the Vienna system involved not only multilateral diplomacy but also early forms of 'polylateralism'.[9] Abolitionist networks and anti-corsairing lobbyists from transnational civil society overlapped and interacted with diplomats in ways that gave diplomacy a 'third dimension' beyond state-level multilateral relations. The process is deeper and more complex in the twenty-first-century era of NGOs and social media but not different in essence.

As I have argued elsewhere, the London ambassadorial conferences also played a part in the internationalization of a universal conception of human rights, that is, promoting awareness and even acceptance of a normative sense of humanity that carried a rights status for members of every nation or race in all areas of the globe.[10] Treaty-making and the efforts of both the British government and the British abolition movement to extend abolition of the slave trade also did so, but the London discussions too were fundamental, partly because of the specific circumstances in which they attempted to highlight links between the cases of European captivity by Barbary corsairs on the one hand and the 'inhuman traffic' in Africans across the Atlantic driven by Europeans on the other. As Castlereagh observed, 'The object [of the negotiations is] to acknowledge and enforce the great principles of justice, humanity, and the Law of Nations mutually between the States and People of Africa and Europe', in order to prevent Europe and Africa 'from having their respective Populations, whether Black or White, forcibly, unjustly, and inhumanly carried away into Slavery.'[11]

To reiterate, the ambassadorial conferences are important in part because they bridge the period of the congress system of 1814–22 and the so-called Concert of Europe that followed. At least one important reason behind the continued stability and success of the Vienna system after the end of the congress phase in 1822 lies in the continued centrality of ambassadorial conferences thereafter. They proved flexible and effective means for solving difficult problems and/or overseeing efforts to implement those solutions once settled. Ambassadorial conferences involving the Russians, British and French as already mentioned helped create the new Greek monarchy separate from the Ottoman Empire in the late 1820s, and before that, the ambassadors of the Great Powers (except Britain) oversaw the restoration of monarchical rule in Naples after the revolution of 1820 and the Congress of Ljubljana, in part to prevent King Ferdinand from pursuing too counter-revolutionary a policy. Following the revolutions of 1830, ambassadorial conferences in London helped secure the independent status of a neutral Belgium after the split from the Kingdom of the Netherlands, while another set in Rome pressured the Papal States to undertake reforms that might hinder renewed revolutionary outbreaks there.[12] The Greek and Belgian conferences in London in particular were shaped as well by mixed-gender political sociability, the Belgian case featuring the French and Russian ambassadorial households of Prince Talleyrand and his hostess the Duchess of Dino and Prince and Princess Lieven, plus the salon of the Whigs Lord and Lady Holland.[13]

A third notable committee from the Congress of Vienna had and continues to have the most direct institutional legacy, namely the Rivers Commission, which helped establish international institutions to superintend a liberalization of commerce on European rivers that flowed through multiple states. First and foremost this applied to the Rhine between Basel and the Netherlands, involving the Great Powers Prussia and France as well as smaller states. The Vienna Congress laid the groundwork for the establishment of the Central Commission for the Navigation of the Rhine (CCNR) from 1816, which endures to this day and is thus the oldest still-functioning intergovernmental organization.[14] Less well remembered is the fact that similar provisions were enacted for traffic on the Elbe and the rivers of partitioned Poland. These moves provided models for the creation of the European Commission of the Danube in the 1856 Peace of Paris, which was revived and restructured in 1921 and 1948 after the World Wars. Whereas the CCNR and other bodies (including one for the Danube also created in 1856) drew their membership from the states bordering the river, the European Commission of the Danube went a step further and involved delegates from other powers as well, in this more like the commissions on abolition of the slave trade, which included representatives of non-maritime powers for an issue deemed to affect the interests of the wider international community. The Danube Commission also incorporated hydraulic and other technical experts alongside the diplomats in making and executing its decisions to improve navigation in the delta region where the river met the Black Sea (an area still technically under Ottoman suzerainty).[15]

Having already noted the extensive role of national and international civil society at various points, this chapter will now probe further into the parts played in international relations by activists and unofficial experts. They too were central to the internationalization of conferencing, including seeing the first more public roles for women and people of colour.

The first such organization to discuss again comes from the abolition milieu, which by the 1830s meant the campaign to end not just the slave trade but slavery itself. Britain and the United States possessed the most powerful abolition movements, with the British movement at the height of its power in the build-up to the final abolition of slavery in the British colonies in 1833 and the subsequent end of the transitional, so-called apprenticeship system in 1838. The two antislavery movements had contact with one another and with other smaller groups elsewhere, and in 1840 they organized an event to bring their representatives together more formally. The World Antislavery Convention of 1840 in London has come to be famous as much as anything for its decision to exclude women delegates from official participation, but it also marks an advance in the internationalization of international civil society, both in the sense of multinational participation and in integrating people of colour across the colour line. The formerly enslaved Henry Beckford of Jamaica, for example, claimed a prominent place in the foreground of Benjamin Robert Haydon's painting commemorating the event (see Figure 2.1) and was among the speakers on the first day. The biracial Samuel Jackman Prescod of Barbados also spoke and served on a committee, three years before he became the first person of African descent elected to the Barbadian Parliament. Delegates too were the African-American abolitionist Charles Lenox Remond and representatives from France, Mauritius, Sierra Leone and independent Haiti (the latter also a person of colour).[16]

Even regarding women, there is more to say. That the question of women's participation in the World Antislavery Convention was raised at all attested to just how integral women had become to the antislavery movement on both sides of the Atlantic. During the 1820s it was women such as the Quaker Elizabeth Heyrick and the women's antislavery societies who helped push the British movement from supporting a gradual end to slavery to demanding immediate abolition, and they also did much to boost the numbers of the petition campaigns to Parliament and to the young Queen Victoria. Already in 1814 at the time of the negotiations after Napoleon's defeat, British abolitionists mustered almost a million signatures against the slave trade; by the 1830s, antislavery petitions amassed over 1.3 million signatures, this time with hundreds of thousands from women. In the petition of 1837–8 against apprenticeship in the colonies, over two-thirds of the 1.1 million signatures came from women. The campaign in the United States in those same years gathered over 400,000 signers, well over half of whom were women. In the United States the women's position was strengthened by the fact that the more radical Garrisonian abolitionists

Figure 2.1 'The Anti-Slavery Society Convention', 1840, by Benjamin Robert Haydon. Oil on canvas, 1841. NPG 599 © National Portrait Gallery, London/Alamy.

were also radical in their support for women's rights, hence the presence of numerous women delegates to the Antislavery Convention in 1840 and the support for their participation from Garrison and others when the debate over their admission erupted. The conservative gender ideals of separate spheres among the new British and Foreign Antislavery Society and the moderate American abolitionists won out in this debate, but the female delegates were still allowed to attend, and they were depicted in Robert Haydon's portrait. Moreover, while the women delegates were forbidden to speak in the meeting or to vote, they also still met among themselves in parallel sessions and mingled with the men in the social venues surrounding the Convention, in this not unlike the salonnières and their visitors during the Congresses of Vienna, Aachen or Verona, or the diplomats' wives, partners and/or daughters in London or Paris.[17]

The list of would-be women delegates to the World Antislavery Convention includes on the US side Lucretia Mott and Elizabeth Cady Stanton, and on the British, Elizabeth Pease and Anne Knight. It is important to observe that women's activity in the abolition movement, plus their combined presence and exclusion in the Antislavery Convention, helped launch the international movement for women's rights in the 1840s and after, with figures such as Mott, Stanton and Knight prominent in the latter as well and profiting from the connections already made and experience gained. The internationally successful abolitionist orator Frederick Douglass in turn helped convince delegates to adopt a platform of women's suffrage in 1848 at the Seneca Falls Convention in the United States.[18]

In considering the peace congress movement in civil society, with its calls for a reorganization of international relations to ban war as a means of resolving conflicts, it is significant that in part through the prominent presence of members of religious networks, there was also considerable overlap with abolition networks and again a crossing of racial lines. Ideas for perpetual peace or international governance were already much discussed around the Vienna Congress, and when the Vienna settlement failed to satisfy these hopes, not only new pamphlets but also new organizations emerged in 1815 and succeeding years. When the second World Antislavery Convention met in London in 1843, it was this time followed by the first International Peace Congress, which featured representatives of peace societies from Britain, Europe and the United States. The presence of so many pacifists in abolition circles and vice versa made it quite practical to hold the meetings in tandem. The African-American pastor James Pennington, like the British abolitionist leader Joseph Sturge, was among the double delegates at the two gatherings. Peace congresses were held again in Brussels in 1848 just after the outbreak of the revolutions, in Paris in 1849 and in Frankfurt in 1850.[19] Among the activists in Paris in 1849 were the African Americans William Wells Brown and, again, James Pennington. Brown, a successful abolitionist lecturer in the United States, Britain and Ireland like Charles Remond and Frederick Douglass, also promoted international peace and other social reform issues during the 1840s and appeared at several reform meetings in conjunction with the World Exhibition at the Crystal Palace in London in 1851, including the newest Peace Congress and a meeting of Fugitive Slaves at Exeter Hall.[20]

In between, at the Frankfurt Congress in 1850, the militant African-American abolitionist Henry Highland Garnet spoke in favour of the peace resolution on the first day, as part of the official American delegation. Garnet and Pennington also addressed an antislavery rally in Frankfurt, and Pennington received an honorary doctorate from the University of Heidelberg through the German scholar Friedrich Wilhelm Carové, whom he had met at the Paris congress. The more noted incident then and since was the speech of Revd. George Copway [Ka-ge-ga-gah-bowh] of the Ojibwa nation in Canada, who in Frankfurt became the first Indigenous representative to address an international venue. Copway dramatically presented the meeting's local president, the Hessian professor, official and parliamentary delegate Carl Jaup, with a calumet peace pipe as well as proposing a resolution in favour of non-intervention that could redound to the benefit of Native American nations as well. Women, as with the abolition campaign, played important organizational roles in the peace movement and were stalwarts in fundraising, but as at the Antislavery Convention, they attended the peace congresses but were not official delegates. Anne Knight tried but failed to be accepted as a delegate at the London Peace Congress in 1851.[21]

In addition to specifically political movements, academic conferences too proved significant in processes of internationalization, not just for their contribution to forging international contacts but also for their engagement with broader international questions. While international congresses of scholars in physics, medicine or other fields emerged later in the nineteenth century, and helped to promote scientific standardization and transnational exchange through international bureaus, here too the roots of such phenomena lay in the first half of the century. These precursor organizations did have primarily national origins and goals, but international participation was also prominent, and even the notion of national played out differently in the states of the German Confederation or the Italian peninsula, with their growing movements for national unification, than in France or Britain. Unlike royal academies, these organizations were self-organized, emphasized interpersonal exchange and moved strategically from city to city for their annual meetings. In Britain one may think first of the British Association for the Advancement of Science (BAAS), founded in 1831, but the equally peripatetic Association of German Scholars of Nature and Doctors (Gesellschaft deutscher Naturforscher und Ärzte) emerged even earlier, founded by Lorenz Oken in 1822, and in fact helped inspire the British creation. The national goals were clearly met by encouraging communication and networking across the boundaries of the various states of the not-yet-fully united German lands, even including aspirations towards a Greater Germany that would include the Habsburg realm, as when the organization met in Vienna in 1832, Prague in 1837 and Graz in 1843.[22] But the networking went beyond the national into the international realm. In Graz, for instance, scholars assembled not just from the German states and the German-speaking parts of the Habsburg Empire but also from Hungary, Bohemia and Polish Galicia. Moreover, the approximately 700 attendees in Graz included scientists from beyond the German powers as well, most numerous from Denmark and from Italy as far south as Naples, but also from Russia, Britain, France, Belgium and Switzerland. The Egyptian scholar Abdelrahman Muhammed presented on mineralogy at the meeting, and though admittedly he was already studying at the university in Graz, five other Arab visitors from Egypt, and one from Jerusalem, also attended.[23]

The Congresses of Italian Scientists (Riunioni degli scienziati italiani) began in Pisa in 1839, with its associations of Galileo and the Leaning Tower, and among the foreign guests was the same Lorenz Oken who had founded the German association in 1822. There too appeared the statistician Adolphe Quetelet, who on the back of the Great Exhibition in London in 1851 went on to organize the first International Statistical Congress in Brussels in 1853, an organization which did even more to mix learned and political or governmental circles in an assembly of experts. Among the foreign participants in Turin for the follow-up meeting in 1840 was Charles Babbage, demonstrating his 'analytical machines' to some enthusiasm. Babbage had been among the early proponents of the BAAS, which itself already emphasized the dimension of internationalism, even linking it to international understanding and peace. BAAS pillar David Brewster, fresh off his appearance as president of the BAAS meeting in 1850, also presided over the London Peace Congress in 1851.[24] The idea that scientists would join to communicate across national boundaries dated to the earlier Republic of Letters and learned academies from the seventeenth and eighteenth centuries, but now it became more possible for scholars not just to serve as corresponding or honorary members but to travel and participate directly, thus giving a more interpersonal, face-to-face and affective character to the networks. Quetelet, for instance, had already participated in BAAS meetings as astronomer and statistician before attending the gatherings in Italy, and while in Britain he cooperated with Babbage in getting statistics accepted as a disciplinary section in the BAAS, against the wishes of some Tory physical scientists who considered statistics too political a subject.[25]

The scholarly associations already offered some functional specialization and differentiation by breaking up into such sections on specific fields, as the German *Naturforscher* had done since the 1820s, and most later organizations followed suit. In this way these bodies were not so qualitatively different from the specialist scientific and professional congresses and organizations of the 1850s and after, but rather helped prefigure and establish them. The same holds for the International Association for the Progress of the Social Sciences in the 1860s, whereby Christian Müller has emphasized its character as an umbrella organization covering a range of disciplines and social reform issues, which served as a bridge between specialized nationally based organizations and later international foundations, including the late nineteenth-century peace movement.[26]

As the case of the Social Science Association therefore also underscores, scholarship and social reform causes could go hand in hand. The modern organization Historians against Slavery, for example, still looks back to the World Antislavery Conventions as progenitors and stresses how much scholarship on slavery in all parts of the world fed their programmes and *Proceedings*. Similarly, those who attempted to get the new discipline of ethnology accepted in the BAAS at that time shared many of the aims of the British Aborigines Protection Society.[27]

To take an even tighter instance of the interlocking of politics and academics, Carl Mittermaier, Edouard Ducpétiaux and Georg Varrentrap helped launch the Penal Reform Congresses in Frankfurt in 1846 and Brussels in 1847 as part of the drive for prison reform in the 1840s. In part a scholarly congress, these gatherings and networks also strove to construct 'epistemic communities' of experts that involved government officials and political figures as well as academics and prison administrators.[28] Efforts to stage international discussions of penal reform had already begun in the medicine and hygiene section of the Congresses of Italian Scientists during the early 1840s, spurred by Mittermaier and his Piedmontese correspondent the state councilor Count Carlo Petitti.[29] In the context of expert communities it is important to remember that the ranks of governmental and non-governmental figures sometimes overlapped not only through conference attendance but also because the same individuals at various times assumed both roles, in sequence or simultaneously: thus the government ministers François Guizot and Alphonse de Lamartine from the peace movement or Ducpétiaux, Petitti and Heinrich Julius as scholars and officials in prison reform.[30] At the same time, these networks made their primary goal the persuasion and mobilization of public opinion to build pressure for leveraging their policy initiatives. In the case of the penal reform movement, this meant that what had been a debate about the various options for communal, cell-based and mixed forms of incarceration and rehabilitation by the congresses of the late 1840s became an effort to establish a consensus around the cellular, solitary system. The second Penal Reform Congress in Brussels in 1847 was also planned to coincide with the Congress of Economists, which itself considered not only issues such as free trade but also international peace, again pointing to the organizational overlap among the various movements and constituencies.[31]

Having mentioned networks several times, while space does not permit elaborating on specific insights of networks-based approaches, I would like to flag the benefits of analysing connections and trends in terms of small-world networks defined by relatively weak ties, rather than only through tightly drawn networks of strong ties such as intermarriage, kinship and patronage. In addition, it is helpful to think in terms of bimodal or bipartite networks, that is, to trace the connections between, say, people or correspondents on the one hand and on the other those between the places, institutions and events in which such connections occur. Making these two moves allows, for example, visualization of interlocking organizational personnel, as with the abolition and peace movements, or peace movements and social science congresses – the spread of ideas and organizational techniques was that much easier and more rapid through such looser networks and interconnected movements.[32] Even individuals can stand out in such an approach. Carl Mittermaier, for example, was through his web of correspondents and academic journal projects a central node in multiple international networks, including not just penal reform but also the international comparison and codification of civil law, and German liberalism. Thus he served as president of the Penal Reform Congress of 1846 in Frankfurt and was a prominent participant in the first Germanist Conference of legal, historical and literary scholars, also in Frankfurt that year, and during the revolution of 1848 he presided at the Pre-Parliament in Frankfurt. Quetelet represents another such nodal figure linking networks.[33]

Finally, a central feature of the scholarly congresses was the accompanying social programme. I have so far said little about this aspect of the diplomatic conferences and gatherings from civil society, but there were almost always some planned activities and tourist programmes to support amicable sociability and to show off local attractions, alongside the spontaneous socializing among visitors and local hubs of social life. The Congress of Vienna represented a pinnacle of such sociability, but even, for instance, the Congress of Ljubljana in 1821 had its sociable moments, and the peace congresses emphasized their social programmes as well. If anything the role of sociability was even greater among scholars, as the mere fact of meeting one another and overcoming often acrimonious scholarly feuds was an important motivation for the gatherings. Not infrequently they even published special guidebooks, though not all were as grand as Gustav Schreiner's lavishly illustrated compilation for the occasion of the meeting of German doctors and scientists in Graz in 1843.[34]

To conclude this discussion of the trajectories of internationalization across the nineteenth century, some scholars such as Douglas Maynard have stressed the congresses of the 1840s as the early front of a continuous wave of development of international movements and organizations that saw what he called geometric growth into the 1850s and beyond. More recent scholars such as Mark Mazower have tended to emphasize a caesura between the early peace congresses and the later ones, with a break after the 1848 Revolutions and the Crimean War, the US Civil War and the Franco-Prussian War.[35] There is some truth to both points of view, with a break perhaps most notable for the specific example of the peace congresses, but even there I would stress the overlap between the peace movement and the various social reform movements and scholarly congresses across the 1840s, 1850s and 1860s. Examining the wider venues of politics and sociability as they interlace across government institutions and civil society reveals these continuities all the more clearly. As the possibilities for international travel, communication and associational life grew over this same period of accelerating social and technological change, new organizations were able to build on the foundations laid by their predecessors, in terms of organization, interpersonal networks and ideologies. It has already been noted that several groups coalesced around the Great Exhibition in London in 1851, just as they would around later World Expos, with the founding of the organization for statisticians in 1853, as well as the welfare congresses of the 1850s. For the Paris World Exposition of 1889, fully 101 of the 111 meetings of international organizations that year took place in Paris, profiting from the event's magnetic pull and facilities. The founding of the Red Cross in turn drew upon connections in the International Statistical Congresses of the 1860s.[36]

Summit-level congresses and monarchical meetings featured in the later nineteenth century as well, and so too did ambassadorial conferences or other gatherings bringing together specialists from further down the diplomatic hierarchy to solve specific problems or to address pressing crises, above all concerning the so-called Eastern Question of the Ottoman Empire and the protection of Christian and Jewish minorities there in the various humanitarian and imperialist interventions of the 1860s and after. The Brussels conference of 1889–90 on the African slave trade was itself a larger-scale ambassadorial conference, with the follow-on supervisory bureaus it created in Brussels and Zanzibar also incorporating the resident diplomatic personnel there, while the Permanent Court of Arbitration established following the Hague Peace Conference of 1899 similarly drew its membership from the diplomatic representatives to the Netherlands, again pointing to links between ambassadorial conferences and the origins of intergovernmental organizations.[37] And in 1920, following the Paris treaties, a standing ambassadorial conference oversaw the implementation of a new peace settlement and of the occupation of western Germany in a way similar to the Allied Council in Paris during the occupation of France after 1815. The extension of the river commission framework from the Rhine and Elbe to the Danube has already been mentioned.

The congresses and conferences, as the work of Davide Rodogno, Abigail Green and others makes clear, also continued to involve a complex mixture of input from activists, lobbyists and increasingly from academic experts as well, as part of efforts to sway public and governmental opinion, and to inform policy through establishing matters of fact as well as expanding transparency. Even with the later peace congresses that led to the Hague Conventions of 1899 and 1907, combinations of civil society activists, scholars of international law and government officials and sponsoring states built on the networks and templates created by the penal reform and other social reform movements and the International Statistical Congresses and social science organizations of the mid-century, while also bringing back the calls for legal codification and arbitration from the earlier peace congress movement, and expanding on the circumscribed public roles for women activists seen in the abolition and peace movements of the 1840s. The ties with formerly enslaved or colonized peoples seen in these same circles in the 1830s and 1840s continued as well and helped promote the formation of activist groups of primarily people of colour, as in the Pan-African Congress movement of Henry Sylvester Williams, W. E. B. DuBois and others in 1900 at the time of the protests against conditions in King Leopold's Congo and again after the two World Wars.[38] As I hope this chapter has revealed, a surprisingly rich and interconnected basis of international governance and international civil society emerged in the first half of the nineteenth century, centred on influence politics and conferencing, and establishing spaces and models for the continued development of internationalization through the end of the century and beyond.

Notes

1. Emphasizing the late nineteenth century, inter alia: Mark Mazower, *Governing the World: The History of an Idea* (New York: Penguin, 2012); Madeleine Herren, 'Governmental Internationalism and the Beginning of a New World Order in the Late Nineteenth Century', in *The Mechanics of Internationalism: Culture, Society, and Politics from the 1840s to the First World War*, eds. Martin H. Geyer & Johannes Paulmann (Oxford: Oxford University Press, 2001), 121–45; F. S. L. Lyons, *Internationalism in Europe 1815-1914* (Leyden: Sythoff, 1963).
2. Brian E. Vick, *The Congress of Vienna: Power and Politics after Napoleon* (Cambridge, MA: Harvard University Press, 2014).
3. On the commissions, see Reinhard Stauber, *Der Wiener Kongress* (Vienna: Böhlau, 2014), 63–78, and Charles Webster, *The Congress of Vienna 1814–1815* (1919; London: Bell, 1950), 88–91.
4. On Poland and Cracow, Vick, *The Congress of Vienna*, 320; on Greece, Jennifer Mitzen, *Power in Concert: The Nineteenth-Century Origins of Global Governance* (Chicago: University of Chicago Press, 2013), 170–6; Miroslav Šedivý, *Metternich, the Great Powers and the Eastern Question* (Pilsen: University of West Bohemia, 2013), 258–60.
5. Mitzen, *Power in Concert*; Robert Jervis, 'From Balance to Concert: A Study of International Security Cooperation', *World Politics* 38, no. 1 (1985): 58–79, 71–5, 79; Dan Lindley, *Promoting Peace with Information: Transparency as a Tool of Security Regimes* (Princeton, NJ: Princeton University Press, 2007), Ch. 3.
6. C. K. Webster, *The Foreign Policy of Castlereagh, 1812-1815: Britain and the Reconstruction of Europe* (London: Bell, 1931), 420.
7. Beatrice de Graaf, 'The Allied Machine: The Conference of Ministers in Paris and the Management of Security, 1815-18', in *Securing Europe after Napoleon: 1815 and the New European Security Culture*, ed. de Graaf, Ido de Haan & Brian Vick (Cambridge: Cambridge University Press, 2019), 130–49; de Graaf, *Fighting Terror after Napoleon: How Europe Became Secure after 1815* (Cambridge: Cambridge University Press, 2020); Christine Haynes, *Our Friends the Enemies: The Occupation of France after Napoleon* (Cambridge, MA: Harvard University Press, 2018); Jacques-Alain de Sédouy, *Le concert européen. Aux origines de l'Europe 1814-1914* (Paris: Fayard, 2009), 48–68.
8. Brian Vick, 'The London Ambassadors' Conferences and Beyond: Abolition, Barbary Corsairs and Multilateral Security in the Congress of Vienna System', in *Securing Europe*, ed. de Graaf, de Haan, & Vick, 114–29, 119–21; Wayne Ackerson, *The African Institution (1807-1827) and the Antislavery Movement in Great Britain* (Lewiston, NY: Mellen, 2005).
9. Geoffrey Wiseman, '"Polylateralism": Diplomacy's Third Dimension', *Public Diplomacy* 4, no. 1 (2010): 24–39.
10. Brian Vick, 'Power, Humanitarianism, and the Global Liberal Order: Abolition and the Barbary Corsairs in the Vienna Congress System', *The International History Review* 40, no. 4 (2018): 939–60.

11 Haus- Hof- und Staatsarchiv (Vienna) Ges. London Varia M-P, 145, Protokolle 1815-1816, Nr. 2.
12 Naples, Giuseppe Galasso, *Il Regno di Napoli. Il Mezzogiorno borbonico e risorgimentale (1815-1860)* (Turin: UTET, 2007), 243–56, 272–6; Belgium, Paul W. Schroeder, *The Transformation of European Politics, 1763-1848* (New York: Oxford University Press, 1994), 675–91, 693–6; Sédouy, *Le concert européen*, 188–215; Papal States, Alan J. Reinerman, *Austria and the Papacy in the Age of Metternich*, 2 vols. (Washington, DC: Catholic University of America Press, 1979-1989), vol. II, 24, 35–7, 145–6; Günther Heydemann, *Konstitution gegen Revolution: Die britische Deutschland- und Italienpolitik 1815-1848* (Göttingen: Vandenhoeck & Ruprecht, 1995), 177–206.
13 Linda Kelly, *Talleyrand in London: The Master Diplomat's Last Mission* (London: Tauris, 2017); Emanuel Waresquiel, *Talleyrand: le prince immobile* (Paris: Fayard: 2006), 569–95; Glenda Sluga, 'Women, Diplomacy and International Politics, Before and After the Congress of Vienna', in *Women, Diplomacy and International Politics since 1500*, ed. Sluga & Carolyn James (London: Routledge, 2016), 120–36, 127–30; Judith Lissauer Cromwell, *Dorothea Lieven: A Russian Princess in London and Paris, 1785-1857* (Jefferson, NC: McFarland, 2007), chs. 13–15; John Charmley, *The Princess and the Politicians: Sex, Intrigue and Diplomacy, 1812-1840* (New York: Viking: 2005).
14 Joep Schenk, 'The Central Commission for the Navigation of the Rhine: A First Step towards European Economic Security?' in *Securing Europe*, eds. de Graaf, de Haan & Vick, 75–94; Robert Mark Spaulding, 'Revolutionary France and the Transformation of the Rhine', *Central European History* 44, no. 2 (2011): 203–26; Spaulding, 'Anarchy, Hegemony, Cooperation: International Control of the Rhine River, 1789-1848' (2007), 2, www.ccr-zkr.org/files/histoireCCNR/21_anarchy-hegemony-cooperation.pdf (accessed 19 April 2019).
15 Luminita Gatejel, 'Imperial Cooperation at the Margins of Europe: The European Commission of the Danube, 1856-65', *European Review of History* 24, no. 5 (2017): 781–800, 782–3.
16 Howard Temperley, *British Antislavery 1833-1870* (London: Longman, 1972), 85–92; Douglas H. Maynard, 'The World's Anti-Slavery Convention of 1840', *Mississippi Valley Historical Review* 47, no. 3 (1960): 452–71; *Proceedings of the General Anti-Slavery Convention Called by the Committee of the British and Foreign Anti-Slavery Society and Held in London from Friday, June 12th, to Tuesday, June 23rd, 1840* (London: Ward, 1840), 22–3 for Beckford's speech, 43, 105, 403–5 for Prescod's engagement.
17 Temperley, *British Antislavery*, 87–90; Seymour Drescher, *Abolition: A History of Slavery and Antislavery* (New York: Cambridge University Press, 2009), 249–51, 258, 295; Maynard, 'Anti-Slavery Convention', 456–61, 466; and esp. Clare Midgley, *Women Against Slavery: The British Campaigns, 1780-1870* (London: Routledge, 1992), Chs. 3, 6, 7.
18 Midgley, *Women Against Slavery*, 155–63; Maynard, 'Anti-Slavery Convention', 452; Hannah-Rose Murray, 'A "Negro Hercules": Frederick Douglass' Celebrity in Britain,' *Celebrity Studies* 7, no. 2 (2016): 264–79; S. Jay Walker, 'Frederick Douglass and Woman Suffrage', *The Black Scholar* 4, nos. 6/7 (1973): 24–31, 26.
19 On the peace movement and peace congresses, see W. H. van der Linden, *The International Peace Movement, 1815-1874* (Amsterdam: Tilleul, 1987). Other double attendees included Thomas Clarkson, William Allen and Lewis Tappan.

20 On Pennington, Mischa Honeck, 'Liberating Sojourns? African American Travelers in Mid-Nineteenth-Century Germany', in *Germany and the Black Diaspora: Points of Contact, 1250-1914*, eds. Honeck, Martin Klimke & Anne Kuhlmann (New York: Berghahn, 2013), 153-68, 154-60. On Brown, Mazower, *Governing*, 34-6; William Wells Brown, *Three Years in Europe* (London: Charles Gilpin, 1852), 23-35, 40-55, 219-22, 237-50; idem, *The American Fugitive in Europe: Sketches of Places and People Abroad* (Boston: Jewett, 1855), 216-22.

21 George Copway, *Running Sketches of Men and Places, in England, France, Germany, Belgium, and Scotland* (New York: Riker, 1851), 208-53 on the Frankfurt Congress, a 'large number of ladies' attending (211), 217-19, 221-4 on Copway's speech and resolution. Generally, see Van der Linden, *Peace Movement*, 328-39 (Paris), 339-45 (Frankfurt) and the published reports, Edmund Fry and A. R. Scoble, eds., *Report of the Proceedings of the Second General Peace Congress, Held in Paris, on the 22nd, 23rd, and 24th August 1849* (London: Charles Gilpin, 1849), and Henry Richard, ed., *Report of the Proceedings of the Third General Peace Congress, Held in Frankfort, on the 22nd, 23rd, and 24th August 1850* (London: Gilpin, 1851). For women's involvement and Anne Knight, David Nicholls, 'Richard Cobden and the International Peace Congress Movement, 1848-1853', *Journal of British Studies* 30, no. 4 (1991): 351-76, 373-4.

22 R. Hinton Thomas, *Liberalism, Nationalism and the German Intellectuals 1822-1847: An Analysis of the Academic and Scientific Conferences of the Period* (Cambridge: Heffer, 1951); Jack Morrell and Arnold Thackray, *Gentlemen of Science: Early Years of the British Association for the Advancement of Science* (Oxford: Clarendon Press, 1981).

23 L. Langer and A. Schrötter, eds., *Amtlicher Bericht über die einundzwanzigste Versammlung deutscher Naturforscher und Aerzte in Gratz im September 1843* (Graz: Leykam, 1844), 126-7 for Muhammed.

24 For materials relating to the Riunioni degli scienziati italiani, https://mostre.museogalileo.it/congressiscienziati/indice.html (accessed 14 December 2018); and see Maria Pia Casalena, 'The Congresses of Italian Scientists between Europe and the Risorgimento (1839-1875)', *Journal of Modern Italian Studies* 12, no. 2 (2007): 153-88. On internationalism and the BAAS, Morrell & Thackray, *Gentlemen*, 138-9, 373; Margaret Maria Gordon, *The Home Life of Sir David Brewster* (2nd ed. Edinburgh: Edmonston and Douglas, 1870), 209, 217-23.

25 Morrell and Thackray, *Gentlemen*, 291-6, 374-5.

26 Christian Müller, 'The Politics of Expertise: The Association Internationale pour le progrès des Sciences Sociales, Democratic Peace Movements and International Law Networks, 1850-1875', in *Shaping the Transnational Sphere: Experts, Networks, and Issues from the 1840s to the 1930s*, eds. Davide Rodogno, Bernhard Struck & Jakob Vogel (New York: Berghahn, 2015), 131-51.

27 Historians against Slavery, www.historiansagainstslavery.org/main/the-world-antislavery-convention-of-1840/ (accessed 14 May 2019). On ethnology and protection of indigenous peoples, Morrell and Thackray, *Gentlemen*, 283-6.

28 Making the connection between the scientific societies in Britain, Germany and elsewhere, and stressing the overlap among the various congress movements, Chris Leonards & Nico Randeraad, 'Building a Transnational Network of Social Reform in the Nineteenth Century', in *Shaping the Transnational Sphere*, ed. Rodogno et al., 111-30, esp. 114-17, including the central roles of Mittermaier, Ducpétiaux and Varrentrapp in other congresses as well.

29 Lars Hendrik Riemer, *Das Netzwerk der 'Gefängnisfreunde' (1830-1872). Karl Josef Anton Mittermaiers Briefwechsel mit europäischen Strafvollzugsexperten*, 2 vols (Frankfurt am Main: Klostermann, 2005), vol. I, 43, 115–16.

30 Van der Linden, *Peace Movement*, 73 (Guizot), 207 (Lamartine); Bert Vanhulle, 'Dreaming about the Prison: Édouard Ducpétiaux and Prison Reform in Belgium (1830-1848)', *Crime, Histoire & Sociétés/Crime, History & Societies* 14, no. 2 (2010), http://journals.openedition.org/chs/1196; DOI: 10.4000/chs.1196 (accessed 14 May 2019); Thomas Nutz, 'Global Networks and Local Prison Reforms: Monarchs, Bureaucrats and Penological Experts in Early Nineteenth-Century Prussia', *German History* 23, no. 4 (2005): 431–59.

31 Martina Henze, 'Transnational Cooperation and Criminal Policy: The Prison Reform Movement, 1820s-1950s', in *Shaping the Transnational Sphere*, ed. Rodogno et al., 197–217, 200 on Mittermaier; Vanhulle, 'Ducpétiaux', paragraphs 28–9.

32 On networks, see Vick, *Congress of Vienna*, 112–19, and literature cited there. See also Brian Uzzi, Luis A. N. Amaral & Felix Reed-Tsochas, 'Small-world Networks and Management Science Research: A Review', *European Management Review* 4, no. 2 (2007): 77–91; the latter suggests that group affiliations in bipartite networks may be more statistically significant than individual 'superconnector' actors as circulatory nodes in networks: 83–6.

33 Emphasizing Mittermaier and Quetelet, Leonards and Randeraad, 'Transnational Network', 117.

34 Hinton Thomas, *Conferences*, 34–8; Gustav Schreiner, *Grätz. Ein naturhistorisches-statistisches–topographisches Gemählde dieser Stadt und ihrer Umgebungen* (Graz: Fersil, 1843). Similarly impressive, L. Pareto et al., *Descrizione di Genova e del Genovesato*, 3 vols. (Genoa: Ferrando, 1846). On the role of locality and social programmes in the BAAS, see Charles W. J. Withers, *Geography and Science in Britain, 1831-1939: A Study of the British Association for the Advancement of Science* (Manchester: Manchester University Press, 2010), ch. 2.

35 Douglas Maynard, 'Reform and the Origins of the International Organization Movement', *Proceedings of the American Philosophical Society* 107, no. 3 (1963): 220–31; Mazower, *Governing*, 37–8.

36 Claude Tapia & Jacques Taieb, 'Conférences et Congrès Internationaux de 1815 à 1913', *Relations Internationales* 5 (1976): 11–35, 15; Red Cross, Lyons, *Internationalism*, 297.

37 Johannes Paulmann, *Pomp und Politik. Monarchenbegegnungen in Europa zwischen Ancien Regime und Erstem Weltkrieg* (Paderborn: Schöningh, 2000); Permanent Court of Arbitration, Lyons, *Internationalism*, 32; Suzanne Miers, *Britain and the Ending of the Slave Trade* (London: Longman, 1975), 229–38, 284–6.

38 Lyons, *Internationalism*, 320–61; Sandi E. Cooper, 'Women's Participation in European Peace Movements: The Struggle to Prevent World War I', in *Women and Peace: Theoretical, Historical and Practical Perspectives*, ed. Ruth Roach Pierson (London: Croom Helm, 1987), 51–75; Jonathan Schneer, *London 1900: The Imperial Metropolis* (New Haven, CT: Yale University Press, 1999), 201–26.

3

Contesting representations of indigeneity at the First Inter-American Indigenista Congress, 1940

Joanna Crow

Introduction

The First Inter-American Indigenista Congress, also referred to as the First Inter-American Conference on Indian Life, took place in Pátzcuaro, Mexico, in April 1940.[1] Policymakers and scholars of the Americas had been discussing the so-called Indigenous question across and beyond national boundaries long before 1940 – for example, at the International Sanitary Convention of the American Republics (beginning in 1902), at the Pan-American Child Congress (beginning in 1916) and at the Inter-American Conference on Education (beginning in 1928), as well as in Europe-based forums such as the International Labour Office (created in 1919) and the International Committee on Intellectual Cooperation (established in 1922) – but it was not until 1938, at the VIII International Conference of American States, held in Lima, Peru, that delegates resolved to dedicate an entire conference to this 'question'. The question was a complex one, with cultural, economic, political and social dimensions, but in broad terms government agencies and interested scholars were deliberating how best to integrate the previously excluded Indigenous people into national society. 'Integration' was the keyword, and, in many cases, it was equated with transformation into useful, productive workers. The question became a major subject of public debate in countries where Indigenous people constituted the majority of the population (e.g. in Bolivia, Guatemala, Mexico and Peru), but – as the documentation related to the conference in Pátzcuaro makes clear – it was deemed to be relevant to all countries in the region.

Approximately 250 delegates, representing eighteen different countries in the Americas, travelled to Pátzcuaro in 1940 and over the course of ten days they debated the details of and possible resolutions to the problems afflicting Indigenous peoples. More than one hundred papers were presented at the conference. These were organized into five different working sections – anthropology, biology, education, law and socioeconomics – and were followed by discussion sessions, from which emerged a series of resolutions and conclusions. After much deliberation, the vast list of findings was whittled down into an *Acta Final* [Final Act] comprising seventy-two recommendations – 'a kind of road map', in the words of Laura Jiraudo, 'for a program of intervention and joint action around the continent'.[2]

As will be shown later, the Pátzcuaro conference was a government-sponsored and government-run event. In this context, it has been widely criticized for exhibiting a stereotypically colonialist and paternalist view towards Indigenous peoples; it was, in many ways, a conference full of white men talking *about* rather than *with* Indigenous peoples.[3] Building on the work of scholars such as Laura Jiraudo and Jennifer Jolly, who underscore the ambiguities of the political games being played at the conference, not least the neo-imperial pretensions of the United States and Mexico's efforts to defy such pretensions,[4] this chapter interrogates the possibilities opened up for and through subaltern agency in Pátzcuaro. It analyses the physical spaces that the conference occupied and the social spaces that it created (focusing on the histories and political narratives performed through the conference), as well as the people who participated in the conference – who they were, how their participation came about and what kind of involvement they had. Despite the major and obvious limitations of the forum, which will be elucidated further, there were some important Indigenous representatives present in Pátzcuaro, who gave papers and who then later drew on the agreements signed at the conference to put pressure on their governments back home to acknowledge and enact legislation defending Indigenous rights. This was the case with Venancio Coñuepán and César Colima, leaders of a Mapuche political organization called the Araucanian Corporation (established in 1938), who went to Pátzcuaro as official representatives of the Chilean state – an intriguing story, given that Chilean state authorities were renowned at the time for denying their country's Indigenous heritage.[5] Drawing on the published conference proceedings, journals founded at the conference, foreign newspaper reports on the conference, letters from delegates during the conference and subsequent national congressional debates, my chapter tells the story of Chilean participation at the conference and explores how it helps us to understand some of the multiple, entangled and oft-competing ideas about indigeneity that were circulating in mid-twentieth-century Latin America. Its innovative contribution lies in the great variety of different (official and non-official) primary sources drawn together, which in turn allows us to hear a greater range of voices, beyond those of the oft-scrutinized US and Mexican representatives.

The physical and social spaces of the conference

The conference was originally scheduled to take place in La Paz, Bolivia, but – as Jiraudo has explained – the death of the country's president Germán Busch in August 1939 and the precarity of its new government led the president of Mexico, Lázaro Cárdenas (1895–1970), to offer to host the event.[6] Cárdenas had been a general in the Constitutionalist Army during the Mexican Revolution (1910–20).[7] He was elected in 1934, becoming the forty-fourth president of Mexico since independence and is renowned for presiding over the most radical phase of reform led by the revolutionary state. Among other things, he revived agrarian reform (expropriating large landed estates and redistributing to smallholders and peasant collectives), nationalized the oil industry and promoted an ambitious socialist education programme in public schools. Reputed to be of Indigenous descent himself,[8] Cárdenas spoke of the urgency of incorporating the Indian into Mexico's modern economy, aimed to harness ethnographic knowledge in order to do this, and in the process allowed for a degree of cultural pluralism.[9] By hosting (and dominating the agenda of) the First Inter-American Indigenista Congress, Cárdenas seemingly aimed to establish Mexico as an international role model on social reform and on Indigenous rights.

Cárdenas chose Pátzcuaro, a small town in his home state of Michoacán, as the location for the conference. The Peruvian daily *El Comercio*, reporting on preparations for the conference in April 1940, outlined both the practical reasons for this choice and the symbolic significance of the place.[10] It described a 'picturesque and legendary' town that was only a few hours by automobile from Mexico City and enormously popular with both local and foreign tourists. This was because of its 'magnificent climate'; its beautiful location, set on the shore of Lake Pátzcuaro and surrounded by 'immense orchards with a great variety of fruits and flowers'; and the fact that it was 'inhabited by Tarasco Indians' from whom visitors could buy the region's 'famous hand-painted bowls and cups'. It was, in other words, home to a living Indigenous community whose handicraft industry was thriving. What better inspiration for delegates attending a conference focused on the question of how to successfully integrate Indigenous peoples into national society?

Pátzcuaro was not represented exclusively as Indigenous, however. Mexico's *criollo* founding fathers (people of Spanish descent born in the Americas) and their struggles against Spanish colonial rule were made visible through the 'famous statue of the Great General José María Morelos, military genius of the independence movement of 1810', located on Janitzio, an island in the middle of Lake Pátzcuaro.[11] The town also paid homage to the Spanish priests, who fought to protect the rights of Indigenous peoples during the long dark days of colonialism: it 'has the distinction', Peruvian delegate José Angel Escalante commented, 'of having been the centre from where the virtuous bishop Don Vasco de Quiroga initiated an energetic and effective apostolic campaign – the first of its kind – in defence of the Indian, cruelly despoiled by the Spanish conquistador'. Reporting back on the conference to the Chamber of Deputies in Lima on 11 September 1940, Escalante described this 'praiseworthy priest' as the 'first *indigenista* of the continent'.[12] This was the reason, he said, that Pátzcuaro was chosen as the location for the First Inter-American Indigenista Congress.

Pátzcuaro was founded in the 1320s, as the capital of the Indigenous Tarascan state. It was conquered by the Spanish two hundred years later. This heritage was recalled by the venue in which President Cárdenas inaugurated the conference: the recently opened Caltzontzin Theatre.[13] 'Caltzontzin' is the Tarascan word for supreme leader. The theatre had been commissioned by Cárdenas in 1936 – in line with other state-led celebrations of Mexico's Indigenous heritage through art, architecture and public monuments – and built on land previously occupied by an Augustinian convent. The preliminary session and many of the working groups that spoke to the five key themes of the congress took place in the Gertrudis Bocanegra library next door, originally a temple of the same Augustinian order which dated back to the sixteenth century. The very buildings which brought together conference delegates for their formal discussions thus embodied the history of *mestizaje* – the cultural and biological mixing of the Indigenous and Spanish 'races' – which became the dominant, state-sponsored narrative of Mexican nationhood in the early twentieth century.[14] As performed through the local craftsmanship and architecture on display at the conference, the Spanish conquistadors had imposed their government on the pre-Columbian Tarascan state, but did not manage to eradicate the people (who were alive and producing beautiful pottery in mid-twentieth-century Michoacán) or to destroy their culture (expressed and commodified in that same pottery and emblazoned in the names given to new public buildings).

In his inaugural address on 14 April 1940, President Cárdenas presented himself and his government as less paternalistic than previous administrations (in both Mexico and beyond) by attacking the prevailing 'formulation "to incorporate the Indian into civilisation"' as 'a remnant of old systems that tried to hide de facto inequality' and, indeed, to 'de-Indianize' the Indian – uprooting 'regional dialects, traditions [and] customs'. What he promoted in Mexico, he said, and hoped to see in other countries that were represented at the conference, was respect for the Indian's 'racial personality, his conscience, and his identity', but he also made it clear that no one could 'expect a resurrection of the pre-Cortesian Indigenous systems or a stagnation that is incompatible with the flux of life today'.[15] Cárdenas attempted to make the conference a stage to celebrate Mexico's (and especially Michoacán's) cultural, political and social achievements, and thereby secure its position as leader of a continent-wide struggle for Indigenous rights.

Alongside the formal discussion sessions, delegates were encouraged to attend numerous cultural festivals, to travel to the nearby Indigenous communities of Tirindaro, Naranja y Tarajero, which were part of a 'special [government reform] programme', and to visit the Indigenous Agricultural Vocational School in Paracho.[16] And, at the end of the conference – which was marked by a ceremony at the Monument to Tanganxuan II, the last chief of the Tarascan state[17] – they were invited (courtesy of the Mexican State Department of Indigenous Affairs) to go to see the Mezquital Valley and the *poblaciones* of Ixmiquilipan, Nith and Pueblo Nuevo in the state of Hidalgo, and (courtesy of the Ministry of Public Education) to visit the famous museum of San Juan Teotihuacán.[18] Outside the plenary and working sessions of the conference, delegates were therefore treated to a touristic experience par excellence. During their stay in Pátzcuaro, they encountered the exotic, heroic Indigenous of the past and the authentic trinket-making Indigenous of the present. They also got to see what could be accomplished in terms of social reform (particularly community education and agriculture) if led by a committed and energetic government. In this regard, there is little doubt that Mexico, under Cárdenas, sought to trump the United States and its 'Indian New Deal' – an official rejection, initiated during Franklin D. Roosevelt's first term as president, of the forced assimilation and land allotment policies in effect since the 1880s and a turn towards the concept of limited self-rule.[19]

Leadership of and participation in the conference

As highlighted in *The Final Act* of the Pátzcuaro conference, which established the set-up for subsequent conferences, the Organising Government was responsible for sending out invitations 'via the proper diplomatic channels', setting the agenda and paying 'the expenses of organising and carrying out the conference'.[20] In Mexico in 1940 it was the then president of the country Lázaro Cárdenas who opened the conference and – indeed – who served as honorary president of the event. His government invited twenty countries to send delegations to Pátzcuaro and seventeen obliged.[21] The onus was then on each participating government to pay for the travel and subsistence costs of their nominated representatives. In total, the *Final Act of the First Inter-American Conference on Indian Life* included the names of fifty-four official delegates. In many cases, these were ambassadors to Mexico at the time. All but one of them were men.[22] Most of them were non-Indigenous or at least did not openly self-identify as Indigenous. The exceptions, as mentioned in the introduction to this chapter, were the two Mapuche political activists Venancio Coñuepan and César Colima. Beyond the official delegates, participating countries also sent teams of 'technical advisors', a distinct marker of modern conferencing, as discussed by Brian Vicks in this collection. More women attended in this capacity, particularly from the United States. Some countries also sent specifically labelled 'Indian delegates': there were thirty-two from Mexico, fourteen from the United States and one from Panama. In addition, there were people with a 'recognised interest in Indian affairs' who attended independently, authorized – but not paid for – by their respective governments.[23] With these different groups added together, we reach the total agreed by most existing studies of approximately 250 attendees.

So, the majority of participants at the First Inter-American Indigenista Congress were not Indigenous. Not for nothing did the *New York Times* publicize it as a 'Meeting *on* Indians' (my emphasis), rather than an Indian Meeting, or a Meeting *of* Indians.[24] Many contemporary scholars have already commented on this irony, hypocrisy and major limitation, which transfers to criticisms of *indigenismo* more broadly as a discourse and movement (rising to prominence in the 1920s) that, in the words of Jorge Coronado, sought to reshape society 'by the inclusion of vast swathes of the marginalised indigenous population' but simultaneously refused 'to relinquish its tutorial attitude toward those that it sought to protect'.[25]

In her excellent book *Creating Pátzcuaro, Creating Mexico*, art historian Jennifer Jolly remarks that the only Indigenous people who attended the conference were included last-minute (hence them being from Mexico and the nearby United States and Panama), and that their interventions were not recorded in the published proceedings. 'The guiding assumption', she argues, 'was that it was the job of government bureaucrats to save the continent's Indians'.[26] Some of the agreements included in *The Final Act* certainly exemplify a paternalistic discourse of salvation. The aim, overall, was to 'elevate' the Indians' 'moral' as well as material standards of living.[27] A 'broad education program' was recommended, for example, to 'acquaint the native peoples with the personal and social advantages of legally registering their marriages'.²⁸ They were perceived not as individual human beings but as a 'problem' to be solved. One resolution that focused on Mexico spoke of the necessary 'resettlement of indigenous groups' and proposed that one or two communities should be set up as 'model colonies'.²⁹ Despite Cardenas's opening remarks to the congress, the language of civilization and barbarism continued to predominate in many of the discussion sessions and agreements that emerged from them.

Building on her previously cited point about Indigenous voices being excluded from the official record, Jolly also asserts that Indian delegates had to stay at the local boarding school, while government delegates were put up in hotels.³⁰ In these ways, they were present but treated as second-class participants, indeed quite literally as children. Venancio Coñuepán and César Colima seem to have been the exception, for they attended not as 'Indian delegates' but as representatives of the Chilean government. However, they too confronted challenges. According to letters that the country's other official delegate, Manuel Hidalgo (recently appointed Chilean ambassador to Mexico), sent to the Minister of Foreign Affairs in Santiago during the conference, these Mapuche leaders' ongoing stay in Mexico was unsustainable because they had not been given sufficient funds to cover their costs. Hidalgo urged the government to send the money they had been promised so that Coñuepán and Colima could pay for their return travel to Chile.³¹

We do not know exactly how or why Coñuepán and Colima were designated official representatives of the Chilean government. It is possible that they themselves made it happen. They were both highly vocal political activists in southern Chile at the time. As a wealthy landowner, leader of the increasingly prominent Araucanian Corporation and president of the Popular Freedom Alliance of Cautín, which had helped to secure crucial votes for the then president Pedro Aguirre Cerda (1938–41), Coñuepán in particular had the capacity to make state officials listen.³² It is also possible that the Chilean government was willing to send Indigenous political leaders as official representatives to Pátzcuaro precisely because it sought to flaunt Chile as a country which had already resolved its (or had never really suffered from an) 'Indian problem'. In other words, it had nothing to fear by sending them. What is more, their presence could testify to the supposed superiority of Chilean social legislation. This seems to have been the narrative promoted by Ambassador Hidalgo, who – as Amelia Marie Kiddle has shown – was critical of Mexico's purported hemispheric leadership.³³ Indeed, as Kiddle tells it, he spotlighted Mexico as a country that was ill-equipped to work rationally towards social and political change. Why? Because the majority population was Indigenous.³⁴ According to Hidalgo, Mexico's indigeneity was holding it back.

If Hidalgo attended the Pátzcuaro conference in order to gain visibility for Chile and its supposed achievements – as opposed to properly engaging with discussions about Indigenous rights – it appears he was successful, at least according to one report published in *El Comercio* of Peru. On 24 April 1940, this newspaper commended the important agreements adopted by the working section on socioeconomics, particularly with regard to Indigenous women. The Chilean delegation, it said, had enlightened delegates about the 'specific circumstances of the female Araucanian population' as well as about 'the living conditions of the country's indigenous people in general'.³⁵ 'At the request of the delegations of Mexico, Colombia and Peru', the Chilean government was then given 'a round of applause for its ample indigenista work'. In this sense, discussions were as much about what had already been done as about what delegates hoped or planned to do in the future. Participating member states were notably keen to congratulate each other for recent accomplishments. Sometimes official delegates also heaped praise on their *own* governments: just prior to the Chilean delegation's presentation on the 'female Araucanian population', Peruvian representatives had 'informed the assembly about their country's highly progressive legislation, which granted extensive protection to indigenous and peasant women'.[36] There was, in short, a lot of backslapping going on in Pátzcuaro. This in and of itself is interesting because it indicates how a country's cultural and political prestige had by this time become linked – at least in part – to how its government was seen to be treating Indigenous people. Perhaps more significantly, if read alongside the research of Jennifer Jolly, and indeed alongside primary source materials documenting Indigenous protests against abuse and exclusion in mid-twentieth-century Latin America, we also get a sense of the disconnect arising between the propaganda surrounding a state's progressive position vis-à-vis Indigenous rights and the reality of Indigenous people's lived experiences.[37]

Indigenous agency, voice and resistance

As shown earlier, Indigenous people were in a minority at the Pátzcuaro conference, their interventions (beyond the touristic performances) were largely excluded from the published proceedings and press coverage, and their accommodation was (at best) substandard. And yet – like subaltern actors in many other parts of the 'Global South' – they embraced the chance to be part of a conversation about the possibility of alternative pathways to modernity.[38] Almost fifty attended, despite the short notice. Furthermore, according to Kiddle, Indigenous representatives far beyond Mexico had been aware of the *indigenista* endeavours of Cárdenas's government several years before he presided over this congress, and they were keen to communicate with him directly. In November 1936, for example, Cardenas received a greeting in Quechua from an Indigenous group in Peru that admired his work, and in 1938 he received a message of appreciation from some Mapuche supporters in Chile, sent through the then *chargé d'affaires* in Mexico City.[39] Perhaps the latter included Coñuepán or Colima, or both.

It looks as if Coñuepán and Colima co-presented a paper approximately fifteen minutes in length to delegates at the conference.[40] In some respects, their presentation was very much in line with mainstream 'official' *indigenista* discourses, in that they spoke of the Indian's 'cultural backwardness' and of the need to 'lift' the Indian out of his 'economic prostration'. Indigenous 'people could easily be incorporated into national civilisation', they proclaimed, but only with 'effective direction and support from the state'. Possibly, they made such statements because they thought it was what the delegates in attendance wanted to hear. These Mapuche political leaders also made sure they praised the efforts of the Chilean administration that had sent them to Pátzcuaro. 'The Indian cherishes the hope', they said, that 'the government of his Excellency Don Pedro Aguirre Cerda will tackle, once and for all, the problems related to land, education, economics and justice'. Those hopes were founded on 'the work already undertaken by this government, with the building of rural schools, the establishment of an Inspectorate of Indigenous Education (led by an indigenous person), and the creation of an Indigenous Museum in the city of Temuco'.

Coñuepán and Colima contrasted such positive developments, however, with a long history of neglect, if not abuse, on the part of the state, and thereby took advantage of the *indigenista* congress as a space to denounce the realities of neo-colonialism in Chile.[41] In their narrative, it was Chilean legislation of the nineteenth century which had left their people with too little land to make a living: 475,000 hectares, they stated, for 200,000 people. The Indian Courts, created in the 1920s, with a purported aim of protecting the little lands communities had left, were useless. The state had also failed in its duty to provide an education. Its 'disinterest' in this area meant that 'Catholic and Protestant missionaries had been the only civilisers of the race'. Interweaved with their denunciations were demands for fundamental changes which would help to combat the legacy of such neglect. These included: new legislation decreeing the return of 'the thousands of hectares usurped by whites' and the increase in individual land quotas; the creation of a state bank dedicated to providing credit to Indigenous farmers; an increased national budget for education to build new primary schools in rural areas, two teacher training colleges for Indigenous students, a vocational school for women, an agricultural school and a school of Indigenous craftsmanship; and the establishment of a State Department of Indigenous Affairs. Their argument, overall, was that the 'Indian problem' could not be tackled by isolated measures; the state needed to deal with it in a holistic manner, addressing the key issues of land ownership, economic structures and education together.

Coñuepán and Colima also made it clear that the Indigenous constituencies they represented – as Indigenous people themselves and as leaders of the Araucanian Corporation, the most prominent Indigenous political organization in Chile at the time – were by no means passive. These activists narrated a story of resistance to the delegates present in Pátzcuaro, a story of a burgeoning *indigenista* movement in Chile that had been defending Indigenous rights for more than thirty years. And they asserted that the 'state urgently needed to adopt *the suggestions of indigenous organisations* in order to create new laws that will resolve our problems in a definitive and satisfactory way' (my emphasis). Moreover, Indigenous people were to take a leading role in the changes that Coñuepán and Colima advocated for Chile. According to their vision, teaching staff in the new Indigenous schools should be Indigenous, teaching should be carried out in the Indigenous language where possible, and the Department of Indigenous Affairs should be run by someone 'of indigenous blood'. Of course, Indigenous people could learn from others; this was not discounted by Coñuepán and Colima, but their point was that they were also very capable of speaking for themselves and actively driving forward the necessary changes.

Of the two Mapuche delegates, Coñuepán seemed to get the most out of his time at Pátzcuaro, or at least we have access to more details of his story because of what he went on to do after the conference, and the fact that this is recorded in official documents available in the Library of Congress of Chile. While in Mexico, Coñuepán took the opportunity to visit its northern neighbour to see for himself the impact of the new legislation introduced as part of Roosevelt's 'New Indian Deal', and – as Jorge Iván Vergara and Hans Gundermann have noted – he spoke very favourably of this state-led initiative when he returned to Chile.[42] In particular, he celebrated the US government's defence of Indigenous community lands and of the resources (timber, oil, water) found on these lands. According to Coñuepán, Roosevelt described the 'New Indian Deal' as 'no more than a powerful nation's obligation of honor to a people who live among us and depend on our protection'. Through such legislation, Coñuepán said, the 'great men of this great country' secured the 'solidarity of the Indians as members of the political state'. In contrast, what the Mapuche mainly heard from Chilean ruling elites were 'petty, demagogic, and hypocritical attitudes'.[43]

Coñuepán also made specific reference to the First Inter-American Indigenista Congress to validate his campaign for Indigenous rights and, indeed, to validate himself as an important transnational political figure. He used the Pátzcuaro conference for resistance years *after* it took place, thereby expanding its temporal scope. In 1945, Coñuepán was elected deputy to the Chilean National Congress, and in one parliamentary debate of 25 November 1947, he almost scolded his peers for not seeing that the 'old theory of "civilising the Indian"' was merely a 'pretext for the oppression of indigenous peoples'. This had been firmly rejected, he said, 'by the representatives who met in Pátzcuaro, at the Indigenista Congress of Mexico', which he 'was able to attend'.[44] To be a modern, democratic nation, he implied, Chile needed to live up to and adhere to international protocols. Perhaps more crucially, he wanted his fellow congressmen to know that he had been involved in the elaboration of such protocols.

Coñuepán was able to make a reality some of the reforms proposed in his (and Colima's) paper in Pátzcuaro, which in many cases coincided with the recommendations included in *The Final Act* signed by each country's leading delegate. Such enacted reforms can therefore be understood as a legacy of the conference. In the late 1940s, as congressman, he succeeded in re-imposing constraints upon Indigenous land sales, and as Minister of Lands and Colonization in 1952–3, he set up a new credit scheme for Indigenous people. He also established a Department of Indigenous Affairs (DASIN), was its first director between 1953 and 1958, and in this capacity managed to change existing legislation in order to exempt Indigenous peoples from the payment of property taxes. As he himself later said, this was 'the first time in the history of the country that an Indian had taken on the great responsibility a ministerial post'.[45]

Coñuepán made the above pronouncement in Chile's National Congress in 1965. He did so in response to accusations from a fellow (non-Mapuche) congressman that he had done nothing for 'his race' while in a senior government position.[46] By this point, Coñuepán was no longer the most prominent Mapuche leader in Chile. His time as director of DASIN finished when Ibáñez left office in 1958, and – in line with broader political developments in Chile – a leftist tendency, led by adversaries of Coñuepán such as Martín Painemal, had become dominant within Mapuche activist circles.[47] As early as the mid-1950s, at the peak of Coñuepán's power, Painemal and other urban leftist Mapuche had condemned him as a hypocrite and traitor to the Mapuche cause. To them he was an affluent, right-wing landowner, who failed to defend his people's rights in congress and who went 'on and on about the race question' just to get votes, when it was class inequality that urgently needed to be addressed.[48] His participation in the First Inter-American Indigenista Congress stood for little. Indeed, it is likely that they aligned him with the 'Yankee imperialism' that they continually and vehemently decried, given the prominent role played by the United States at this conference, and the fact that Coñuepán praised the US government's Indigenous rights policies after travelling there post-Pátzcuaro. We could say this Indigenous leader was drawn into the world of the international elite that he had previously sought to challenge, and that his radical campaigning potential (in the early 1940s) was blunted or neutralized in the process. However, Coñuepán is not easily categorized as 'subaltern' or radical even in the early 1940s. He was Indigenous 'by blood' and he self-identified as Indigenous, meaning he was 'subaltern' in a racial sense, but in terms of economic and social status, he was part of the elite, which might help to explain why the Chilean government was willing for him to speak as its representative in Mexico. And – as I have outlined elsewhere – the reforms he advocated, with their focus on the practical needs and 'development' of the rural communities, only ever sought to reorder the relationship between the Mapuche people and the state in rather subtle and indirect ways.[49]

Moreover, underscoring Coñuepán's perceived treachery or selling-out is just one way of reading local responses to him and his political strategizing. According to the main newspaper of Temuco in southern Chile, thousands of Mapuche people turned out to pay tribute to him when he visited Nueva Imperial shortly after being incorporated into the upper echelons of the state apparatus in 1953.[50] And the news of Coñuepán's death in early May 1968 was greeted by widespread public mourning. The day after his funeral, *El Diario Austral* described the grand cortège which accompanied his coffin to the General Cemetery in Temuco: it included not just local army regiments, police troops (regional and national), government officials and school children but also many Mapuche political leaders and 'an extraordinary number of people from Mapuche communities all over the region'.[51]

Conclusion

Scholarship on the Inter-American Indigenista Congresses, which took place intermittently from 1940 until the early 2000s, largely reaffirms recent critiques of continental *indigenismo* more broadly, in that it highlights the inherent limitations of a mainly non-Indigenous movement which sought to improve the lives of Indigenous peoples without really listening to or engaging with the demands of Indigenous peoples themselves. To a certain extent, the primary source materials that I have scrutinized in this chapter concur with such an interpretation of the Pátzcuaro conference. Beyond the touristic encounters, Indigenous peoples *are* largely absent from the historical records pertaining to it. This is not surprising. Pátzcuaro was a state-led and state-sponsored encounter. It was unlikely that social and racial hierarchies were going to be questioned or challenged. However, the central strand of this chapter's argument is that Indigenous peoples are not *entirely* absent from the records. The case of Coñuepán shows that while in a minority and often treated as lesser delegates, Indigenous people *did* participate in international and transnational conversations about race and indigeneity, and that they could use these conversations to their advantage on the national political stage.

What is more, Coñuepán was not the only Mapuche to draw on Pátzcuaro to try to advance the cause of Indigenous rights in mid-twentieth-century Chile. In 1943, the *Boletín Indigenista* – one of the official mouthpieces of the Inter-American Indigenista Institute (III) in Mexico City – received an 'extensive and highly interesting report by Sr J. Andrés Aguayo Paillalef, inspector of Indian education in Temuco, Province of Cautín'.[52] It was impossible, the editor(s) said, to reproduce the report in full, but they nonetheless quoted two pages of 'urgent improvements which Sr Aguayo recommends for the benefits of the Indian population'.[53] After arguing for the restitution of Indian lands and a guarantee of their inviolability, the increase of credit facilities for Indigenous communities, the conservation and industrialization of Indian crafts and better provision of technical and educational services, Aguayo Paillalef urged the Chilean government to ratify the Pátzcuaro Convention, to celebrate 'every year on April 19 the "Day of the Indian"' (one of the resolutions of the congress), and to establish a National Indigenista Institute. The latter, he reportedly said, should work to defend 'the race without exercising tutelage or monopolising the Indian program'.[54] This Mapuche education inspector thereby appropriated Pátzcuaro to put pressure on the Chilean government to enact new legislation, but also challenged the narrative – seemingly perpetuated by delegates at the conference in Mexico – that Indigenous peoples needed saving or were somehow incapable of speaking for themselves.

The broader lesson to take from the material presented here is that when we are studying conferences we need to go beyond their principal organizers, leading delegates and keynote speakers, and scrutinize as wide a range of actors and interventions as possible. We need to listen for traces of the marginal voices in the archival records, which in turn prompt us to interrogate the precise context and nature of participants' marginality. Finally, we need to pay attention to not only what happens or what is said at a conference but also how people cite it afterwards and how it shapes the lives of those who take part.

Notes

1 In Spanish, the language of most participating countries, the conference was known as the Primer Congreso Indigenista Interamericano. In *The Final Act* produced by the US Office of Indian Affairs in Washington in 1940, it was entitled the First Inter-American Conference on Indian Life, but I use a closer English translation – the First Inter-American Indigenista Congress. After Mexico, the conference was held in many different countries but intermittently: for example, Cuzco, Peru, hosted the conference in 1949 and then La Paz, Bolivia, in 1954. The last conference was celebrated in the early 2000s.
2 Laura Jiraudo, 'Neither "Scientific" nor "Colonialist": The Ambiguous Course of Inter-American *Indigenismo* in the 1940s', *Latin American Perspectives* 39, no. 5 (2012): 14.
3 Jiraudo, 'Neither "Scientific" nor "Colonialist"'; Jennifer Jolly, *Creating Pátzcuaro, Creating Mexico: Art, Tourism, and Nation-Building under Lázaro Cardenas* (Austin: University of Texas Press, 2014).

4   It is worth noting that the published conference proceedings make no reference to the Second World War. The outbreak of the conflict is mentioned in some letters relating to the organization of the conference, it is covered (as a separate news story) in US and Latin American newspapers that reported on the conference and scholars have commented that it was one of the reasons why the resolutions of the congress were not prioritized in the following years, particularly in the United States (why it took a long time to get the Inter-American Indigenista Institute off the ground, for example), but it does not seem to have been a major topic of conversation at the congress itself. Clearly, this event exemplified a distinctly American – and in some ways, *Latin American* – circuit of internationalism, where Europe did not feature very much, either in terms of participants or as a reference point.
5   The Chilean poet Pablo Neruda was serving as Chilean consul in Mexico City in 1940. While there he set up a new magazine to educate Mexicans about Chilean culture. It was entitled *Araucanía* and dominating the front-cover of its first issue was the smiling face of an old Mapuche woman. What happened next has now been widely reported and commented: when he sent copies back to Chile, hoping for increased funding for the initiative, he was reprimanded and famously told to suspend the publication immediately, on the basis that Chile was 'not a country of Indians!'. See Adam Feinstein, *Pablo Neruda: A Passion for Life* (London: Bloomsbury, 2004), 159.
6   Jiraudo, 'Neither "Scientific" nor "Colonialist"', 28.
7   For a useful overview of the Mexican Revolution 'as a complex, multisided process subject to many possible interpretations', see John Foran, 'Reinventing the Mexican Revolution: The Competing Paradigms of Alan Knight and John Mason Hart', *Latin American Perspectives* 23, no. 4 (Autumn 1996): 115–31.
8   Robert Alexander, 'Lázaro Cárdenas', in *Encyclopaedia Britannica*, available at https://www.britannica.com/biography/Lazaro-Cardenas (last accessed 15 September 2019).
9   See Karin Rosemblatt, *The Science and Politics of Race in Mexico and the United States, 1910-1950* (Chapel Hill, NC: University of North Carolina Press, 2018), especially chapter 4, 135–68.
10 'Se ultiman los preparativos para el Congreso Indigenista Interamericano q' se celebrará en Paztcuaro [sic], Mexico', *El Comercio*, 13 April 1940, 13.
11 'Se ultiman los preparativos . . .', 13.
12 *La Cámara de Diputados del Perú y el Primer Congreso Indigenista Interamericano: Exposición ante la Cámara, del señor diputado por Espinar, doctor José Angel Escalante, presidente de la Delegación Peruana al Congreso Indigenista; pedidos que la determinaron, y otras intervenciones* (Lima: Librería Gil, 1940).
13 *The Final Act of the First Inter-American Conference on Indian Life* (Washington: US Office of Indian Affairs, 1940), 11.
14 There exists an abundant and very rich scholarship on discourses of mestizaje in Mexico and Latin America. Particularly helpful overviews are Florencia Mallon, 'Constructing Mestizaje in Latin America: Authenticity, Marginality, and Gender in the Claiming of Ethnic Identities', *Journal of Latin American Anthropology* 2, no. 1 (1996): 170–81; and Lourdes Martínez-Echazábal, 'Mestizaje and the Discourse of National/Cultural Identity in Latin America, 1845–1959', *Latin American Perspectives* 25, no. 3 (1998): 21–42.
15 Cardenas's inaugural speech is partially reproduced in English in Rosemblatt, *The Science and Politics of Race*, 135–6.
16 'Ha sido confeccionado el programa de labores del Congreso Indigenista Panamericano que se realizará en México', *El Comercio*, 14 April 1940, 10.

17 According to Jennifer Jolly, this involved burying a copy of the conference agreements at the monument. 'Two members of an (unspecified) indigenous group', she comments, 'interred the documents in an urn at the monument's feet.' See Jolly, *Creating Pátzcuaro*, 199.
18 'Ha sido confeccionado el programa . . . '
19 See Lawrence Kelly, *The Assault on Assimilation: John Collier and the Origins of Indian Policy Reform* (Albuquerque, NM: University of New Mexico Press, 1983) and Robert Fay Schrader, *The Indians Arts and Crafts Board: An Aspect of New Deal Policy* (Albuquerque: University of New Mexico Press, 1983). On the complexities of the Mexican–US relationship in this regard, see Rosemblatt, *The Science and Politics of Race*.
20 *The Final Act of the First Inter-American Conference on Indian Life*.
21 These were Argentina, Bolivia, Brazil, Chile, Colombia, Cuba, Dominican Republic, Ecuador, El Salvador, Guatemala, Honduras, Nicaragua, Panama, Peru, the United States, Uruguay and Venezuela. Of course, Mexico had its own delegation. This was the largest delegation. The second largest was that of the United States. The Pan-American Union also sent a representative. Paraguay and Canada did not nominate delegations; they sent apologies in advance. Costa Rica nominated two representatives, but these did not turn up at the conference.
22 The exception was Ana María Reyna, who attended as part of Mexico's official delegation.
23 *El Comercio* of Peru referred to these delegates as 'genuine representatives of the main groups of *indigenista* scholars from each country'. See 'Se ultiman los preparativos . . . '
24 Betty Kirk, 'A Meeting on Indians: An Inter-American Conference Is Held on Shore of Lake Pátzcuaro in Mexico', *New York Times*, 14 April 1940, 139.
25 Jorge Coronado, *The Andes Imagined: Indigenismo, Society and Modernity* (Pittsburgh: University of Pittsburgh Press, 2009), 135. Coronado and other contemporary scholars are in part looking back from the vantage point of the present on the limited, paternalistic nature of *indigenismo*, but – as the scholarship itself highlights – there were also many intellectuals in the early twentieth century who critiqued the perceived hypocrisy of this pro-indigenous discourse and movement. Particularly interesting and impacting in this regard was a dispute between the Peruvian intellectuals José Carlos Mariátegui and Luis Alberto Sánchez that played out in the pages of the Peruvian magazine *El Mundial* in 1927 and to which many others, such as José Angel Escalante, contributed. See Nicola Miller, *In the Shadow of the State: Intellectuals and the Quest for National Identity in Twentieth-Century Spanish America* (London: Verso, 1998), 153–6.
26 Jolly, *Creating Pátzcuaro*, 165.
27 *The Final Act*, resolution IV on 'Irrigation Projects', 14.
28 *The Final Act*, resolution VII on 'Marriage and Free Union', 15.
29 *The Final Act*, resolution LI on 'Resettlement of Indian Groups', 30.
30 Jolly, *Creating Pátzcuaro*, 165.
31 Hidalgo wrote two letters dated 12 and 25 April 1940. These are accessible in the Archivo Histórico del Ministerio de Relaciones Exteriores in Santiago (Fondo Histórico Vol. 1807, 1940), and Jorge Vergara and Hans Gundermann make reference to these letters in 'Chile y el Instituto Indigenista Interamericano, 1940-1993: Una visión del conjunto', *Chungara, Revista de Antropología Chilena*, 2016, 1–16.
32 In November 1938, Aguirre Cerda wrote to Coñuepán thanking him for his loyalty and enthusiasm, which he said were crucial to his electoral victory. He addressed

Coñuepán as his 'esteemed friend'. The letter is cited in Fabián Almonacid Zapata, *La agricultura chilena discriminada (1910-1960): Una mirada de las políticas estatales y el desarrollo sectorial desde el sur* (Madrid: Consejo de Superior de Investigaciones Cientícas, 2009), 219.

33 Amelia Marie Kiddle, *La Politica del Buen Amigo: Mexican-Latin American Relations during the Presidency of Lázaro Cárdenas, 1934-1940* (Tucson, AZ: University of Arizona Press, 2010), 222.

34 Kiddle, *La Política del Buen Amigo*, 222.

35 'El Congreso Indigenista Interamericano adoptó importantes acuerdos', *El Comercio*, 24 April 1940, 10.

36 'El Congreso Indigenista Interamericano . . .', *El Comercio*.

37 On the ongoing reality of racist abuse and exclusion in twentieth-century Latin America (as well as indigenous responses to, protests against and survival despite it), see, for example, Joanna Crow, *The Mapuche in Modern Chile: A Cultural History* (Gainesville, FL: University Press of Florida, 2013; Marisol de la Cadena), *Indigenous Mestizos: The Politics and Culture of Race and Culture in Cuzco, Peru, 1919-1991* (Durham, NC & London: Duke University Press, 1991); Laura Gotkowitz (ed.), *Histories of Race and Racism: The Andes and Mesoamerican from Colonial Times to the Present* (Durham, NC & London: Duke University Press, 2012); Alan Knight, 'Racism, Revolution and Indigenismo: Mexico, 1910-1940', in *The Idea of Race in Latin America, 1870-1940*, ed. Richard Graham (Austin, TX: University of Texas Press, 1990), 72–114.

38 Focusing on Julius Nyerere, president of newly independent Tanzania (1964–85), Jo Sharp describes how post-colonial African leaders sought 'to find a voice within a world order that actively sought to silence those in the South and that [. . .] was structured in such a way that it would ensure their continued economic, political and epistemological marginality'. 'Through the spatial politics of nation-building and Pan-African, non-aligned cooperation', she continued, leaders like Nyerere 'sought to interrupt the system that created such inequalities'. See Jo Sharp, 'Practicing Subalternity: Nyerere's Tanzania, the Dar School, and Post-Colonial Political Imaginations', in Tariq Jazeel & Stephen Legg, *Subaltern Geographies* (Athens, GA: University of Georgia Press, 2019), 74–93. To be sure, indigenous participants at Pátzcuaro were not state leaders. They were subaltern within their nation states, which in turn were relegated to the peripheries of the existing world order, but they too embraced continental or hemispheric – as well as national – political spaces to try to make their voices heard and to protest against a long history of economic and social marginalization rooted in colonialism.

39 The original source was the ANA, RREE, Vol. 4047, Miguel Cruchaga Ossa to Minister 23 July 1938. It is cited in Kiddle, *La Politica del Buen Amigo*.

40 Venancio Coñuepán & Cesar Colima, 'El problema indígena de Chile' (1940). I would like to thank Jorge Iván Vergara for sharing this document with me.

41 The Mapuche were one of the few indigenous peoples in the Americas to defeat the Spanish conquistadors on the battlefield and to successfully defend their political and territorial independence throughout the colonial period. This was recognized in a series of treaties signed between representatives of the Spanish crown and Mapuche community leaders from 1641. The Chilean state also recognized Mapuche sovereignty in the early independence years, through the treaty of Tapihue signed in 1825. However, plans for conquest of the rich, fertile lands of the southern regions were set in motion in the 1850s. Military intervention started in earnest in 1862 (with

the occupation of Angol) and concluded in 1883, when Villarrica, the last bastion of indigenous resistance, was taken over by the Chilean army. For more on the historical background, see Pilar Herr, 'The Nation According to Whom?' *Journal of Early American History* 4, no. 1 (2014): 66–94. For current examples of marginal groups transforming conferences into spaces that can work to their advantage, see Fiona McConnell's work on the Unrepresented Nations and Peoples Organization (UNPO): 'Liminal Geopolitics: The Subjectivity and Spatiality of Diplomacy at the Margins', *Transactions of the Institute of British Geographers* 42, no. 1 (2017): 139–52.

42 Vergara & Gundermann, 'Chile y el Instituto Indigenista Interamericano'. Coñuepán was not the first Mapuche political activist to visit and learn from the experience of the United States. Arturo Huenchullán – who alternated with Manuel Aburto Panguilef as President of the Executive Committee of Araucanía, bringing together several different Mapuche organizations in southern Chile – travelled to the United States in the late 1920s to investigate and report back on indigenous education policy and practice there. See Arturo Huenchullán, 'La educación de indígenas en los Estados Unidos', *Revista de Educación* (October 1929), 759–62.

43 All these quotes are taken from *Sesiones de la Cámara de Diputados*, Congreso Nacional, Sesión 19 Extraordinaria, 25 November 1947, 829–65.

44 *Sesiones de la Cámara de Diputados*, 25 November 1947, 861.

45 *Sesiones de la Cámara de Diputados*, Congreso Nacional, Sesión Especial 45, 1 September 1965, available at www.bcn.cl.

46 *Sesiones de la Cámara de Diputados*, 1 September 1965.

47 This was during the centre-left Christian Democrat government of Eduardo Frei Montalva (1964–70). Five years later, Salvador Allende, leader of the Socialist Party of Chile and candidate for the Popular Unity coalition, would win the national elections. Painemal was a member of the Communist Party. In 1953, he co-founded and became leader of the Asociación Nacional Indígena [National Association of Indigenous People].

48 Crow, *The Mapuche in Modern Chile*, 121. The quoted words are those of Painemal.

49 Crow, *The Mapuche in Modern Chile*, 121.

50 'Indígenas rinden hoy homenaje a congénere Primer Sec de Estado', *El Diario Austral*, 1 January 1953, 18.

51 'Imponentes funerales del diputado Coñuepán', *El Diario Austral*, 4 May 1968, 9.

52 'Chile: Proposed Benefits for the Indians', *Boletín Indigenista* 3, no. 1 (1943): 23. This journal was a bilingual (Spanish–English) publication. The other journal linked to the Inter-American Indigenista Institute, which was created at the conference in Pátzcuaro, was *América Indígena*. Reports in the latter were mainly published in Spanish.

53 'Chile: Proposed Benefits . . .', 25.

54 'Chile: Proposed Benefits . . .', 25.

4

Awe and espionage at Lancaster House

The African decolonization conferences of the early 1960s

Peter Docking

Introduction

The location of a conference as an object of study is often overlooked. As Henrikson has noted, the focus of scholars is usually on participants and outcome. Where, precisely, the conference takes place tends to be taken-for-granted.[1] Yet an analysis of conference location can bring rich pickings, revealing the wider political strategies of the organizers and telling us something too about the objectives and motivations of the parties that agreed to attend. A study of a conference location helps contextualize the whole event. Why a conference was called, what happened during its proceedings, the relationship between conference actors, how the conference affected those living in its surround, the conclusions the conference reached and the effects these had are of course all important. But to fully understand the significance of a particular conference, who decided on the venue, why and why this was accepted by those who attended give us a more rounded picture of the event.

This chapter looks at the 'decolonization' constitutional conferences which took place during the early 1960s for British colonies in east and central Africa. These were conferences to discuss the next stage of constitutional advance for a particular colony. The constitutional discussions varied depending on the colony and the time. Some of the conferences (particularly in the early part of the period) debated matters such the enfranchisement of a greater number of African voters and more African ministers being appointed to the executive council of the colonial government. Others, however, discussed dates for a colony's move to self-government and to independence. Agreed outcomes were never formally binding on the British government, but in practice were always accepted. All but one of the sixteen conferences took place in London.[2] The chapter will show the perceived value to the British government of hosting these events at the capital of empire. For the most part, it had clear conference objectives and outcomes firmly in mind, and London was chosen to help facilitate these aims. Holding conferences away from the African colonies would, it was thought, insulate delegates from the offstage pressures of their supporters and allow 'good influences' to be brought to bear on them. Many of the conferences were held at Lancaster House, a venue chosen to awe delegates as the chapter will go on to show. Holding the events in London also permitted the use of espionage to find out delegates' thinking and generally gave the British a firm grip over proceedings. Yet for the most part, African delegates were happy enough to travel to London. The conferences offered them a relatively fast route to power and rocking the boat by holding out for an African venue would not have been good politics. Moreover, a conference held many thousands of miles away provided African politicians with opportunities to turn the events to their advantage.

The secondary literature on the African constitutional conferences and decolonization is fragmented. Many of the conferences have been given brief mentions in general works on the last days of the British empire in Africa and appear also in a variety of texts written, for example, about British and African politicians, as well as the histories of African countries and their constitutions.[3] There are no works, however, which interrogate comprehensively how British and African actors made use of the London decolonization conferences of the early 1960s.

Background to the conferences

By the early 1960s, the British were finding 'hard' methods of colonial management more difficult. The British and colonial governments had long employed a wide range of both 'hard' and 'soft' methods to govern. But by 1959, in the wake of prisoner deaths at the Hola camp in Kenya, and following the heavy-handed introduction of a state of emergency in Nyasaland, hard measures were no longer so feasible.[4] Influential ministers and Colonial Office officials appreciated that territories could no longer be held by force. In part this was because of logistical difficulties. A shift in emphasis in military strategy from conventional forces to nuclear weapons following the defence review of 1957 and the planned end of conscription in 1960 served as potential constraints. Both Iain Macleod, appointed colonial secretary in October 1959, and his prime minister, Harold Macmillan, also wished to avoid the sort of long and costly campaign which France had endured in Algeria. There was now an acute sensitivity about offending world opinion.[5] Hard measures had not completely disappeared; a state of emergency was declared, for example, in Zanzibar in 1961.[6] But in general, emergency control measures were generally seen as 'having had their day'.[7] Instead, negotiation became the order of the day, and commissions and conferences became the vehicles through which such bargaining took place.

Holding a constitutional conference was not new to the 1960s. In the colonial context, the modern origins of the African conferences can be found in the three Indian Round Table Conferences of the early 1930s. Important conferences were also held for Nigeria, Malaya and other colonies in the 1950s. Yet it was not until Macleod's tenure that conferences became a frequent event. Of the twenty-two calendar months between January 1960 and October 1961, only five were without conferences. Macleod's biographer, Robert Shepherd, notes how conferences were sometimes held simultaneously in London, each one chaired by Macleod, and how the colonial secretary 'realized that the constitutional conference had to be his main instrument if he was to achieve relatively peaceful decolonization'.[8] Shepherd himself offers no explanation as to why Macleod favoured conferences, but it is easy to see why, in general terms, the colonial secretary felt predisposed towards conferences as a constitutional mechanism. Confident of his own abilities and secure in his intellect, his former Cabinet position of Minister of Labour had sharpened Macleod's skills around the negotiating table, where meetings with employers and trade union organizations had been commonplace.[9] Macleod, an expert bridge player, was also prepared to take risks if the reward seemed worth it.

Sometimes there were technical reasons which made it expedient to set up a conference. This is a feature of the 'independence conferences' for Kenya, Northern Rhodesia and Uganda, where time-consuming and sometimes awkward post-independence issues could be dealt with under the one roof. Thus for Kenya, an 'independence conference' was always seen as necessary by the British government to make the technical changes to Kenya's self-governing constitution which independence would require and also to deal with other matters such as defence issues and financial.[10] At other times, the African conferences were constitutionally unavoidable. The British government was committed, for example, some years in advance to hold a review conference for the Central African Federation of the Rhodesias and Nyasaland. But by far the most common reason for holding the conferences was an attempt by the British to seize the initiative and to manage outcomes – to give the British and colonial governments breathing spaces.

The British and colonial governments had firm objectives at most of the African conferences, including making what were seen as small constitutional advances in order to delay independence, conceding self-government but in return for concessions which would further delay the independence process, imposing British-desired terms at independence conferences, securing a hoped-for East African federation and, on two occasions, using conferences to divest itself speedily of the territory concerned. All of these objectives were employed by the British government to control and manage the pace and trajectory of decolonization: to slow down the process when that was considered desirable, to depart on terms it wanted or to divest itself of territories considered awkward.

The London advantage: Control, influence, expertise, infrastructure and espionage

To achieve its conference objectives, the British government employed a range of tactics. Prominent among these was to insist that the conferences be held in London. The location of a conference that involves diplomacy and negotiation is often of high importance to one or more of the parties. Thus in deciding on the venue for the peace conference at the end of the First World War, Clemenceau insisted upon Paris, with the French prime minister having 'wept and protested so much' that Britain and the United States gave way.[11] The French argument was that it was France which had particularly suffered during the war and it was only right therefore that Paris should host the conference. Revenge was in the air.[12] Bandung, chosen to host the Asia-Africa Conference in 1955, had special significance for the Indonesians. Many of the post-colonial Indonesian elite had spent their earlier years in that city as 'freedom-fighters'.[13]

Alan Henrikson identifies some twelve types of diplomatic sites. One of these is 'my place': where conditions of interchange can be controlled and where there is 'territorial dominance' at play at both the psychological and organizational levels. The converse of 'my place' is 'your place', where certain deference is shown to the other side by the gesture of journeying. The trip can signify inequality, yet going to the other party's place can result in gains.[14] The east and central African conferences of the early 1960s fitted into this pattern: 'my place' for the British and 'your place' for the African leaders.

Discussions in Whitehall over the venue for the first Kenyan conference, to take place in January 1960, set the tone. Sir Leslie Monson, head of the Colonial Office's Africa Department, felt strongly that the conference should be in London. This, he thought, would insulate delegates from offstage pressure from their supporters and give the British government a greater control over the discussion.[15] This was to become a recurring theme. When deciding on the venue for the 1960 Federal Review Conference, for example, holding the event anywhere in the Central African Federation was rejected by London as this 'would expose delegates to local pressures inhibiting any spirit of compromise' and also attract demonstrations. Holding the conferences in London, on the other hand, would mean, as the deputy governor of Nyasaland observed, that African political leader Dr Hastings Banda would 'be exposed to the many good influences which can be brought to bear on him there'.[16] Similar observations were made for other conferences.[17]

The 'good influences' comment is somewhat Delphic, but a clue as to its meaning can be gleaned from subsequent action taken by the British government in the run-up to and at certain of the conferences. British ministers used the opportunity afforded by delegates travelling to London to weaken their resolve. Key actors were sometimes invited to meet with members of the British and colonial governments on home soil before a conference began in order to secure their agreement to British objectives. Thus shortly before the Federal Review Conference at the end of 1960, Sir Roy Welensky, the prime minister of the Central African Federation who had been acting as a thorn on the side of the British, was invited to Chequers so that the British government could 'have this opportunity of working on Welensky in advance'.[18] Similar techniques were used for Hastings Banda. Before the first Nyasaland conference, Macleod wanted to find a reliable 'third party' who might be lined up to influence Banda, convincing him on the benefits of compromise. The names of Oliver Woods of *The Times* and the Fabian Sir Jock Campbell were put forward.[19] The Colonial Office took up the suggestions, with Campbell telling Monson that he 'would do his best to influence Dr. Banda' to accept the sort of constitutional settlement that the Colonial Office contemplated.[20]

Having the conference in London meant also that key British actors would be on hand and could be brought into the conference arena to variously flatter, cajole and influence delegates. When delegates needed reassurance or the British government wanted them to feel important, it was appreciated that the status of the office of prime minister and the personal charm of Macmillan himself could be used to good effect. At the first Kenyan conference, to coax along the newly formed multiracial group of

Michael Blundell, Macleod enlisted the prime minister's help, especially when the group baulked at the colonial secretary's new proposals;[21] the message to be given to the Blundell's group, Macleod told Macmillan, should be *'Courage, mes braves'*.[22] At the first Nyasaland conference, when the European leaders were concerned at the concessions to be made to Banda, Macleod suggested that Macmillan be asked to meet them as the prime minister's 'reassurance . . . would be enormously helpful'.[23] Macmillan was otherwise engaged but the chancellor, Lord Kilmuir, stepped in, reading out the prime minister's words of support.[24] Banda was also subjected to the Macmillan treatment at the Federal Review Conference, the Nyasaland leader telling assembled crowds on his return that having walked out of the conference, he had been persuaded to return to the table following a 'fatherly' talk from Harold Macmillan, adding that 'I could not disappoint a man like that. His great humanity made a deep impression on me', and that 'If my trip did nothing else it allowed me to meet a great Prime Minister'.[25] Macmillan was actually only four years older than Banda, and the latter's description of the British prime minister as a father figure shows the paternalistic ambience which Macmillan wanted to convey: that he was at hand to help and to guide but was also someone of authority.

Yet hosting the African conferences in London was more than just avoiding inconvenient demonstrations by supporters and softening up participants. Holding conferences in London gave the British the opportunity to control pretty much everything – the minute taking, which delegates should attend the conference, the agenda, the bland press communiques that were issued at the end of each day and the hospitality too. To some extent that would also have been true had the conferences been held in the colonies. After all, at the time at which many of the earlier African conferences took place, the governor of the colony still wielded considerable power. Yet the situation would not have been so predictable had the conferences been held in Africa, where the dynamics and local pressures would have exerted a potent influence. At the very least this would have been a concern to the British, as the example of Tanganyika will show. Formal power structures notwithstanding, holding the conferences in the territories would not have given the British the same clean, undisputed sense of who was boss, a point not lost on British ministers and officials.

A small but nevertheless meaningful example of the confidence felt by colonial secretaries in using London as the conference venue, this can be seen in relation to the first Kenya conference. Macleod faced huge pressure from the African delegates to admit an unexpected guest, Peter Koinage. For the British, Koinage's conference presence was wholly unacceptable, given his association with Mau Mau. Yet without Koinage there, the African delegates refused to participate at the conference. Demonstrations were planned in Nairobi.[26] Macleod resolved the issue by deciding that each group of delegates could have one additional adviser who would not be admitted to the sessions but who could be admitted to the offices of the group at the conference venue. The Africans accepted this, as, reluctantly, did the Europeans. Had the conference taken place in Nairobi, it is easy to imagine that the whole situation would have been far more volatile. Thousands of miles away from the fierce glare of party supporters, it was easier for the European and African delegates to compromise and to accept the proclamation of the colonial secretary.

Having the conference in London also meant that Whitehall Colonial Office lawyers were on hand to take over the drafting of outlined constitutions agreed at conferences. There was a much easier rationale for doing this if the conference was held in London. At the Northern Rhodesia independence conference, its African government was invited to submit the first draft of their desired constitution, but there was no question of the Northern Rhodesian government drafting the final constitution (although it would be consulted). 'Following normal procedure' was the reason given for this process to be in British hands, but it is easy to imagine that issues concerning the British government's perceived superior drafting ability and also an innate need to direct the situation were factors too.[27]

Ruth Craggs has argued that hospitality is an important diplomatic institution, facilitating information gathering, communication and negotiation. Diplomacy often happens outside the office. Craggs has shown how when Nkrumah attended a drinks reception given by the Royal Commonwealth Society, shortly after Ghana's independence, the event also 'elevated and reinforced diplomatic conventions, assumptions and power relations'.[28] Much the same points can be made about official British hospitality at the African conferences. Each of the conferences had a bar which would open at the end of the proceedings. It was considered by the Colonial Office, only half-jokingly, that conferences 'might not be altogether successful without one' and that it was '[their] experience that this facility contributes materially to the successful outcome of negotiations'.[29] The bar was to be open for half an hour before lunch and for half an hour in the evening.[30] Formal drinks receptions were also held for delegates shortly after the conferences opened, often at Lancaster House and hosted by the prime minister and other Cabinet members. This hospitality was no doubt given, as the Colonial Office staff intimated, because they thought it would aid discussion. But the drinks receptions were also, as Craggs has argued, designed to make the delegates feel important, and to instil in them a sense of responsibility, that an agreement had to be reached. Moreover, the hospitality reinforced British hegemony: it was the British government that decided how long the bar should be open for, paid the bills and who, outside of the delegations, was invited to the conference receptions.

There was also a more sinister and basic reason for the British wanting to hold the African conferences in London: it facilitated better surveillance. One of the most eye-catching tactics which the British used to gather information for a conference was to make use of the British intelligence service to bug the conference venue, hotel rooms and telephone lines, spy on delegates and intercept their letters. In his 1987 book *Spycatcher*, former senior intelligence officer Peter Wright recounts how he set up an extensive operation installing microphones at Lancaster House. The Colonial Office had agreed to this enthusiastically and the system was used whenever high-level negotiations took place. More recently, Christopher Andrew, who had access to MI5 restricted files (which he was not permitted to reference), notes how surveillance was carried out on colonial delegations which visited London and in particular the intelligence which was gleaned for the third Kenyan conferences.[31]

More recently still, several 'KV series' files have been released to the National Archives which show just how widespread the surveillance operation was.[32] These files provide details of the surveillance of delegates at the second and third Kenyan conference, the Federal Review Conference and both Nyasaland conferences. There may well have been more occasions when this was done, with the further material not having yet been released. For the London conferences, and from the files we have, the emphasis, not surprisingly, was on finding out the thoughts of the key African actors. The hotel room and telephone calls of Kenyan delegate Oginga Odinga were bugged at the second Kenya conference. In the application for the telephone check, it was suggested that this was done not just to keep a watch on the African politician's communist activities but because 'it is of the utmost importance [that] . . . the Secretary of State for the Colonies should have in advance the fullest access throughout the course of the Conference to the views and intentions of the delegations and individuals concerned.'[33] For the third conference, it was not just Odinga who was closely observed. MI5 were requested by the colonial secretary to 'give full coverage to certain of the delegates who will be attending the Kenya Independence Conference', with one of its operatives noting, 'It is the view of the Colonial Office that there will be questions of great importance to her Majesty's Government arising at the Conference, and it will be of vital importance to the Secretary of State to have the fullest access throughout the Conference to the views and intentions of the various parties.'[34] Andrew has observed from the files to which only he had access that Colonial Secretary Duncan Sandys made use of the information he received for the third of the Kenyan Conferences.[35]

Hastings Banda was the subject of surveillance before and during the London conferences he attended. Clearly the British government had reservations about how far they could trust the enigmatic African leader, but they also wanted to remain one-step ahead of Banda. Nyasaland intelligence authorities were able to report before the first Nyasaland conference of information that indicated a 'preparedness to compromise'.[36] Banda's post was also intercepted by security services as it was 'desired to investigate his activities and contacts before and during the conference', and his phone lines were tapped for the same reason.[37] As an MI5 briefing note recorded: 'Almost anything that Dr. BANDA says or does may be helpful in assessing his attitude to the conference and in trying to discern his intentions.'[38]

'The Lancaster House treatment'

Another important reason for holding the conferences in London was because of the venues it offered and in particular Lancaster House. In London, the African conferences were held at one of three venues, ranked by the British government in terms of status: Lancaster House, then Marlborough House and lastly and less glamorously a room at the Colonial Office. Lancaster House was the prestigious venue. James Yorke, who has devoted a whole book to the building, describes it as 'this monumental edifice' and one whose 'splendid interiors have dazzled many a VIP'.[39] The building, a neoclassical mansion designed by the Duke of York in 1825, had hosted many leading events, including Queen Elizabeth II's coronation banquet in June 1953.[40] The three-floored building with its huge pillars, sweeping staircase, Louis XIV style furnishings and historic paintings, is located on The Mall, almost opposite and only a stone's throw away from Buckingham Palace. A testament to Lancaster House's grandeur and size is that it was used as a stand-in for the Palace in the 2010 film *The King's Speech* and for the Netflix series, *The Crown*.[41] The largest and most important of the African conferences were held at this venue: the first Kenyan conference, the first Nyasaland conference, the first Ugandan conference and the Federal Review Conference.

Lancaster House was chosen to awe delegates and to remind them of Britain's power. Invitations to such a prestigious venue were no doubt also intended to flatter delegates. Alan Lennox-Boyd captured this mixture of motives in 1956, telling a colleague that

> Both the Malayan and West Indian conferences are of enormous importance . . . and I just want to let you know how greatly we value our being able to have them in Lancaster House. I am quite certain that the dignity and splendour of the building will not only make an immediate and favourable impact on the delegations we have to negotiate with, but exert a potent and helpful influence throughout the discussions. I won't attempt to analyse why this is, but I think you will know what I mean.[42]

This was a common view among British ministers. When requesting the building for the first Nyasaland conference Macleod told Lord Hope, Minister of Works, that 'apart from the administrative convenience, the prestige attaching to a conference at Lancaster House in the eyes of some of our visitors would be an additional earnest of the seriousness of our intentions, and could itself make a contribution to the successful outcome of these important discussions'.[43] Sir John Martin, deputy undersecretary of state at the Colonial Office, could see value in the 'mystique' of Lancaster House as a venue for the first Nyasaland conference and when it transpired that the building was not available for the timeslot first desired, the territory's governor was told that it would be 'better that we should accept a short postponement in order to give the Conference full Lancaster House treatment'.[44]

Not all delegates were taken in by the 'Lancaster House treatment'. Both Julius Nyerere, the leader of the Tanganyika African National Union, and Hastings Banda seemed to see through the use of the venue to impress and cower. The Colonial Office noted that Nyerere thought the 'Lancaster House technique a lot of Ballyhoo',[45] and Banda told the first Nyasaland conference on its opening day that if he returned to Nyasaland empty-handed and his people had come inside and looked at the Lancaster House building, then they 'would accuse us of having been dazzled by the beauty, magnificence, and other things that I see about in this building'.[46] What other delegates made of the building and whether the 'Lancaster House' treatment actually worked is difficult to gauge. Certainly one of the New Kenya Group party was impressed. Mrs Hughes observed how the conference had opened in a 'beautiful and stately room'.[47]

Marlborough House was also an impressive venue, having been furnished as a 'Commonwealth centre' with the Commonwealth Prime Ministers' conferences as its main function.[48] Built in the early eighteenth century, commissioned for the Marlborough family, and located also on The Mall it too is undoubtedly a prestigious venue.[49] At the time of the African conferences, the building was owned by the Crown. Further away from Buckingham Palace and having a more functional appearance, it lacks, however, the same allure as Lancaster House. It is striking how many of the *second* conferences for a particular African territory in the wind of change era were held at this venue – those for Uganda, Northern Rhodesia and Nyasaland. These conferences were more functional, workaday than the initial ones. There was no need at that stage to awe delegates, who would already have experienced the glamour and prestige of Lancaster House at the first of the territories' conferences. Moving further down the scale was the Colonial Office itself. This hosted the Swaziland and Basutoland conferences, both of which were seen as minor and both of which were seen by the British government as possibly ending in failure. For these events, the emphasis of the British government was on discreet, behind-the-scenes negotiation and influence, not the oxygen of publicity which Lancaster House (and even Marlborough House) would have attracted. Quite what the delegates attending these smaller conferences made of the inferior venue is, unfortunately, not known.

London, then, offered the British government the opportunity to control proceedings in a systematic, comprehensive way. An illustration of just how important this was, and just how lost the British were when conferences were held outside of London, can be seen in the case of the Tanganyika Conference of 1961. Macleod gave no reason for his willingness to travel to Dar es Salaam. One factor may have been that he did not anticipate major areas of disagreement, but it was also the case that Julius Nyerere, who by now had considerable leverage, was not at all keen on the idea of coming to London for a conference, no doubt fearing, as mentioned earlier, that this would give the British the upper hand.[50] Lacking the usual and familiar conference scaffolding, Macleod wanted the Dar es Salaam Conference to be as short as possible, with contentious decisions being put off until Nyerere could come to London for talks later on in the year (and which the Colonial Office were careful not to label a 'conference'). The Dar es Salaam Conference, which had been planned for four days, lasted for an even shorter time than anticipated. In the event it comprised one meeting from 10 am to 4 pm, one from 3 pm to 4.15 pm and a final one from 9.20 am to 10 am.[51] The *Tanganyikan Standard* observed at the close of proceedings: 'It must surely be unique in recent colonial history for such a conference to have ended early.'[52] The paper attributed that to a spirit of compromise. In truth it was because the British, fearing a loss of control in unfamiliar surroundings, had managed events so that there was nothing difficult to discuss.

Travelling from Africa

While it is evident why the British wanted the conferences held in London, it is not so obvious why African nationalist politicians agreed to travel to London. There is little to suggest that they put up much resistance. At one level, they had little choice, the London conferences being take-it-or-leave-it opportunities. Yet that Macleod had been willing to travel to Tanganyika shows that there was potential flexibility on the part of the British. On further analysis it is not too hard to see why London may have appealed to African politicians. First, and somewhat paradoxically, the act of travelling to and from a conference could be used to shore up political support. The airport send-offs and arrivals were particular acts of theatre, where vast crowds sometimes gathered.

Whether these were spontaneous acts of admiration or whether the crowds had been organized by party machinery is not known, but either way some of the numbers are impressive. After the third Kenyan conference, for example, more than 5,000 people met Kenyatta at Nairobi airport on his return from London. The *East African Standard* reported that some had travelled from upcountry areas and some had started to arrive some seven hours before Kenyatta's jet had landed. Later the Kenyan leader spoke to a mass rally, attended by an estimated crowd of 150,000, described by the police as the biggest ever gathering in Nairobi for a political meeting.[53] On Kenneth Kaunda's return to Lusaka from the second Northern Rhodesia conference, the *Northern News* reported how around 2,000 people were at the airport to greet Kaunda and outside a crowd of more than 15,000 lined the two-mile stretch of road to UNIP's headquarters, receiving the UNIP leader with 'thunderous cheers'.[54] But most startling are the airport crowds for Hastings Banda. On his return from the 1960 Nyasaland conference, some 10,000 gathered at the airport to welcome back the leader with 40,000 attending a later meeting at Blantyre which he addressed.[55] Then, for the second conference, crowds estimated at between 100,000 and 150,000 arrived to see the MCP leader return, many of these waiting at the airport itself.[56] The *Nyasaland Times* reported in advance of the arrival that every available bus, truck and lorry in the country had been seconded to bring in people from far afield.[57] The London conferences, then, gave an opportunity to rally support.

Returning politicians, out of the gaze of local eyes, could also exaggerate the part they played in conference proceedings, telling supporters on their return about their importance and their successes. This may have been harder to do had the conference been held in the colony. In overstated claims, Banda spoke after Nyasaland Conference of 1960 in terms of the conference having agreed on self-government, pointing out that Nyasaland was now to be recognized as an African state, and that no time restrictions had been imposed on the next stage of constitutional advance.[58] A party conference was arranged for late September at which Banda's 'victory' at Lancaster House was to be celebrated.[59] Some Africans, having given the conference agreement scrutiny, were disappointed with the results, but the acting publicity secretary of Banda's party, J. D. Mosonthi, probably spoke for others when he said that the party had every confidence in Dr Banda and his team and that he was sure that as they had accepted the proposals, they would be good for Nyasaland.[60] As Short observes, Banda had little difficulty in presenting the 1960 Conference as a success.[61]

Moreover, African politicians sometimes used the location away from home to pursue their own tactics to demonstrate support and power. One of these was the use of telegrams from supporters from home. The telegram sending came to prominence with the Federal Review Conference of 1960 at which Kenneth Kaunda sought to bolster his position, telling the British that tension was mounting back home and that he had received fifty-three telegrams about it, but also that he had asked his people to stay calm and dignified.[62] Kaunda used a similar device at the Northern Rhodesian conference that followed shortly afterwards, broadcasting that he had received more than 250 cables from supporters which made it clear that unless the British government stood firm against Welensky, there would be an explosion of a far-reaching nature which he may not be able to control, which would make Mau Mau look like 'a childish picnic'.[63]

Travelling to and from London conferences also enabled travelling African politicians to pursue wider opportunities. One example is the Kenyan communist Oginga Odinga. Recently released British security service files show how, while in London for two of Kenya conferences, Odinga met with Idris Cox, a senior official of the Communist Party of Great Britain.[64] Odinga was also invited to visit East Berlin twice during the duration of the second Kenya conference. It was reported that apart from wanting to hear about the conference, the East Germans were anxious to discuss the provision of training facilities including instruction in state security and intelligence, military matters and the organization of party cadres.[65] The Kenyan was also said to have met with Russian and Chinese officials, with the latter too offering training facilities.

Another example of delegates making use of the London conferences to pursue their own agenda is Milton Obote. On the back of the Uganda conference of 1961, Obote spent around a month after the conference ended attending various conferences and meetings in Europe, seeking also to raise funds for this party's forthcoming election campaign.[66] Sometimes travelling politicians would also no doubt have enjoyed the experience of visiting London for other reasons. It gave them the occasion to address societies in Britain, to meet with friends and supporters, and to pursue publishing opportunities. Reasons could be more domestic. Kenyatta, for example, while attending the Kenya independence conference, visited his son who was studying at the University of Cambridge and also Windsor Castle with which he was 'very impressed'.[67]

Conclusion

This chapter has sought to add to the small but growing literature on conferences, in particular by building on Henrikson's work to demonstrate the importance of conference location to the parties that attend. There is always a reason for the choice of a particular venue. For the British government 'my place' was important for both the concrete and softer benefits on offer. London provided the British with a comforting sense of control over the African conference proceedings in terms of matters such as the setting of the agenda, press management and not least surveillance. But there was more to it than that: London offered other less tangible but nonetheless crucial benefits. In particular, the conference location was chosen with the objective that delegates, travelling to the capital of the British Empire and taken to historic, prestigious venues, would absorb a reverence that would somehow make them more malleable and submissive. African delegates might also be influenced by the office and character of the prime minister and could be worked on by other collaborators. As the chapter has also shown, African delegates who attended were also not averse to travelling to 'your place' for the power and opportunities on offer, not least the chance to drum up support at the airport send-offs and return, and the latitude a far-away event gave to exaggerate outcomes and the parts they played. Travelling to London also opened up welcome networking opportunities. Location, as this chapter has sought to illustrate, should not be seen as a sterile point on the map where a conference event happened to be held. Rather, it should be asked why, precisely, the event took place where it did. What the organizers and delegates each hoped to gain from the location, and how they used the location to their advantage, helps us to more fully contextualize the whole event.

Notes

1. Alan Henrikson, 'The Geography of Diplomacy', in *The Geography of War and Peace: From Death Camps to Diplomats*, ed. Colin Flint (Oxford: Oxford University Press, 2005), 369–94.
2. The sixteen conferences concerned Kenya (1960), Somaliland (1960), Nyasaland (1960), the Federation of Rhodesia and Nyasaland (1960), Northern Rhodesia (1961), Tanganyika (1961), Uganda (1961), Kenya (1962), Zanzibar (1962), Uganda (1962), Nyasaland (1962), Kenya (1963), Zanzibar (1963), Swaziland (1963), Basutoland (1964) and Northern Rhodesia (1964).
3. The texts are too numerous to mention here in any detail. For general texts, see, for example, Frank Heinlein, *British Government Policy and Decolonisation 1945-1963: Scrutinising the Official Mind* (London: Routledge, 2002); Robert Hyam, *Britain's Declining Empire: The Road to Decolonisation 1918-1968* (Cambridge: Cambridge University Press, 2006); and John Darwin, *Britain and Decolonisation: The Retreat from Empire in the Post-War World* (Basingstoke: Macmillan, 1988). Of the texts on specific actors, see, for example, Robert Shepherd, *Iain Macleod* (London: Hutchinson, 1994), which gives some coverage to the conferences organized by Macleod as Colonial Secretary. The conferences for Kenya receive some analysis in terms of delegates' competing aims in Robert Maxon's two books: *Britain and Kenya's Constitutions 1950-1960* (New York: Cambria Press, 2011) and *Kenya's Independence Constitution: Constitution-Making and End of Empire* (Madison: Fairleigh, 2011).
4. Kate Kennedy, 'Britain and the end of Empire: A study in colonial governance in Cyprus, Kenya and Nyasaland against the backdrop of internationalisation of empire and the evolution of a supranational human rights culture and jurisprudence, 1938-1965', Unpublished PhD thesis, University of Oxford, 2015.
5. Peter Docking, 'The Wind Has Been Gathering Force': Iain Macleod and His Policy Change on Tanganyika', *Journal of Imperial and Commonwealth History* 46, no. 2 (2018): 367–95, 376.
6. Samuel G. Ayany, *A History of Zanzibar: A Study in Constitutional Development 1934-1964* (Nairobi: African Literature Bureau, 1971), 85–9.
7. Kennedy, 'Colonial Governance', 295.
8. Shepherd, *Macleod*, 165–7.
9. Shepherd, *Macleod*, 122–42.
10. The National Archives, Kew, United Kingdom ('TNA'), PREM11/4328, Note from Trend to Prime Minister, 21 June 1963.
11. Alan Sharp, *The Versailles Settlement: Peace-Making after the First World War 1919-1923, Third Edition* (London: Palgrave, 2018), 20–1. The words in quotation marks are those of Lloyd George.
12. V. N. Khana, *International Relations*, Fifth Edition (New Delhi: Vikas Publishing House, 2013), 66.

13 Naoko Shimazu, 'Diplomacy as Theatre: Staging the Bandung Conference of 1955', *Modern Asian Studies* 48, no. 1 (2014): 225–52, 235.
14 Henrikson, 'The Geography of Diplomacy', 372.
15 TNA, CO822/1427, Draft Telegram from Monson to the Governor, 13 August 1959.
16 TNA, CO1015/2335, Telegram from Nyasaland Government to Colonial Secretary, 24 October 1960; CO1015/2338, Note from Macleod to Macmillan, 26 October 1960.
17 See, for example, TNA, CO822/2422, Letter from Chief Secretary to Webber, 8 March 1961, in which it was suggested that the Uganda Conference of 1961 be held in London as it would be away from local political influences and distractions.
18 TNA, CO1015/2338, Telegram from Colonial Secretary to Hone, 11 November 1960.
19 TNA, CO1015/2268, Letter from Macleod to Welensky, 30 May 1960.
20 TNA, CO1015/2241, Memorandum from Monson to Macleod, 19 July 1960.
21 TNA, PREM11/3030, Telegram from Macleod to Macmillan, 8 February 1960; TNA, CO822/2354, Note from Macleod to Macmillan, 17 February 1960.
22 TNA, CO822/2354, Note from Macleod to Macmillan, 17 February 1960.
23 TNA, DO35/7567, Note from Macleod to Macmillan, 2 August 1960.
24 TNA, PREM11/3077, Note for the record, 3 August 1960.
25 *Nyasaland Times*, 'Conference to Stop Trouble', 20 December 1960, 1.
26 TNA, CO822/2356, Telegram from Acting Governor to Colonial Secretary, 20 January 1960.
27 TNA, DO183/77, Telegram from Whitley (CRO) to Hone, 22 April 1964.
28 Ruth Craggs, 'Hospitality in Geopolitics and the Making of Commonwealth International Relations', *Geoforum* 52 (2014): 90–100, 94.
29 TNA, CO1015/2375, Letter from Reynolds to Watson, 17 June 1960. From the bar bill at the end of the conference, gin and tonic was by far the favoured drink: letter from Strachan to Reynold, 8 August 1960.
30 TNA, CAB21/3119, Letter from le Tocq to J. L. Clark at the Treasury, 28 November 1960.
31 Peter Wright, *Spycatcher: The Candid Autobiography of a Senior Intelligence Officer* (New York: Del Publishing, 1987), 73. Christopher Andrews, *Defence of the Realm: The Authorized History of MI5* (London: Penguin Books, 2009), 467. Drawing on Andrew and Wright's observations, Calder Walton notes this practice too in relation to Kenya: Calder Walton, *Empire of Secrets* (New York: William Collins, 2013), 269.
32 The KV series files are records of the British security services.
33 TNA, KV2/4085, Note by G. R. Mitchell, 7 February 1962.
34 TNA, KV2/4088, File note by E.2.B, 4 September 1963.
35 Andrew, *Defence of the Realm*, 467.
36 TNA, KV2/4075, Extract from Nyasaland Intelligence Report for May, May 1960.
37 TNA, KV2/4075, Intelligence Reports, 4 July 1960 and 11 July 1960.
38 TNA, KV2/4075, A.2.A. Briefing sheet, 13 July 1960. Banda was subject to checks at the second Nyasaland conference: see KV2/4077, Letter from R. G. Holden to N. A. Hawkins, 2 November 1962, and also the Federal Review Conference: see TNA, KV2/4075, Letter to Major A E Denman, 29 November 1960.
39 James Yorke, *Lancaster House: London's Greatest Town House* (London: Merrell, 2001), 15, 175.
40 https://www.gov.uk/government/history/lancaster-house, accessed 26 February 2019.
41 https://blogs.fco.gov.uk/stories/film-and-television/, accessed 9 August 2019.
42 Quoted in Yorke, *Lancaster House*, 171. Reference given is PRO Work12/444, Boyd to Buchan-Hepburn MP, 4 February 1956.

43 TNA, CO1015/2375, Letter from Macleod to Hope, 10 May 1960.
44 TNA, DO35/7567, Telegram from Colonial Secretary to Armitage, 25 May 1960.
45 TNA, CO822/2413, Memorandum from Monson to Morgan, 23 January 1961.
46 TNA, CO1015/2379, Minutes of Meeting, 25 July 1960.
47 KNA MSS13/57, Undated Memorandum of Mrs Hughes.
48 TNA, FCO141/18390, Letter from Webber to Coutts, 3 May 1962.
49 http://thecommonwealth.org/marlborough-house, accessed 1 August 2019.
50 TNA, CO822/2413, Memorandum from Monson to Morgan, 23 January 1961.
51 TNA, CO822/2415, Minutes of meetings, 27–29 March 1961.
52 *Tanganyika Standard*, 29 March 1961, 'Conference reaches "agreement on a wide variety of points"', 1.
53 *East African Standard*, 21 October 1963, 'Vast Crowd Gives Three Promises', 1.
54 *Northern News*, 27 May 1964, 'Kaunda Home in Triumph', 1.
55 TNA, CO1015/2241, Note by Jones, 16 August 1960.
56 TNA, DO183/59, Letter from Jones to Butler, 4 December 1962; *Malawi News*, 7 December 1962, 1.
57 *Nyasaland Times*, 30 November 1962, 'Malawi Flag to Be Hoisted for Dr. Banda', 1.
58 TNA, CO1015/2241, Account of Press Conference, 10 August 1960 and excerpt from *Malawi News*, 20 August 1960.
59 Joey Power, *Political Culture and Nationalism in Malawi: Building Kwacha* (Rochester: University of Rochester Press, 2010), 152.
60 *Nyasaland Times*, '100,000' Voters', 1.
61 Philip Short, *Banda* (London: Routledge and Kegan Paul, 1974), 138.
62 *Northern News*, 15 December 1960, 'Constitutional Conferences May Open This Week', 1.
63 *Northern News*, 10 February 1961, 'Africans Dissatisfied with Progress of Talks', 1.
64 TNA, KV2/4085, 'CPGB Interest – Kenya Constitutional Conference', 21 February 1962.
65 TNA, KV2/4085, Report on Kenya Constitutional Conference, 21 February 1962.
66 *Uganda Argus*, 6 November 1961, 'U.P.C. Leader Back from Europe', 1; TNA, FCO141/18363, Letter from Special Branch Kampala to Secretary for Security and External Relations, Uganda, 24 November 1961.
67 *East African Standard*, 30 September 1963, 'Invigorated by Drive', by Arnold Raphael and David Jones, 1.

Part II

Science, civil society and the state

5

Conferencing the aerial future

Martin Mahony

It needs no prophetic ability to suggest that when the next Imperial Conference is held one of these airships will call for and collect all the Dominion delegates in London in the space of a fortnight, circumnavigating the globe while picking them up.[1]

The Imperial Conference will then become an annual affair, and what is more, the way will be paved for the setting up of a Commonwealth Parliament which shall be in permanent session like the League of Nations at Geneva.[2]

The interwar period saw both the conference and the airship emerge as joint technologies of international world-building. Aviation held out great hope both to internationalists who dreamed of peaceful coexistence and to imperialists who dreamed of empires united under criss-crossed skies. Rapid transport would feed a sense of cultural affinity, whether international or imperial, while also greatly expediting the circulation of important people between the conferences which would enable new forms of international governance. Indeed, in the case of the airship, its apparent ability to sedately traverse great distances suggested that the craft itself could become a site of international conferencing, as it wended its way between capitals and conferences with its cargo of chattering statesmen.

This chapter explores this joint emergence of the conference and the airship as technologies of international world-building through the lens of British imperial internationalism. Three conferences – the 1926 and 1930 Imperial Conferences, and an intervening Conference of Empire Meteorologists – illuminate how the technical and performative aspects of world-building were distributed across these different kinds of gathering. I examine how the political technology of the conference was used to enact an empire-spanning system of airship communications, but also how the resistances which were given space by the conference format – from delegates, critics, infrastructure and the weather – illuminate wider challenges in the building of an aerial empire. This mutual relationship between the airship and the conference as joint technologies of world-building sheds new light on how conferences serve as nodal points in both the social and technical networks of hegemonic internationalisms[3] while also highlighting how fragile such networks could be.

The international atmosphere

When approached as an object of political thought, the atmosphere can seem an exemplary space of internationalism. As dreams of powered human flight took root in the nineteenth century, the political affordances of imagined aerial technologies were painted either in happy, cosmopolitan colours of social connection and cultural exchange or in rather more doom-laden, monochromatic shades of authoritarian international government-from-the-air.[4] In both cases, the atmosphere offered an almost inevitable transcendence of not only the earthly limitations of the human body but also the nation state as the natural unit of political action and community.

For those for whom the atmosphere was an object of scientific study, the late nineteenth century saw the maturation of ideas about spatial patterns, interconnections and flows which rarely mapped neatly onto national cartographies.[5] Meteorology and allied sciences began to chase internationalist ideals of free exchange and cooperation, in which the pursuit of knowledge was subordinated not to provincial or national aims but to the broader benefit of an international society. However, the late nineteenth and early twentieth centuries were also a period of high imperialism in atmospheric science and technology. Despite professing internationalist ideals, many atmospheric scientists nonetheless 'embraced imperial expansion and fought among themselves for supremacy over colonial observer networks'.[6] European imperial networks represented unique resources for meteorologists: telegraph networks gave them global reach and vision, overseas territories gave them direct access to little-known, often tropical climates and the economic interests of empire – shipping, agriculture, health – furnished strong arguments for institutional support.[7] Immediately after the Great War, aviation rose to the top of the list of meteorological priorities, and for atmospheric scientists in settings like Great Britain efforts to make the atmosphere safe to traverse, through the observation and forecasting of weather phenomena, meant that new ways of practising and coordinating meteorology were needed.

It is in this period that we can observe the emergence of 'airspace', a form of social and spatial organization which can be usefully thought of, following Liz Millward, as something which needs to be *produced*: that is, airspace does not 'pre-exist its articulation in culture or its delineation through techniques of territorialisation such as mapping, defining, observing, writing about and occupying'.[8] While the rhetoric of air and atmosphere as something 'free' and 'indivisible' informed interwar articulations of atmospheric politics, the act of actually inhabiting and traversing the atmosphere involved complex negotiations of the links between earthly territory and the aerial spaces aloft.[9] Meteorologists were engaged in one part of the technical production of airspace, but their efforts were paralleled by the cultural work of transforming the atmosphere from a threatening, unknowable 'atopia' into a domesticated space where human life and mobility could proceed contentedly.[10]

Producing airspace is thus a form of world-building, and as Heather Anne Swanson and colleagues have recently argued, the conference is a key site where world-building, as a hybrid of the cultural and the technical, the scientific and the political, takes place.[11] We can think of this world-building in the sense of fairly prosaic matters like technical standardization – how should we count and measure things? How to make one local way of doing things interchangeable with another? But world-building is also a matter of performance – of persuasion, hospitality[12] and the physical and material actualization of futures.

In 1924 the short-lived Labour government enacted an airship development programme whereby two crafts would be built to serve empire routes – initially, to Canada and India. Britain had operated military airships during the war – largely for naval scouting – but scepticism over their wider military and civilian utility, especially from the young Royal Air Force, meant that most had been mothballed by the early 1920s. Airship boosters thus 'fell back on the support that was coming from the Dominions'; indeed, it was the Agent General of Tasmania who produced, in 1921, the first plan for an airship mail and passenger service 'for the Commonwealth and Empire'.[13] This helped cement the idea of their imperial utility, but other dominions refused to co-fund a scheme. However, in 1923 Charles Dennistoun Burney, an enterprising naval engineer and Conservative MP, proposed a programme of development to be driven by private capital and state subsidy, whereby the development of six new airships would be pursued. When Labour came to power in January 1924 the new secretary of state for air, Lord Thomson, approved a revised scheme whereby two ships would be built, one by the Vickers company at Howden in Yorkshire (R.100) and one directly by the Air Ministry (R.101) at Cardington in Bedfordshire – the historic home of British airshipping and the place name Thomson chose for his new peerage.

The imperial airship scheme was couched rhetorically as a means of uniting the empire, culturally and economically, and of securing (or perhaps recapturing) Britain's global hegemony. But airship travel was also seen by its proponents as both a harbinger and steppingstone to a more peaceful, even liberal internationalism. Aviation and internationalism were frequently paired together in this period, although different versions of which one lead to the other make for an interesting study in changing conceptualizations of the relationship between technology and geopolitics.[14] For the British airshippers, imperial aviation would lay the Anglophone foundations of a new, peaceful internationalist order while also securing the economic reproduction of British imperialism.[15] In the United States, by contrast, airships remained a largely military venture, but aviation more broadly was central to emerging imaginaries of a new US hegemony – a projection of national power outwards, rather than a knitting-together of an already dispersed polity.[16] German airship development had proceeded rapidly during the Great War but was stunted by the Versailles Treaty; nonetheless, by the mid-1920s airships became wrapped up in visions of national renewal, a source of technological pride and a means of forging new alliances in regions such as South America.[17] Elsewhere, though, airships and aeroplanes were conceived of in more avowedly internationalist terms – as vehicles of peaceful exchange, trade and scientific exploration. In Scandinavia, for example, the airship took on a more politically 'neutral' hue of scientific internationalism, although projects of aerial exploration usually demanded cooperation with more nationally minded communities of scientists and aviators, such as those of Germany or Italy, and nationalism and internationalism coexisted uneasily.[18]

It is thus difficult to tease apart the threads of nationalism, imperialism and internationalism that were woven into the tapestry of interwar aviation discourse. With this in mind, in this chapter I focus on three ostensibly imperial conferences as sites where a British aerial future was summoned into being. Focusing on the constitution of the space of the conference – field trips, circulating texts, the arrangement of meeting rooms – brings into view the resistances which were met with by those who would remake British imperialism and build a new international future with the airship. Doing so enables us to see how imperial and international futures were conceived and how historical actors sought to make such visions a reality, and helps us to position the conference as a key nodal point, as well as a finely textured political space, within the map of interwar internationalism.

Aerial futures at the 1926 Imperial Conference

The 1926 Imperial Conference came at a key moment in the development of British airshipping. This was the seventh in a series of periodic gatherings of the prime ministers of the dominions dating back to 1887, all of which had taken place in London under British chairmanship with the exception of an 1894 conference in Ottawa. The venue was 10 Downing Street, the heart of British executive power, and the 1926 meeting was to be significant for producing the Balfour Declaration, which established that the dominions were not subordinate to the UK but rather equal and 'autonomous communities within the British Empire'.[19] Amid the increasing assertiveness of the dominions, the potential for air travel to hold together and unify the empire was particularly important to the British. The two airships were by then under development and pointed towards Canada, India and Australia. But the scheme itself, and a wider vision of an aerial future for empire, still needed to secure broader backing from the dominions themselves. By this point Samuel Hoare had returned to government as the Conservative secretary of state for air, eventually becoming the longest serving of the interwar air ministers. In introducing his topic he was careful not to appear fanatical, but nonetheless strove to paint a rosy picture of an aerial future as distinct from the airborne 'horror' of the Great War and the 'limitless terrors of any future war'.[20] A couple of weeks prior to the conference Alan Cobham had returned from his mammoth Australia flight, landing on the Thames in front of an enthusiastic crowd of some one million onlookers.[21] On the same day, a French airliner serving the Paris–London route crashed, killing seven. Balancing the promises and risks of aviation was thus a delicate task.

Hoare spoke at the conference in soaring terms of constructing a 'long chain of great tensile power', with aeroplanes and airships acting as instruments for 'making closer and more constant the unity of Imperial thought, Imperial intercourse, and Imperial ideals'.[22] His remarks indicate 'not just that political and economic connection could be imagined concretely' in this period of rapid aeronautical advances but also 'that concreteness itself had taken on an important political and economic function'.[23] That is to say, the material connections of empire were becoming new objects of political concern, and attempts to materially and visually enact such connections, in an anticipatory mode, were becoming a key strategy of persuasion of what a post-Great War imperial future would look like. During this period the British Empire was increasingly being conceived and visualized not as a disparate collection of remote territories but as a 'space of flows' – of bodies, of knowledge and information, of capital.[24] New cartographic forms emerged in scientific, political and public circles to give form to this new geographical imagination of empire and to offer it as 'a paradigm of global integration': that is, as a hegemonic mode of imperial internationalism. This paradigm demanded a space that was 'fully contiguous . . . fully tensile: one link clasping, and flexed against, the next'.[25] Maps of possible imperial aviation routes, which could be regularly spotted in mid-1920s newspapers, offered just such a spatial image, with their dashed lines connecting the shaded blocks of British territories.[26] But for these links to become fully tensile, to move from the page to the concrete reality of imperial flows, much diplomatic work was required.

A text prepared by the Air Ministry for the Imperial Conference became a particularly important agent of this diplomacy. Hoare later recalled that 'It proved in fact to be one of the official documents that chiefly caught the attention of the Dominion Premiers'.[27] The text, carefully crafted by a young assistant of Hoare's, Geoffrey Lloyd, analysed aviation developments at home and abroad, while the account of the Imperial Airship Scheme in particular was deliberately structured to counter the memories of previous airship disasters. The loss of the USS *Shenandoah* in September 1925, which broke in two as a result of a violent vertical disturbance over Ohio, loomed large over the discussions. Lloyd's text stated:

> The airship at the time was cruising over an area of the US where severe squalls are known to occur . . . the meteorological officer had suggested a change of course to the south some hours before the accident occurred. This advice was not, however, acted upon.[28]

By recasting this accident as being not the result of the fundamental vulnerability of airships to external aerodynamic forces but rather as a failure to heed meteorological advice, the Air Ministry was able to make an argument that the careful attention being given to meteorological matters in the British airship programme would mean that British imperial airspace would be considerably safer than that in which the *Shenandoah* perished. What was overlooked in the report of the inquiry into the loss of the *Shenandoah*, whether deliberately or not, was the claim that this accident was not the result of unheeded meteorological advice but of an encounter with forces which meteorology could not at that time comprehend. As one critic of the British programme put it, 'The pilot in the air becomes involved in conflict with these forces without warning.' Echoing a formulation used commonly by Hoare to point back to Britain's earlier command of the seas, the airship sceptic argued that 'It is absolutely impossible to chart the air'.[29]

However, the Air Ministry report highlighted new research in aerodynamics, structural design and meteorology, to convince any sceptical readers that the Ministry was taking a rigorously empirical approach to developing new forms of airship technology. The text was a key intervention in the discursive management of risk and a reminder of the intentionally performative role of technical information in constructing the feasibility of technological innovation.[30] Furthermore, while the text was originally meant for official use only, public demand eventually saw it go on sale for five shillings a piece, and it seems to have shaped wider public as well as official opinion. It was serialized in *The Times*, and the *Spectator* argued that its content had given Britain 'the tonics of faith and hope'.[31] The unusually wide circulation of this conference text illustrates how the technical production of airspace was always bound up with its cultural articulation, the engineering of a new imagination of empire as a space of aerial flows (see Figure 5.1) co-evolving with the technical means of domesticating such a space as an object of knowledge and as an environment made safe for technology.

At the conference itself, the schedule followed the emerging tradition of the field trip as a key part of any gathering, and the premiers were whisked up to the airship base at Cardington where they could go 'behind the curtain' and 'peep into the future' inside the shed where one of the new airships was being put together.[32] Despite the performative barrage of technical information, the Home Government and the media played up the secrecy under which the ships were being built, and it was only the premiers who were allowed to visit a completed section of the hull.[33] Much to Hoare's

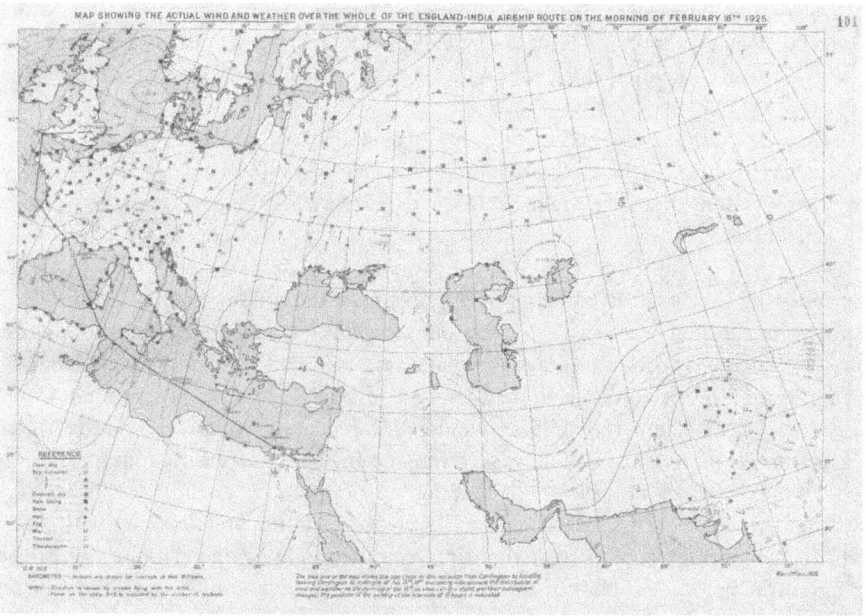

Figure 5.1 The empire as a space of aerial flows: Meteorological conditions along the England–India route. Source: UK National Archives MPI 1/410/6.

embarrassment, however, a planned flight on one of the older airships had to be cancelled when some light wind meant it couldn't initially be taken out the shed – an undercutting of the idea that more and better science could render airships safe from the vagaries of things like the weather.

The weather wasn't the only source of resistance the conference stage-managers met with. The new infrastructures of airship flight also failed to cooperate, with the elevator in the new mooring mast breaking down. But Australian prime minister Stanley Bruce, who was still thoroughly impressed by the whole spectacle, enthusiastically lead the others up the stairs to the top where he 'examined every detail' of the mast and pledged that Australia would be building one as soon as trials of the completed craft had been successfully undertaken.[34] New Zealand's premier was apparently less taken in by it all, perhaps as he waited to be reassured that any airship line wouldn't terminate in Australia, while the Indian government insisted that it 'would not be dictated to about new imperial projects'. They intended to be treated as an equal partner in consultations, a principal in commercial contracts and as the sole owner of any aviation infrastructure.[35] But in Australia, the press echoed their prime minister's enthusiasm while also reflecting on the airship's potential to help populate the dominion's 'empty spaces . . . with the promptitude that is eminently desirable in order to establish our moral right to this vast continent'.[36] The airship was a malleable technology, whose political potential, even within the confines of an Imperial Conference, could be bent to a variety of projects of imperial world-building.

Resistance to an airship future, as well as to the particular conduct of the Imperial Conference, also arose from the booming aviation commentariat. One of the loudest critics of the airship scheme, the appropriately named naval engineer and military novelist Edward F. Spanner, took aim in a range of publications not only at the technology of the airship but also at the technology of the conference as a means of getting it off the ground. In his harrumphingly indignant *This Airship Business*, penned shortly after the 1926 Imperial Conference, Spanner argued that

> people of this country have a very important responsibility towards all guests who come to our shores in an official capacity, but particularly towards those who come to us from the Dominions, to sit in conference with members of our own Government upon questions of tremendous import.

This responsibility extended to ensuring that those sitting in conference could deliberate freely in an informed manner with their hosts. Yet, he suggested,

> If one has had any experience of conferences of any description, it becomes easy to realise that individual Dominion representatives, attending an Imperial Conference from distant parts, must . . . feel a little diffident about expressing strong views upon any subject, unless it be the case that they have been specifically charged with some duty of putting forward . . . some quite definite point of view.[37]

They couldn't be expected to do so on the topic of the airship scheme, though, as the Air Ministry had armed itself with the rhetorical slings and arrows of the 'latest science' and technical know-how. Spanner surmised that only a dominion representative 'of very strong character, having the ability to argue his case in great technical detail, and fired with the altruistic desire to put the Mother Country right in this matter, would have had the temerity to issue a bold challenge' to the airship scheme, not least after it had been introduced 'with such a resounding Statement as that made by Sir Samuel Hoare'. Any delegate who wanted to challenge the Air Ministry line 'would have had to spend a great deal of time searching around in this country for technical papers, official publications, and other data to enable him adequately to arm himself for the contest'. Such an undertaking would be near impossible for a busy conference delegate, and therefore they were reliant on whatever was presented to them by the Air Ministry. As such, Spanner interpreted the relatively consensual nature of the discussions of the Imperial Air Communications Special Sub-Committee (the Indian position notwithstanding) as an inevitability engendered by this particular format of imperial diplomacy. The British government had engineered it, Spanner suggested, so that the proceedings 'were at no time in the slightest danger of being diverted from the path *which had been predetermined for them by the Air Ministry*'.[38]

Spanner suggested that the Imperial Conference was a fait accompli, but that British politicians would nonetheless use the dominions' general agreement with the scheme as a means of sharing out responsibility for it between the Air Ministry and the Imperial Conference, 'a subterfuge which may do much in time . . . to weaken the respect felt for the Mother Country by the Dominions'. Spanner was on the side of the latter: 'responsibility for the grandiose schemes of the Air Ministry cannot be fairly laid upon the shoulders of those Dominions Representatives' who signed off the agreements of the Air Communications subcommittee; they were merely innocent, perhaps slightly naive bystanders, hoodwinked by the Air Ministry's monopoly on technical arguments and by the 'fanciful, imaginative decorations' with which they were adorned.[39]

Spanner was speculating of course both about the motivations and expertise of the dominion representatives, and about how responsibility and blame would be apportioned when it all went wrong – which he believed to be inevitable. His cynical reading of the conference as a political technology nonetheless bears consideration, resonating as it does with more analytical readings of the performative power of conference texts, atmospheres and material arrangements in directing deliberations towards certain outcomes.[40] But we might also turn the analysis around, to consider not just how the functions of the conference were used to bolster airshipping but also how the potentials of the airship were anticipated to bolster conferencing.

As discussed earlier, much of the imaginative rhetoric around imperial airships concerned their ability to knit together the empire, but in practice that was taken by many to mean simply the elites of imperial governance, allowing the accelerated circulation of heads of governments and their representatives, speeding up processes of decision-making and, it was assumed, encouraging those decisions to tend towards imperial unity rather than fragmentation. *The Queenslander* breathlessly predicted that the next imperial conference would begin with an airship calling for all the dominion delegates and delivering them to London in just a few days.[41] Another Australian newspaper reported that while visiting the new mooring mast at Cardington, Bruce was confidently told 'that he would not only fly to the next Imperial Conference but that he would probably have 100 passengers accompanying him', all of whom could enjoy 'lounges, a smokeroom, a dining room, hot baths and 6-course meals, and there might even be a newspaper published on board'.[42] That the promised luxuries of airship travel were aimed in part at the dominion premiers themselves was illustrated too in a model of the proposed interior of one of the craft, which was made available for the delegates to inspect. Together with the glimpses of the actual craft under construction, the delegates 'had a vision, which is expected to materialise within the next year or eighteen months, of the time when it will be as comfortable to travel by air from Britain to the uttermost parts of the Empire . . . [with] luxuries undreamed of by Jules Verne and H.G. Wells'.[43] For Burney, the ability of imperial politicians to float around the globe in the utmost luxury meant that the Imperial Conference would 'become an annual affair', paving the way for 'a Commonwealth Parliament which shall be in permanent session like the League of Nations at Geneva'.[44] The airship could remake empire by remaking the practices of imperial conferencing, adapting the emerging practices of internationalism for a thoroughly imperial future.

Weather permitting: The 1929 Conference of Empire Meteorologists

From the light wind which spoiled the show at Cardington to the mid-air destruction of the *Shenandoah* by a violent updraft, the period of British airship development offered numerous lessons in the dependency of airships upon the medium through which they travel. This, along with a distinct anxiety about flying in tropical rather than just temperate climates, motivated a new urgency which took hold of meteorologists as they were enrolled into efforts to produce imperial airspace. Interwar meteorology operated under what Paul Edwards has called a mode of 'voluntary internationalism', whereby countries could sign up to standardized rules and procedures if they wanted to, but governments were under no compulsion to conform.[45] This meant that achieving technical standardization in modes of observing, reporting and forecasting the weather was difficult, although cooperation between neighbouring meteorological services – such as those of Britain and France – had been accomplished as short-distance aeroplane flights rose in frequency, an early example of airspace as a 'cosmopolitan commons'.[46] But airships represented a different prospect, with their globe-spanning routes meaning that they would pass non-stop not only between different climatic zones but also through multiple zones of meteorological responsibility. Furthermore, the apparent vulnerability of airships to atmospheric disturbances meant that not only did the atmosphere need to be considered on a newly global scale[47] but fine-scale patterns of motion needed to be accounted for and, if possible, predicted. For an imperial airship scheme, a new mode of imperial meteorology was called for.

A new aerial imperialism required a newly imperial science – meteorology – which in turned required a new form of conferencing. During this period the conference was becoming a central tool of British imperial science policy. In disciplines such as forestry, entomology and mycology, London hosted a succession of events which paired the technical demands of imperial standardization with quixotic rhetoric of imperial unity. The notion of direct imperial coordination had lost some of its earlier lustre amid colonial calls for equal treatment, and imperial cooperation was thus the primary goal, the mechanism of which, as Roy MacLeod has shown, 'was not to be the formal command, but the informal conference'.[48] In part these imperial conferences echoed the international science conferences which were becoming more frequent in this period, not least in meteorology. But, as shown below, their imperial nature led to very particular outcomes.

In August 1929, after several abortive attempts, the empire's meteorologists were gathered together for the first time, at the Air Ministry on Kingsway. As the meeting approached, debate was had within the Air Ministry as to whether it would be sufficient to just repeat a 1919 meeting of dominion meteorologists. When consulted, the dominions argued for the colonies to be included. But the fact that the Air Ministry favoured a smaller conference is revealing of meteorological priorities in this period. Aviation was to get top billing at the conference, and it was believed by the Air Ministry that the burgeoning weather services in the dominions could largely handle the demands of aviation meteorology on their own, producing airspace through meteorological observations and predictions which extended beyond their own terrestrial borders. The minutes of the proceedings and subsequent correspondence offer the impression that the Air Ministry might have regretted expanding the delegate list to the colonies and protectorates. For the Ministry, the chief aim of the conference was to 'bring before the Empire meteorologists the problems of Empire meteorology and to show how they were being dealt with in Great Britain'.[49] But rather than the colonial and dominion meteorologists quietly noting these examples of 'best practice', Air Ministry and Meteorological Office staffers were met instead with cantankerous choruses of dissent. Unlike at the Imperial Conference, where dominion delegates perhaps acquiesced in the superior technical knowledge of the Home Government, here was a cast of experts on doing meteorology in the empire's furthest corners, arrayed often in the furthest corners of the conference room (see Figure 5.2), and determined to resist the inappropriate extension of imperial schemes.

The air minister was present again to open proceedings and sell the image of an empire remade by aviation. The cultural work of producing airspace as an object of imagination was as essential here as at the political events, because here was a group of meteorologists for whom aviation could represent an unwelcome distraction from local colonial priorities – fitting agriculture better to tropical climates or warning shipping of approaching storms. As with most of the conference topics, the aviation discussion began with a detailed outline of British practices, reinforced by visits to Croydon aerodrome and the now customary visit to the Cardington airship works. Subcommittees then delved into regional detail and demands, and it was through this format that the colonial meteorologists could voice their displeasure for metropolitan presumptuousness. Often this was simply about reconciling the demand for observational standardization with the variety of the empire's climates. Disagreement reigned on the correct way to monitor and record thunderstorms, for example, whose violence and intermittency posed challenges to airship navigation. How to even define a colonial thunderstorm? Relying on sighted lightning could cause confusion with

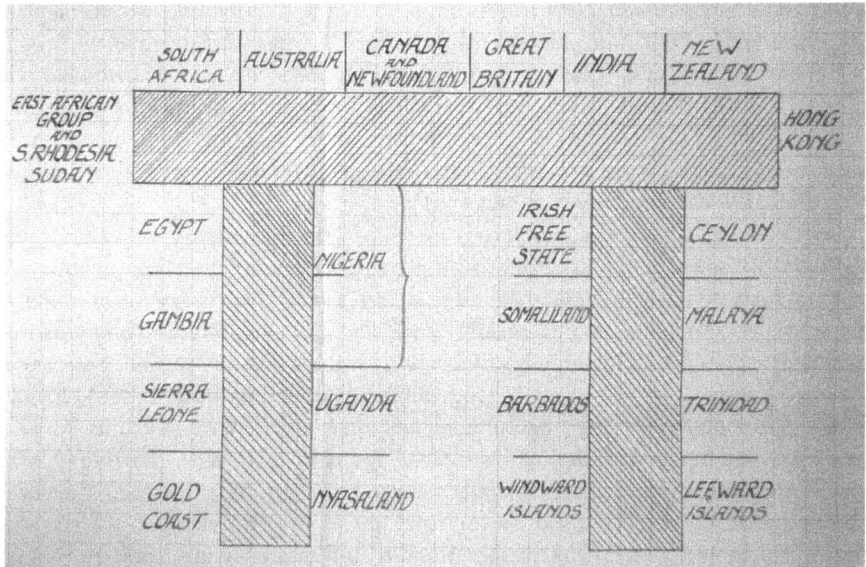

Figure 5.2 The arrangement of the main conference room at the 1929 empire meteorology gathering. Source: UK National Archives BJ 5/19.

the sparks of new electric trains, but sometimes there would be no audible thunder to record instead. Precipitation was an unreliable signifier as dry South African storms were among the most dangerous. New Zealand's representative thought that the audible occurrence of thunder would be 'satisfactory for natives to observe', but thunder could be heard almost every day in Malaya, which rendered problematic the British suggestion of simply recording the number of days on which thunder was heard. Across Malaya and neighbouring regions of Southeast Asia, 'the frequency of actual thunderstorms' observed visually was recorded by lighthouses and steamships, but this chafed against an emerging British practice of recording, for the benefit of airships, the audibility of thunder – a strategy which offered information for a wider area.[50]

In the end, the conference agreed that 'the specification of frequency of thunder heard should be adopted, but that observations should be supplemented by the frequency of thunderstorms and possibly by observations of lightning'.[51] The pattern of this discussion set the template for the rest of the conference – metropolitan calls for imperial standardization, met with colonial pleas for flexibility; colonial geography used to refute imperial categories. Compromise was then generally reached, framed with ungainly caveats catering to the manifold ways in which weather was or could be recorded in diverse colonial settings. Significantly, these caveats found their way into the very media by which meteorological data were starting to circulate the globe. The empire conference became a site where the applicability of, for example, new, Eurocentric wireless codes to the climates and weather systems of the rest of the world could be contested. New codes proposed by the International Meteorological Organization (IMO) had no place for things like an Egyptian dust storm or the squalls of the East African coast. Railing against global homogeneity, and against what one colonial director acidly called the 'methods laid down by the pundits who pontificated from Kingsway',[52] the colonial delegates proposed new code formations which allowed for local flexibility. These formations were subsequently adopted by the International Meteorological Conference which met a couple of weeks later.

As Helen Tilley has argued, imperial scientific institutions in this period 'occupied an interstitial space that was neither national nor international'.[53] In their negotiation of emerging international standards and practices, the 1929 and subsequent imperial meteorology conferences were a means by which a global calculative apparatus was being constructed *through* empire. Metropolitan globalists saw in the conferences a confederation of largely like-minded individuals united by both imperial loyalty and a global outlook, while the colonial meteorologists saw opportunity to gain new influence in international conversations. Many of them didn't have their own seat at the IMO table (indeed, for many the empire meeting was their first ever 'international' conference),[54] so by influencing the British delegates, their voices could find their way into the deliberations of international meteorology.[55] More broadly, this reflects Joseph Hodge's argument that imperial science became in the interwar period a site where the pursuit of universalist aims – such as 'development', or the hoped-for internationalism of the aerial age – occurred through new ways of dealing with local specificities.[56] In the case of British imperial meteorology the conference was the key technology for doing so, a nodal point in new networks of knowledge-making which sought to reconcile the global and the local, the national and the international.

By the end of the proceedings, the project of technical harmonization in service of airship travel was nearing completion. By that point, the 'private' airship R.100 had successfully travelled to Canada and back, piling pressure on the rival 'state' ship, R.101, and its builders. R.101's maiden flight had been delayed as its petrol engines were swapped for diesel, thought to be considerably safer in tropical climates. The new, heavier engines required the elongation of the frame and the insertion of an extra gas bag, and it seemed that late 1930 would be the earliest date for its first flight to India.

Rehearsing the aerial future: The 1930 Imperial Conference

The 1930 Imperial Conference saw the dominion delegates returning to Downing Street with the chief intention of turning the Balfour Declaration into a substantive legal framework. This resulted in the 1931 Statute of Westminster, which essentially established the dominions as independent legislative entities. Also high on the agenda was the issue of imperial preference trading tariffs, proposed as a means of remaking the empire as a unified space of economic flows, even as it was fragmenting politically. Meanwhile, the prospect of a successful airship flight to India, with the return leg coinciding with the conference itself, was hoped to secure further agreements and financial commitments for imperial aviation. Lord Thomson had again replaced Samuel Hoare at the Air Ministry in June 1929, having enthusiastically given the airship scheme the go-ahead in 1924. Thomson's apparent desire to be the next Viceroy of India, and the role of that ambition in the scheduling of R.101's maiden flight to coincide with the Imperial Conference, was to prove controversial. The engineer-novelist Nevil Shute, who worked on R.100, suggested that

> he wished to visit his new empire in the new vehicle of Imperial communications that he had a hand in producing, arriving from the skies in a manner unknown to any previous Viceroy.[57]

At the Imperial Conference itself, amid fractious tariff debates, the premiers were to be persuaded to continue investing in airship infrastructure to secure what was taken to be one of the chief means of imperial unity. The spectacle of the air minister returning safely and speedily from India to chair proceedings would be a perfect sequel to the promises made in 1926 that airship travel would greatly smooth and accelerate 'imperial intercourse'.

Much ink has been spilled on the last-minute work to ready the ship according to the minister's schedule – the lack of all-weather test flights, the expansion of the gas bags to increase the available lift, the granting of an air worthiness certificate just two days before the departure.[58] Those responsible for readying the ship were acutely aware of the political pressure, with Director of Airship Development R. B. Colmore reportedly remarking to a friend that 'If the ship doesn't get back in time for the Imperial Conference, I understand that not only will there be no money for future airship work, it just won't be *asked* for'.[59] The ship took off from Cardington on 4 October, weighed down by heavy expectations of a bright new imperial future, as well as by the accoutrements of ministerial hospitality – Persian rugs for a banquet at the Egyptian waypoint, extra fuel so the dinner guests wouldn't have to comport over the sounds and smells of refuelling. The final forecast had suggested moderate wind, but the weather refused to follow the script. After a few hours struggling against unexpectedly strong wind and rain, a heavy blast of wind seemingly caused a tear in the outer fabric and a dive into a French hillside, whereupon the airship burst into flames, killing all but six of those onboard, including Lord Thomson.

The disaster rocked the conference and created, however briefly, a new atmosphere of unity focused around paying tribute to those who had given their lives for the cause of imperial progress. For one participant and observer of the conference proceedings, 'It seemed ordained that the Dominions' delegates should be together when the terrible catastrophe struck the nation, but they continued their work with courage and determination'.[60] Thomas Simm was a member of the Canadian delegation and an airship enthusiast who had seen the R.100 over his home during its visit to the dominion. Simm recalled how, for the conference delegates, 'The initial shock was not the greatest. It was the realisation that the vast project of linking the Empire by air had suffered, if not its deathblow, for the present decade, at least, it had received a serious setback for years to come', yet another 'great problem for the Imperial Conference to try to solve'.[61] A new technical memorandum on developments in imperial airshipping, once considered for public sale like its predecessor, instead became overnight a submission to the Court of Inquiry set up to investigate the crash. A sentence proclaiming how fortunate it was that the completion of the airship programme coincided with the Imperial Conference was hastily excised from the text. And some months later, the Inquiry noted that it was

> impossible to avoid the conclusion that the R.101 would not have started for India on the evening of October 4th if it had not been that matters of public policy were considered as making it highly desirable that she should do so.[62]

Here was a thinly veiled critique of Thomson's motivations for pressuring the start of the airship's maiden voyage. The question of whether Thomson was using conference diplomacy to bolster airshipping, or using airshipping to bolster his own diplomatic manoeuvrings in relation to India, remains a matter of debate among historians. Simm recalled how at the conference 'there was a general feeling that the work of proving the practicability of rigid airships must go on',[63] but such efforts to make concrete the imagination of aerostatic imperial connection never recovered from the R.101 disaster, and the aeroplane soon took over as the new means of hastening the development of imperial intercourse.[64]

Conclusion

I've suggested in this chapter that the particular characteristics of interwar conferencing importantly shaped the making and unmaking of imperial and international futures. As spaces of not just text and talk but of performance, witnessing and experience, conferences functioned here as spaces where the cultural and technical work of producing airspace could be conducted with a particular intensity – whether in the public circulation of laudatory texts, stage-managed visits to the sites where the future was being made concrete or the tortuous negotiation of meteorological codes. Conferences were an important resource in producing imperial airspace, where persuasion could take place through combinations of quixotic rhetoric and technical overload, and where dreams of a unified empire and a unified airspace could be tested against the experiences and knowledges of those charged with representing the many links in Hoare's 'great tensile' chain.

Focusing on the conference also foregrounds how the future of imperial and international governance was conceived in relation to technology.[65] Airship enthusiasts reckoned that the Imperial Conference could become an annual affair, or even that an Imperial Parliament might sit in permanent session, while others thought it more likely that 'the future development of television and wireless telephony' would enable dominion parliaments to interact with each other while 'sitting at ease in their own Chambers',[66] obviating the need for any Imperial Conferences at all.[67] Internationalism and imperialism were future-oriented discourses, and attending to how the futures of their political technologies were conceived – whether the airship, the wireless or the conference itself – can shed new light on the links between imagination and reality in the making of international worlds.

Notes

1 'Civil Aviation', *The Queenslander*, 8 January 1927, 9.
2 Charles Dennistoun Burney, *The World, the Air and the Future* (London: A.A. Knopf, 1929), 50.
3 Fred Halliday, 'Three Concepts of Internationalism', *International Affairs* 64, no. 2 (1988): 187–98.
4 Waqar H. Zaidi, '"Aviation Will Either Destroy or Save Our Civilization": Proposals for the International Control of Aviation, 1920-45', *Journal of Contemporary History* 46, no. 1 (2011): 150–78.
5 Deborah R. Coen, *Climate in Motion: Science, Empire, and the Problem of Scale* (Chicago: University of Chicago Press, 2018).
6 Gregory T. Cushman, 'The Imperial Politics of Hurricane Prediction: From Calcutta and Havana to Manila and Galveston, 1839-1900', in *Nation-States and the Global Environment*, eds. Erika Marie Bsumek, David Kinkela & Mark Atwood Lawrence (Oxford: Oxford University Press, 2013), 139.
7 Martin Mahony, 'For an Empire of "All Types of Climate": Meteorology as an Imperial Science', *Journal of Historical Geography* 51 (2016): 29–39.
8 Liz Millward, *Women in British Imperial Airspace: 1922-1937* (Montreal & London: McGill-Queen's University Press, 2007), 17–18. Millward's arguments bear comparison with Elden's efforts to historicize political notions of territory: Stuart Elden, *The Birth of Territory* (Chicago: University of Chicago Press, 2013).
9 See, for instance, Stuart Banner, *Who Owns the Sky? The Struggle to Control Airspace from the Wright Brothers On* (Cambridge, MA: Harvard University Press, 2008).
10 See Peter Adey, *Aerial Life: Spaces, Mobilities, Affects* (Chichester: Wiley-Blackwell, 2010); Siobhan Carroll, *An Empire of Air and Water: Uncolonizable Space in the British Imagination, 1750-1850*, (Philadelphia, PA: University of Pennsylvania Press, 2015).
11 Heather Anne Swanson, Nils Bubandt & Anna Tsing, 'Less Than One But More Than Many: Anthropocene as Science Fiction and Scholarship-in-the-Making', *Environment and Society* 6, no. 1 (2015): 149–66.
12 See Ruth Craggs, 'Hospitality in Geopolitics and the Making of Commonwealth International Relations', *Geoforum* 52 (2014): 90–100.
13 Samuel John Gurney Hoare, *Empire of the Air: The Advent of the Air Age, 1922-1929* (London: Collins, 1957), 220.
14 Compare the discussion in Duncan Bell, *The Idea of Greater Britain: Empire and the Future of World Order, 1860-1900*, (Princeton, NJ: Princeton University Press, 2007), chapter 3.
15 See especially Burney, *The World*.
16 Jenifer Van Vleck, *Empire of the Air: Aviation and the American Ascendancy* (Cambridge, MA: Harvard University Press, 2013).
17 Guillaume de Syon, *Zeppelin! Germany and the Airship, 1900-1939* (Baltimore, MD: Johns Hopkins University Press, 2002).
18 See John Duggan & Henry Cord Meyer, *Airships in International Affairs, 1890–1940* (Basingstoke: Palgrave, 2001). On the broader relations between aviation and liberal internationalist thought in the interwar period, see Zaidi, 'Aviation'.
19 The Oireachtas, *Imperial Conference, 1926. Summary of Proceedings* (Dublin: Stationery Office, 1926), 13.
20 Hoare, 'Statement on Imperial Air Communications', in *The Approach Towards a System of Imperial Air Communications* (London: HMSO, 1926), xi.

21 Alan Cobham, *Australia and Back* (London: A. & C. Black, 1926).
22 Hoare, 'Statement on Imperial Air'.
23 David Trotter, *Literature in the First Media Age: Britain Between the Wars* (Cambridge, MA: Harvard University Press, 2013), 17.
24 Michael Heffernan, 'The Cartography of the Fourth Estate: Mapping the New Imperialism in British and French Newspapers, 1875-1925', in *The Imperial Map: Cartography and the Mastery of Empire*, ed. James R. Akerman (Chicago: University of Chicago Press, 2009), 293.
25 Trotter, *Literature*, 17.
26 See, for instance *The Times*, 15 December 1926, 10.
27 Hoare, *Empire of the Air*, 221.
28 *The Approach*, 12.
29 E. F. Spanner, *About Airships* (London: E. F. Spanner, 1929), 108.
30 See Mads Borup, Nik Brown, Kornelia Konrad & Harro Van Lente, 'The Sociology of Expectations in Science and Technology', *Technology Analysis & Strategic Management* 18, no. 3-4 (2006): 285-98.
31 Quoted in Gordon Pirie, *Air Empire: British Imperial Civil Aviation, 1919-39* (Manchester: Manchester University Press, 2009), 101.
32 'Giant Liner of the Air: Dominion Premiers See Flying Hotel', *Evening Telegraph* (Dundee), 18 November 1926.
33 'Luxurious Airships', *The Cumberland Argus and Fruitgrower's Advocate*, 21 January 1927, 14.
34 'By Air to Next Conference?', *The Sun* (Sydney), 18 November 1926, 1.
35 Pirie, *Air Empire*, 100.
36 'Civil Aviation', *The Queenslander*, 8 January 1927, 9.
37 E. F. Spanner, *This Airship Business* (London: Williams and Norgate, 1927), 64.
38 Spanner, *Airship Business*, 65.
39 Spanner, *Airship Business*, 66-8.
40 See Stephen Legg, '"Political Atmospherics": The India Round Table Conference's Atmospheric Environments, Bodies and Representations, London 1930-1932', *Annals of the American Association of Geographers* 110, no. 3 (2020): 774-92; Florian Weisser, 'Practices, Politics, Performativities: Documents in the International Negotiations on Climate Change', *Political Geography* 40 (2014): 46-55.
41 'Civil Aviation', *The Queenslander*, 8 January 1927, 9.
42 'By Air to Next Conference?' *The Sun* (Sydney), 18 November 1926, 1. The smokeroom, slung beneath five million cubic feet of hydrogen, was to be lined with asbestos and feature cigarette lighters chained to the tables.
43 'Giant Liner of the Air: Dominion Premiers See Flying Hotel', *Evening Telegraph* (Dundee), 18 November 1926.
44 Burney, *The World*, 50. This reflects broader trends in British conferencing which saw the decidedly liberal internationalist conference techniques honed at the League of Nations being translated or appropriated for openly imperial means. See Stephen Legg, 'Imperial Internationalism: The Round Table Conference and the Making of India in London, 1930-32', *Humanity* 10, no. 1 (2020): 32-53.
45 Paul N. Edwards, 'Meteorology as Infrastructural Globalism', *Osiris* 21, no. 1 (2006): 229-50.
46 Eda Kranakis, 'The "Good Miracle": Building a European Airspace Commons, 1919-1939', in *Cosmopolitan Commons*, eds. Nil Disco & Eda Kranakis (Cambridge, MA: MIT Press, 2013), 57-96.

47 As Friedman points out, the hemispheric vision of the 'Bergen School' was motivated in large part by the interwar craze for trans-Atlantic flight, rather than being derived initially from theoretical propositions. See Robert M. Friedman, *Appropriating the Weather: Vilhelm Bjerknes and the Construction of a Modern Meteorology* (Ithaca, NY: Cornell University Press, 1993). On the scalar politics of atmospheric knowledge-making, see also Coen, *Climate in Motion*.
48 Roy MacLeod, 'Passages in Imperial Science: From Empire to Commonwealth', *Journal of World History* 4, no. 1 (1993): 117–50, 140.
49 Bennett to His Majesty's Stationery Office, 17 December 1929. BJ 5/19, The National Archives, Kew.
50 *Report of the Conference of Empire Meteorologists* (1929) (London: HMSO, 1929), 16. See also the discussion in Mahony, 'For an Empire'.
51 Conference of Empire Meteorologists, 16.
52 Albert Walter, *Echoes of a Vanishing Empire, being the Memoirs of a Meteorologist and Civil Servant in the Colonial Empire* (1968), MSS Brit. Emp. R.9 and r.10, Commonwealth and African Collections, University of Oxford, 357–8.
53 Helen Tilley, *Africa as a Living Laboratory, 1870-1950* (Chicago: University of Chicago Press, 2011), 10.
54 And some were surprised at how tedious such an affair could be – see Mahony, 'For an Empire'.
55 The empire meteorology conferences were deliberately timed to coordinate 'the imperial position' in advance of international conferences. When the association morphed in the post-war period into the Conference of Commonwealth Meteorologists its role switched – meetings were scheduled after the international ones and presented as more of a social occasion.
56 Joseph Morgan Hodge, *Triumph of the Expert: Agrarian Doctrines of Development and the Legacies of British Colonialism* (Athens, OH: Ohio University Press, 2007).
57 Nevil Shute, *Slide Rule* (New York, NY: Vintage Classics, 2009), 37.
58 See references in Martin Mahony, 'Historical Geographies of the Future: Airships and the Making of Imperial Atmospheres', *Annals of the American Association of Geographers* 109, no. 4 (2019): 1279–99.
59 Quoted in James Leasor, *The Millionth Chance: The Story of the R.101* (London: Hamish Hamilton, 1957/2015), n.p.
60 Thomas Simm, *Britain's Tragedy: A True Story of R-101 Tragedy and the Imperial Conference, London, England* (London: A. H. Stockwell, 1932), 59.
61 Simm, *Britain's Tragedy*, 31.
62 *Report of the R-101 Inquiry* (London: HMSO, 1931), 95–6.
63 Simm, *Britain's Tragedy*, 36.
64 Mountbatten became the first Indian Viceroy to arrive from the air in 1947, shortly before Indian independence. On the links between British aviation strategy and the onset of decolonization, see Peter John Brobst, '"Icarian Geography": Air Power, Closed Space, and British Decolonisation', *Geopolitics* 9, no. 2 (2004): 426–39.
65 See also the chapter by Su Lin Lewis, this volume.
66 Spanner, *Airship Business*, 69.
67 On visions of the future League of Nations in which aviation was combined with wireless technology to allow permanent discourse, see Waqar H. Zaidi, 'Liberal Internationalist Approaches to Science and Technology in Interwar Britain and the United States', in *Internationalism Reconfigured: Transnational Ideas and Movements Between the World Wars*, ed. Daniel Laqua (London: I.B. Tauris, 2011), 17–43.

6

Scientific internationalism in a time of crisis

The Month of Intellectual Cooperation at the 1937 Paris World Fair

Jonathan Voges

Introduction: Paris 1937 – A huge 'waste of time'?

The Dutch cultural historian and critic Johan Huizinga wrote rather disappointedly to his fiancée Auguste Schoelvinck on 3 July 1937 about his trip to the Paris World Fair.[1] He went to the French capital not just as a tourist but as a member of the International Committee on Intellectual Cooperation (ICIC),[2] which held its annual meeting in Paris that year, as part of a more all-embracing *Mois de la Coopération Intellectuelle*.[3] But for him the proceedings of the meeting were '99 per cent chitchat and paper, and one per cent tangible results'.[4] Ironically, he told Schoelvinck, he presided over a subcommittee on cinematographic questions without being an expert on film. His stay in Paris was for him just: 'A waste of time, a waste of time!'[5]

The *Exposition Internationale des Arts et Techniques dans la Vie Moderne* of 1937 is today more known for the confrontation of the totalitarian ideologies of the first half of the twentieth century (communism and fascism) by architectural means.[6] The German and Soviet pavilions positioned on either side of the main boulevard of the exhibition leading towards the Eiffel Tower were the expressions in stone, concrete and marble of the strength and self-confidence of the 'hyper-nationalism' of the 1930s. Huizinga considered such 'hyper-nationalism' to be the 'plague-spot of our time', exacerbated by the 'monstrous ulcer' of propaganda.[7] He described to his fiancée the 'sky high pretentious Hitler temple' which for him was nothing more than a 'monument of national haughtiness that makes my heart drop'. Huizinga understood the Soviet pavilion to be a mere copy of Albert Speer's German pavilion. Together, they formed a 'brutal contrast'.[8]

While the World Fair of 1937 is remembered for those representations of nationalism in an internationalist setting, it could also be interpreted as a rather impressive rearing of liberal internationalism – in the form of the League of Nations. Elements of this liberal or progressive internationalism were 'self-determination, reduction of armaments, and free trade'. Mediation in cases of conflicts, cooperation in times of peace as a means to prevent conflicts and even wars, democratic institutions and social and economic justice were part of the liberal internationalist vision too, as one of its main protagonists, the American president Woodrow Wilson, defined it at the end of the First World War.[9]

One way to explore liberal internationalism at the *Exposition Internationale des Arts et Techniques dans la Vie Moderne* is to show how it, too, found material manifestation at the exposition, in the pavilion of the ICIC which was built up (under guidance mainly of the French national committee on intellectual cooperation) in ten rooms of the newly built *Musée d'Art contemporain*.[10] An alternative approach, adopted here, is to focus on the broader *Mois de la Coopération Intellectuelle*.

From the very first World Fairs, international scientific congresses had been a typical feature of the exhibition programme.[11] What happened in Paris in 1937 could therefore be interpreted as a mere continuation of a tradition reaching back to the middle of the nineteenth century. However, I would argue that the organizers in Paris tried to achieve something more. They not only arranged several congresses for different disciplines of scientific research, where scientists from all over the world were invited to present new findings in their specific field of research to an international professional audience.[12] More than this, the *Mois de la Coopération Intellectuelle* gathered together international congresses, both closely and loosely connected to the League of Nations' work on intellectual cooperation, under one roof. This gathering was presented as an impressive expression of the achievements, potential and strength of international cooperation – even in a time of crisis of the League of Nations.[13]

This chapter concentrates first on the organization of the Month of Intellectual Cooperation in general; in a second step I take a closer look at the *Congrès Mondial de la Documentation Universelle* (World Congress of Universal Documentation) as one example of a conference taking place at the World Fair of 1937 without an official connection to the work of the League of Nations Organization for Intellectual Cooperation but with a similar aim – fostering intellectual cooperation. The chapter concludes by framing these contrasting studies within the understandings of internationalism that were present in Paris 1937.

The Month of Intellectual Cooperation: A guardian angel for world peace?

The image that the organizers of the *Mois de la Coopération Intellectuelle* chose for the official programme carried a strong message: it showed a guardian angel holding in its arms the representations of art (brushes, a lyre, a quill) and science (a globe, a book, a circle). The meaning of this allegory was rather simple, signifying the deep relationship between peace and scientific and cultural progress.[14] The series of conferences started in late June 1937 with the tenth session of the *Conférence Permanente des Hautes Études Internationales*, dealing with the question of the peaceful settling of international conflicts, and continued with meetings of different civil society groups close to the League of Nations and the annual meeting of the ICIC, an advisory organization for the League. The ICIC's Permanent Committee on Arts and Letters gathered to discuss the future of literature, and the second general meeting of the national committees on intellectual cooperation took place from 5 to 9 July.[15]

All in all, nine different congresses of international significance were organized by the International Institute of Intellectual Cooperation (IIIC), the executive branch set up to translate the ICIC's proposals into action. The IIIC's offices were located in the Montpensier Wing of the Palais Royal in Paris, both a gift and a condition of the French government's offer to fund the new organization, agreed in 1925 (though only after some highly fraught debate in the International Committee about the danger of too strong a French influence).[16] After a reform of the League structure in the early 1930s, both the ICIC and IIIC sat within the larger League of Nations Organization for Intellectual Cooperation, which contained all the different institutes, committees and the section of the secretariat dealing with intellectual cooperation.

The organizers of the *Mois de la Coopération Intellectuelle* made clear that the congresses were not just work meetings but also social events. Prominent persons from French politics or society were invited to give welcome addresses to the international audiences. *Soirées* or breakfasts had to be offered, the Foreign Office dedicated a 'garden-party' to the participants of the Permanent Conference of International Studies and on the last day they even got a guided tour through the Louvre. Other participants of the *Mois de la Coopération Intellectuelle* were invited to attend an 'official visit' of the 'Intellectual Exchanges around the world' pavilion, which was hosted by the French national committee on intellectual cooperation.[17] And the participants understood the combination of work meetings and social events; Gilbert Murray, who was president of the ICIC at that time, was very upset to have to tell Henri Bonnet, director of the IIIC, that unfortunately his wife was not able to accompany him especially at the reunions in the evenings, the garden parties and breakfasts because of sickness.[18] To facilitate delegates' stays in Paris the Institute asked the Commissaire general au Tourisme in Paris to publish a brochure which would include everything that made a trip to Paris agreeable ('prices of hotels, travel opportunities, possibilities to get discount at theatres', etc.). One thousand copies of the brochure were printed and given to the participants of the *Mois de la Coopération Intellectuelle*.[19]

All international participants of the congresses were given free passes for the exhibition ground for the duration of their time in Paris.[20] All in all, 815 people took part in the nine events which formed the *Mois de la Coopération Intellectuelle*; most of them attended the meeting of the *Conférence Permanente des Hautes Études Internationales* (300), 150 came from the different national committees and 200 gathered to discuss the internationalization of higher education.[21] All of them had to be transported to Paris, accommodated and fed – not only a logistical problem for the IIIC but also a financial one. Setting the costs of the participants aside, interpreters, secretaries and stenographers were also needed. Nine members of the Section for Intellectual Cooperation at the Secretariat of the League of Nations had to travel to Paris to do all the organizational work – which alone cost nearly 60, 000 francs.[22]

What was the significance of bringing together these 800 people from all over the world at one place in the late 1930s? In June 1938 the *Commissaire Général de l'Exposition*, Edmond Labbé, asked the IIIC for a short report about the *Mois de la*

Coopération Intellectuelle, which could be included in the final report for the World Fair. Labbé suggested that the great importance of this series of congresses necessitated their inclusion, and a special place was reserved in the document to honour them.[23]

The resulting submission was twelve pages long; beside a short abstract of all of the congresses organized as part of the *Mois de le Coopération Intellectuelle*, its author mainly tried to highlight the importance of the interconnectedness of the whole series. 'The "*Mois de la Coopération Intellectuelle*" – and that is what gives this ensemble its true significance and value – for the first time gave the International Committee on Intellectual Cooperation the possibility of gathering nearly all of the institutions that constitute the International Organisation of Intellectual cooperation.'[24] Normally all the committees and subcommittees met at different places over the year: 'This year it was possible to assemble them at the same time and in the same place.' That led – the author was convinced – to 'a coming-together of work and personal contacts which is eminently beneficial for the work itself, its development and its success'. All of 'the manifestations that the "Mois" included were inaugurated and closed with *éclat* by the most prominent representatives of French public life'. Several hundred participants benefitted from the heartfelt hospitality of the French capital: 'they were recipients of the most delicate attentions from the French Government, the General Commissariat of the Exposition and of the city of Paris.'[25]

The message that the League of Nations Organization for Intellectual Cooperation wanted to send to the world is quite obvious – and it was an optimistic one: the gospel of internationalism went on. The gathering of more than 800 people from the international intellectual elite all at one place was marketed[26] as a strong symbol of the ongoing vitality and strength of 'internationalism in the time of nationalism'.[27] The paper which summarized the *Mois de la Coopération Intellectuelle* for the official final report emphasized even in the shorter abstracts of the several congresses the mere fact that the respective meeting took place in Paris as one part of the series and said much less about the actual proceedings.

And the same message could be found in the discussions of the meetings as well. For example, Paul Valéry, the president of the Permanent Committee on Arts and Letters, opened the meeting of this organization by referring to an 'eminently spiritual concert, a concert not lacking in dissonances'. But these dissonances were not what was important for him, he portrayed them as the elements which make the music interesting in the first place; what was important for the French writer was that the meeting took place, and he was sure that the 'work of the mind tends to enlarge the capacity of mutual comprehension that is the necessary fundament of every society'. And he concluded:

> That is the reason why we have sent invitations to every person with good will, in every country [...] to enter into discussions with them – in a polite and friendly manner, as always [...] One of the major benefits of these meetings consists in the relations that will be instituted between the members of these *Entretiens*.

And Valéry did not hesitate to send a heartfelt appeal to the gathered intellectuals: 'We are here for listening to each other and for loving each other.'[28]

While the German and the Soviet pavilion were both expressions of their respective forms of 'hyper-nationalism' (to use Huizinga's word), the 'Mois' was presented as a forum of internationalism and a symbol of the advantages of international cooperation – the first of the two leading principles in the preamble of the Covenant of the League of Nations.[29] At the same time the *Mois de la Coopération Intellectuelle* was also a means for France to present itself as the cultural capital of the world – even in rougher times.[30] It was the French national committee on intellectual cooperation which did most of the planning for the representations of intellectual cooperation at the World Fair; it was they who acted as host for the 'capital event' of this series of congresses, the second general conference of the national committees of intellectual cooperation.

The World Congress of Universal Documentation 1937: Non-utopian internationalism?

The inquiry that the *Deutsche Kongreß-Zentrale*[31] sent to the IIIC in April 1937 was far from polite. Without any kind of salutation a Mister Blume asked for 'five copies of your already-printed publications, preferably in German, which reveal the concrete programme of the meeting, the names of the speakers etc'.[32] The reason that the Germans had to send such a request to Paris was rather simple: because all the congresses and conferences of the *Mois de la Coopération Intellectuelle* were connected to the League of Nations and the German government, after the exit of Nazi Germany from the League of Nations in 1933, had forbidden any German from taking part in any League of Nations activity.[33] No German was invited to any of the events (apart from Thomas Mann who was a member of the Permanent Committee on Arts and Letters, but he was already living in exile at that time).[34]

Nevertheless, Germans found their stages in Paris – not only in Speer's pavilion architecture but also at the international congresses. However, this was not in the part of the programme which was officially declared to be the *Mois de la Coopération Intellectuelle* but at the other conferences and congresses which took place at the World Fair. The *Mois* consisted only of the events that were organized by institutions that were part of (or at least very close to) the League of Nations Organization for Intellectual Cooperation. The other conferences and congresses that took place in Paris in 1937 were held by international non-governmental organizations (e.g. International Congress of the Ancient Combatants), by economic lobby groups (e.g. the Congress of the Association for the Defense of Industrial Property, the Congress of Milk and the Meeting of the International Alliance of Hotel Businesses), by professional associations (e.g. architects) and by international scientific organizations (e.g. chemists, physicists or biologists).[35]

All of them were international in their participation but did not adhere necessarily to the progressive model of internationalism aforementioned. Their understanding of internationalism (with the exception of the ancient combatants) was more or less technically defined. And that was a form of internationalism Nazi Germany had no problem participating in. I want to focus in the following on the World Congress of

Universal Documentation because one of the main speakers at this event was a former German member of the ICIC who left the committee in 1933 and who afterwards was keen to build up new international networks outside the realms of the League of Nations.

Hugo Andres Krüss came into contact with the ICIC via one of its numerous subcommittees. Krüss was the general director for the Preußische Staatsbibliothek and was therefore invited to take part as an expert in the work of the subcommittee on libraries and bibliographical questions.[36] Under his guidance (and with the help of the funding of the German national committee on intellectual cooperation) the subcommittee was able to publish the second edition of its ambitious 'Index Bibliographicus', which was meant to be a 'bibliography of bibliographies' and which demanded the cooperation of libraries from all over the world.[37]

Since the late 1920s he had acted as a substitute for Albert Einstein, who was a member of the ICIC but had to miss more and more of its sessions because of illnesses. Krüss was far from being satisfied with this role as a standby for the well-known physicist and took over more and more tasks which connected him ever closer with the widely diversified League of Nations Organization for Intellectual Cooperation. In the early 1930s he got into disputes with Einstein, who did not like Krüss's sympathies for the right-wing members of the committee, Gonzague de Reynold and especially Alfredo Rocco from fascist Italy, with whom Einstein himself had some quarrels in the meetings of the committee.[38] When Einstein decided to leave the committee, he tried hard to prevent Krüss from becoming his successor and asked renowned figures from German cultural life like Harry Graf Kessler and Fritz Haber to replace him.[39]

But the committee no longer followed its own guidelines from the early 1920s; instead of an independent intellectual with an international reputation the Council of the League of Nations appointed bureaucrats with close connections to national administrations (Alfredo Rocco from Italy would be another example of this recruiting policy).[40] There were few people who were as well integrated into the German apparatus of state concerning questions of science and culture as Hugo Andres Krüss, and no one who had a 'biographie croisée'[41] of similar prominence in the international sphere too.

For some time around 1933 Krüss seemed to be rather careful with his international contacts; he had to defend himself for taking part in the activities of the League of Nations in the first place. But as early as 1933 the now national-socialist German Foreign Office started to try to use Krüss as an informant at all the international organizations the Germans were still allowed to take part in. In April 1933, for example, Krüss refused at first to travel to Paris for a meeting of the Executive Committee of the IIIC. But the German Foreign Office convinced him to go, explaining that: 'In a situation like the present one, every one of us who has possibilities of influence in foreign countries must look out for any opportunity to get into contact with others.'[42]

Krüss also took part in international organizations which were not part of the League of Nations committees. One such example was the International Library Association, to whose meeting he was in 1934 sent by the German Foreign Office despite again initially refusing to travel because he was unsure about the official position regarding international contacts. In Madrid a memorandum by the IIIC dealing with its activities in the realms of libraries and bibliography was discussed.

> After that there was a discussion about whether German libraries or some German librarians were able to contribute to the works of the institute again. The German delegates declared that there was no such opportunity, because Germany had distanced itself from any form of cooperation with the League of Nations. However, the German libraries are all the more ready to take part in all tasks and undertakings of the international association.[43]

Subsequently, Krüss travelled around the world to talk at international librarians' conventions,[44] and it was in this role that he travelled to Paris in 1937. He was a member of the advisory council of the German pavilion,[45] and he was also one of the main speakers – his was the opening speech, after the general greetings – of the World Congress of Universal Documentation which took place in August 1937 at the Paris World Fair.

The title of his presentation that he gave in German was far from modest; what he talked about was the 'Mastery of Knowledge' (Beherrschung des Wissens) and he gave a short insight – mainly in German – on attempts to create the means to control the ongoing publication of new books and articles. In front of an international audience of library experts, Krüss outlined his vision of intellectual cooperation. He defined its aims as purely technical without any political or ethical surplus value in the sense of the liberal internationalism that the League of Nations stood for. 'We can be sure that we fulfil a useful and important task when we modestly take our rightful place in the armoury of intellectual work.'[46]

Besides Krüss, a considerable number of German delegates and participants attended the congress and functioned as cultural ambassadors of Germany – and they experienced nearly the same forms of international get-togethers as the intellectuals that were in Paris for the *Mois de la Coopération Intellectuelle*: a daytrip to Versailles, receptions, visits at the Hôtel de Ville and so on.[47] But the understanding of internationalism in this case was purely technical:

> The goal for this congress was to investigate the problem of documentation in all its extent; to give an overview of all its existing forms, to compare the different principles of documentation, the different programs and methods. It wants to provoke exchanges of views over the different results that were already accomplished; and to discuss a work schedule and the services that every organisation dealing with documentation has.[48]

This strictly technical definition of international cooperation made it possible for even participants from Nazi Germany to take an active role in the meetings without getting into conflict with their convictions or the government.

The ICIC itself had in fact been troubled by the dispute about the meaning of international intellectual cooperation since its beginning in the early 1920s. The Swiss conservative literary historian and intellectual Gonzague de Reynold was one of the pronounced critics of any form of intellectual cooperation that went beyond technical assistance in specific areas of scientific research. He argued that there were certain members of the committee who – in his view – wanted to use intellectual cooperation as 'an instrument of propaganda in favour of the pacifist and humanist idea'. That was something he denounced as utopian and even dangerous and he knew exactly which of his colleagues were part of this group; prominent members in this camp included Albert Einstein and Marie Curie.

For de Reynold, a right-wing conservative Catholic, such people were on the verge of taking over the idea of international cooperation and infiltrating it with socialist, freemasonic and 'Jewish' ideas – whatever that might mean.[49] He denounced liberalism and democracy and at the same time modern science which he characterized as 'analysis until the truth is decomposed, relativization of the human mind and an unhealthy interest in the unconscious'. These could be rather surprising comments from someone who declared himself at the same time to be the 'most faithful and eager servant' of the committee.[50] But de Reynold had his own idea of intellectual cooperation – one which was popular in conservative circles in the 1920s and one which would get even greater momentum in the 1930s when institutions like the League of Nations had to think about how to uphold or recreate connections to the European dictatorships in Italy and especially Germany.[51]

Gonzague de Reynold did not only write polemics against liberal internationalism in the organization for intellectual cooperation; he also outlined his own vision of internationalism: intellectual cooperation 'of sense and possibility'.[52] That meant concentrating on simple questions of scientific – not humanitarian – progress: 'Resistance against all magnificent, utopist projects, especially the dangerous and impracticable; instead: united force for less wondrous, but clearly defined, useful, executable projects'.[53] Again, de Reynold was not just anyone, he was the longest serving member of the ICIC who participated in its work from 1923 until the late 1930s.

De Reynold's vision of intellectual cooperation was exactly what his good friend Krüss put forward in 1937. The Paris World Fair therefore was the stage for pragmatic-technical internationalism and idealistic-liberal internationalism at the same time – and even with partly the same audience, because the IIIC also participated at the World Congress of Universal Documentation. Its director, Henri Bonnet, was one of the six vice-presidents of the 'Comité technique' of the congress and at the same time the president of the working group that dealt with the question of a 'global network of documentation'. The IIIC was also listed as one of the international institutions that took part in the congress.[54]

Conclusion: Internationalism, networking and the benefits of chitchat

What happened in Paris in 1937 highlights broader questions of locating internationalism in the last years before the Second World War. On the one hand one can see the German attempt to use their presence at the *Exposition Internationale des Arts et Techniques dans la Vie Moderne* and their participation at the scientific congresses in the French capital to build up new nodes of international networks – networks that were meant to leave out the League of Nations as far as possible. On the other hand, for people like Krüss, these newly formed networks constituted an opportunity to extend the transnational life of an internationally renowned cultural manager that he had become accustomed to while working in the subcommittees and for the ICIC, and which was hampered by the German refusal to cooperate with the League of Nations. Thinking about one's own career was compatible with pursuing the interest of the state for a form of international recognition that departed from the League of Nations' internationalism.

At the same time the *Mois de la Coopération Intellectuelle* was meant to send a strong signal to the world that liberal internationalism was far from declining. And this was a signal that was sent by the League of Nations, which – in the words of Glenda Sluga – 'was less and less at the center of influential internationalist activities' in the second half of the 1930s.[55] With pride and self-confidence, the IIIC made it possible for an international elite of intellectuals, scientists, writers and artists to gather in Paris.

They discussed the present state and the future of international intellectual cooperation at several conferences and had numerous possibilities to meet in more informal surroundings. 'Chitchat', in the words of Huizinga, was surely part of the atmosphere of these meetings of intellectuals – but it was that 'chitchat' that perhaps bound people (and even intellectuals) closer together than many of the more formal aspects of the conference agendas. Huizinga complained bitterly that the participants of the conference of the Permanent Committee on Arts and Letters did not have time to read the papers that were circulated in the meeting – 'and if one tries to read them, they are unreadable'.[56]

The American writer Thornton Wilder, who like Huizinga participated in the eighth meeting of the Permanent Committee on Arts and Letters which was held as part of the *Mois de la Coopération Intellectuelle* in Paris, wrote several letters to his dear friend Gertrude Stein from Paris. Even though he gently mocked his own situation (calling himself, for example, 'a provincial little intellectual')[57] and the conference in general (he called the agenda of the conference a 'sort of hit or miss'),[58] he found rather warm words for the idea of gathering intellectuals from all over the world. 'We had a Ministre, and Herriot and the Bibliotheque [sic]. Lots of "amitiés" and lots of "culture française" and lots of wit.'[59] And he thought it important to tell Stein that the meeting was far from being a stiff academic event: 'Mr. Gilbert Murray and Mr. M. E. Forster [i.e., E.M.] laughed delightedly and M. Valéry turned with pleased amusements to his right and his left.'[60]

The officials of the IIIC were keen to make known to the world that these gatherings of intellectuals took place in Paris. Thornton Wilder's attendance of the meeting was reported directly to a journalist of the *New York Times*: 'Many eminent Americans, from which Professor Shotwell, who is the president of the American Committee on Intellectual Cooperation, and the writer Thornton-Wilder [sic] participated in its [the Mois de la Coopération Intellectuelle; J.V.] works, in which they had a great interest […].'[61]

And the French organizers did their best to offer possible spaces for 'chitchat' – not only in the breaks of the conferences but also at all the different social events, day trips and receptions mentioned earlier. For a historian with a Weberian-like 'protestant work ethic' who was longing to be reunited with his fiancée, all this may have been a 'waste of time'. Indeed, this was long the orthodox historical verdict on interwar liberal internationalism: that it amounted to an ineffective and idealistic talking shop, which sowed the seeds for its own failure. However, for the ICIC and the League of Nations in general the sociability of conference life in Paris was an important proof of the attractiveness of the idea of liberal internationalism, able to bring together eminent figures from around the globe. A careful re-evaluation of conference life in Paris in the summer of 1937 prompts us to ask whether, despite Huizinga's misgivings, the very prevalence of chitchat might also have constituted a source of strength and a contribution towards the renewal of the internationalist mission to develop a new kind of politics.

Notes

1 J. Huizinga, *Briefwisseling III. 1934-1945*, eds. Léon Hanssen, W.E. Krul & Anton van der Lem (Utrecht & Antwerp: Veen Tjeenk Willink, 1991), 185-6.
2 For Huizinga's work for the League of Nations Committee on Intellectual Cooperation, see Kurt Köster, *Johan Huizinga, 1872-1945* (Oberursel, Taunus: Europa-Archiv, 1947), 53; Christoph Strupp, 'A Historian's Life in Biographical Perspective: Johan Huizinga', in *Biography Between Structure and Agency: Central European Lives in International History*, eds. Volker R. Berghahn & Simone Lässig (New York: Berghahn Books, 2008), 103-18, 113; Anton van der Lem, *Johan Huizinga. Leven en werk en beelden & documenten* (Amsterdam: Wereldbibliotheek, 1993), 257; Anne-Isabelle Richard, 'Huizinga, Intellectual Cooperation and the Spirit of Europe, 1933-1945', in *Europe in Crisis: Intellectuals and the European Idea 1917-1957*, eds. Mark Hewitson and Matthew d'Auria (New York: Berghahn Books, 2015), 243-56; Christoph de Voogd, 'Johan Huizinga en de Coopération intellectuelle internationale. "Een intellectueel ambassadeur" van Nederland in de crisisjaren', *De gids* 168 (2005): 159-69. For the Organization for Intellectual Cooperation in general, see Jean-Jacques Renoliet, *L'UNESCO oubliée. La Société des Nations et la coopération intellectuelle (1919-1946)* (Paris: Publications de la Sorbonne, 1999).
3 Month of Intellectual Cooperation. All translations are the author's own.
4 Letter from Johan Huizinga to Auguste Schölvinck, 3 July 1937, in Huizinga, *Briefwisseling*, 185. For a similar critique to Huizinga's contemporary complaint about the attempts of the League of Nations to foster intellectual cooperation from a historian, see Mark Mazower, *Governing the World: The History of an Idea* (London: Penguin, 2012), 143.
5 Letter from Huizinga to Schölvinck, 3 July 1937, in Huizinga, *Briefwisseling*, 186.
6 Arthur Chandler, 'Paris 1937', in *Historical Dictionary of World's Fairs and Expositions, 1851-1988*, ed. John E. Findling (New York, NY: Greenwood Press, 1990), 283-90.
7 Johan Huizinga, 'Geistige Zusammenarbeit der Völker', in *Verzamelde Werken VII*, ed. J. Huizinga (Haarlem: Tjeenk Willink, 1950), 436-40 (first published in *Neue Freie Presse* (Vienna), 1937).
8 All quotations from a letter to Schölvinck, 6 July 1937, in Huizinga, *Briefwisseling*, 188.
9 Thomas J. Knock, *To End All Wars: Woodrow Wilson and the Quest for a New World Order* (Princeton, NJ: Princeton University Press, 1995), 57.

10 See Jonathan Voges, 'The International Institute for Intellectual Co-Operation at the World Fair 1937 in Paris: Profiling Internationalism in a "Hyper-Nationalistic" Context?' in *World Fairs and International Exhibitions: National Self-Profiling in an International Context, 1851-1940*, eds. Eric Storm & Joep Leerssen (Leiden: Brill, forthcoming). For the discussions about the pavilion on intellectual cooperation, see also the different proposals in UNESCO Archives AXII 10: Exposition International Paris 1937; Participation de l'Organisation int. de cooperation intellectuelle.

11 Anne Rasmussen, 'Les Congrès internationaux liés aux Expositions universelles de Paris (1867–1900)', *Mil neuf cent. Revue d'histoire intellectuelle* 7 (1989): 23–44.

12 For a complete list of all the scientific conferences taking place in Paris at the time of the World Fair, see UNESCO Archives AXII 9: Exposition International Paris 1937; Commission de la Synthèse et de la Coopération Intellectuelle.

13 For the crisis years of the League of Nations, see Michel Marbeau, *La Société des Nations. Vers un monde multilateral, 1919-1946* (Tours: Presses Universitaires François-Rabelais de Tours, 2017), 169–89; Ruth B. Henig, *The League of Nations: The Peace Conferences of 1919-1923 and Their Aftermath* (London: Haus Publishing, 2010), 134–73; Martyn Housden, *The League of Nations and the Organisation of Peace* (Harlow: Longman, 2012), 93–110.

14 Mois de la Coopération Intellectuelle. Organisé par L'Institut Internationale de Coopération Intellectuelle. Sous les Auspices de L'Organisation de Coopération Intellectuelle de la Société des Nations. Programme des Réunions. 28 Juin-28 Juillet 1937. UNESCO Archives AXII 10: Exposition International Paris 1937; Participation de l'Organisation int. de coopération intellectuelle.

15 The series of conferences of the permanent committee for arts and literature would be an interesting field of research, too. From 1932 until the late 1930s, intellectuals from different parts of the world gathered in different cities (mainly in Europe but one time in South America) to discuss the most pressing topics of their time.

16 See Jonathan Voges, 'Eine Internationale der Geistesarbeiter? Institutionalisierte intellektuelle Zusammenarbeit im Rahmen des Völkerbundes', in *Grenzüberschreitende institutionalisierte Zusammenarbeit von der Antike bis zur Gegenwart*, eds. Christian Henrich-Franke, Claudia Hiepel, Guido Thiemeyer & Henning Türk (Baden-Baden: Nomos, 2019), 355–84.

17 Liste des cérémonies et réceptions pendant le Mois de Coopération Intellectuelle. UNESCO Archives AXII 10; Exposition International Paris 1937; Participation de l'Organisation int. de coopération intellectuelle.

18 Letter by Gilbert Murray to Henri Bonnet, 19 May 1937, UNESCO Archives AXII 10; Exposition International Paris 1937; Participation de l'Organisation int. de coopération intellectuelle.

19 Letter by Henri Bonnet to Roland-Marcel, Commissaire général au Tourisme, 25 February 1937, UNESCO Archives AXII 10; Exposition International Paris 1937; Participation de l'Organisation int. de coopération intellectuelle.

20 Letter by the Ministère du Commerce et de l'Industrie to Henri Bonnet, 6 June 1937, UNESCO Archives AXII 10; Exposition International Paris 1937; Participation de l'Organisation int. de coopération intellectuelle.

21 Letter by Daniel Sécrétan to Boissard from the Ministère du Commerce et de l'Industrie, 8 June 1938, UNESCO Archives AXII 10; Exposition International Paris 1937; Participation de l'Organisation int. de coopération intellectuelle.

22 Letter from Montenach from the secretariat of the League of Nations to the director of the International Institute for Intellectual Cooperation Henri Bonnet, 14 November

1936, UNESCO Archives AXII 10; Exposition International Paris 1937; Participation de l'Organisation int. de coopération intellectuelle.
23   Letter from E.V. Letzgus, secretary to Labbé, to the International Institute for Intellectual Cooperation, 4 June 1938, UNESCO Archives AXII 10; Exposition International Paris 1937; Participation de l'Organisation int. de coopération intellectuelle.
24   D. Sécrétan, Mois de la coopération intellectuelle, Manuscript; UNESCO Archives AXII 10; Exposition International Paris 1937; Participation de l'Organisation int. de coopération intellectuelle; 1.
25   Ibid. Actually Huizinga complained about all the breakfasts and social events which distracted the group of intellectuals from concentrated work. See Huizinga, *Briefwisseling*, 186 (Letter from Huizinga to Schölvinck, 3 July 1937).
26   For the idea to use the vocabulary of economic theory to analyse international relations, see Jessica C. E. Gienow-Hecht, 'Nation Branding', in *Dimensionen internationaler Geschichte*, eds. Jost Dülffer & Wilfried Loth (München: Oldenbourg, 2012), 65–83.
27   Glenda Sluga, *Internationalism in the Age of Nationalism* (Philadelphia, PA: University of Pennsylvania Press, 2015).
28   Paul Valéry, 'Introduction', in *Le Destin Prochaine des Lettres*, ed. International Institute for Intellectual Cooperation (Paris: International Institute for Intellectual Cooperation, 1937), 11–16.
29   'In order to promote international co-operation and to achieve international peace and security'.
30   For France's role as the capital of European civilization before 1914, see Bernard Wasserstein, *Barbarism and Civilization: A History of Europe in Our Time* (Oxford: Oxford University Press, 2007), 9; for the 1930s, Olivier Bernier, *Fireworks at Dusk: Paris in the Thirties* (Boston: Little, Brown and Company, 1972), 38–66; Piers Brendon, *The Dark Valley: A Panorama of the 1930s* (London: Jonathan Cape, 2000), 492.
31   For the Deutsche Kongreß-Zentrale, see Arnd Bauerkämper & Grzegorz Rossoliński-Liebe, 'Introduction: Fascism without Borders. Transnational Connections and Cooperation between Movements and Regimes in Europe, 1918-1945', in *Fascism without Borders: Transnational Connections and Cooperation between Movements and Regimes in Europe from 1918 to 1945*, eds. Arnd Bauerkämper & Grzegorz Rossoliński-Liebe (New York: Berghahn Books, 2017), 1–38, here 7; Madeleine Herren & Sacha Zala, *Netzwerk Außenpolitik. Internationale Kongresse und Organisationen als Instrumente schweizerischer Außenpolitik 1914-1950* (Zürich: Chronos, 2002); Madeleine Herren, '"Outwardly ... an Innocuous Conference Authority": National Socialism and the Logistics of International Information Management', *German History* 20, no. 1 (2002): 67–92.
32   Blume of the Deutsche Kongreß-Zentrale to the International Institute for Intellectual Cooperation, 2 April 1937, UNESCO Archives A XII 10.
33   See, for example, an article in a German science magazine which told its readers 'that after the German exit from the League of Nations every cooperation in committees and every scientific connection to any organisation, institute or committee that is linked to the League of Nations has to be stopped'. 'Anfragen des Völkerbundes betr. Internationale Organisation', *Deutsche Wissenschaft, Erziehung und Volksbildung* 6, no. 18 (1940): 428–9.
34   Actually, Thomas Mann did not travel to Paris in 1937. See Thomas Mann, *Tagebücher 1935–1936*, ed. Peter de Mendelssohn (Frankfurt am Main: S. Fischer, 1978), 349. Entry into his diary, 11 August 1936.

35 Calendrier des Congrés Internationaux Assurés au 15. Novembre 1935; in UNESCO Archives AXII 9: Exposition International Paris 1937; Commission de la Synthèse et de la Coopération Intellectuelle.
36 For the nomination of Krüss as general director of the *Preußische Staatsbibliothek*, see Werner Schochow, 'Hugo Andres Krüß – letzter Generaldirektor der Preußischen Staatsbibliothek', *Mitteilungen der Staatsbibliothek zu Berlin/Preußischer Kulturbesitz* 4, no. 1 (1995): 47–59.
37 Joris Vorstius, 'Der Plan einer Neuauflage des "Index Bibliographicus"', *Zentralblatt für Bibliothekswesen* 47 (1930): 130–3.
38 Albrecht Fölsing, *Albert Einstein. Eine Biographie* (Frankfurt am Main: S. Fischer, 1995), 677.
39 'Einstein asked me if I would take over the post as his deputy in Geneva at the "Coopération Intellectuelle", if it was offered to me. He is very unsatisfied with his present deputy Krüs [sic] (Staatsbibliothek). He seemed to be very happy when I answered with a conditional yes.' Entry into his diary, 15 July 1930; Harry Graf Kessler, *Das Tagebuch. Neunter Band 1926-1937*, eds. Sabine Gruber & Ulrich Ott (Stuttgart: Cotta, 2010), 370.
40 Paolo Ungari, *Alfredo Rocco e l'Ideologia Giuridica del Fascismo* (Brescia: Morcelliana, 1963).
41 For the term, see Johannes Großmann, *Die Internationale der Konservativen. Transnationale Elitenzirkel und private Außenpolitik in Westeuropa seit 1945* (München: De Gruyter, 2014). Hugo Andres Krüss still deserves a biography which takes these transnational aspects of his life seriously and which does not only deal with the question if he was or was not a Nazi in the second half of the 1930s. For such approaches, see, for example, Eberhardt Gering, *Die Gründer und Mitbegründer der Deutschen Gesellschaft für Dokumentation im NS-Staat. Biographische Skizzen: Geheimrat Prof. Dr. Hugo Andres Krüß (1879-1945)* (Berlin: Selbstverlag, 2007); Werner Schochow, 'Hugo Andres Krüß und die Preußische Staatsbibliothek. Seine Berufung zum Generaldirektor 1925 und die Folgen,' *Bibliothek. Forschung und Praxis* 19 (1995): 7–19.
42 Letter from von Schmieden from German Embassy in Paris to Kamphöver of the Foreign Office, 4 April 1933; Politisches Archiv des Auswärtigen Amtes R 65745 Das Pariser Institut.
43 Hugo Andres Krüss, 'Die Tagung des internationalen Bibliotheksausschusses. Madrid 1934', *Zentralblatt für Bibliothekswesen* 51 (1934): 495–9.
44 See, for example, for one of his visits to the United States, Hugo Andres Krüss, 'Die Jahresversammlung der American Library Association und die Tagung des internationalen Bibliotheksausschusses in Chicago, 1933', *Zentralblatt für Bibliothekswesen* 51 (1934): 129–45.
45 See Reichskommissar für die Internationale Ausstellung Paris 1937, *Internationale Ausstellung Paris 1937 für Kunst und Technik. Deutsche Abteilung/Section Allemand/ German Section* (Berlin: Ala Anzeigen A.G, 1937), 125.
46 Hugo Andres Krüss, 'Die Beherrschung des Wissens', in *Congrès Mondial de la Documentation Universelle. Paris, 16-21 Août 1937. Compte Rendu des Travaux/Sitzungsberichte/Proceedings*, ed. Secrétariat du Congrès Mondial de la Documentation Universelle (Paris: Congrès Mondial de la Documentation, 1937), 31–3.
47 Secrétariat du Congrès Mondial de la Documentation Universelle, 'Le Congrès Mondial de la Documentation Universelle', in *Congrès Mondial de la Documentation*

Universelle. Paris, 16-21 Août 1937. Compte Rendu des Travaux/Sitzungsberichte/ Proceedings, ed. Secrétariat du Congrès Mondial de la Documentation Universelle (Paris: Congrès Mondial de la Documentation, 1937), 5–10, 7.
48 Secrétariat du Congrès Mondial de la Documentation Universelle, 'Le Congrès Mondial', 5.
49 See Gonzague de Reynold, 'La Reconstruction intellectuelle, les Catholiques et la Société des Nations', *La revue Générale* (June/July 1922): 617–33.
50 Gonzague de Reynold, 'Der katholische Gedanke und die gegenwärtige Zeit', *Das Neue Reich* 13 (1924): 293–8.
51 For the realm of international cultural cooperation in the 1930s and 1940s, see Benjamin G. Martin, *The Nazi-Fascist New Order for European Culture* (Cambridge & London: Cambridge University Press, 2016); Benjamin George Martin, '"European Literature" in the Nazi New Order: The Cultural Politics of the European Writers' Union, 1941-1943', *Journal of Contemporary History* 48, no. 3 (2013): 486–508.
52 Gonzague de Reynold, 'La Cooperazione Intelletuale', *Rivista di Filosofia del Dirito* 7 (1927): 381–97, here 385.
53 Gonzague de Reynold, 'Der Anteil der Schweiz an der internationalen geistigen Zusammenarbeit', *Schweizerische Rundschau* 27 (1927): 227–36. For the role of de Reynold in intellectual cooperation of the interwar years, see Aram Mattioli, *Zwischen Demokratie und totalitärer Diktatur. Gonzague de Reynold und die Tradition der autoritären Rechten in der Schweiz* (Zürich: Orell Füssli, 1994); Aram Mattioli, 'Propagandist und gescheiterter Chef der "nationalen Revolution"', in *Intellektuelle von rechts. Ideologie und Politik in der Schweiz 1918-1939*, ed. Aram Mattioli (Zürich: Orell Füssli, 1995), 135–56; Paul König, *Gonzague de Reynold. Der europäische Gedanke* (Hildesheim: Olms, 2003), 89; Urs Altermatt & Martin Pfister, 'Gonzague de Reynold. Gegen den Rassenantisemitismus und gegen die Juden', *Zeitschrift für Schweizerische Geschichte* 92 (1998): 91–106.
54 Secrétariat du Congrès Mondial de la Documentation Universelle, 'Bienfaiteurs et donateurs du Congrès', in *Congrès Mondial de la Documentation Universelle. Paris, 16-21 Août 1937. Compte Rendu des Travaux/Sitzungsberichte/Proceedings*, ed. Secrétariat du Congrès Mondial de la Documentation Universelle (Paris: Congrès Mondial de la Documentation, 1937), 11–24, here 12 and 15.
55 Sluga, *Internationalism*, 76.
56 Letter from Johan Huizinga to Auguste Schölvinck, 6 July 1837, in Huizinga, *Briefwisseling*, 188.
57 Letter by Thornton Wilder, 22 June 1937, in Gertrude Stein & Thornton Wilder, *The Letters of Gertrude Stein and Thornton Wilder*, eds. Edward Burns & Ulla E. Dydo, with William Rice (New Haven & London: Yale University Press, 1996), 148.
58 Letter by Wilder, 30 May 1937, in Stein & Wilder, *Letters*, 145.
59 Letter by Wilder, 20 July 1937, in Stein & Wilder, *Letters*, 158.
60 Letter by Wilder, 20 July 1937, in Stein & Wilder, *Letters*, 158.
61 Letter by J. Beline from the International Institute of Intellectual Cooperation to Waldemar Kaempffert from the *New York Times*, without date; UNESCO Archives AXII 10; Exposition International Paris 1937; Participation de l'Organisation int. de coopération intellectuelle.

Between camaraderie and rivalry

Geopolitics at the eighteenth International Geographical Congress, Rio de Janeiro, 1956

Mariana Lamego

Introduction

By the time the curtain closed on the 18th International Geographical Congress, held in Rio de Janeiro (Naval School), we were convinced that if it depended on geographers the world would live in peace. And I am not suggesting a 'cold peace' of indifference, because geographers would maintain a world in a mood of mutual interest and camaraderie. At least, that was the atmosphere at the Congress of Geography. Russians and Americans, Egyptians and English, Poles, Czech-Slovaks, Hungarians, Brazilians, Chinese (nationalists, since the others, the red ones, did not come), finally, men of all races and different ideologies, discussed, talked to each other about their ideas and discoveries.[1]

It was with these words that *Manchete* magazine started its special report on 25 August 1956, under the evocative title 'Geographers' world has no frontiers'. The magazine article reported on the eighteenth International Geographical Congress (IGC), which was held in Rio de Janeiro from 8 to 19 August 1956 under the auspices of the International Geographical Union (IGU). The passage reproduced here has multiple layers of meaning that, at first glance, can go unnoticed. However, an attentive reading can reveal the political significance subsumed in the careful selection of some of its words – such as the use of 'cold peace', which both invoked and inverted the 'cold war'. Or the choice of the sequence of nationalities in the final sentence, which juxtaposed Russians with Americans in reference to the indirect conflict that involved the two political and military powers in a bipolar world at the time, and Egyptians with English, referring to the diplomatic situation of Suez Canal that at that time extensively occupied the international pages of the main Brazilian newspapers. Although clearly celebrating the atmosphere of camaraderie that was seen at the IGC, the magazine article also depicted the international geopolitical textures of the congress, reinforcing Cold War tensions that were softened and even vanished in participants' discourse and performance during the conference, as I want to show here.

The presence of so many nationalities gathered for a large international congress in the city justified the media interest in the Rio IGC, and this international scientific meeting is worthy of attention by scholars as well. And there are many reasons for it. First, it was the first and still the only time in the IGU's international conference history that a Latin American country was chosen as the host. It also was the last time in the history of the IGU's international conferences that six official languages were accepted.[2] From 1956 onwards, we can see a tendency towards the current hegemony of English as the lingua franca of scientific communication. In this respect, the Rio IGC can be seen as the dawn of the global expansion of North American disciplinary rhetoric and geographical practice. Finally, the Rio IGC clearly manifests some of the most controversial international geopolitical issues of the period. The meeting dynamics expressed a divided world, although its performance tried to propagate a rhetoric of global reconciliation, as highlighted in the text from *Manchete* magazine earlier. This chapter aims to expose and understand the geopolitical implications underlying the media coverage of the conference.

The importance and scale of the Rio IGC were impressive, with 1,084 participants attending the conference from fifty-seven different nations. Of the seventeen international geographical congresses previously held, only five had attracted over 1,000 participants.[3] However, its existing Brazilian historiography is scarce, and it mostly falls into a celebratory disciplinary narrative. The conference has been portrayed as a landmark in the improvement and development of geographical knowledge in and of Brazil.[4] Almost exclusively, the main historical source used is the official material produced for the Rio IGC, such as the four volumes of its proceedings, published between 1959 and 1966, the catalogue for the geographical and cartographical exhibition and the guide books for its field trips throughout the country. These documents are regarded as the ultimate proof of the ability and capacity of the production of geographical knowledge by Brazilian geographers.[5]

The focus of Brazilian historiography is largely on the beneficial impacts or outcomes of the Rio IGC, the afterlife of the meeting detracting attention from the happening itself, from what actually had occurred during those intense congress days. The few records beyond official documents that exist are mostly recollections from attendees who were, at that time, young Brazilian geographers. Sourcing these recollections, mainly through interviews, can help provide some notes on the spirit of the time, when the excitement caused by the arrival of distinguished visitors blended with a great sense of responsibility for the hosts. The main intention of organizers was to show how geographical practice in Brazil was of equal merit to that of so-called great geographical knowledge-producing centres, notably university departments of geography in North America and Western Europe.[6]

One of these oral accounts comes from the eminent Brazilian geographer Milton Santos, at that time a young new professor at the Catholic University of Bahia. For Santos, the Rio IGC opened 'world doors to Brazilian geographers, with the arrival of key figures of geographical knowledge'.[7] Milton Santos was one of many Brazilian geographers who stepped through those open doors in the years following the congress when he went to Strasbourg for his PhD studies under the supervision of the French geomorphologist Jean Tricart, whom he had become close to during the Rio IGC.[8] The Brazilian geomorphologist Aziz Ab'Saber credited the Rio IGC with the improvement of his theoretical formulations. According to Ab'Saber his theory of refuges to explain Amazon and Atlantic forests patterns was inspired by 'contact with the great German, Belgian, French, Polish and Russian geographers [. . .] Suddenly a plane full of geographers, authors of the books I read, arrived in Brazil. It was a festival'.[9] The Brazilian historian and geographer Manuel Correia de Andrade, likewise, suggested that it was from his contact with 'the authors whose books he was constantly handling' that he developed his career in geography.[10]

There is no doubt that such oral accounts must be considered important historical sources, especially in providing more intimate and embodied narratives. As the three examples gathered earlier show, these accounts are often accompanied by all sorts of perceptions and feelings embedded in the personal trajectory, professional networks and disciplinary visions of each interviewee. However, some questions remain unaddressed, especially those regarding how dynamics and performances at Rio IGC embodied geopolitical issues. Fortunately, there was an abundance of press coverage. The Rio IGC occupied several pages of main newspapers in Rio de Janeiro city that reported the day-to-day activities, circulating a diverse range of information on the nature of the presented theses, going behind the scenes of the assemblies of the IGU to the gossip that ran through the ballrooms prepared for the social events programmed for the participants.

Analysing media coverage of the event opens possibilities of constructing a new picture of the Rio IGC that could plug gaps in the existing literature, offering new narratives that can deflate certain overly celebratory and outcome-focused ones. However, we cannot neglect the analysis of the media's role in producing its own narratives, which themselves influence both how the event is received and the course of the event itself. That is why in this chapter, the media is understood as both an archive and an agent of conferencing, using press reports as a historical source while at the same time treating the press as an active presence in the unfolding of the conference, beholden to its own interests and capable of influencing proceedings by helping to shape certain narratives and scripts.

Geopolitics is understood in this chapter as a discursive practice by which actors '"spatialize" international politics and present it as a "world" characterized by particular types of places, people and dramas'.[11] My contribution seeks to expand the cast of those able to write such 'geopolitical scripts' – that is, sets of representations, descriptions, scenarios and attributes which are deemed relevant and appropriate to defining a place in foreign policy – to include the press, conference organizers and the delegates themselves.[12] Insofar as geopolitical reasoning 'is reasoning by means of consensual and unremarkable assumptions about places and their particular identities',[13] this chapter intends to show how (and what kind of) geopolitical reasoning structures the scripts visible in media coverage during the Rio IGC.

The chapter is organized into two parts. The first looks at the spaces of the media (column inches) through the lens of the conference. The press coverage is contextualized with reference to Brazil's geopolitical situation in the 1950s, and its treatment of the conference before, during and after the event is analysed. The second part inverts this perspective and looks at the spaces of the conference through the lens of the media. This refocuses attention on the events of the conference but does so with an eye on how 'practical geopolitical reasoning' – that is, informal geopolitically inflected thinking – was a constant presence that was guided, amplified and at times revealed by the press coverage.

Media narratives on the eighteenth IGC

The focus on geographical scientific meetings as eloquent phenomena for the construction of disciplinary narratives is well established.[14] Bringing them from the periphery to the core of historical scholarship, scientific meetings have been subjected to a new analytical gaze, one that scrutinizes them considering intricate relationship between knowledge and power. Moreover, these new approaches have promoted a geographical sensibility regarding the politics of location of international scientific meetings.[15] In addition, the perspective of the conference as a geopolitical event[16] can highlight performances which reinforce its geopolitical nature.[17] Those performances became object of media coverage and reflected a wide diversity of geopolitical discourses at play during the Rio IGC.

Those geopolitical discourses, in turn, express the voice of distinctive social actors engaged in the Rio IGC. In general terms, it is possible to identify three main actors: (1) the delegates whose performances sought to express their commitment to science detached from any political content; (2) the press, which often created tension with scientific discourse by exploring international and national political issues; and finally, (3) the State, whose discourses sought to explore how the scientific achievements of the meeting could contribute to its own political cause, associating the congress triumph with the rhetoric of the dawn of a new political and economic moment for the country.

Brazil in 1956 had a newly sworn president, Juscelino Kubitschek ('JK'). The president took office in January 1956 in a troubled election that was contested and threatened by conservative national political sectors. In 1956 the atmosphere was still one of great adversity and internal political instability, and JK often used the press to gain public support as a way of securing his post. New developmentalist rhetoric had been consolidated into a set of thirty objectives to be achieved in various sectors of the economy, mainly the energy and transport sector. During his five years as president, Kubitschek opened the Brazilian economy to international investments, mainly through the modernization of the Brazilian industrial complex. In foreign policy, the early years of the JK administration did not signal any substantial change compared to the policy of its predecessor Getúlio Vargas, which was a political and military alignment with the United States.[18]

Analyses of media coverage by the reading and interpretation of articles published in newspaper and magazines must consider the political positioning, the circulation range as well as the public reception of each media vehicle. Regular news coverage of the Rio IGC occurred in the six main newspapers of the time with strong influence in national politics: *O Correio da Manhã, Jornal do Brasil, A Noite, Tribuna da Imprensa, Diário Carioca* and *O Globo*. Furthermore, special coverage also occurred in magazines, such as *Manchete* and *Revista da Semana*, and in small newspapers with less political influence, such as *Imprensa Popular, Diário de Notícias* and *O Jornal*.

The historiography of the Rio press treats the 1950s as a watershed in the way news was produced.[19] The transformation began with the introduction of new graphic presentation techniques, innovations in journalistic coverage and a shift in the dominant writing style. From 1955, journalism of criticism and opinion shifted towards a more objective and impersonal language avoiding the employment of personal pronouns, judgmental or emotive words, looking for an assumed appearance of impartiality. JK was enthusiastic about modernizing the national press, though this did not stop his government from being harshly criticized in newspapers that contested his election and inauguration.[20] The positions for and against the JK regime among the press can be explained by the political positions taken by the powerful groups that owned and ran the media companies of the time. The relationship between JK and the press had been very close. Carlos Lacerda, who was one of the most influential journalists of the time and also congressman and political enemy of both Getulio Vargas and JK, created the newspaper *Tribuna da Imprensa* in 1949. This newspaper together with *O Globo, Jornal do Brasil* and *Diário de Notícias* were JK's tireless political opponents throughout his presidential term. However, the JK government also had its supporters in the press. Among them was *Manchete* magazine, created in 1952 by journalist Adolfo Bloch, a very close friend of JK. Bloch made *Manchete* magazine one of the main platforms for visibility of JK government policies, being a great promoter of JK's developmental proposals and his famous slogan '50 years in 5'.[21]

The first article on the congress was published four years before the meeting, and the last article was published almost a year after the meeting. Media coverage of the Rio IGC also varied in size and intensity. The space that the meeting occupied in the pages of newspapers ranged from short items to full-length articles, having coverage on some front pages and, depending on the technological status of the newspaper company and its print techniques, sometimes featuring many photos as well. From a thorough survey of newspaper coverage it is possible to identify three main types of articles related to three moments of the meeting: (1) the items published in the four years leading up to the meeting; (2) those published during the period 9 to 19 August 1956 when the eighteenth ICG was effectively news; and (3) the post-event items published from 19 August onwards. For each main type, it is possible to identify themes and patterns:

Main type	Themes	Patterns	Size of articles
Pre-event published items	Expert commentaries on the event realization in Rio	Scientific competency and social and economic opportunity	From short to mid-length items
	Local organizing committee announcements and notes	Prominent visibility strategy	

Event published items	Reports on meeting schedule	Geopolitical script of Cold War tension context	From mid- to full-length (front pages and photographs)
	Summaries of press conference		
	Social events coverage		
Post-event published items	Analyses and commentaries on event's impacts	Global harmonic scientific community	From mid- to full-length

The pre-event period was characterized by stories that generally occupied less than a single column. The main themes were the choice of Rio as the next host of the IGC and the preparation for the meeting. The pre-event media coverage followed two general patterns. The first focused on the importance of the event, stressing that its occurrence in Brazil would convey the quality of Brazilian geographic science to the international scientific elite. Through this media script the event is portrayed in its significance and aftermath both to Brazilian society and to the country's economic development. A second pattern focused on giving the event greater visibility by publishing notes and announcements made from local organizing committee demands. A strong expectancy and enthusiasm were the general tone of the articles.

A good example of this first pattern is found in an article published four years before the event, on 16 August 1952, in the pages of *Jornal do Brasil*. The article reports the selection of Rio as the next venue for the IGC after the realization of the eighth General Assembly of the International Geographical Union at the seventeenth IGC in Washington, DC. Rio de Janeiro was elected to host instead of Edinburgh and Vienna. IGU criteria for the venue choice established that the host country should be in a certain degree of scientific development as well as possessing enough geographers to assure the preparation and development of the congress.[22] Interviewed for the report was the head of the Brazilian delegation at the seventeenth IGC, the pioneer geographer of the Brazilian Institute of Geography and Statistics (*Instituto Brasileiro de Geografia e Estatística*, IBGE) Jorge Zarur, who told the newspaper that 'The Congress of Rio de Janeiro will give a truly worldwide look to the International Geographical Union'. Zarur's words expressed the recognition of one of the internationalization strategies put in place by the IGU, precisely from the Washington Congress. The strategy of '*deseuropeanisation*'[23] (de-Europeanization) that began after the Second World War by including countries outside the European axis[24] reached its climax in selecting a host country in the southern hemisphere in 1956.

Print media attention to the Rio IGC began to increase a year before the conference was held, mainly stressing how the meeting would be suitable for Brazil's international reputation by making it known to the world as a developed country. The importance of the conference was advertised by publishing statements from important scientific figures from abroad. In the article[25] published in 1955, the standpoint of the Portuguese geographer Orlando Ribeiro, at the time first vice president of the IGU, and the French geographer Pierre Monbeig[26] were reported. According to the article, Orlando Ribeiro said, 'I am sure that the Congress to be held in Rio will be a great event in the world of geography, leading Brazil to occupy a prominent place in this field of science definitely.' Pierre Monbeig due to his long-standing involvement with Brazilian geography asked questions that remained throughout the congress, wondering how the popular imagination of the tropical country would be put to the test during the event and how much Rio would be more than just an eccentric and de-centred IGU congress venue. Monbeig said: 'In my view, the choice of Brazil clearly represents the end of exotic myths about the country of indigenous people and snakes and also shows Brazil's integration into the international scientific plan.'

As the date of the conference approached newspapers became an essential vehicle for the diffusion of event propaganda, with brief notes being printed monthly. Examples included the announcement of Switzerland's participation;[27] the reception by the scientific committee of the first abstracts from Japan, Uruguay, the United States and Holland;[28] the finalization of the first field trip guide for the northeast of the country;[29] the launching of the event celebratory postal stamp;[30] the arrival of US maps for the Cartographic Exhibition;[31] the arrival of the Italian and German delegation aboard the ship *Augustus*;[32] and the arrival of British geographer Monica Cole,[33] announced as 'the first congresswoman to reach the city'.

When the congress finally began on 8 August it became the focus of daily newspaper articles. The media coverage during the event became more substantial, with long stories and many photographs. This unofficial archive impresses not only with the amount and size of articles but also with the diversity of subjects that were addressed. Articles covered the opening speech made by President Juscelino Kubitschek;[34] the cheerful folk party after the lunch offered by the City mayor with two typical Brazilian meals, *feijoada* and *vatapá*,[35] and the national cocktail *caipirinha*[36] much appreciated by the guests;[37] the session papers at the Medical Geography Commission, where Brazilian scholars were highly praised;[38] the importance of geography for the USSR in the construction of the Soviet territory;[39] the fertility of Luis Solé-Sabarís from Spain, Carl Troll from Germany and André Cailleux from France, parents of thirty-two children in total;[40] the choice of Stockholm as the next venue for the nineteenth IGC;[41] a long interview with Japanese researcher Masako Sakamoto[42]; and the closing night's *Te Deum* ceremony celebrated by the Archbishop of the city of Rio de Janeiro at the time, Dom Jaime de Barros Câmara, at the Nossa Senhora do Monte do Carmo Church in the downtown area.[43]

Among the three periods, the event period is one in which the relationship between media and participants tightens, allowing us to explore how media scripts can effectively influence delegates' performances. Much more than reporting, the media can also shape events 'both through their practices of news-making, and also through practices which frequently reproduce dominant political assumptions'.[44] That is why the geopolitical script of the tense Cold War context is the pattern that dominates most of the articles published during the event, mainly highlighting the potential tensions between delegates from capitalist countries and those from communist countries. The tone of media coverage in the event period became more analytical, although keeping the enthusiastic tone of the pre-event period coverage.

Finally, there is the third type of media coverage: the articles published in the post-event period. As in the event period, there were a wide variety of themes in the published items, but a great number of reports dealt with the aftermath of the Rio

IGC conference, stressing its strengths and weakness. Although many articles were analytical and critical in tone, the predominant discursive practice was similar to the articles published in the pre-event period. However, if previously, the tone was of great expectation, the tone of the post-event was that of expectations that had been exceeded.

Most of the reports published in the post-event period reached the size of full-length columns, such as the text entitled 'Echoes of Geographical Congress',[45] published two months after the end of the meeting and signed by Virgílio Corrêa Filho, a Brazilian geographer from the IBGE and First Secretary Treasurer of the Local Organizing Committee of the Rio IGC. In the text, Corrêa Filho highlighted what he called an atmosphere of 'comprehensive tolerance in theoretical debates' even when 'ideological divergence may have aroused'. This Brazilian cordiality and spirit of camaraderie was on display not only during the official programme but also in the social events, which were recorded as event highlights. The text concluded with a reproduction of complimentary testimonials from foreign participants who attended the meeting, proving that the Rio IGC 'had expressed its high quality compared with previous meetings held in Europe and North America' and ultimately 'Brazilian culture was enhanced after the test to which it was submitted'.

The geopolitical script of Cold War tension, which was the main pattern found in the event period published items, was softened in the post-event period, and a renewed pattern seemed to occur. The new pattern supported a spirit of global harmonic community among the 'men of science' that could bridge international adversities or even intercommunication obstacles in the Cold War tension context. Regarding the employment of the term 'men of science' by media coverage, it is noteworthy that although there are no records on how many women attended the meeting, a careful look at the names on the Proceedings' extensive list of individual members shows that, although fewer than men, the number of women present at the meeting was significant. In the news there is mention of the large participation of Brazilian women compared to the number of foreign women, and there is also a curious mention of the expressive participation of nuns in the event.[46] However, despite this circumstance, in both newspaper texts and other texts produced for official material, the word 'man' is used as a gendered noun.

In the post-event media coverage, rather than looking for Cold War tension in participant performance, media coverage sought to suggest that there was virtually no such tension among researchers. The text from *Manchete* magazine quoted in the epigraph to this chapter is actually from the post-event period and is the biggest item published on the Rio IGC. Its four pages were illustrated with large photographs showing different meeting moments, including a comic photo of French geographer Max Sorre sleeping during a paper session. Another photograph that illustrates the article reflects how geopolitical script is being lightened for the sake of an atmosphere of international harmony in the world of science: the image of two well-dressed gentleman stood up side by side looking at a piece of paper. They are Professor Leo Alpert from the United States and Professor Feofan F Davitaia from the USSR, described in the photo caption as 'a constant pair'. The photo and the article text reinforce the rhetoric of camaraderie that became the pattern in post-event media coverage.

The presence of USSR delegates at the meeting was extensively covered by the media. This interest is due to the geopolitical script followed by media translation on the Rio IGC. The next section will return to the materials published during the period of the Rio IGC in order to highlight the practical geopolitical reasoning in circulation at that time, in the two primary spaces of performances at the IGC: the conference halls and rooms, and the places of social events and interactions.

Practical geopolitical reasoning at the conference

One of the most controversial events at the Rio IGC, described by press as the 'bitter moment' of the whole meeting, was the ninth General Assembly, which took place on 10 and 18 August in the Naval School's main hall. It is located on Villegaignon Island, a historic little island situated in Guanabara Bay where in the year 1555, the French admiral Nicolas Durand de Villegaignon, under the support of Henry II from France and with the help of the Tamoios Indians, erected the Fort of Coligny when attempting to establish a French colony at the tropics called 'Antarctic France'.[47] The Naval School still today belongs to the Brazilian Marine Force, and at that time, its facilities were made entirely available for congress activities. The Naval School became the meeting headquarters.[48] The facilities were used for all paper sessions and commission meetings as well as for the two sessions of the ninth General Assembly. Male members used the student lodging at no charge, and participants used the student restaurant during the congress. There was also room for the press, a post office, an exchange agency, newspaper stands and a souvenir shop. This mini-city appearance of the Rio IGC venue is mentioned in the congress proceedings as a strategy to overcome the inconvenient insulation. Yet, the official invitation also highlights the advantages of being on an island such as *'un rapprochement plus étroit entre les participants'*.[49] The ninth General Assembly is indeed remembered in the IGU meeting historiography as a truly controversial episode due to the applications for regular membership. In the IGU order of ceremony, the general assembly is the moment when a series of crucial matters related to the functioning of the organization are decided by the votes of the regular members, such as the definition of the new executive committee for the next four years, the entry (or exclusion) of regular members, the creation (or suppression) of committees and the choice of the following international congress venue.

The ninth General Assembly in Rio had two sessions. The first occurred on 10 August, the third day of the congress, and the second session took place on 18 August, the penultimate day. Both sessions were chaired by Professor Dudley Stamp, then president of the IGU. After the first session proceedings, Stamp presented the applications for regular membership and associate membership.[50] There were five applications for regular membership: from Ethiopia (which received twenty-four votes out of a possible twenty-six); the German Democratic Republic (GDR, or East Germany, which received fifteen votes); Hungary (twenty-three votes); Iceland (twenty-four votes) and the USSR (twenty-three votes).[51] The voting system required a simple majority of votes in favour, which meant that all of the applications were successful. According to IGU Statutes III, on General Assembly regarding resolutions on the matter of an administrative character, clause G says that any 'decision shall only be valid if more than 50 per cent of the possible votes, i.e., of member countries present at the General Assembly or eligible to vote via postal ballot, are cast'.[52]

However, by the second session, eight days later, the scenario had changed. The IGU statutes allowed for absent members to vote by letter, and this time the absentee votes would be computed as well. This recalculation increased the total number of voters from twenty-six to thirty-six, which had significant consequences for the result of the GDR application. In the first vote, the GDR's fifteen votes out of twenty-six translated into a majority of 58 per cent, but by taking into account the absence of postal votes in their favour, that percentage dropped to forty-two, beneath the majority required by the statutes. As described in the minutes of the second session, it was decided that 'the election of the German Democratic Republic shall be regarded as *sub judice*, and that the new Executive Committee should be asked to consider the case and make a recommendation to the next meeting of the General Assembly'.[53] It was not until the tenth General Assembly in Stockholm in 1960 that the GDR application was again the subject of discussion, which this time did finally result in the admission of the GDR to the International Geographical Union.[54]

The media coverage of the ninth General Assembly did not let the application of three communist countries as new regular members go unnoticed. The choice of the next venue, Stockholm, was also highlighted in the news. Both issues had gained prominence on newspaper pages following the geopolitical script that emphasized the context of Cold War tension. Under the title 'Russia was admitted at IGU', the article[55] reported on the first session of the ninth General Assembly, at which Stamp had said that 'the IGU is not a political agency and has no political character'. Stamp's talk occurred before the vote and was followed by an unidentified German geographer who 'kindly asked that the vote on the GDR application should be done by ignoring the country's current division'.

A *Manchete* magazine article[56] added both some light and some spice to the controversial GDR application episode mentioned earlier. Without giving further details, the article text suggests 'it was known that Mr. Dudley Stamp, the former president of the IGU [the article was published after the election of the Swedish geographer Hans Wilhelmsson Ahlmann], had manipulated the vote in favour of the USSR and Hungary's admission'. The text went on to say that this manoeuvre had the side effect that the 'GDR was also able to penetrate the body'. This 'unforeseen effect' was then questioned by US delegates who 'did not recognize the GDR' and requested the annulling of the vote. For the article, this would have been the reason why Stamp concocted a recount of the final vote that rendered the election of the GDR sub judice at the second session of the ninth General Assembly. It is clear that the reporter was not present during the two sessions of the General Assembly but had probably been informed by eyewitnesses. Such details and the internal politics brought to light by *Manchete* are suppressed in the minutes of the ninth General Assembly.

In fact, the media spilt a lot of ink trying to both portray how the Cold War tension was felt and distort facts so as to present a particular geopolitical impression. Still having as subject the controversial general assembly, the article, entitled 'In Geography

United States and Russia are together',[57] contains a good example of the active role of media in framing the geopolitical script. According to the article, all regular membership applications would have had unanimity in votes except 'Russia', which would have had three votes against. The newspaper article is mistaken in suggesting that only Russia did not have unanimous votes. In fact, no application had unanimous support.

The text goes further and raises questions on whose could be the three votes against Russia's admission, creating an atmosphere of suspense. This was followed by what was presented as a private interview with the head of the US delegation, Professor Wallace Atwood Jnr. Atwood was asked if the United States could be one of the votes against, causing an embarrassing situation. According to the report, Atwood emphatically replied that 'the Russians, concerning geography, should have been part of the IGU at least thirty years ago, as they should never have departed since science knows no political boundaries'. The newspaper's strategy seems to be an attempt to show that there is a conflict between facts – three countries had voted against USSR – and statements – US delegate under pressure ensures that the United States has not voted against, but he could be dissembling – fully exploring the tense atmosphere created by the Cold War context.

The same strategy appears in *A Noite* article[58] which chronicles the events of the ninth General Assembly, focusing on the choice of Stockholm as the next IGC venue and the election of Professor Hans Wilhelmsson Ahlmann, member of the Royal Swedish Academy of Sciences, as the new president of IGU Executive Committee, succeeding Dudley Stamp. Ironically entitled 'The King is dead. Long live the King!' in reference to the shifting of IGU presidency from one monarchist country to another, the article text suggests that the choice of Ahlmann should be seen as a geopolitical strategy by featuring an interview with Professor Nafis Ahmad, from University of Dacca, Pakistan. In the interview, Ahmad declared that the choice of the new president of IGU shows 'the skilful blow by English science, which is following with keen attention the foreign policy directions of your Majesty's Prime Minister'. Ahmad believed that the strategy of IGU direction in choosing Ahlmann was to become 'closer to the Soviets since the Norse can handle them very well'. Concluding his understandings of the episode, Ahmad suggested that if 'in the Middle Ages the Hanseatic League had been created, now the Nordic League is created'.

The interview with Ahmad was immediately followed by an interview with Dudley Stamp who was asked the reason why Ahlmann was chosen, in a clear intention of the newspaper to load some geopolitical ink in the episode. In fact, the choice had not been Stamp's decision but an open vote decision at the General Assembly. Clearly wanting to avoid further controversy, Stamp explained to the journalist that the choice would have been due to the beauty of Stockholm, 'the only capital that could compete with the beauty of Rio de Janeiro'. Stamp's shrewdness was again highlighted by the newspaper article's praise for the great ability he led the General Assembly. Visibly interested in getting some political positioning from Stamp, the reporter commented on how quickly decisions were made at the General Assembly, chaired by Stamp. In a demonstration of quick-witted humour, Stamp replied, 'well, it is the world press itself that celebrates British democracy as the most perfect in the world, isn't it?'

In addition to the official spaces where the conferences, symposiums, IGU committee meetings, paper sessions took place, the Rio IGC also made use of other, semi-official spaces such as the fancy ballrooms that housed the social events or the many vehicles that transported participants across the city in their daily detachments for the city tours. Media coverage of these semi-official spaces introduced new shades of the geopolitical rivalry script. In the many articles published on social events, it is possible to catch much of the atmosphere of the Rio IGC. Reporters had been present as eyewitnesses at all social events, such as the fancy cocktail evening offered by the Brazilian Equestrian Society at the Brazilian Hippodrome in which a night horse race was provided exclusively for the visitors and the official lunch offered by the City mayor ending in a celebration of traditional folklore performance with music and dance. The qualities of the Brazilian foods and drinks appreciated by foreign visitors were the subject of reports in the press. Among the delicacies, black beans stood out. According to *Tribuna da Imprensa*,[59] North American delegates 'confessed that they had never eaten as much starch as in Brazil, with rice, beans, potatoes and bread, served in practically all meals offered'. Regarding beverages, the *mate*, made from the yerba mate infused and served cold, was highlighted. However, according to the newspaper's text, the most popular drink was coca-cola, 'which would have been a great success among Russian delegates and other communist countries' delegates'.

There were nine field trips offered to delegates. Four of them happened before the meeting, from mid-July to early August, and the rest of them took place after the conference, from mid-August to early September. The field trips' average length was fifteen days, with the shortest excursion being an eight-day tour of the coastlines and sugar-producing region of Rio de Janeiro State and the longest being a twenty-four-day trip to the Amazon Region. All excursions resulted from a great effort made by Brazilian geographers who did preliminary fieldwork and had produced a series of brand new maps, photographs and images to illustrate the pages of the guide books. There was also a mid-conference tour in the form of a boat trip to Bahia da Guanabara, and a visit to Paquetá Island with an unplanned Brazilian carnivalesque closing also became object of media coverage. In the boat trip from Paquetá, a group of young people embarked and during the return trip to the continent, started playing Brazilian music.[60] According to the article, this unexpected spectacle created a catchy atmosphere capable of 'making serious Professors get pleasantly drawn into the evolution of samba'.

The media acted as an eyewitness of the events even in the daily shuttle-bus journeys made by the congress' participants. An *O Globo* article[61] covered the intense first day of work in the congress when all delegates were welcomed by political representatives, from the mayor of the city to President Kubitschek. The reporter wrote about some 'relaxed moments' that occurred inside the bus during the visits. He mentioned that some delegates could communicate using different languages, and sometimes a weird blend of French and English could be heard. He also described a passionate dispute between delegates from the United States, France, Cuba and the Soviet Union about the best alcoholic beverage in the world, with each naturally defending their own national product. Here the celebration of a global harmonic community appeared side-by-side with a geopolitically scripted one, since the newspaper article depicted the dispute between whisky and vodka as the hardest to settle.

Sometimes media coverage explored even subtler communication strategies or, in some cases, no communication strategies. Social events were highlighted as places where 'everyone speaks an average language' or a 'common language' and even with differences, everyone 'understands each other'.[62] However, language could also be used to avoid embarrassing situations and controversial geopolitical issues. The article from *Correio da Manhã* read the cocktail evening offered by the Brazilian Equestrian Society using a geopolitical script. By describing the 'environment of intense cordiality and camaraderie' of the party, the text reports that:

> several chat groups were formed with participants from various nationalities. No one was left isolated. Not even the Russians, though hardly anyone knew their language. The Russians communicated with the others in reasonable English that always became confusing when the subject began to approach political issues. A true strategic language that allowed the Russians a discreet retreat at critical moments.[63]

In describing strategies[64] and narrating their perceptions of the meeting, journalists framed delegates' interactions in their own scripts. Even with explicit selectivity, these reports are a key source to study delegates' performances during the Rio IGC, considering both official spaces such as the meeting rooms and semi-official spaces such as restaurants, boats and buses.

Final words

> *In such meetings, there is always a hint of international politics in everything. Especially in hall conversations. And the most commented subjects were: 1- Communist China did not come. The nationalists did; 2- The East and West German delegations were together. It seems the Americans didn't like it; 3- Russia, which did not participate in the last two congresses, were represented by a delegation of six members; 4- the Hungarian representative elected to participate in an IGU council had his candidacy opposed by West Germany; 5- and, among other things, the fact that Russia had given as a present for the congress a very modern collection of maps.*[65]

The analysis of media coverage of the eighteenth IGC held in Rio de Janeiro city in 1956 discussed in this chapter focuses on the geopolitical scripts that guided its narratives in order to understand both the intricate relationship between reporters and men and women of science and the relation between practice and rhetoric. The official and semi-official spaces of the Rio IGC were objects of media narrative showing how deeply Cold War tension was embedded in delegate performances despite many attempts to remove, at least in discourse, its immanent political content.

Geopolitics is a key element in understanding the dynamics and practices of international geographical congresses. However, the task of highlighting geopolitical aspects in academic relations brings with it fundamental methodological challenges. As argued in this chapter, media coverage can be an important source for identifying and exposing the major geopolitical tensions that overtook the Rio IGC. This source, however, has limitations and potentialities. By shaping political events through news-making practices,[66] on the one hand, media coverage tried to fit different phenomena into the same script, often subverting the facts to run through a binary narrative associated with the Cold War. On the other hand, journalists' accounts may reveal nuances and practices that are hardly accessible in official documents that can provide alternative narratives.

They also reveal the complex ways in which the geopolitical script was filtered through the reportage of camaraderie at the conference. Likewise, one cannot isolate these reports of camaraderie at the conference without acknowledging that they were invariably filtered through the lens of geopolitics. By focusing on the Rio IGC, we can see not only the saturation of the conference in geopolitical scripts but also the breadth of those scripts, extending from the more blatant power struggles at the conference to what at first sight might seem like the more peripheral aspects of conference life. The abundance of column inches devoted to the conference demonstrates that the event was a significant moment not just in the development of Brazilian geography, but also how its staging of international geopolitics in microcosm generated waves that, inflated by the interplay between the spaces of the conference space and its presence in the press, reverberated out beyond the event itself and into Brazilian society at large.

Notes

1 All translations are my own. *Manchete*, 25 August 1956.
2 The Rio IGC was the last of three conferences to have six official languages; after 1960, only English and French were officially featured in International Geographical Congresses. See Chauncy D. Harris. 'English as International Language in Geography: Development and Limitations', *The Geographical Review* 91, no. 4 (2001): 675–89.
3 George Kish, 'International Geographical Union: A Brief History', *GeoJournal*, 26, no. 2 (1992): 224–8.
4 Carlos Augusto de Figueiredo Monteiro, *A geografia no Brasil 1934-1977: avaliação e tendências* (São Paulo: Edusp, 1980) and Helio de Araujo Evangelista, 'O XVIII Congresso Internacional da União Geográfica Internacional – UGI Rio de Janeiro, 1956', *Revista geo-paisagem* 3, no. 5 (2004).
5 XVIIth International Geographical Congress, 1956. Abstract of papers. Comptes rendus du dix–huitième congrès intrenational de géographie, Rio de Janeiro, 1956 (Rio de Janeiro: Comité National du Brésil, 1959–1966) 4 vol.: t.I, 1959. XXI + 383p., fig., cartes; t.II, 1960. VIII + 613p., fig., phot., cartes; t.III, 1965. VIII + 655p., graph., phot., cartes, don't 3 dépl. h. t.; t. IV, 1966, 659 p., graph., tabl., phot., cartes dont 2 dépl. 9 livrets – guides de excursions; Geographical and cartographical exhibition, catalogue (Rio de Janeiro: IGU, 1956).
6 Fabio de Macedo Soares Guimarães & Orlando Valverde, 'XVIII Congresso Internacional de Geografia', *Revista Geográfica do Instituto Pan-Americano de Geografia e História* 19, no. 45 (1957): 1–7, 3.
7 Milton Santos, 'Entrevista com Milton Santos', *GEOSUL*, n.12/13 (1991/1992): 170–201.

8   Pedro de Almeida Vasconcellos, 'Milton Almeida dos Santos (1926-2001)', in *Geographers: Biobibliographical Studies*, v. 37, eds. Elizabeth Baigent & André Reyes Novaes (London: Bloomsbury, 2018), 41–68.
9   Aziz Ab'Saber, 'Entrevista com o Professor Aziz Ab'Saber', *GEOSUL*, n.14 (1992): 170.
10 Manuel Correia de Andrade, 'Entrevista com o Professor Manuel Coreia de Andrade', *GEOSUL*, n.12 (1991): 132.
11 Gearóid Ó Tuathail & John Agnew, 'Geopolitics and Discourse: Practical Geopolitical Reasoning in American Foreign Policy', *Political Geography* 11, no. 2 (1992): 190–204, 192.
12 Ó Tuathail & Agnew, 'Geopolitics and Discourse'.
13 Ó Tuathail & Agnew, 'Geopolitics and Discourse', 194.
14 Ruth Craggs & Martin Mahony, 'The Geographies of the Conference: Knowledge, Performance and Protest', *Geography Compass* 8, no. 6 (2014): 414–30, Marie-Claire Robic, 'À propos de transferts culturels. Les congrès internationaux de géographie et leurs spatialités', *Revue Germanique Internationale*, 12 (2010): 33–45; Charles W. J. Withers, Diarmid Finnegan & Rebekah Higgitt, 'Geography's Other Histories? Geography and Science in the British Association for the Advancement of Science, 1831-c.1933', *Transactions of the Institute of British Geographers* 31, no. 4 (2006): 433–51, Charles W. J. Withers, Rebekah Higgitt & Diarmid Finnegan, 'Historical Geographies of Provincial Science: Themes in the Setting and Reception of the British Association for the Advancement of Science in Britain and Ireland, 1831-c.1939', *British Journal for the History of Science* 41, no. 3 (2008): 385–415, Charles W. J. Withers, *Geography and Science in Britain, 1831-1939: A Study of the British Association for the Advancement of Science* (Manchester: Manchester University Press, 2010), Charles W. J. Withers, 'Geographies of Science and Public Understanding? Exploring the Reception of the British Association for the Advancement of Science in Britain and Ireland, c.1845-1939' in *Geographies of Science*, eds. Peter Meusburger, David Livingstone & Heike Jöns (Heidelberg: Springer Verlag, 2010).
15 Rob Kitchin, 'Commentary: Disrupting and Destabilizing Anglo-American and English-Language Hegemony in Geography', *Social & Cultural Geography* 6, no. 1 (2005): 1–15, Dominique Volle, 'La carte des États: vers la couverture du monde?' in *Géographes Face au Monde. L'Union Geographique Internationale et Les Congrès Internationaux de Géographie*, eds. Marie-Claire Robic, Anne-Marie Briend & Mechtild Rössler (Paris, Montréal: L'Harmattan, 1996), 41–62; Dominique Volle, 'L'Universalité et ses limites', in *Géographes Face au Monde. L'Union Geographique Internationale et Les Congrès Internationaux de Géographie*, eds. Marie-Claire Robic, Anne-Marie Briend & Mechtild Rössler (Paris, Montréal: L'Harmattan, 1996), 63–82.
16 Naoko Shimazu, 'Diplomacy as Theatre: Staging the Bandung Conference of 1955', *Modern Asian Studies* 48, no. 1 (2014): 225–52.
17 Ruth Craggs, 'Postcolonial Geographies, Decolonization, and the Performance of Geopolitics at Commonwealth Conferences', *Singapore Journal of Tropical Geography* 35, no. 1 (2014): 40–56.
18 Celso Lafer, *JK e o programa de metas (1956-1961): processo de planejamento e sistema político no Brasil* (Rio de Janeiro: Editora FGV, 2002).
19 Alzira Alves de Abreu, *A imprensa em transição: o jornalismo brasileiro nos anos 50* (Rio de Janeiro: Editora FGV, 2008) and Nelson Werneck Sodré, *História da imprensa no Brasil* (Rio de Janeiro: Civilização Brasileira, 1966).
20 Abreu, *A imprensa em transição* and Sodré, *História da imprensa no Brasil*.

21 Rose Mary Guerra Amorim, 'O Governo JK e a revista Manchete: a criação do mito dos anos dourados' (MA diss., Fundação Getúlio Vargas, 2008).
22 Philippe Pinchemel, 'La localisation des congrès', in *Geography through a Century of International Congresses*, ed. IGU Commission on History of Geographical Thought (International Geographical Union, 1972), 30.
23 Pinchemel, 'La localisation des congrès', 29.
24 Robic, 'À propos de transferts culturels', Volle, 'La carte des États', & Volle, 'L'Universalité et ses limites'.
25 *Diário Carioca*, 5 March 1955.
26 Monbeig had lived in Brazil between 1935 and 1946 and was responsible for the creation of the first Chair of Geography at the newly created University of São Paulo, at São Paulo state.
27 *A Noite*, 4 January 1956.
28 *Tribuna da Imprensa*, 6 January 1956.
29 *Jornal do Brasil*, 18 January 1956.
30 *Tribuna da Imprensa*, 30 April 1956.
31 *Diário Carioca*, 23 May 1956.
32 *O Jornal*, 4 August 1956.
33 *Correio da Manhã*, 5 April 1956.
34 *A Noite*, 10 August 1956.
35 The dinner guests had *feijoada* and *vatapá*. The first, made with black beans, pork and beef stew, is very typical of Rio de Janeiro and is considered one of the oldest typical meals of the country that mixes Portuguese and African cuisine. The *vatapá* is very typical from the northeast of the country, made of bread, ginger, red pepper, coconut milk, peanuts, palm oil with fish. Unlikely *feijoada*, *vatapá* is considered a representative of African cuisine with adaptations according to the ingredients found in Brazil.
36 Made with *cachaça*, a sugarcane hard liquor, sugar, lime and a generous amount of ice.
37 *O Globo*, 13 August 1956.
38 *O Correio da Manhã*, 14 August 1956.
39 *Imprensa Popular*, 15 August 1956.
40 *Correio da Manhã*, 16 August 1956.
41 *A Noite*, 17 August 1956.
42 *Revista da Semana*, 18 August 1956.
43 *Correio da Manhã*, 19 August 1956.
44 Simon Dalby, 'Reading Rio, Writing the World: The New York Times and the "Earth Summit"', *Political Geography* 15, nos 6–7 (1996): 593–613, 594.
45 *Jornal do Comércio*, 21 October 1956.
46 *Tribuna da Imprensa*, 20 August 1956.
47 Maria Fernanda B. Bicalho, 'A França Antártica, o corso, a conquista e a "peçonha luterana"', *História* 27, no. 1 (2008): 29–50.
48 Charles B. Hitchcock, 'The Eighteenth International Geographical Congress, Rio de Janeiro, 1956,' *Geographical Review* 47, no. 1 (1957): 118–123.
49 Comptes rendus du dix-huitième congrès intrenational de géographie, 49.
50 It was during at the ninth General Assembly that the new associate membership category was introduced. This category was understood as the first attempt of the IGU to open its frontiers to independent recent countries from the 'Third World' (Volle, 'L'Universalité et ses limites'; Robic, 'À propos de transferts culturels'). In the occasion of the ninth General Assembly, six countries applied for associate membership: Iraq;

Kenya; Nigeria; Sudan; Uganda; and French West Africa – which disintegrate itself two years after, in 1958.
51 Comptes Rendus du XVIIIe Congrès International de Géographie, 186.
52 Available at www.igu-online.org/organization/statutes/#statute3.
53 Comptes Rendus du XVIIIe Congrès International de Géographie, 186.
54 Volle, 'La carte des États'.
55 *O Correio da Manhã*, 11 August 1956.
56 *Manchete*, 25 August 1956.
57 *O Globo*, 12 August 1956
58 *A Noite*, 17 August 1956.
59 *Tribuna da Imprensa*, 20 August 1956.
60 *Jornal do Comércio*, 21 October 1956.
61 *O Globo*, 10 August 1956.
62 *Correio da Manhã*, 14 August 1956.
63 *Correio da Manhã*, 17 August 1956.
64 Similar strategies in communication between US and USSR delegates were explored in the case of the Bretton Woods Conference in Giles Scott-Smith & J. Simon Rofe (eds), *Global Perspectives on the Bretton Woods Conference and the Post-War World Order* (London: Palgrave Macmillan, 2017).
65 *Tribuna da Imprensa*, 20 August 1956.
66 Dalby, 'Reading Rio, Writing the World'.

Part III

Permanent institutions

8

Spectacular peacebuilding

The League of Nations and internationalist visions at interwar World Expos

Wendy Asquith

The interwar years have long been considered an era of political and economic crisis characterized by the ascendance of belligerent nationalisms, simmering anti-colonialist tensions and world economic collapse. Though the 1920s had seen the emergence of the League of Nations, the world's first major intergovernmental organization, 'a distortion of historical vision has featured nationalism [and particularly ultranationalist aggression] in the foreground' of narratives recounting the era.[1] Substantiating such accounts, historians and political scientists have spotlighted the League's faltering, taciturn or ineffective responses to processes such as the Manchurian Crisis, the Italian invasion of Abyssinia, global rearmament and the rise of communism and fascism: events that emphasized the era's politically fractious nature. A newer wave of studies has contested this view. Spurred by the transnational turn in historical study, these accounts have begun to illuminate the period's importance as a seedbed for internationalism by exploring the organizational structures, societies, movements and 'technical' work of the League that laid the groundwork for the rapid expansion of internationalist working in the second half of the twentieth century.[2]

This chapter contributes to revisionist work on internationalism in the late 1930s. Like the surrounding chapters, it moves away from dematerialized accounts of diplomatic negotiation but pushes our focus beyond the bounds of conventional understandings of international conferencing to explore the visual and material culture of two exhibitions representing the League of Nations at the much more open mass gatherings of people at two World Expositions. The histories of international conferencing and of World Expos are intimately intwined. The latter have always served as sites for the staging of a vast array of conferences, congresses and meetings that various international organizations, associations and interest groups have scheduled to coincide with them.[3] Moreover, the League's first secretary general, Eric Drummond, described the organization's Secretariat as 'nothing more and nothing less than a permanent conference of representatives'.[4] Therefore, by focusing on exhibits of the League of Nations at World Expos, this chapter analyses the materiality of the twentieth century's first self-confessed unending conference, though rearticulated within the spectacular register of the World Expo circuit. In doing so, our focus is shifted away from the forging of internationalisms in Geneva and the restricted conferencing spaces of the political elite. Instead, this study draws our attention to the public sphere and the ways in which the League of Nations advocated a range of internationalisms to attract and sustain a broad community of international supporters.

Specifically, this chapter foregrounds an analysis of the spaces, sights and sounds of two projects supported by the League's Department of Public Information: the *Pavillon de la Paix* staged at the *Exposition Internationale des Arts et Techniques dans la Vie Moderne* held in Paris in 1937 and the League of Nations' Pavilion produced for the New York World's Fair of 1939. In each case, time and place inflected the range of internationalisms that the League was willing to be associated with, so that across the two expositions a significant shift can be discerned in the ideologies advocated and aesthetics deployed within displays promoting the organization. While it was shrewd in the context of the pre-war exposition of 1937 in Paris – overseen by the leftist alliance of the Popular Front government – to celebrate internationalist sentiments and styles associated with socialism, two years later in the United States it was not. The New York World's Fair had been dedicated to the 'world of tomorrow', but increasingly after the event's opening the pavilions of the phantom states of Europe – including Czechoslovakia, Poland and Belgium – came to haunt the Expo's landscape.[5] In this atmosphere of uncertainty, the League opted for a more politically ambivalent and conservative aesthetic.

Like all world's fairs and *expositions internationales* since their emergence in the mid-nineteenth century, the major World Expos of 1937 in Paris and 1939 in New York were enthusiastically promoted by their host nations as exemplary sites for fostering internationalism: spaces invested with audacious global aspirations in which causes and challenges beyond the reach of single nations could be pursued. Edmond Labbé – *Commissaire General* of the Paris Exposition – declared, for example, that the event under his charge 'must serve the interests of the world economy and the cause of peace' while the New York World's Fair operated under the motto, 'building the world of tomorrow'.[6] Yet, despite organizers' internationalist aspirations, analyses of these two expositions have echoed the tone of broader histories of the interwar era, judging them to be ill-fated or contrived expressions of peace that purposefully camouflaged simmering hostilities, jingoistic nationalisms and even outright threats of war between states.[7] Indeed, scholars have generally dismissed the statements of fraternal goodwill routinely adopted by host nations of international expositions across their broad history as empty gestures: sentiments 'ridiculed by displays of military technology, imperial conquest and abject racism' woven in and among the melee of competing national exhibits.[8] While it is patently clear that the built environments of international exhibitions are replete with the competitive architectural gestures of participant nations, which have drawn much attention in the existing historiography, this chapter will demonstrate that major World Expos at the end of the interwar period also attest to 'the vitality [and multiplicity] of internationalism[s]' extant in the late 1930s, through an exploration of the plural internationalisms advocated by the League of Nations in Paris and New York.[9]

War and peace at the Paris Exposition of 1937

Between May and November 1937, the gates at the *Exposition Internationale* in Paris recorded a total of 31.5 million entries to the fairgrounds.[10] At the heart of the exhibition stood the Eiffel Tower, which had been erected as the gateway to the *Exposition Universelle* of 1889. Four decades later, the viewing platforms within this iconic Parisian landmark once again offered scores of visitors an elevated platform from which to gaze out in all directions at the vast cultural spectacle feted by organizers as a great space of international exchange promoting peace among nations, itself situated in an interwar Paris of 'exhilarating cosmopolitanism'.[11] Yet for those who gazed out in a north-westerly direction towards the new *Palais de Chaillot*, panoramic views of the built environment were disturbed by a scene of confrontation.[12] Here, as many contemporary sources registered, was an alarming face-off between the thrusting Soviet and towering Nazi pavilions on the far-side of the Seine.

On 15 July 1937, the right-wing Parisian weekly *Candide* published a full page of satirical cartoons about the expo by popular illustrator Albert Dubout.[13] In the bottom left-hand corner was an image bearing the caption 'It's them fighting again!' (Figure 8.1). Above, a line drawing shows animated versions of the Nazi and Soviet pavilions in conflict: the eagle atop the Nazi pavilion screeching in alarm as the (un)idealized socialist figures surmounting the Soviet pavilion lunge towards it, causing the whole building to lean comically forwards. In Dubout's rendering, the elevated, architectural hostilities cause a commotion in the boulevards below where anxious fairgoers run into one another in panic or leap into the Seine to avoid the ruckus.[14] This image has been repeatedly analysed and reprinted in case studies examining the pavilions constructed by Germany and Russia in 1937, but a key detail has remained unnoticed in each instance. At the centre of this chaotic image of bilateral confrontation, diminutive but unmistakably present, is the representation of another specific pavilion erected for the 1937 exposition, a pavilion that embodied international accord: the *Pavillon de la Paix* or Peace Pavilion.[15]

The Peace Pavilion was situated on the Place du Trocadero and comprised a semi-circular building partially surrounding a 50-metre-high pillar, topped by an illuminated star, known as the *Colonne de la Paix* or Peace Column. The pavilion's interior exhibits dramatized the longue durée of modern war and peace and were split into three main sections: 'the destruction of war'; 'the efforts of humanity for the maintenance of peace'; and 'the coordination of peace forces'.[16] Particularly in its latter sections, the pavilion's exhibits advocated for specific organizations and concrete actions that could constitute an international movement for peace. Chief among these was galvanizing support to strengthen the League of Nations. One room was dedicated entirely to the League but displays that championed the organization and its key principles could be found throughout the pavilion's interior as well as on its façade. A passionate case was made for the League as the crucial vessel through which the principles of international cooperation and collective security could be pursued thereby enabling a permanent peace. While subsequent scholarly accounts of the 1937 exposition seem to have all but forgotten the Pavillon de la Paix, a range of contemporary sources show that exposition organizers, international journalists and leading French politicians as well as large

Figure 8.1 'It's them fighting again!' Detail from 'Dessins de A. Dubout: A L'Expo', Candide, 15 Juillet 1937. Bibliothèque Nationale de France, Département Droit, économie, politique, JOD-125 [ark:/12148/bpt6k46894901].

swathes of the visiting public saw it as a powerful symbol of shared anti-war sentiment across national borders.

Aerial views, offered by the many fairground maps published in souvenir guidebooks, brochures and leaflets, show the Peace Pavilion located at the apex of the exposition site directly opposite the *Entrée d'Honneur*, the main gateway into the fairgrounds.[17] The Peace Pavilion's Organizing Committee decided to cover the interior concave surface of its external façade with decorative features celebrating the League of Nations, which were floodlit for ease of viewing by day or by night. These included a large-scale world map with shaded areas showing member and non-member states, and all twenty-six articles of the League of Nations' Covenant engraved upon a series of large stone-like slabs embedded within the wall's surface. By this means, every visitor who entered the exposition via the *Entrée d'Honneur* would have unavoidably encountered this monument to peace and internationalism with its cartographic depiction of League principles and advocates.

Coverage of the Peace Pavilion's inauguration gave a sense that it had obtained a position of special significance within the context of the exposition.[18] Marcel Cachin, leading communist politician and editor of *L'Humanité*, took this opportunity to publish his take on the pavilion's symbolic significance. On 8 July 1937, Cachin declared the pavilion to be a powerful 'sign of Universal Peace' and a vital monument to 'the defence of collective security and the necessary solidarity of all'. He went on to assert that the Peace Pavilion would not only act as a symbol of solidarity but – like the many fairground venues that would host international conferences and congresses during the period of the exposition – it would also function as an active site of internationalist working, where 'the representatives of groups who want to fight effectively against the war all over the world [would convene]'.[19]

Figure 8.2 Carte Postale showing the exterior of the Peace Pavilion captioned 'Cher . . . . Le Pavillon ou la nuit – avec un immense foule d'Ancien Combattants . . .'. Source: Rassemblement Universel pour la Paix Archives, International Institute for Social History (Amsterdam).

While entrance to the exposition cost six Francs, the Peace Pavilion – standing just outside the boundary of the fair – was accessible to all, admitting visitors free of charge.[20] Its accessibility meant that the pavilion quickly became a rallying point for pacifists and anti-war activists just as Cachin had prophesied (see Figure 8.2). Coverage in the French press highlighted two events as particularly noteworthy. Just over a month after the inauguration of the Peace Pavilion, in mid-August, a large demonstration was held there by representatives of youth for peace organizations from up to twenty-five different nations, with many donning national costume to highlight the rally's international nature.[21] The marches coordinated by these groups involved the laying of wreaths at the foot of the Peace Column and then culminated in the delivery of anti-war addresses by three youth delegates from India, Belgium and France.

A month or so later, on 8 September 1937, First World War veterans' organizations arranged for a particularly poignant anti-war ceremony to take place adjacent to the Peace Column. In the presence of various dignitaries and gathered international publics 'the torch that transported the famous flame of the Arc de Triomphe [from the tomb of the unknown soldier] to the ossuary of Douaumont . . . was deposited at the foot of the Peace Column'.[22] In doing so, this ceremony admitted the exposition's ephemeral monument to Peace into a circuit of sacrosanct memorial sites, revealing the tone of public response to this new landmark as well as the emotional investment made in it, however temporarily, by a range of anti-war campaigners drawn from many different nations worldwide. Yet just beneath the apparent open, anti-war internationalism enabled by the Peace Pavilion, a more politically partisan internationalism of the left was also being promoted at this site.

A pavilion in partnership: The League and the RUP's proletarian internationalism

Leftist leanings could be discerned in various elements of the Peace Pavilion's displays. Across its five rooms socialist ideals and a broad proletarian internationalism were implicitly championed through the use of communist- or Marxian-style rhetoric and the adoption of visual conventions that approximated Socialist Realism. One of the most notable examples of such left-wing advocacy could be found in the pavilion's third – and largest – room, which was assigned the theme 'the great peace forces'.[23] Here the pavilion's Organizing Committee planned, as the room's central feature, 'a huge painting representing the seven great divisions of mankind: peasants, workers, intellectuals, ex-soldiers, religion, women and youth'.[24] Expanding on their design brief, the committee gave further instruction as to the specific social settings in which these 'great divisions' should be represented as having acted. They explained, 'for the Section concerning Workers' and Peasants' Movements we should like to give the impression of a factory, of a harvest field, of a co-operative store'. This delineation of peace movements into schematic social and spatial typologies is telling. The vision it intended to offer viewers – with the transnational social categories of 'peasant' and 'worker' clearly playing a central role – was one of collective international struggle populated by the familiar stock figures of a global communist imaginary. Moreover, the committee suggested that 'the important dates of the different congresses of the First, Second and Third Internationals' should be explicitly commemorated. Notably, given this volume's focus on conferencing, ambitious early proposals for the 'interior arrangement' of the wider space which would house this painting suggested that it could take the form of 'an immense congress chamber' in order to give visitors an immersive experience of a congress in-session as well as permitting 'special use [by] approved organisations' during the exposition.[25]

In its final form it seems the pavilion contained no such mock congress chamber, though the 'huge painting' set to represent the 'seven great divisions of mankind' was actually arranged as seven separate painted panels.[26] The panel representing 'Youth' strongly approximated visual conventions of Socialist Realism, which had recently become the Russian Soviet state's artistic style of choice (Figure 8.3). For visual arts in the Soviet Union, what this resulted in was 'the production of a visual super-reality' in which realist styles were used to create highly idealized scenes that uncritically glorified Soviet life.[27] The panel depicting youth in the Peace Pavilion's 'Grand Salle' conformed to many facets of this aesthetic style.[28] At its centre, it depicted a group of vivacious, youthful figures. Some wore workers overalls; others were clothed as stereotypical peasant figures including a woman right-of-centre wearing a long tunic and headscarf. Several of the figures carried farming or labouring tools, among them both a sickle and a hammer. As the group marches forward with purpose towards the viewer, beaming smiles and bright eyes adorning the face of

Figure 8.3 Mural depicting youth movements for peace within the 'Grand Salle' of the Peace Pavilion. Detail from a promotional booklet published by the RUP. Source: Rassemblement Universel pour la Paix Archives, International Institute for Social History (Amsterdam).

each figure gazing outwards, the idealized scene conveys a mawkish optimism every bit the equal of cloying artworks that depicted Stalin among the cheery youth of the Soviet Union.[29] Its sense of collective movement also unmistakably resembles the forward progression embedded within Vera Mukhina's sculptural duo *Worker and Kolkhoz Woman* that topped the nearby Soviet pavilion. Leaving no room for confusion as to the politically partisan message being visually championed here, the panel representing youth peace movements was topped with the tagline 'Youth of the world unite to defend peace': an unquestionable echo of the Communist Manifesto's famed final lines.[30]

That the visual and discursive clues outlined earlier, and threaded throughout the pavilion, were promoting a proletarian internationalism is shown to be all the more plausible when we scrutinize the organization chiefly responsible for the Peace Pavilion project. It was led by a fairly new, short-lived and long-forgotten pacifist organization known in French as the *Rassemblement Universel pour la Paix* (RUP) and in English as the International Peace Campaign (IPC). The RUP had been publicly founded little more than six months prior to the opening of the Paris Exposition, in September 1936. Yet, by the time of the expo's opening in May 1937 the RUP had apparently expanded exponentially. It now claimed a membership of more than four hundred million adherents worldwide and a very prominent space on the exposition fairgrounds. Historian Rachel Mazuy reveals that France's Socialist prime minister Léon Blum played a crucial role in allocating a permit and subsidy to the Peace Pavilion's Organizing Committee ensuring both this structure's existence and prominent location.[31] Mazuy also shows that key personalities within the (French) communist sphere played a crucial but deliberately obscured role within the RUP's founding: notable among these were Pierre Cot, socialist politician and government minister who became president of the RUP, and Louis Dolivet, an adept propagandist with links to the Comintern.

Like the very existence of the RUP itself, the partnership between this organization and the League to deliver the Peace Pavilion was very much a collaboration of convenience born out of a specific historical moment. While the popular front government was leading in France and with the prospect of world war looming large – threatening to undercut the League's raison d'etre – a collaboration with the RUP to achieve a noteworthy presence at the Paris Exposition was expedient. Just as advantageous for the League, two years later, at the New York World's Fair of 1939 was an alignment with quite different values and interest groups.

An appeal to American psychology? The League at the New York World's Fair of 1939

In January 1938 just six months after the inauguration of the Peace Pavilion in Paris the League's Supervisory Commission submitted a report for consideration by the Council. In this document the views of a group of anonymized 'prominent and representative'

Americans were compiled vis-à-vis the desirability of staging a League pavilion at the New York World's Fair of 1939.³² Summarizing these views, the document advised, 'to be effective and to avoid all possible criticism [the League] should be housed in a separate pavilion and stand entirely on its own, and should not in any case be combined with any other efforts such as those of various peace or other organisations'.³³ Given that the League had collaborated with the RUP – a prominent peace organization – only six months earlier, it's hard not to see this sentiment as a direct reflection on the compromises made and partisan allegiances revealed during that project.

While signing up as a solo exhibitor for the New York World's Fair may have ensured that the League was more likely to be seen as politically impartial by American fairgoers, it did mean that the full weight of the project's expense would fall squarely on the organization's shoulders. In retrospect the League calculated that actual expenditure on the New York project totalled two million Swiss Francs.³⁴ Significantly more than the estimated 12,500 Swiss Francs that the League had contributed to the Peace Pavilion project staged in Paris.³⁵ Though quite restrained in the scheme of the fairgrounds, the League of Nations pavilion staged in New York offered visitors six full rooms of visually rich, floor to ceiling exhibits, while the pavilion's exterior was designed to convey grandeur and dignity. Aesthetically, it took on a monumental neoclassical style akin to contemporary American civic and memorial architecture clearly intended to be an imposing and significant addition to the fairgrounds (Figure 8.4).³⁶

In 1939, with its membership shrinking and the outbreak of war in Europe, the drive to gain broad US support for a League of Nations seems to account for the organization's much heavier investment in the New York World's Fair. In early 1939 a member of the League's Information Section observed 'Roosevelt moves to the front as leader of the democracies ... in the new League, whatever form it may take, the United States is bound to be prominent'.³⁷ This context of expected future leadership from the United States is a crucial point. While Woodrow Wilson had been a key architect of the League and Americans had undertaken significant collaborative projects with it through both public and private channels, the United States had never become a member.³⁸ Through the New York fair key League personnel hoped to convince US audiences that the best way to continue their collaborative relationship was through US membership of the League. To this end League officials preparing the organization's pavilion for New York continually underscored the importance of 'appealing to American psychology'.³⁹

In their quest to achieve cultural resonance with the fair's host nation, League personnel consulted with pavilion commissioners from past Expos as well as notable Americans.⁴⁰ Arthur Sweetser, a key member of the League's Information Section (1919–42) and an American national himself, took a leading role in these discussions. Among those he consulted was New York-born author, playwright and diplomat Clare Boothe Luce, who is remembered as a staunch advocate of Catholicism. Luce suggested that 'the idealistic and philosophical heart' of the League should take centre stage within the pavilion. She opined that American visitors would be 'com[ing] in off the street rather exhausted; they would appreciate a cool, quiet, religious-like place in which to repose for a moment; they would then immediately get the atmosphere

Figure 8.4 Artist's impression of the League of Nations' Pavilion, New York World's Fair. Source: League of Nations Archives, United Nations of Geneva.

and spirit of the League'.[41] Given her well-documented religious allegiance, it stands to reason that Luce was more specifically proposing that the League design an exhibit that would resonate with New York's Catholic, and strongly anticommunist, majority who were 'a powerful force in city political and cultural affairs'.[42] Like many American Catholics at that time, Luce harboured strong anticommunist sentiments. Indeed, the 'American Roman Catholic Church' has been identified as the 'backbone of American anticommunism for most of the movement's history'.[43] With this audience in mind, the influences of both anticommunism and Roman Catholicism can be discerned in the content both presented within and absented from the League's US pavilion.

In Room One, the pavilion's displays opened with an exhibit representing the 'long historical process which culminated in the League of Nations'. Beginning with Pharaoh Rameses II, this section offered a selection of 'portraits, quotations and documents recall[ing] some of the great men and historical events' that had furthered international cooperation.[44] Yet socialist activities were notably absent. In the League's gendered narrative of internationalist history staged in New York 'great men and historical events' associated with communist internationalism found no mention in direct contrast to plans for its Parisian Peace Pavilion.[45] Instead, in 1939, the League's origins story contained prominent references to a range of religious figures, including St Augustine, Erasmus, Francisco Suarez and the Abbé de Saint-Pierre. Elsewhere in the pavilion explicit religious references continued.

Among the Health Section's exhibits in Room Two were allusions to figures from Christian scripture. Above a cartographic panel showing the global networks facilitated by the League's 'creat[ion of] an international epidemiological intelligence service' was a bas-relief in wood showing a man carrying a wounded figure: with the title 'The Good Samaritan' (Figure 8.5).[46] The association of these two figures – a hero and a victim of biblical genealogy – with the medical work of the League conforms to an ossified iconography of humanitarian action. This iconography is particularly associated with narratives of 'humanitarian medicine', dating back to the late nineteenth century, which built upon the tried and tested tropes of a visual culture developed alongside missionary and reformer activities stretching back centuries.[47] Moreover, this bas-relief alluded to historically significant representations of Christianity's most sacred and central characters. The entwined composition of the sculpture's two central figures aped the shape and form of Michelangelo's *Pietà*: a Renaissance-era marble representing the Virgin Mary cradling the body of Christ after the crucifixion, which has been part of the Vatican's art collection since the sixteenth century.

The aesthetic links between the pieta and that created for the League pavilion in New York signal a much more direct influence by the Roman Catholic Church upon the League's Expo project, courtesy of the French Catholic priest Père de Reviers de Mauny, a Jesuit known for his creative endeavours.[48] Reviers was the commissioner of the Vatican pavilion (*Pavillon Pontifical*) at the 1937 Paris Exposition and after informally advising the League for a time, he quickly became a key player within the their New York pavilion project team.[49] In July of 1938, Secretary General Joseph Avenol informed all departments that he had retained the services of Reviers 'as [a] technical adviser, to draw up complete plans for an appropriate League exhibit and Pavilion.'[50] Working with a group of artists and architects in Paris, Reviers set about transforming each League department's vague plans into striking multimedia displays. Some of these were the same artists who he had worked with on the Vatican pavilion for the 1937 Expo and there were clear transferences from one context to the other.

There were striking similarities between the aura and architectural dimensions of spaces created within each pavilion. The floor plan for the League's 1939 pavilion shows five antechambers that formed an outer ring surrounding the central rotunda space. This circular sixth room was described by organizers and in press releases as 'the culminating point' of the pavilion. It was carefully designed to encourage reverence for the League's 'ideal and objective' of collective security via international cooperation through creation of a religious-like shrine that venerated this work as 'the apotheosis of human solidarity.'[51] The high-ceilinged room was dimly lit. At its centre stood an elevated sculptural group of five female figures with their arms outstretched forming a protective ring within which was placed 'a tree in wrought metal' (Figure 8.6). This collection of symbolic forms was intended to 'represent the five continents, forming a circle to protect

Figure 8.5 'The Good Samaritan', a bas-relief in wood which was displayed among the Health Section's exhibits in Room Two of the League Pavilion at the New York World's Fair. Source: League of Nations Archives, United Nations of Geneva.

the Tree of Peace'. The pavilion's elevated external peristyle was situated directly above this room and so the sculptural group at centre was seen 'under the full light falling from the dome'.[52] Correspondence between the League's Finance and Information Sections gives insight into the sonic dimensions of the space. These archival documents explain that 'on the advice of Father de Reviers' there was 'a loud speaker installed hidden in the ceiling of room six' which facilitated the 'play[ing of] some good classical music . . . to enhance the impression' made upon visitors by the exhibits in this room.[53]

Figure 8.6 Installation view of Room Six within the League Pavilion at the New York World's Fair, showing lighting and architectural features surrounding central sculpted figures (here at left). Source: League of Nations Archives, United Nations of Geneva.

There was a very similar use of height, light and sound in the Vatican pavilion of 1937. Its form followed centuries-old patterns of Roman Catholic architecture – replete with high altar, baptistry, crypt, cloisters, a free-standing bell tower and a sanctuary – with the latter particularly standing out as a model for Room Six of the League pavilion. Summing up the main features and effects of this space in his introductory statement for the published guide to the Vatican pavilion, Reviers effused, 'before the altar, at the call of the Light, feel the universality and the holiness'.[54] It is telling that these words alluding to the supranational allegiances that the curatorial team hoped would be inspired by the Vatican pavilion's sanctuary could easily have been describing notable features and the atmosphere created within Room Six in the League's pavilion at New York: key elements of which had been influenced by Reviers's own sense of what constituted an impactful sacred space. Clearly, architectural conventions and iconographies drawn from Roman Catholicism provided a significant blueprint for the League pavilion's central space, though they were not the only influence here.

A technical League: Accommodating multiple internationalisms

On the 'dark' wall surrounding the League pavilion's shrine-like sanctuary in Room Six were a series of 'four frescoes representing scourges such as War, Famine, Epidemics and Exile'.[55] These allegorical depictions were intended to represent major global threats to the League's central goal of world peace through collective security. The fresco depicting war was particularly striking. The bottom third of the image shows the ruins of warfare. Angular buildings jut from the ground on the left which is covered in a tangled mess of figurative forms suggesting multiple casualties. At its centre, a figure clutches at the child in their arms while bending backwards in an unnatural way in an attempt to avoid the inescapable aerial bombardment descending from above. At top, endless planes fill the air with smoke and projectiles as they race across sky. The descending barrage is anthropomorphized as the huge and terrifying forms of the four men of the apocalypse hurtling with alarming speed towards the victims below.[56] The fresco offers a forceful and passionate indictment of war, but not of any conflict in particular.

Though the aggressive actions of the Axis Powers in Asia, Africa and Europe had set in motion a spiraling global conflict, the League offers no direct condemnation of these contemporary acts, only a repudiation of the notion of war. This reluctance to confront the most flagrant examples of war-making to hand, even within a fair that ultimately found no place for a Nazi pavilion, confirmed that the League could be persuaded to a taciturn response in the face of significant acts of aggression and suggested that the League was willing to advocate a politically indiscriminate internationalism.[57] This abstracted denunciation of war also marked a significant departure from the curatorial choices made in executing the Peace Pavilion at the Paris Exposition in 1937. In Paris, a pavilion entirely dedicated to the themes of war and peace housed emotive exhibits explicitly condemning aggressive actions by Nazi Germany and fascist Italy including the invasion of Abyssinia and the bombing of a school in the Spanish city of Getafé. Both used photographic images to show the actual environmental and human devastation resulting from these incidents.[58]

Reticence to explicitly confront contemporary political disputes in the League's New York pavilion has been interpreted as a move to secure US support. The League was keen not to lay itself open to the 'charge of attempting propaganda in a non-member state' and even sought to reassure US audiences, by press release in 1938, that 'nothing in the nature of political propaganda' would be contained among its exhibits.[59] In his analysis of the League's New York pavilion, historian David Allen argues this project was part of a public process of League reform, which actually sought to recast the

League 'as a less political body' focused on facilitating technical cooperation between states with much greater scope for non-member involvement.[60] The picture of League reform intimated by the New York pavilion – with its focus on accomplishments in the social, economic and health spheres – was very much in line with the League's internal Bruce Report of 1939, recommending that it focus on 'technical' (rather than political) work. Both have been interpreted as 'aligning the League more consciously with prevailing American policy toward it'.[61] Preparing the League, or its already anticipated successor, for US leadership in the post-war era was undoubtedly a key motivation behind this organizational recasting. Yet in the uncertain era of world war, some anticipated the emergence of an alternate world order headed by fascist powers. A developing strand of scholarship compellingly argues that in steering the organization away from entanglement in political disputes through a programme of reform key League personnel – right up to the secretary general himself – had this future in mind.[62] Marco Moraes has recently revived enquiry into the purported fascist leanings of Joseph Avenol, the League's secretary general and top official from 1933 to 1940.[63] He contends, among other events, that Avenol's fascist sympathies were revealed through his leadership of the League's administrative response to aggressive imperialist actions by the Japanese in Manchuria. He suggests Avenol reduced League activities there at the time of the crisis in order to facilitate Japanese annexation in contradiction of the Covenant. Actions which, at best, reveal Avenol to be one of the interwar era's arch-appeasers and, like many of his colleagues, a chronic imperialist.

Echoing the imperialism advocated by its leading bureaucrat, the League's New York pavilion also offered a prosaic display on the work of its Permanent Mandates Commission (PMC, see Figure 8.7). The PMC was the branch of the League created to oversee imperial administration of African, Pacific and Middle Eastern territories taken from the German and Ottoman Empires in the course of the First World War. For key stakeholders the aim of this committee was the internationalizing of the imperial system.[64] The panel representing this work in the League's New York pavilion was located in Room Three, centred on a cartographic mapping of mandated territories and, undoubtedly for the benefit of the gathered American audience, was headed by a plaque containing an extract from Woodrow Wilson's fifth point. 'Colonel' House, Wilson's chief advisor at the Paris Peace Conference of 1919, explained that this point was concerned with making 'colonial administration . . . a matter of international concern' by instating 'a code of colonial conduct' and was therefore, in part, a basis for the creation of the PMC.[65] In the decades to follow, both the Wilsonian moment and the fora generated by the PMC were successfully exploited by anti-imperialists and anti-colonial nationalists to validate their causes. Yet neither Wilson's framework for peace nor the PMC had been devised as tools to dismantle the imperial system.[66] Rather, each for their own ends sought to make competing colonial systems 'more humane', more transparent and more open (to other imperial powers) thereby lending the imperialist world order greater legitimacy.[67]

Though the League's pavilion panel on the work of the PMC made no direct comment on broader systems of colonial administration, it nevertheless betrayed the organization's subscription to an imperialist world order. For instance, this display featured at its centre a large map of Africa with the words 'wards of civilization'

Figure 8.7 Installation view of Room Three within the League Pavilion at the New York World's Fair, showing display panel titled 'Wards of Civilization' representing the work of the Permanent Mandates Commission. Source: League of Nations Archives, United Nations of Geneva.

emblazoned across its entirety. Though League mandates in Africa accounted for only a small minority of its landmass, what the inclusion of this civilizational language signified was the PMC's advocacy of a system of imperialist internationalism stretching across the whole continent. Indeed, most members of the twelve-person commission were 'retired diplomats or former colonial officials' for whom the 'language of civilizational stages, of 'backward peoples' and Western guidance', was second nature.[68] Indeed, Article 22 of the League's Covenant – concerned with the reasoning behind the mandates system, the terms of mandatory administration and the creation of the PMC – was suffused with this language: decreeing that the mandatory powers or 'advanced nations' were bound by 'a sacred trust of civilization' to guard the 'well-being and development' of mandates, 'inhabited by peoples not yet able to stand by themselves under the strenuous conditions of the modern world'. The League's PMC display in New York, and indeed the material form of the pavilion itself, exemplified this world view and its justifications.

A caption attached to an early artist's impression of the League's New York pavilion explained that it was designed to 'symbolis[e] the fundamental philosophies of the [League, being] . . . composed of two parts. The lower section is pentagonal, signifying the five continents and five races of man. The upper structure is a circular colonnade typifying unity and cooperation'.[69] Even at this base level, then, the League's pavilion and core philosophy were revealed to rest upon a notion of global racial divisions: an understanding of humanity that had been routinely organized into a discriminatory, white supremacist, hierarchy for centuries. Continuing this pattern of thinking inside, below the PMC's cartographic display, was another large panel bearing the dual title 'Mandates – Slavery'. The implicit connection here was that endeavouring to completely suppress slavery in all its forms and minimize use of forced labour was an obligation impressed upon mandatory powers from the outset.[70] The left-hand side of this panel offered a paraphrased listing of key obligations and principles from Article 22. The right-hand side presented a record by date of key actions taken to eliminate slavery worldwide, before and during the tenure of the League. The conjoining of these two lists – under the title 'Mandates – Slavery' – exemplifies a sleight of hand, widely employed by imperial powers of the time, that presented imperial(ist) rule as a form of humanitarian work aimed at casting colonial (and in this case mandatory) systems as progressive spaces in which social justice and economic development were pursued on behalf of local populations guarded by the 'sacred trust of civilization'. Indeed, this panel ended with the somewhat premature claim that 'the council of the League of Nations concluded in 1939 that slavery and the slave trade were approaching extinction'.[71] The reality was quite different: as historian Susan Pedersen confirms, 'mandated territories were not better governed than colonies across the board and in some cases were governed more oppressively' with practices of forced labour actually expanded in certain mandates under PMC oversight.[72] Pedersen claims that 'by 1939 the mandates system had very few defenders' and given the popularity of anti-imperialist rhetoric in the United States alongside the championing of national self-determination by key political figures we might expect that it would find no welcoming party in the Big Apple either.[73] Yet, the gap between rhetoric and reality can be capacious. Though Americans had a long history of disavowing – and selectively forgetting – their nation's imperialist activities it was nonetheless a colonial power in the late 1930s, which justified its extraterritorial activities using a racialized developmental world view, one which colonized peoples and their domestic allies in the United States recognized and lobbied against.[74] This tension between American imperialist ambitions and their disavowal was perfectly reflected in the awkward presence of the PMC panel within the League's New York pavilion, which seemed to want to champion internationalist imperialism, yet was unsure about how to articulate its achievements and aspirations.

At the New York World's Fair the League offered a pavilion project that had been managed in-house by its own Department of Information. Yet this did not result in advocacy of a more unified or coherent set of internationalist philosophies. Advocating anti-war sentiment remained a prominent element of the 1939 pavilion's exhibits, reflecting the League's founding raison d'être of collective security. Yet sensitivity to the non-member status of the United States and its conscious distancing from the mounting European conflict, as well as the possibility of an Axis victory, resulted in the abstraction and diffusion of this message. What came to the fore in the League's New York pavilion was a functionalist internationalism that accommodated a range of ideologies and movements including a form of religious internationalism, courtesy of a special advisor from the Roman Catholic Church, as well as an unsurprising nod to the Wilsonian moment and an awkward restatement of imperialist internationalism.

Conclusion

In the post-war-era landmark conferences at Bretton Woods, Yalta, San Francisco and the like once again became the spaces in which heads of state hammered out the terms of peace. It was at such gatherings too that the League was finally decommissioned in 1946 following the inauguration of a new United Nations in 1945. In these moments of future-focused anticipation, the spectacular pre-war sites of internationalist dreaming at World Expos in Paris and New York may have been distant memories, yet they had played their part in rehearsing the alignments and foregrounding the agreements made later. Indeed, this study shows how the delicate diplomatic negotiations that underpin the very existence of much internationalist working can take place in the visual, as well as verbal, register and in open public, as well as restricted private, fora.

In the late 1930s the world was in flux as was the League of Nations. The habitually shifting sands of the global political economy had become feverishly accelerated due to the manoeuvres of belligerent fascist and communist states, as the period also hailed the arrival of an irreversible tide of anti-colonial nationalisms. Yet this warmongering, uncertainty and advent of post-colonial nation states did not result in a vacuum of internationalism but rather a proliferation of internationalist movements, philosophies and systems. The World Expos held in Paris in 1937 and New York in 1939 drew much of this internationalist activity momentarily together in peerless sites of spectacular display uniquely configured to reflect the geographic specificities of the host nation. For the League, which had previously been reticent to take part in such public extravaganzas, these events became valuable spaces in which to experiment with various internationalist alignments. With the League's future very uncertain, League bureaucrats, external advocates and expo officials in favour of the organization's World Expo participation were able to push it beyond its customary risk-averse stance and realize two such projects to significant financial cost in the space of a few years. Reflecting the highly selective global vistas on display at each of these interwar World Expos the internationalist visions that the League inhabited at each changed as the organization travelled, responding to the unique geopolitical configuration of each event.

Notes

The author was a Leverhulme Early Career Fellow while conducting research and writing for this chapter and so would like to acknowledge the generous support of the Leverhulme Trust.

1 Glenda Sluga, *Internationalism in the Age of Nationalism* (Philadelphia, PA: University of Pennsylvania Press, 2013), 8.
2 See, for example, Glenda Sluga & Patricia Clavin (eds), *Internationalisms: A Twentieth Century History* (Cambridge: Cambridge University Press, 2017); Daniel Laqua (ed.), *Internationalism Reconfigured: Transnational Ideas and Movements Between the World Wars* (London: I.B. Tauris, 2011).
3 Each of the two Expo editions that are the focus of this chapter provided venues for hundreds of such events. The Paris Expo of 1937, for example, hosted the IIIC's International Studies Conference on Peaceful Change and the First International Yiddish Culture Congress. Among those held at the New York World's Fair were meetings of the International Youth Congress and the International College of Surgeons. See Nick Underwood, 'Exposing Yiddish Paris: The Modern Jewish Culture Pavilion at the 1937 World's Fair', *East European Jewish Affairs* 46, no. 2 (2016): 160–75; New York World's Fair 1939 and 1940 Incorporated Records, Manuscripts and Archives Division, The New York Public Library.
4 Eric Drummond, 'The Secretariat of the League of Nations', *Public Administration* 9 (1931): 228–9.
5 Marco Duranti, 'Utopia, Nostalgia and World War at the 1939-40 New York World's Fair', *Journal of Contemporary History* 41, no. 4 (2006): 663–83.
6 'Les Participations Étrangères à l'Exposition Internationale de Paris', 23 Juillet 1936, *Participations Étrangères Généralités*, Archives Nationales de France (hereafter ANF) F^{12} 12143. Translation by the author.
7 Rika Devos, Alexander Ortenberg & Vladimir Paperny (eds), *Architecture of Great Expositions 1937-1959: Messages of Peace, Images of War* (Farnham: Ashgate, 2015), 1–22; Robert H. Kargon, Karen Fiss, Morris Low & Arthur P. Molella, *World's Fairs on the Eve of War: Science, Technology, and Modernity, 1937–1942* (Pittsburgh, PA: University of Pittsburgh Press, 2017), 83–107.
8 Paul Greenhalgh, *Ephemeral Vistas: The Expositions Universelles, Great Exhibitions and World Fairs, 1851-1939* (Manchester: Manchester University Press, 1988), 17.
9 Daniel Laqua, 'Preface', in *Internationalism Reconfigured: Transnational Ideas and Movements Between the World Wars*, ed. Daniel Laqua (London: I.B. Tauris, 2011), xii.
10 Shanny Peer, *France on Display: Peasants, Provincials and Folklore in the 1937 Paris World's Fair* (Albany, NY: State University of New York Press, 1998), 30.
11 Les Participations Étrangères', *Participations Étrangères Généralités*, ANF: F^{12} 12143; James D. Herbert, *Paris 1937: Worlds on Exhibition* (London: Cornell University Press, 1998); Michael Goebel, *Anti-Imperial Metropolis: Interwar Paris and the Seeds of Third World Nationalism* (Cambridge: Cambridge University Press, 2015).
12 See Andre Devambez, *The Exhibition of 1937, View of the Eiffel Tower* ([Painting] 1937) oil on canvas, 217x189cm, Rennes Museum of Fine Arts.

13 Though Dubout himself did not share these right-wing leanings.
14 'A L'Expo: Dessins de A. Dubout', *Candide*, 15 Juillet 1937, 9.
15 See, for example, Danilo Udovički-Selb, 'Facing Hitler's Pavilion: The Uses of Modernity in the Soviet Pavilion at the 1937 Paris International Exhibition', *Journal of Contemporary History* 47, no. 1 (2012): 13–47, 18; Karen Fiss, *Grand Illusion: The Third Reich, the Paris Exposition, and the Cultural Seduction of France* (Chicago, IL: University of Chicago Press, 2009), 58; Devos et al., *Architecture of Great Expositions*.
16 'Visit the Peace Pavilion', RUP 137, IISH.
17 *Exposition Internationale de Paris 1937: Arts et Techniques* (Paris: L'illustration, 1937); 'Visit the Peace Pavilion' RUP 137, IISH.
18 'French President Lebrun Opens the International Exposition 1937', *Our Roving Camera Reports*, 25 July 1937, Reuters Archive – British Pathé, Film ID: VLVA7C4I71IT94GRWCAWIV9US7D7G; 'Paris Exhibition Opened', *Pathe Gazette*, 1937, British Pathé Archive, Film ID 941.16; 'Le Pavillon de la Paix a été inauguré hier après-midi à l'Exposition', *Le Peuple*, 10 Juillet 1937; 'L'inauguration du Pavillon de la Paix', *L'Humanité*, 8 Juillet 1937; 'Le Monument de la Paix', *Le Petit Journal*, 10 Juillet 1937, Pavillon de la Paix, ANF F^{12} 12143.
19 'L'inauguration', *L'Humanité*, ANF F^{12} 12143.
20 'A l'Exposition', *L'Humanité*, 26 Aout 1937, ANF F^{12} 12143.
21 'Au pied de la colonne de la Paix', *Excelsior*, 15 Aout 1937, ANF F^{12} 12143.
22 The Douaumont ossuary, inaugurated in 1932, contains the material remains of at least 130,000 unidentified French and German soldiers who died in the Battle of Verdun. 'Le Flambeau de la Paix,' *L'Humanité*, 10 Septembre 1937; 'La Flambeau de Verdun au Pavillon de la Paix,' *L'Homme Libre*, 10 Septembre 1937, ANF F^{12} 12143 (Paix, Pavillon de la).
23 'Visit the Peace Pavilion', RUP 137, IISH.
24 'International Peace Campaign: The Message of the Peace Pavilion', RUP 137, IISH.
25 'Suggestions for interior arrangement of the Peace Pavilion', RUP 137, IISH.
26 No congress chamber is mentioned or depicted within the many souvenir postcards and brochures produced to promote the Peace Pavilion nor is it mentioned within related press coverage on file at the Archives Nationales de France, ANF F^{12} 12143. 'Cher... Voici la grande salle', RUP 137, IISH.
27 Evgeny Dobrenko, 'The Epic Retreat: Political Culture and Cultural Policy in 1930s Stalinist Russia', in *Red Cavalry: Creation and Power in Soviet Russia between 1917 and 1945*, ed. Rosa Ferré (Madrid: Casa Encendida, 2011), 372; Andrew Ellis, *Socialist Realisms: Soviet Painting 1920–1970* (Milano: Skira, 2012), 37.
28 'La Jeunesse', *Le Pavillon de la Paix* (Paris: Editions du RUP, 1937), RUP 140, IISH; Agnès Humbert, 'Expo 1937', *La Vie Ouvriere*, 19 Aout 1937, RUP 136, IISH.
29 See, for example, Vassili Svarog, *I.V. Stalin and Members of the Politburo among Children in Gorki Park* ([Painting] 1939), oil on canvas, 200×300cm. Tretjakov Gallery, Moscow.
30 Karl Marx & Friedrich Engels, *The Communist Manifesto* (New Haven: Yale University Press, [1848] 2012), 102.
31 Rachel Mazuy, 'Le Rassemblement Universel pour la Paix (1931-1939): Une organisation de masse?' *Matérieux pour l'histoire de notre temps* 30 (1993): 40–4.
32 Those consulted were listed as Admiral Stanley, Mr Johnson and Mr Holmes and Mr Whalen of the Fair Corporation as well as Norman H. Davis, Shotwell, Haskell, Fosdick, Eichelberger, J. C. Dunn and Mrs H. G. Leach.

33 'Participation of the League of Nations in the New York World's Fair (1939): Annex to the Report of the Supervisory Commission', 27 January, 1938, International Exhibition New York, 1939: Place for Participation of the Secretariat, General and Miscellaneous, League of Nations, (50-31578-26744 [R5764]) United Nations Archives. Hereafter GM, LN (Reg. no.) UNA.
34 'Aide-mémoire' (Conversation Pelt/Field)', 17 August 1967, New York World's Fair: Demolition of the League Pavilion, GM (50-40163-26744 [R5770]) UNA.
35 'Participation du Secretariat a l'Exposition de Paris 1937': Exposition Internationale des Arts et Techniques dans la Vie Moderne, Paris 1937, GM (5B-28829-14775) UNA.
36 See, for example, the New York County Courthouse (completed 1927); the Montsec American Monument (dedicated 1937); and the Washington DC Jefferson Memorial (begun 1939).
37 Correspondence John H. Hall to Adrian Pelt, 20 April 1939, New York World Fair, 1939: Installation of Room I, GM (50/36746/26744 [R5770]) UNA.
38 Pitman B. Potter, 'Note on the Distinction between Political and Technical Questions', *Political Science Quarterly* 50 (1935): 264–71.
39 Correspondence John B. Whitton to Adrian Pelt, 28 September 1937, Invitation and Acceptance, GM, LN (50-26744-26744 [R5764]) UNA; Report by the Director of the Information Section: Annex 1, 23 December 1937, International Exhibition: Participation of the Secretariat, GM (50-31578-26744 [R5764]) UNA.
40 These included the commissioners of pavilions for Switzerland, Norway, Finland, the Netherlands, Hungary, Canada and the Vatican at the Paris Expo of 1937, as well as 'Government officials, political leaders, officers of several foundations, representatives of peace organisations, officials of the New York Fair Corporation'.; Report by the Director of the Information Section: Annex 1, 23 December 1937; Correspondence Noel H. Field to Joseph Avenol, 25 December 1937, International Exhibition: Participation of the Secretariat, GM (50-31578-26744 [R5764]) UNA.
41 Correspondence Arthur Sweetser to Adrian Pelt, 19 June 1938, International Exhibition: General Correspondence respecting participation, GM, LN (50-31578-26744 [R5764]) UNA.
42 'Catholics in New York: Society, Culture and Politics 1808 to 1946,' *Museum of the City of New York*, https://www.mcny.org/exhibition/catholics-new-york accessed 20 November 2020.
43 Richard G. Powers, *Not Without Honor* (New Haven: Yale University Press, 1998), 51; Patrick J. McNamara, *A Catholic Cold War: Edmund A. Walsh, S.J., and the Politics of American Anticommunism* (New York: Fordham University Press, 2005); 'Clare Boothe Luce dies at 84', *New York Times*, 10 October 1987.
44 'Building World Order – Glimpses of History', Pavillon de la SDN Salle No.1, Cab4, dra4, LN, UNA; 'III. League of Nations Pavilion at the New York World's Fair', *Monthly Summary of the League of Nations*, 19, 3, March 1939, 113–24.
45 'Suggestions for Interior', RUP 137, IISH.
46 'Salle II: Bas-relief d'Honoré (sur bois)', Cab4, dra4, LN, UNA; 'League of Nations Pavilion' [Leaflet], New York World's Fair: Publicity for the League Exhibit, GM, LN, (50-35195-26744 [R5764]) UNA.
47 Sonya de Latt & Valérie Gorin, 'Iconographies of Humanitarian Aid in Africa', in *Learning from the Past to Shape the Future: Lessons from the History of Humanitarian Action in Africa*, eds. Christina Bennett, Matthew Foley & Hanna B. Krebs (London: Humanitarian Policy Group, ODI, October 2016), 15– 29; Davide Rodogno & Thomas

David, 'All the World Loves a Picture: The World Health Organisation's Visual Politics, 1948-1973', in *Humanitarian Photography: A History*, eds. Davide Rodogno & Heide Fehrenbach (Cambridge: Cambridge University Press, 2015), 223–48; Michael Barnett (ed.), *Sacred Aid: Faith and Humanitarianism* (Oxford: Oxford University Press, 2012).
48 Reviers was the author of *Paysans de l'Eau* (1932) showcasing an extraordinary collection of photographs he had taken while on a mission in China.
49 *Guide du Pavillon Pontifical à l'Exposition 1937* (Paris: éd. De l'Art sacré, 1937); Bibliothèque Nationale de France (hereafter BNF): FRBNF40364716: https://catalogue.bnf.fr/ark:/12148/cb40364716h.
50 'Appointment of Technical Adviser' [Memo] 16 March 1938, New York World's Fair: Services of Rev. Père de Reviers de Mauny as Expert, GM, LN (50-33181-26744 [R5764]) UNA.
51 'III. League of Nations Pavilion', *Monthly Summary*, 124; NYWF Press Department, Release 668, UNA; Room Six was designed by H. Le Roy who also designed the Vatican pavilion's Crypt for the 1937 Exposition: 'League of Nations Pavilion' [Leaflet], UNA; *Guide du Pavillon Pontifical*, 29, BNF.
52 'III. League of Nations Pavilion', *Monthly Summary*, 124.
53 Correspondence Adrian Pelt to John Bieler, 7 July 1939, International Exhibition: Participation of the Secretariat – Finances, GM, LN (50-32763-26744 [R5764]) UNA.
54 Père de Reviers de Mauny, 'Au Visiteur du Pavillon Pontifical', *Guide du Pavillon Pontifical*, 5, BNF.
55 'III. League of Nations Pavilion', *Monthly Summary*, 124.
56 'Salle VI 'La Guerre' Fresque de M. Untersteller' [Photograph] Salle VI, Cab4, dra4, LN, UNA.
57 See James J. Fortuna, 'Fascism, National Socialism, and the 1939 New York World's Fair', *Fascism* 8, no. 2 (2019): 179–218.
58 'Travel with I.P.C.', RUP 137, IISH.
59 New York World's Fair Press Department, News Release: 296, International Exhibition, GM, LN, (50-31578-26744 [R5764]) UNA.
60 David Allen, 'Internationalist Exhibitionism: The League of Nations at the New York World's Fair, 1939-1940', in *International Organizations and the Media in the Nineteenth and Twentieth Centuries: Exorbitant Expectations*, eds. Jonas Brendebach, Martin Herzor & Heidi J.S. Tworek (London & New York: Routledge, 2018), 91–116.
61 Allen, 'Internationalist Exhibitionism', 94–5.
62 Madeleine Herren, 'Fascist Internationalism', in Sluga & Clavin, *Internationalisms*, 191–212; Kargon et al., *World's Fairs*, 83–107; Rika Devos, Alexander Ortenberg & Vladimir Paperny, 'Introduction: Messages of Peace and Images of War', in Devos et al., *Architecture of Great Expositions*, 1–22.
63 Marco Moraes, 'Competing Internationalisms at the League of Nations Secretariat, 1933-1940', in *The League of Nations – Present Perspectives*, eds. Karen Gram-Skjoldager & Haakon A. Ikonomou (Aarhus: Aarhus University Press, 2019); James Barros, *Betrayal from Within – Joseph Avenol, Secretary General of the League of Nations, 1933-1940* (New Haven, CT: Yale University Press, 1969). Also see Elisabetta Tollardo, *Fascist Italy and the League of Nations, 1922–1935* (London: Palgrave Macmillan, 2016).
64 Susan Pedersen, *The Guardians: The League of Nations and the Crisis of Empire* (Oxford: Oxford University Press, 2015).

65 United States Department of State, *Papers Relating to the Foreign Relations of the United States, 1918, Supplement 1, The World War*, I (Washington DC: US Government Printing Office, 1930), 405–13.
66 Erez Manela, *The Wilsonian Moment: Self-Determination and the International Origins of Anticolonial Nationalism* (Oxford: Oxford University Press, 2007), xii; Miguel Bandeira Jerónimo, 'A League of Empires: Imperial Political Imagination and Interwar Internationalisms', in *Internationalism, Imperialism and the Formation of the Contemporary World: The Pasts of the Present*, eds. Miguel Bandeira Jerónimo & José Pedro Monteiro (Basingstoke: Palgrave Macmillan, 2017), 87–126, 107.
67 Pedersen, *Guardians*, 3–4.
68 Pedersen, *Guardians*, 2–3.
69 Artist's impression of League Pavilion, New York World's Fair Press Department, News Release 668, International Exhibition, GM, LN (50-32763-26744 [R5764]) UNA.
70 Though the PMC spent much time debating what was meant by these clauses: Pedersen, *Guardians*, 233.
71 'Mandates – Slavery' [photograph: credit Jannelise Rosse] Cab4, dra4, LN, UNA.
72 On the expansion of forced labour in Rwanda, see Pedersen, *Guardians*, 4, 233–60.
73 Pedersen, *Guardians*, 12.
74 See Raphael Dalleo, *American Imperialism's Undead: The Occupation of Haiti and the Rise of Caribbean Anticolonialism* (Charlottesville, VA: University of Virginia Press, 2016); Brenda Gayle Plummer, 'The Afro-American Response to the Occupation of Haiti, 1915-1934', *Phylon* 43, no. 2 (1982): 125–43.

Re-situating Bretton Woods

Site and venue in relation to the United Nations Monetary and Financial Conference, June 1944

Giles Scott-Smith

I take it everybody is in a good humor. It is a nice sunny day. We will have some fun as well as some work.[1]

'Bretton Woods' has long been a metonym for the international financial order following the Second World War. The United States – and the US$ – became the fulcrum for currency values and transactions, and the International Monetary Fund (IMF) and International Bank for Reconstruction and Development (IBRD) oversaw currency stability and global modernization respectively. The 'end of Bretton Woods' is therefore often evoked as the moment when President Nixon removed the fixed value of $35 to one ounce of gold in 1971. This association of 'Bretton Woods' with the apparatus of global financial governance has overshadowed the physical reality of Bretton Woods, a resort located in the state of New Hampshire. Removed from context and personal experience, it has been absorbed almost as a normative trope in the literature on economic management. This chapter seeks to reconnect the site with the everyday social realities of a remarkable multinational group of several hundred financial ministers, civil servants, bankers, media and support staff who congregated for three weeks during mid-summer 1944. Recent studies continue to describe it as 'the most important international gathering since the Paris Peace Conference of 1919'.[2] Whereas most histories focused on the horse-trading between the main players, in recent years studies have begun to emphasize the global character of the conference.[3] By reviving attention for the choice, timing, background and organization of the diplomatic site, the emphasis can be placed on the human experience more than the policy outcomes. Such a 'new diplomatic history' approach portrays Bretton Woods as a lived occasion interwoven with the well-chronicled processes of policy-relevant negotiation and deliberation that took place there.

Bretton Woods is usually treated as an example of 'conference diplomacy', which focuses on the historical evolution, negotiation processes and power differentials involved in formal interstate encounters.⁴ This orthodox approach focuses on forms of interstate interaction. Thus Meerts defines this field as 'multiparty diplomatic negotiation' and Kaufmann more distinctly as 'not only public meetings, but also private, often informal meetings held before, during and after international conferences'.⁵ Individual experiences are largely reduced to the techniques applied by diplomats as they seek to secure a deal. In contrast, Neumann conducts a cultural and spatial switch, emphasizing not the high politics of state-led interaction but the designated 'diplomatic site' as 'a place where something happens'. It is necessary to

> foreground the more concrete processes that turn social place into diplomatic site. This move, I think crucially, also brackets the state and diplomacy as being 'up there', for it identifies a certain group of state personnel and turns the scholarly focus not 'upwards', but horizontally, onto what they do every day, on the same level at which we live out our lives, namely the social one.⁶

Neumann thus collapses the vertical power structure that situates the state and its representatives somehow 'above' social life, deflating these processes, protocols and professionals by reconnecting them with the everyday and the mundane:

> Infrastructure must be overhauled; transport, sleeping quarters, restrooms. Food and drink must be at hand. Places for what diplomats call bilaterals (conversations à deux) and for fringe meetings must be available. Comings and goings must be regulated. Security must be in place. Diplomatic practice is imbricated in general social life.⁷

Neumann's 'spatial turn' has been complemented by studies of venues as 'the institutional setting in which a variety of international actors interact'.⁸ The venue becomes the basis for analysing the membership, mandate, output status, rules of procedure/operating procedures and legitimacy of a particular interaction. Choice of venue is also relevant, such that every venue must involve a cost calculation, in terms of both material arrangements and symbolic capital should the negotiations not deliver the intended outcome.

The official record of the United Nations Monetary and Financial Conference, held at the Mount Washington Hotel, Bretton Woods, between 1 and 22 July 1944, is quite detailed. In 1948 the State Department issued a two-volume set of *Proceedings and Documents*. In 2014, to mark the seventieth anniversary of the conference, the Center for Financial Stability posted a host of additional documents, ranging from telephone directories and secretariat notices to the daily news bulletins on the war in Europe and the Pacific. Deemed of secondary importance at the time of compiling the *Proceedings*, they do add an extra layer of quotidian materials to the historical record.⁹ Alongside these official records, several recent publications have sought to turn the arcane details of financial negotiation into a historical drama of epic proportions, focusing on the main protagonists to emphasize the contribution of vision, leadership and power.¹⁰ Of these, it is Conway who has gone furthest 'to portray the experience of the negotiators', arguing that other works 'tend either to ignore the pressure-cooker atmosphere of the

Figure 9.1 The scenic location of the Mount Washington Hotel, surrounded by the White Mountains. Source: Rae Elizabeth / Getty Images.

conference, or to treat it as an incidental detail, rather than something endogenous that might have affected the agreement itself'.[11] Building on the 'social turn' in the historiography, this chapter will first explore the relevance of 'site' and 'venue' in terms of the decision to go to the New Hampshire mountains, followed by an analysis of the social atmosphere during the conference itself.

Timing/site/venue

Volume one of the *Proceedings* included the working papers from the conference sessions, while volume two included supplementary materials such as press releases and lists of media personnel. It begins with a brief introduction to the conference setting itself:

> Bretton Woods, New Hampshire consists solely of the Mount Washington Hotel and its appendages. The hotel community is surrounded by the scenic White Mountain National Forest, which covers nearly one million acres and is dominated by Mount Washington, highest peak of the Presidential Range.[12]

The *Proceedings* continue with insights into the accommodation arrangements. Room charges were meticulously arranged. An $11 a day flat rate was instituted for all guests (including meals), with surcharges added for additional requirements such as *en suite* bathroom (to put this in context, the hotel had instituted a $10 rate at its opening in

1902).¹³ This daily rate was split into 'four six-hour quarters' so that someone arriving or leaving at a certain time would not be charged for the full twenty-four-hour period of the day in question. Swimming pool, tennis courts and 'motion picture theatre' were included, whereas the golf course and riding facilities were extra. An Episcopalian and a Catholic church were close by, but there is no mention of accommodating other religions.¹⁴ Bretton Woods, as van Dormael noted later, 'was only a stop on the railway. . . . The hotel was self-sufficient with its own power plant, dress shops, beauty parlour, bowling alleys, barber shop, and stock ticker-tape'.¹⁵

The choice of Bretton Woods and the Mount Washington Hotel came out of apparently light-hearted, confident exchanges between Franklin Roosevelt and his closest advisors. On 18 May 1944, at a White House meeting between FDR, Treasury Secretary Henry Morgenthau and Treasury's chief negotiator Harry Dexter White, Morgenthau stated that May had been the preferred month, but this was ultimately unattainable due to ongoing deliberations within the British government and the dominions on the proposed IMF. US–UK discussions on post-war economic planning had begun already in 1941 in the context of the Lend Lease agreement, and by 1944 the respective schemes of Morgenthau and White on one hand and John Maynard Keynes on the other were ready to be presented in a wider international setting. Effectively, the future of British economic power was at stake, since the Americans had aimed at opening up the British imperial system to competition already with Lend Lease. As late as 3 May, Morgenthau had secured Soviet acquiescence for an end-of-the-month conference, and everything rested on London's decision. Failure to secure it in time made early July the next option, with a preparatory conference in Atlantic City planned for late June.¹⁶ In contrast to the world-defining issues on the agenda, Morgenthau's diary entry for 18 May records the following exchange:

> The President wanted to know why not have it at the end of June. The Secretary replied that that might interfere with the Republican convention, which opens on the 19th of June. The President smilingly replied that he didn't see why that should interfere. 'We ought to provide our guests with some entertainment', he laughingly said.¹⁷

At this late stage, various possible locations were still being thrown around with equal merit:

> The President asked where the conference is going to be held and the Secretary replied that we do not know yet, that French Lick had been suggested but that it was hot there in the summer. The President said, 'How about Portsmouth, New Hampshire?' The Secretary thought that might be an excellent place.¹⁸

The French Lick Springs Hotel in southern Indiana had been bought by the Democratic mayor of Indianapolis, Tom Taggart, and in the first decades of the twentieth century he turned it into a luxurious spa resort. FDR knew it well, since Taggart, as Democratic Party Chairman and thereafter as 'backroom kingmaker', had a hand in major appointments within the party through the 1920s, turning the hotel into an unofficial political headquarters. In 1931 Roosevelt used a conference of Democratic governors there to round up support for his presidential bid. But temperatures were regularly in the low 30s centigrade in July, causing Morgenthau's hesitation.

The final decision on the starting date and location came on 25 May, following discussions between Morgenthau, White and the State Department's representative Dean Acheson. 'In an excellent humor', the president 'approved wholly of the program presented him', and invitations were sent out at the end of the day.[19] Skidelsky records it as being Morgenthau who proposed 'Maine or New Hampshire' to White, who was feeling the pressure of John Maynard Keynes not to hold the event in Washington DC in mid-summer. Having to cope with the heat and humidity of the US capital, according to the Englishman, 'should surely be a most unfriendly act'.[20] Others have noted that 'In a world before air-conditioning was commonplace, the closest site to Washington with bearable summer weather was New England'.[21] Bearing in mind the conference outcome and the American triumph in blocking Keynes's designs, one might conclude that determining the location was ultimately the Englishman's greatest victory.

Bretton Woods, New Hampshire, was ultimately chosen due to the sizeable accommodation offered by the Mount Washington Hotel. Morgenthau recorded his approval of the 'excellent hotel facilities in a cool, handsome and accessible environment'.[22] The Washington was part of a number of Gilded Age 'grand' hotels that dotted the White Mountains region. Predominantly wooden structures, in 1979 a local historian recorded that of nineteen of the largest (those able to accommodate over 200 guests), ten had been destroyed by fire and another six were either torn down or standing empty, indicating the precariousness of investing in these imposing structures.[23] Completed in 1902, the Mount Washington was the creation of Joseph P. Stickney, a Pennsylvania coal magnate who moved into hotels in the late nineteenth century. Stickney had already obtained the Mount Pleasant Hotel nearby in 1894 and had set about modelling not only the building itself but also the surrounding landscape, creating trails and log cabins in the woods for guests.[24] Stickney's ambitions for the Mount Washington went several steps further, with 250 Italian craftsmen brought in to ensure a refined quality to all of the interior design. It was Stickney himself who effectively christened the location as Bretton Woods by reviving the original name given to the valley.[25] The aim was to be as self-sufficient as possible in terms of power, recreation and health provision. With a capacity of 550 guests (two per room) by 1944 and a white stucco, steel-framed structure giving it an imposing stature, the Mount Washington was immediately a landmark site of real prominence. It is worth reflecting on Neumann's comment that 'An important aspect of diplomacy is to inculcate into the other party some kind of vision of how things could be different . . . [This may] be done by staging an event which is so overwhelming that the guests are simply knocked out. In such cases, sites melt away in an act of sublimation'.[26] Both the French Lick and Bretton Woods sites involved hotels not simply of excessive capacity but also as deliberate demonstrations of wealth, luxury and leisure. This significant detail aligned with the US government's determination to use the conference to cement its status as the world's number one financial power.

Stickney died in 1903 and his wife Caroline ran the business until 1936 when she passed both hotels to her nephew F. Foster Reynolds. Deciding that two hotels were not worth the upkeep, Reynolds had the Mount Pleasant demolished in 1939. The Depression and changing holiday patterns due to car transport were already undermining the turn-of-the-century glamour of the White Mountain resorts, and once the United States entered the war in late 1941, the Mount Washington was effectively mothballed.[27] In 1944 Reynolds sold it to a Boston business group for an estimated $450,000, and it was these new owners who dealt with the upcoming conference.[28] This sale involved a significant twist. Pre-Second World War anti-semitism in New England meant that many of these hotel resorts did not accommodate Jewish guests. The Boston group, which included Jewish businessmen, removed this ban, opening up the hotel to a prosperous Jewish middle-class clientele.[29] It also ensured no embarrassment regarding the July conference. The front man for the group was Boston Jewish businessman David Stoneman, who reportedly received a healthy $300,000 from the US government as payment for the conference block-booking 'shortly after buying the run-down palazzo'. Conway, who has looked the furthest into this issue, calls the selection of the hotel 'something of a mystery', adding that 'both Morgenthau and White had faced the humiliation of being turned away from New England hotels in the past because they were Jewish'. Stoneman's business field was movie theatres, but Conway also describes him as a 'venture capitalist', as if to suggest that a sudden large investment in a vast decrepit New Hampshire hotel in wartime somehow made sense. But a large hotel, located in a temperate zone in mid-summer and open to all faiths, was indeed needed in a hurry. With such high stakes at play, ensuring the right result by calling on open-minded business associates to provide the necessary solution would be a perfectly logical move.[30]

Having said that, politics inevitably also played a role. Roosevelt knew that any deal emerging would need to be maneuvered through Congress, and so support from Republicans was essential. New Hampshire Republican senator Charles Tobey was facing re-election in November 1944, giving him every reason to desire a high-profile event in his home state. Tobey also happened to be the ranking Republican on the Senate Banking and Currency Committee, an influential platform considering the level of resistance among the bankers to the kinds of regulatory controls or state-led financial management expected to be made public at Bretton Woods. It was Acheson, aware of the potential political battles to come, who talked Morgenthau into allowing Tobey on to the US delegation.[31] Tobey duly made full use of the event by giving an address over the radio on 4 July, cementing his association with the conference and effectively tying him to ensure its success. Nevertheless, Morgenthau recorded FDR's advice in his diary: 'I should remember that Senator Tobey was a little cracked.'[32] Roosevelt didn't trust Tobey's political acumen, whatever the advantages of his presence.

The decision of 25 May left little over a month to transform the vacant hotel into a habitable residence. Levy provides a typical account of the ensuing mayhem: 'There were the usual auxiliary conference personnel – shorthand reporters, typists, interpreters, and the like for whom sleeping, dining, plenum, and committee meeting space was also needed ... arrangements had to be made to have [the hotel] reopened, temporary hotel staff hired, the quarters made ready for guests, food and beverages bought, and timely delivery arranged.'[33] Parts of the hotel were uninhabitable due to weather damage, and without the intervention of the US government, in the form of 150 military personnel and some German prisoners of war, basics such as roofing, plumbing and telephone lines would have been lacking.[34]

Dean Acheson, attending as representative of the State Department, chose a safer option:

> Bretton Woods had been chosen both for the beneficent climate of the White Mountains and the availability there of a summer hotel of adequate size and condition. However, having been closed for three years, it presented problems of staffing and operation in wartime that had not been fully considered. Having at least recognized them, I did not stay in the hotel myself but in a comfortable inn at nearby Crawford Notch.[35]

Crawford Notch was actually four miles away, and transportation was not available according to the twenty-four-hour conference cycle. As a result, Acheson recorded to his son, 'when we got through work about two o'clock in the morning we couldn't get home and to bed. This led to excessive alcoholism.'[36] Acheson's aside is confirmed by a 4 July memo from the conference secretariat which stated that 'The last bus to the Crawford House leaves at 1.30am', after which the 'Military Barracks' would need to be called for any 'emergency'. The memo apologetically ended by emphasizing that 'transportation cannot be supplied each individual at all hours . . . under present wartime conditions'.[37] Lunch and dinner were meant to be taken by Crawford residents at their own hotel, but the awkwardness of constantly needing to be on the move led the secretariat to arrange for lunches at the Mount Washington for those who requested it. This was presented as 'a very special concession' and 'generous in view of the difficulties under which the hotel managers are operating'.[38] Traces of 'conference memory' can be found from those who were working at the hotel at that time.[39]

Social atmosphere

The overriding atmosphere portrayed in the official statements on Bretton Woods is one of harmony. There was clearly a coordinated effort to present the proceedings as an almost perfect merger of national and common interest. Volume I of the *Proceedings* includes the following in its preface:

> The Bretton Woods Conference worked in a spirit of complete cooperation and harmony. All the nations represented at Bretton Woods were interested in finding the best means for cooperation in dealing with international monetary and financial problems. Every country realized that the effectiveness of its own economic policies depended to a considerable extent upon removing the monetary disorders and obstructions that stifled world trade in the 1930's. At the same time, every country represented at Bretton Woods was concerned with protecting its

own interests. In this atmosphere of enlightened self-interest the United Nations found the basis for their mutual advantage.[40]

The language indicates that great power rivalries and power differentials were not entirely absent, but claims in turn that they gave way to a common desire for economic progress. Diplomacy, as the resolving of conflicting interests, ultimately triumphed. This aura of harmony was emphasized at every official opportunity. FDR had stipulated to Morgenthau that 'The responsibility which you and the other delegates of the American Delegation will undertake is the responsibility for demonstrating to the world that international post-war cooperation is possible'.[41] FDR's welcoming statement on 1 July, read out by Morgenthau, stated that the conference should 'set a pattern for future friendly consultations among nations in their common interest'. The president's closing words on 22 July claimed that the previous three weeks had laid the 'foundation stones for the structure of lasting peace and security'. Morgenthau himself added that 'the only enlightened form of national self-interest lies in international accord'.[42] Keynes did his best to confirm this interpretation, lauding in his closing speech the fact that 'a concourse of 44 nations are actually able to work together at a constructive task in amity and unbroken concord'.[43] Such an aura obviously elided the fact that two rival plans were being presented, those of the United States and Britain, on the post-war financial architecture. Instead the United States was positioning itself as the benevolent hegemon, both calling international agreement into life and ensuring that those agreements fit its desired outcomes.

Roosevelt left the conference entirely in the hands of Morgenthau, deciding not to appear and only communicating via his Treasury Secretary. He left Washington for his residence at Hyde Park on the Hudson river in upstate New York already on Friday 30 June, only returning to the White House on 5 July. Having been briefed on the latest developments by Morgenthau on the morning of 6 July, Roosevelt received a string of ambassadors and a state visit from General de Gaulle before departing once again on 13 July for a five-week 'military inspection trip', departing San Diego for Hawai'i and the Aleutian Islands, covering 13,900 miles under a news blackout to hide his location.[44] FDR had requested to be kept up to date on developments, but his schedule was in no way adapted to accommodate the Bretton Woods event. His next full engagement would be to receive the delegates to the Dumbarton Oaks conference on United Nations Organization on Wednesday 23 August.

Morgenthau went out of his way to ensure this harmonious atmosphere was communicated to the press corps at the conference. Opening his first hotel press conference at 10.15 am on 1 July, Morgenthau called on the journalists 'to help make this Conference a success in the eyes of the world, and what is more important, in the eyes of our enemies'. The secretary also praised his special assistant, Michael J. McDermott: 'considering the circumstances, that since we really only had one or two hotels to pick from in the entire East, the State Department has done very well'. Extra efforts were made to ensure that communication lines were up and running in time. Whether by accident or design, the wire service, bar and bowling alley were all within 'a hundred feet' of each other, causing much merriment among the press.[45]

Figure 9.2 John Maynard Keynes and Henry Morgenthau confer on the hotel veranda following the opening of the conference, 1 July 1944. Source: Alfred Eisenstaedt / The LIFE Picture Collection / Getty Images.

Just as FDR left it to Morgenthau, so too did Morgenthau leave the daily management of the conference to his trusted lieutenants, Dexter White and Edward Bernstein, with McDermott ensuring the infrastructure and administration held up. White, without consulting other delegations, applied an open-all-areas approach to press scrutiny in a bold move to ensure media acquiescence. Since Roosevelt had previously maintained very cautious relations with the press regarding the developing plans for the United Nations and the post-war world for fear of triggering resistance in the Senate, White's gambit was an evident expression of confidence in the outcome.[46] Every effort was therefore made to integrate the press corps into the daily life of the hotel. A barrage of news bulletins provided by the Office of War Information covering progress on the European and Pacific fronts were provided on a daily basis, many of which have been preserved on the Center for Financial Stability's website. Most of the press corps were lodged at the Twin Mountain Hotel six miles away, which meant many nights involved journalists taking any available space to catch some sleep at the Mount Washington.[47]

Morgenthau would make one further appearance at the press conference, on 8 July, when he complimented everyone 'on the very excellent way they have been handling this Conference'. His first post-conference assessment on 27 July was also geared to maintaining the positive atmosphere:

> Q: Mr Secretary, has any time been set for the first meeting of the Executive Council of the Fund?
> A: I am the only man from the Treasury who was at Bretton Woods who is working. The rest are all recovering!
> Q: So is the press!
> Q: Is it true that you slept in the woods, Mr Secretary?
> A: Well, I slept in the Hotel, which was in the woods.
> Q: We got reports that you went out and had an outing in the woods with Mr Fred Smith [M. Frederik Smith, Treasury Department] one evening, just to try roughing it.
> A: No.
> Q: Did you get your socks?
> A: Did we get the socks!
> Mrs Klotz [Henrietta Stein Klotz, Assistant to the Secretary]: Which socks?
> A: I think there is a story that other people slept in the woods, but I didn't – if anybody wants that for background! [Laughter]
> Q: Mr Secretary, seriously . . .
> A: I was serious![48]

Morgenthau's *bonhomie* was needed, because FDR had instructed him to hold off on presenting any proposals from the conference until after the November elections.[49] He was still stone-walling an eager press pack a month later.[50]

Every effort was made to enable the delegates to enjoy the surroundings in between the relentless committee meeting schedules. An agenda for Wednesday 12 July records that meetings began at 9.30 am, but 'working breakfasts' were already active two hours before that. The final formal session began at 8.30 pm. Yet in among this there was still time for a tennis tournament, 'the Monetary Conference doubles', with 'Trophies awarded to winners'. Delegates therefore had to check in with the secretariat and the sports shop to ensure a complete view of the upcoming day's itinerary.[51] The menu of the closing dinner on Saturday 22 July has been preserved: Fruit Supreme was followed by Potage Lisette and a main course of Half Roast Chicken with potatoes and peas, the meal closing with Meringue Glace and Demi Tasse.[52] While not obviously celebratory in style, it was also far from frugal for those delegates, such as from Britain, who had withstood wartime rationing.

But behind the public expressions of harmony lay a reality of relentless schedule, fatigue and exhaustion. Conway sums this up well: 'it was *extraordinarily* hard work. Most of the delegates at Bretton Woods were perfectly used to long, gruelling days . . . even by their standards, the work at the conference was exhausting, difficult, and emotionally-draining'.[53] Post-dinner recording, drafting and negotiating continued long into the night. Bretton Woods has been typecast as one of the most remarkably successful multilateral conferences, yet it is worth remembering how, underneath the patina of harmony for the outside world, chaos reigned. Emanuel Goldenweiser, director of research and statistics for the Federal Reserve's Board of Governors, reminds us in a brief memoir how it took place 'up in the White Mountains in a hotel that had been closed for two years'.[54] Morton Blum, drawing on Morgenthau's diary, noted how 'The physical environment at Bretton Woods contrasted vividly with the conditions of poverty and war. The hills and woods of New Hampshire's vacation-land invited delegates to leisure their duties precluded'.[55] B. K. Madan of the Indian delegation recalled later that the event was 'one crowded moment of history', where the delegates 'had all the amenities for relaxation and recreation except the leisure to use them!' Nevertheless, he maintained the mythologized image of diplomatic harmony by claiming 'the total setting had at least something of the air of a papal election'.[56]

Language was an additional obstacle. Delegates from forty-four nations had to overcome linguistic barriers in order to communicate, let alone agree on the fine details of legal text and financial management. Needless to say, this placed the advantage with the native speakers. Some resisted, notably the French, who, despite the delegation not representing a recognized government and France still a battleground, presented themselves as *cultural* equals by speaking only in their own language.[57] However, the delegation's leader, Pierre Mendes-France, did break ranks in order to vent objections at the financial quota assigned to France, which at $450 million was placed fifth behind the United States, Britain, the Soviet Union and China. Junior Treasury official Raymond Mikesell, the source of the arcane, politically motivated formula that produced these rankings, had to withstand a tirade from Mendes-France when the quotas became known. Morgenthau tried to explain, 'whereupon Mendes-France went into a rage, speaking unintelligibly, half in English, half in French'. The secretary calmed his French colleague with some well-meaning obfuscations, but Mikesell, a backroom analyst not keen on an international dispute, 'continued to shake for much of the rest of the day'.[58] If we take Goldenweiser's remark to be true, that Mendes-France 'insisted on speaking in his own language despite knowing English very well', it is clear that the Frenchman was so upset that he was caught between his sense of national pride and his need to express comprehensible indignation.

The Russians were at the other end of the scale, wanting to cooperate but lacking the linguistic skills. Goldenweiser recorded memorable observations on the cultural mix at play:

> The Russians didn't speak English; neither did their interpreters. . . . I could not help feeling that they were struggling between the firing squad on the one hand and the English language on the other. . . . They were really seriously handicapped by language. . . . The Hindus . . . spoke Oxford English with a sort of oriental touch, and were very emphatic and passionate in their pleas. . . . There was a large collection of assorted South Americans, who for the most part spoke something approximating English.[59]

Mikesell, thirty years younger than Goldenweiser, recounted the interaction somewhat differently:

Socially, the Soviets were quite friendly, and I recall being recruited by White on two occasions for a Treasury Department volleyball game with the Russians – who soundly defeated us. They also entered into the spirit of Commission IV, the Bretton Woods hotel nightclub, where we all tried to sing each other's songs.[60]

The Russians clearly had a great time, running the most alcohol-drenched cocktail parties with everyone invited, in contrast to the more 'members-only' approach of the clubby Americans or British.[61] Schild adds the not inconsequential detail that the Soviet Union had exited international financial negotiations after 1917, meaning they suddenly had to match the need for official revolutionary rhetoric with compromises on capitalist regulations.[62] Everything going via a translator, and the need to clear everything with Moscow, gave these negotiations a built-in delay. But it would be wrong to assume the Soviet delegation was therefore handicapped in any way. 'No news from Moscow' may have been a form of savvy diplomatic brinkmanship.[63] Harmony was severely tested in the final days as the Soviet delegation looked to force a favourable outcome on their quota to the future IMF. Yet the American determination to keep the Russians party to the agreements generated a remarkable amount of patience. Morgenthau, closing the final US delegation meeting on 22 July, commented drily that 'The Russian Delegation is on the golf tee, wherever that is, waiting for us'.[64]

Needless to say, Bretton Woods was an overwhelmingly male-dominated affair – if one reduces the occasion to the official photos of the male-dominated delegations. Some wives of delegates were present, and the small army of secretaries and stenographers, overwhelmingly female, was vital for the conference to achieve its goals. Economics professor Mabel Newcomer, the only woman delegate among the Western nations, had to deal with a startled *New York Times* reporter asking 'How . . . does a woman ever get to be an economics professor and qualify as an expert on international finance?'.[65] Conway reminds us that 'cheap sexism of the 1940s variety was rife', something that free-flowing alcohol did not lessen. The Soviet delegation also viewed its female members as 'strategic devices'.[66] Canadian Louis Rasminsky later recalled being approached by a 'good-looking blonde', sent by delegation leader Mikhail Stepanov, to discuss gold deposits.[67]

The dominance of English ensured an inevitable 'Anglosphere' atmosphere at Bretton Woods, and this was further enhanced by the networks of affinity generated by educational background. It is no coincidence that Antonio Espinoza de los Monteros, the Mexican in charge of Committee III, was a Harvard graduate and fully conversant with American ways. The ebullient Hsiang-Hsi Kung, leader of the Chinese delegation, was a graduate of Yale, which undoubtedly assisted in the US effort to talk up the importance of China in global economic management (Kung's delegation also included graduates from Columbia, McGill and Ohio State). Alma mater diplomacy cropped up most visibly in relations between Britain and India. The Indian delegation, backed up by Egypt and some of the Latin Americans, used the conference to press the issue of Britain's sizeable debt to India that had been built up during the war. With sterling being unconvertible, India, fast on its way to independence, was unable to access this resource for its own purposes. Lionel Robbins, faced with efforts to push this highly contentious item onto the agenda, was able to calm things down through a mutual connection with an Indian delegate, Ardeshir Shroff: 'Shroff and I converged as one old LSE [London School of Economics] to another', and according to Robbins, the issue was duly postponed for another day.[68] It is worth recalling that all of the senior figures of the Indian delegation were Oxford, Cambridge or LSE graduates.

In terms of exuding Anglosphere, Keynes was the unquestioned master of ceremonies. With his rather eccentric Russian wife Lydia bringing colourful dress, public bathing sessions, ballet practice and occasional interpreting skills with her, Keynes book-ended the conference with two demonstrations of esprit-de-corps erudition, having also provided the greatest scare of the three weeks with a mild heart attack on 19 June. The first was a private affair, as Keynes held a celebration of the 500th anniversary of the concordat between King's College, Cambridge, and New College, Oxford, on the evening of arrival at the Mount Washington, gathering together some old-school ties for an energetic soiree. The last was his more sober appearance at the closing banquet on Saturday 22 July, where he delivered a gracious speech that confirmed how his presence 'had elevated the gathering to something beyond a major political event'. Historical accounts compete with rival claims as to who kicked off 'For He's a Jolly Good Fellow' as he departed the room, in the wake, appropriately, of the Star-Spangled Banner.[69]

But prejudices and stereotypes do seep out from under the harmonious blanket that was placed over Bretton Woods, mainly through memoirs and unpublished papers. Goldenweiser, writing five months after the conference, could not hold back his judgement that 'The French were a rather pathetic group, because the French inevitably at this time are suffering from a very bad case of inferiority complex'.[70] Even Morgenthau occasionally stooped to stereotypical tactics in currying favourable relations with the American press. Discussing the efforts of a 'silver lobby' pushing for the metal to provide the basis of currency stability in place of gold, the following press conference exchange took place prior to the event:

> Q: Mr. Secretary, can you tell us anything about your conversations with the Mexicans?
> A: No, they came in here to make a courtesy call but Mr Suarez [Eduardo Suarez, head of Mexican delegation] is an old friend of mine. We have done lots of business together.
> Q: Did they indicate they would press claims for silver at the Bretton Woods Conference?
> A: You better ask him.
> Q: Suarez?
> A: Yes, you better ask him.
> Q: How powerful is that silver lobby?
> A: Off the record?
> Q: Off the record.
> A [Goes off the record]: I mean, they have men working here. Are these all press people here?

Q: Yes, sir.
A: I don't know how much fuss they are going to make. Off the record Suarez came in and he said, 'I want just one leetl thing'. [Laughter][71]

Conclusion

'Bretton Woods', reflected Mikesell fifty years later, 'was a drafting meeting.... The committees and commissions at Bretton Woods presented a façade of democratic procedure, but the outcome had been largely predetermined by the U.S. and U.K. delegations'.[72] Yet this 'mere' drafting involved thrashing out, clause by clause, the foundations for both the IMF and the IBRD, which took three weeks of intense deliberation. Meant to be completed on 19 June, the hotel management was overruled and the next batch of guests postponed by five days to ensure an outcome. As a conference that had to succeed, Bretton Woods was far more fragile than the standard interpretations have led us to believe. Interpreting Bretton Woods as an 'evented site', this chapter points to the arbitrariness of the chosen location and the intensity of the occasion. In this way, 'Bretton Woods' as symbol of economic stability is replaced by Bretton Woods, a social event riven by contrasts. The apparently laconic search for an appropriate site was determined more by weather patterns than politics. The luxury hotel that had to be propelled out of mothballs in record time. The American desire to entrench their burgeoning hegemony against the wish to secure that hegemony through consensus. The calculated manipulation of the agenda by Dexter White, balanced by the efforts to maintain an image of democratic openness. The acknowledgement of all parties – including the Soviets – of American intentions, matched by the determined negotiating that actually took place. The often good-natured, sometimes fractious, social interactions that took place as the delegations established themselves in the new 'pecking order' of international finance.[73] The contrasting meanings of 'enlightened self-interest' expressed in the official record. One can add the later revelations of Dexter White being a Soviet informant at the same time as he vehemently defended American national interests.[74] All of these factors augment, if not complicate, the flattened-out history of Bretton Woods as purely a set of well-known agreements. By emphasizing the social environment of the 'diplomatic site', the importance of chance and the ever-present vulnerability held within all diplomatic encounters becomes evident.

Notes

1 Secretary Morgenthau's Press Conference, 1 July 1944, 10.15 am, Bretton Woods, NH, Press Conferences, 1 July 1944–15 March 1945, Henry Morgenthau Papers, Reel 26, Roosevelt Institute for American Studies (hereafter RIAS).
2 Ben Steil, *The Battle of Bretton Woods: John Maynard Keynes, Harry Dexter White, and the Making of a New World Order* (New Haven: Princeton University Press, 2013), 202.

3   Giles Scott-Smith & J. Simon Rofe (eds), *Global Perspectives on the Bretton Woods Conference and the Post-War World Order* (Cham: Springer, 2017); Naomi Lamoreaux & Ian Shapiro (eds), *The Bretton Woods Agreements* (New Haven: Princeton University Press, 2019).
4   A. J. R. Groom, 'Conference Diplomacy', in *The Oxford Handbook of Modern Diplomacy*, eds. Andrew F. Cooper, Jorge Heine & Ramesh Thakur (Oxford: Oxford University Press, 2015), 263–77.
5   Paul Meerts, 'Conference Diplomacy', in *The Sage Handbook of Diplomacy*, ed. Costas M. Constantinou, Pauline Kerr & Paul Sharp (London: Sage, 2016), 499; Johan Kaufmann, *Conference Diplomacy* (The Hague: Martinus Nijhoff, 1988), 2–3.
6   Iver Neumann, 'Sited Diplomacy', in *Diplomatic Cultures and International Politics: Translations, Spaces and Alternatives,* ed. Jason Dittmer & Fiona McConnell (Abingdon: Routledge, 2016), 81–2.
7   Neumann, 'Sited Diplomacy', 82.
8   Katharina P. Coleman, 'Locating Norm Diplomacy: Venue Change in International Norm Negotiations', *European Journal of International Relations* 19, no. 1 (2011): 163–86, 164.
9   See <http://www.centerforfinancialstability.org/brettonwoods_docs.php>.
10 Steil, *Battle*; Elizabeth Borgwardt, *A New Deal for the World: America's Vision for Human Rights* (Cambridge, MA: Harvard University Press, 2005); Ed Conway, *The Summit* (Boston: Little, Brown, 2014); Eric Rauchway, *The Money Makers: How Roosevelt and Keynes Ended the Depression, Defeated Fascism, and Secured a Prosperous Peace* (New York: Basic Books, 2015).
11 Edmund Conway, 'Seeing the Woods for the Trees – Preconceptions and Misconceptions about Bretton Woods', Bretton Woods@70: Regaining Control of the International Monetary System, Oesterreichische Nationalbank (2014), 41. Online: <https://www.oenb.at/en/Publications/Economics/Workshops/2014/Workshop-No.-18.html>.
12 *Proceedings and Documents of United Nations Monetary and Financial Conference, Bretton Woods, New Hampshire, July 1–22, 1944*, Vol. II. Washington DC: Department of State, 1948), 1129.
13 R. Spalding, 'The Grand Hotels, the Glory and the Conflagration', *Outlook: The Magazine of the White Mountains Region of New Hampshire* (1979), 31. Online: <http://www.whitemountainhistory.org/uploads/Hotels_enh.pdf>.
14 *Proceedings*, 1129–30.
15 Armand van Dormael, *Bretton Woods: Birth of a Monetary System* (Basingstoke: Macmillan, 1978), 169.
16 *Foreign Relations of the United States* 1944 Vol. II General: Economic and Social Matters (Washington DC: Government Printing Office, 1967).
17 'Memorandum of a Conference at the White House, May 18 1944, 12.30 pm', Presidential Diaries of Henry Morgenthau, Jr. 1938-1945, Reel 2, Presidential Collections, RIAS.
18 'Memorandum of a Conference at the White House, May 18 1944, 12.30 pm'.
19 J. Morton Blum, *The Morgenthau Diaries: Years of War 1941-1945* (Boston: Houghton Mifflin, 1967), 251. Invitations were sent to all signatories of the Declaration by United Nations and those nations that were assisting with the allied war effort but that had either not signed the Declaration or had not then declared war. This approach was first used with the Hot Springs conference of July 1943. See Harley A. Notter, *Postwar Foreign Policy Preparation 1939-1945* (Washington, DC: Government Printing Office, 1950), 144.

20 Robert Skidelsky, *John Maynard Keynes 1883-1946: Economist, Philosopher, Statesman* (Harmondsworth: Penguin, 2003), 758.
21 Herbert Levy, *Henry Morgenthau Jr: The Remarkable Life of FDR's Secretary of the Treasury* (New York: Skyhorse, 2010), 372.
22 Blum, *Morgenthau Diaries*, 251.
23 Spalding, 'Grand Hotels', 27.
24 'Mount Pleasant House', n.d. Online: <http://whitemountainhistory.org/Mt._Pleasant_House.html>.
25 Conway, *Summit*, 2.
26 Neumann, 'Sited Diplomacy', 83–4.
27 'Mount Washington Hotel', n.d. Online: <http://whitemountainhistory.org/Mount_Washington_Hotel.html>.
28 Bryant F. Tolles, Jr., *The Grand Resort Hotels of the White Mountains: A Vanishing Architectural Legacy* (Boston: David R. Godine, 1998).
29 Joel J. Bedor, *The Mount Washington Hotel & Resort – A Heritage of Optimism*, Address delivered at Bretton Woods, New Hampshire, on 7 September 2002 (New York: Newcomen Society of the United States, 2003).
30 Conway, *Summit*, 8. Steil makes no direct connection between sale and conference, saying only that 'the US government ultimately won Stoneman over by convincing him that the conference was important to humanity and, more important, the hotel's bottom line. Stoneman, misgivings notwithstanding, signed a contract to play host for three weeks', Steil, *Battle*, 11.
31 Dean Acheson, *Present at the Creation: My Years in the State Department* (New York: W.W. Norton, 1969), 82.
32 6 July 1944, Presidential Diaries of Henry Morgenthau, Jr. 1938-1945, Reel 2, RIAS.
33 Levy, *Morgenthau*, 373.
34 Conway, *Summit*, 9.
35 Acheson, *Present*, 82.
36 James Chace, *Acheson: The Secretary of State Who Created the American World* (Cambridge, MA: Harvard University Press, 1998), 97.
37 'The United States Group in Residence at Crawford House', 4 July 1944, Document 67, Unpublished Conference Documents, Center for Financial Stability (hereafter CFS), <http://www.centerforfinancialstability.org/bw/Doc_067.pdf>.
38 'Members of the Conference in Residence at Crawford House', 4 July 1944, Document 68, CFS, <http://www.centerforfinancialstability.org/bw/Doc_068.pdf>.
39 Bob Dunn signed up as a sixteen-year-old bellhop ('figuring the tips would be good'): 'Arrival of all the delegates took place in two days (June 29-30) primarily by trains from Boston, Washington and New York. The lobby, 200 feet long, was loaded with suitcases, and we worked all day and evening getting the delegates and staffs into their assigned rooms. Tips were great for the arrival but then reality set in. I was fortunate to assist the Nationalist Chinese delegation, and they used me for the whole conference. They always tipped for the least service, and I was kept busy running messages back and forth from their office to the various delegate locations each day. . . . The IMF conference was interesting, but for a sixteen year old it would have been better duty to stand around listening to talk about the Red Sox or the Boston Braves. The duty that we had to pull was to stand in the meeting rooms. If any of the delegates needed water or an errand run, they would signal to us. They hardly ever tipped. The economic problems of the world sort of filtered through my dreaming of swimming in the river as I gazed out the window.' See Bob Dunn, 'Reflections on when I Was Wet

Behind the ears . . .', *Rye Reflections* (2005), <http://ryereflections.org/servlet/pluto?state=3030347061676530303757656250616765303032696430303338 3739>

40 *Proceedings*, vi.
41 Treasury Department, 23 June 1944, Press Service No. 42-39, Press Conferences 4 Nov 1943 – 29 June 1944, Henry Morgenthau Papers, Reel 25, RIAS.
42 George Schild, *Bretton Woods and Dumbarton Oaks: American Economic and Political Postwar Planning in the Summer of 1944* (Basingstoke: Macmillan, 1995), 111, 127.
43 Conway, *Summit*, 281.
44 Joseph Lelyveld, *His Final Battle: The Last Months of Franklin Roosevelt* (New York: Alfred A. Knopf, 2016), 168.
45 Secretary Morgenthau's Press Conference, 1 July 1944, 10.15am, Bretton Woods NH, Press Conferences 1 July 1944–15 March 1945, Henry Morgenthau Papers, Reel 26, RIAS.
46 Steil, *Battle*, 202; Townsend Hoopes & Douglas Brinkley, *FDR and the Creation of the UN* (New Haven: Yale University Press, 1997).
47 Conway, *Summit*, 203.
48 Secretary Morgenthau's Press Conference, 27 July 1944, 10.30am, ibid. During his opening press conference on 1 July at the hotel, Morgenthau had expressed a wish for a pair of woollen socks.
49 6 July 1944, Presidential Diaries of Henry Morgenthau, Jr. 1938–1945, Reel 2, RIAS.
50 Secretary Morgenthau's Press Conference, 24 August 1944, 10.30am:

> Q: Any news on the Reconstruction Bank or the Fund?
> A: No, nothing.
> Q: Do you have any idea when it will be brought up in Congress?
> A: No.

Press Conferences 1 July 1944–15 March 1945, Henry Morgenthau Papers, Reel 26, RIAS.

51 'Order of the Day', 12 July 1944, CFS, <http://www.centerforfinancialstability.org/bw/Doc_301.pdf>.
52 'Farewell Dinner', 22 July 1944, CFS <http://www.centerforfinancialstability.org/bw/MenuFarewellDinner.jpg>.
53 Conway, 'Seeing the Woods', 44.
54 'Bretton Woods', 22 November 1944, Box 4, E.A. Goldenweiser Papers, Library of Congress (hereafter EG).
55 Blum, *Morgenthau Diaries*, 257.
56 B. K. Madan, 'Echoes of Bretton Woods', *Finance and Development* 6, no. 2 (June 1969): 30–1. This was a special issue of the IMF-World Bank publication celebrating 25 years since Bretton Woods.
57 Conway, *Summit*, 217–18. The conference took place only a month after the constitution of the Provisional Government of the French Republic (PGFR) by the French Committee of National Liberation in Algiers. Roosevelt, unwilling to grant de Gaulle any official authority, only sanctioned the recognition of the PGFR on 23 October, along with Britain and the Soviet Union. See Eric Monnet, 'French Monetary Policy and the Bretton Woods System: Criticisms, Proposals and Conflicts,' in *Global Perspectives on the Bretton Woods Conference and the Post-War World Order*, ed. G. Scott-Smith & Simon Rofe (New York: Palgrave, 2017), 73–87.
58 Raymond F. Mikesell, 'The Bretton Woods Debates: A Memoir', *Essays in International Finance* No. 192, Princeton, Department of Economics (1994), 37.

59 'Bretton Woods', 22 November 1944, Box 4, EG.
60 Mikesell, 'Bretton Woods Debates', 42.
61 Conway, *Summit*, 251.
62 Schild, *Bretton Woods*, 113.
63 Conway, *Summit*, 232.
64 Steil, *Battle*, 245.
65 Steil, *Battle*, 207.
66 Conway, *Summit*, 252, 256.
67 Bruce Muirhead, *Against the Odds: The Public Life and Times of Louis Rasminsky* (Toronto: University of Toronto Press, 1999), 325.
68 Conway, *Summit*, 219–20.
69 Steil, *Battle*, 246. Skidelsky comments only that 'presumably those from the Anglo-Saxon world' started it, but Bernstein later claimed he requested the orchestra to play it, whereas Chace claims it was Acheson. See Skidelsky, *Keynes*, 767; Black, *Levite*, 57; Chace, *Acheson*, 100.
70 'Bretton Woods', 22 November 1944, Box 4, EG.
71 Secretary Morgenthau's Press and Radio Conference, 29 June 1944, Press Conferences 4 Nov 1943–29 June 1944, Henry Morgenthau Papers, Reel 25, RIAS.
72 Mikesell, 'Bretton Woods Debates', 34.
73 Nicolas Pouliot, *International Pecking Orders: The Politics and Practice of Multilateral Diplomacy* (Stanford, CA: Stanford University Press, 2016).
74 John Earl Haynes, Harvey Klehr & Alexander Vassiliev, *Spies: The Rise and Fall of the KGB in America* (New Haven, CT: Yale University Press, 1999).

10

Countenancing and conferencing Japan at the Institute of Pacific Relations, 1945–54

Daniel Clayton and Hannah Fitzpatrick

Introduction

The myriad international conferences of the middle decades of the twentieth century were fleeting yet remarkable meetings that at once captured, helped to constitute and were compromised by the dynamism and fluidity of a world in and out of war. Our focus here is on the Institute of Pacific Relations (IPR), which existed from 1925 to 1960, and through which a good deal of this dynamism and fluidity was refracted. We use a specific reference point, and witness (namely, Pierre Gourou), as a way of thinking about four of the IPR's international conferences (Hot Springs 1945, Stratford-upon-Avon 1947, Lucknow 1950, Kyoto 1954) spanning the most intense period of change in Asia and the Pacific of the twentieth century, involving the defeat of Japan, the rise of anti-colonial, nationalist and pan-Asian movements, the demise of European empires, the Chinese Communist Revolution and the onset of the Cold War.

Our reference point is Japan. We touch on how, at these four conferences, the IPR sought to countenance Japan – that is, to bring it into focus and deal with it – and at the first two of these meetings to do so in its absence. Japan was one of the original members of the IPR but was expelled in 1931 following its invasion of Manchuria and was not readmitted until 1950.[1] However, the country had a central place in Pacific politics and continued to be discussed at IPR international conferences, which from 1931 and until 1947 took place in Western locations. During the 1940s and 1950s the IPR was deemed a pivotal vehicle in the multinational effort to defeat and then reconstruct Japan. But our concern here is with how, at each of these four conferences, the IPR also struggled to keep Japan in focus for a series of contingent reasons that were in fact constitutive of, rather than incidental to, the way this international organization worked.

Our main witness is the French geographer Pierre Gourou (although others are brought into the frame), who was at the conferences of 1945, 1947 and 1950, and chaired the one at Stratford-upon-Avon. Gourou was a renowned expert on the peasant cultures and landscapes of the Far East, and especially Indochina, where he had worked during the 1920s and 1930s. Residing in Brussels and Paris from 1936, he was acquainted with France's Minister of the Colonies, Marius Moutet, and moved in French foreign policy circles. In 1937 he was recruited to the Guernut Commission, which France's Popular Front Government set up to investigate allegations of exploitation in its colonial empire, and Gourou's 1940 survey *L'utilisation du sol en Indochine*, which was lauded as one of the most detailed and sophisticated regional studies of land use and population of its day, was commissioned by the IPR.[2] Gourou played a leading role in bringing Japan into focus at IPR meetings and presented a major paper on the country's importance to post-war international development at the 1950 conference in Lucknow. But we also trace this arc of IPR international conferencing through him because he found himself in a lateral position to what transpired at the conferences he attended. We are interested in the way he witnessed, and lamented, how Japan was pushed out of the international picture due to competing agendas and exigencies. Yet to fully appreciate how the IPR worked in this off-kilter fashion, through the oscillation of (and sometimes gaps between) plan and eventuality, the ideas and influence of some of its chief architects and administrators (especially Edward Carter, John Condliffe and William Holland) also need to be brought into the frame.

This selective focus on Japan and Gourou, via these other central figures, provides some interesting and instructive glimpses into both the tensions that shaped the IPR conferences during this period and a more general set of difficulties surrounding the way international conferencing was grounded in face-to-face interaction. In both regards we see Erving Goffman's 1956 *The Presentation of Self in Everyday Life* as an important contemporaneous prompt. Goffman explored how individuals interact, converse and cooperate through the intercession of presence and absence – or in what he termed 'front' (face-to-face and individual-to-audience) and 'back' (behind the scenes) 'regions'.[3] He was variously concerned with what individuals bring to situations of interaction (assumptions, identities, memories, prejudices, moral codes and social norms and status); how they present (select, fashion and perform – or in his terms 'front', 'feign', 'forfeit' and 'invent') aspects of themselves in those situations and in the way they address an audience (as on a stage); and how the settings in which interactions take place ('the physical confines of a building or plant') exert an influence over what is or can be said or agreed, and on what is kept behind the curtain or said behind someone's back.[4] Goffman did not discuss international conferences. He had commercial, domestic, industrial and leisure settings in mind. However, as Anthony Giddens highlights, he was fascinated by organized settings of collaborative interaction and 'the massively complex question of what copresence [in such settings] actually is', and at a time of wider and intense interest in how social and international collaboration, dialogue and trust needed to be rebuilt as a means of surmounting and averting the authoritarianism and xenophobia of the interwar decades and the Second World War.[5]

The IPR international conferences were vibrant yet volatile spaces in which the rudiments of Goffman's analysis – the swaying of supposition and statement, ambition and eventuality, propriety and transgression, and of resolution and what Gourou saw as *divertissement*, by which he meant entertainment, distraction and digression – were evident.[6] What Goffman identified as 'role enterprise' through 'specialization', 'whereby many performers come to make brief communal use of very elaborate social settings', is of particular relevance here.[7] The point we develop is that it was difficult for IPR actors to perform in their elaborate setting. The case of the IPR also sheds some interesting light on both the value of and the difficulties in pursuing one of this book's key aims: namely, to get inside international conference venues and recover the textures, architectures, conversations that made them vivacious, if fraught, spaces of knowledge and discussion.

Japan and Gourou point to the intercession of presence and absence, and problem of copresence, in the kaleidoscopic outlook and arrangements of the IPR. They are invoked here synecdochically – as means of tracing broader questions about the IPR conferences without having to provide a full description of its archives, actors and agendas. They also bear witness to the difficulties involved in trying to stage-manage (or here, 'conference') interests, norms and expectations – in the present case surrounding peace, security, development and governance in Asia and the Pacific – in internationalist situations of interaction where individuals and groups aimed but struggled to be non-partisan. Finally, the combination of Japan and Gourou – and we shall get to the connections between them presently – points to the core political and moral question that Goffman, and Hannah Arendt, Theodor Adorno and other thinkers at this time posed: of 'what we owe to each other', and particularly their concern about the everyday provenance and reach of authoritarianism.[8] We shall say something first about the set-up of the IPR before attending to Japan and Gourou at the four conferences.[9]

The IPR: A collaborative space?

First, the IPR was a 'non-state agency in international politics', as Tomoko Akami puts it, that emerged during the interwar golden age of international organizations and aimed to include all nations and areas in the Pacific region, including European colonies, the Soviet Union, and Canada and the United States (which have Pacific coasts).[10] It stemmed from a multinational conference held in Honolulu in 1925 organized by American internationalists who felt frustrated by the neglect of the Pacific at the League of Nations, but also upon the initiative of Hawai'ian leaders who dreamt of both creating 'a confederation of Polynesian nations and generating a grand synthesis in East-West philosophy'.[11]

One of the American internationalists involved was Edward Carter, a Harvard graduate who had worked with the International YMCA in Europe and India and was friends with the wealthy Carnegie and Rockefeller families, whose financial backing and letters in support of the organization proved crucial to its fate.[12] Carter fashioned the IPR as an ambitious educational project and with a distinguished scholarly publication series that yielded more than 200 research volumes. The IPR also published a quarterly journal, *Pacific Affairs*, which was edited for a time by Carter, latterly by his successor (and former IPR research secretary) William Holland and for a stint by the renowned American geographer and sinologist Owen Lattimore, who taught from 1938 to 1963 at Johns Hopkins University in Baltimore and from 1963 to 1970 at the University of Leeds in the UK.

Carter was secretary of the IPR from 1926 to 1933, secretary general from 1933 to 1946 and executive vice-chair from 1946 until 1948, when he quit the organization under a cloud of FBI suspicion about his involvement with Chinese and Soviet interest groups.[13] However, he established the IPR as a proficient international organization with a professional, largely American, bureaucratic staff. The organization had an International Secretariat, initially based in Honolulu before Carter lobbied, in 1933, for its relocation to New York, and an executive Pacific Council which included representatives of autonomous IPR National Councils affiliated with international affairs and foreign policy institutes in the different countries, including the Royal Institute of International Affairs in London (Chatham House), Council on Foreign Relations in New York, *Centre d'études de politique étrangère* in Paris and Nankai Institute in Tianjin.[14] Carter presided over the American Council, and our witness, Gourou, was close friends with the figurehead of the French Council, Roger Lévy, an expert on the geopolitics of the Far East.[15]

These national councils organized their own regional conferences, and it was at the American regional meeting in Cleveland, Ohio, in December 1941 that Carter ran into the conference hall from an adjoining room bearing radio news of the Japanese assault on Pearl Harbour, apparently to the utter disbelief at first of the participants.[16] But the IPR is best known for its international conferences every two to four years, which lasted for ten to fourteen days, and were hosted in lavish hotels and organized on a rotating basis by different IPR member countries. The number and size of national delegations attending the IPR's international conferences varied, from five to twenty and from conference to conference, and comprised a cross-section of experts and officials from academia, business, journalism and government ministries.

The IPR regarded itself as a non-partisan outfit that sought to use its conferences and scholarly and educational programmes to promote mutual understanding and equal relations between Pacific countries. It did not seek to make policy. Australia, Britain, Canada, China, France, Holland, Japan, Korea, the United States and USSR, and after 1945 newly independent nations of Indonesia, Malaysia, India, Pakistan and the Philippines, each had national councils. But international organizations were never level playing fields, and by participating in them as part of national councils individuals also became in Goffman's terms 'team players' whose individual 'positions' and 'presence' were 'forfeited' to collective ends and 'back region' agendas.[17] From 1925 until 1954 the American and British national councils dominated at IPR international conferences, and Japan's expulsion also politicized the organization. Moreover, as the British historian RH Tawney intimated with singular foresight at the 1931 Conference in Shanghai, the IPR's engagement with a region that was being shaped by a series of momentous economic, social and political transformations (from agrarianism to capitalism, dynasticism to communism and colonialism to independence), and that was riven by thoroughgoing tensions between nationalism and internationalism, and authoritarianism and democracy, at once defined and compromised the organization's internationalist ambitions and capabilities.[18]

The IPR international conferences had three basic formats: first, addresses from the national councils; second, the presentation of pre-circulated papers on specialist topics (most of which stemmed from independent research projects supported by the IPR); and third, round-table discussions of issues identified by the International Secretariat and Pacific Council. Many of the pre-submitted papers were presented by leading foreign affairs pundits and regional experts, such as Gourou, Lévy and Tawney.

Goffman argued that 'expressive treacherousness is a basic characteristic of face-to-face interaction' and noted how groups strive to mitigate it both by recruiting 'team-mates who are disciplined and will not perform their parts in a clumsy, gauche, or self-conscious fashion' and by settling on 'a complete agenda' beforehand to avoid 'confusions, lulls . . . and hitches in the proceedings'.[19] Gourou and Lévy regarded each other as 'disciplined', 'erudite' and 'cultured' in their contributions to IPR debates, amid what Gourou recalled as the 'the stormy debates taking place around me'.[20] The IPR's first research secretary (from 1926), John Condliffe (a New Zealand economist), grasped the need for discipline in a more general sense. Condliffe had a significant influence on how the IPR conferences, and also the International Studies Conferences (ISC) of the International Institute of Intellectual Cooperation (IIIC), were set up to generate discussion in an unfettered yet disciplined manner.[21] The need for such an unencumbered yet structured space allowing in-depth discussion was prompted by concern that the League of Nations lacked international vision because it was too preoccupied with day-to-day business and crisis management.

For much of the 1930s Condliffe worked for the League of Nations Secretariat and oversaw the production of the first annual World Economic Surveys. He was also interested in conference organization and presented some of his ideas in a 1930 paper presented to the IIIC entitled 'International collaboration in the study of international relations', a detailed review of how international conferences worked as vehicles of foreign policy formation and how the structure of IPR conferences might be regarded as 'best practice'.[22] As a direct result of Condliffe's report, the remaining annual ISCs were reformulated around two-year themes.

Yet the IPR international conferences were private rather than policy-making affairs, and this had an important impact on how Condliffe's plans and structure worked out. While some of the IPR conference proceedings and excerpts from the pre-circulated papers were subsequently published, the conference deliberations themselves took place behind closed doors, in order to preserve the sanctity of frank exchange. There were stenographers and translators at the round-table sessions, and invited onlookers, but no photographers and no press gallery. The press clamoured for news and felt thwarted by the press releases that came from the conference floor, which were tightly controlled by the International Secretariat, and not least Carter himself, and disguised disputes both before and at the conferences over the agenda and ordering of the sessions and papers. They were also solely in English. Group photographs of delegates taken outside conference venues were the 'public face' of these conferences. The few existing photographs of activities inside the conference venues in IPR archival collections (e.g. Figures 10.1, 10.2 and 10.3) remained private.

It is by turning to private memos, commentaries and reminiscences that more of the 'front region' (as well as 'back region') qualities of this international conference space – the apparel, body language, oratory, elisions, interruptions, shuffling of papers and sometimes walkouts – might be brought (albeit still opaquely and furtively) into view. On the one hand, many of the position statements, motions, posturing, threads of conversation and disputes at the round table and panel sessions were influenced

Figure 10.1 Edward Carter (left) and William Holland (right) in China during the Second World War. Courtesy of University of British Columbia Archives (UBC 95.1/1).

by back-stage politicking, gossiping and schmoozing involving people not formally affiliated to the national councils and conference delegations. On the other hand, prominent individuals and personalities sometimes put their own stamp on the conference proceedings and did so in ways that upended back-stage preparations.

Countenancing and conferencing Japan, with Gourou

The IPR international conferences at Hot Springs, Virginia (1945), Stratford-upon-Avon (1947), Lucknow (1950) and Kyoto (1954) point to a series of tensions in the workings of this international organization. The two most important and far-reaching

Figure 10.2 Round-table discussion (future of Japan), IPR International Conference, Homestead Hotel, Hot Springs, Virginia. Courtesy of University of British Columbia Archives, Institute of Pacific Relations fonds, Box 100 – File 100b (2).

Figure 10.3 Pierre Gourou (upper far right) outside the Homestead Hotel, Hot Springs, with conference delegates. Courtesy of University of British Columbia Archives, Institute of Pacific Relations fonds, Box 100 – File 100b (2).

ones were between what the IPR's research secretary, Holland (who succeeded Carter as secretary general in 1948), identified as its different 'private' and 'public' faces, and its 'heterogeneous character' and 'coordinated groups of projects'.[23] Holland and Carter promoted values of political and scholarly independence, and argued that centralized control, particularly over the IPR's research programme, would be 'resisted by scholars' and 'destroy some of the deeper significance' of individual projects.[24] However, they recognized that their international conferences were prone to external political influence, that their central oversight of conference planning was looked upon suspiciously by some and that the 'services of scholars' upon which the IPR relied to buttress its claims to objectivity were 'apt to be in demand by national governments' too and thus were not immune from political pressures and expectations.[25]

Political outlooks and influence were keenly felt at the Hot Springs and Stratford-upon-Avon conferences. And we shall see that Holland's insistence, in reaction to this eventuality, that 'the Lucknow Conference was unofficial', that 'the members attended only in their personal capacities and not as spokesmen for governments or organisations' and that Lucknow was thus the 'high point' of IPR international conferencing for these reasons, was more a wish image than a reality.[26]

Funding of the IPR and its national councils was firmly embedded within a competitive nation-state framework, and myriad papers presented during the organization's history, from Tawney onwards, probed and returned to the question of whether internationalism and nationalism were compatible. It was not simply a case, Jon Davidann suggests, of the American National Council predominating (and with the highest number of delegates usually American and reaching a high point in 1945): US–Japanese relations at the IPR before and after Japan's expulsion were indicative of a wider and disabling 'resistant strain of nationalism' affecting international organizations more generally.[27] The IPR always struggled to live up to its aim of being non-partisan, and non-government 'experts' such as Gourou, working across wider quasi-political reformist networks and assemblages of skilled know-how, were the fragile glue binding non-state agency to nation-state interests. As Carter and Holland knew full well, many of the experts – and particularly academics – who gathered at IPR meetings worked not only through national councils but also as advisors to government.

This tension between non-state agency and nation-state authority shaped how delegates comported themselves at IPR international conferences through a set of what Goffman characterized as 'demands' and 'forfeits': 'When an individual projects a definition of the situation and thereby makes an implicit or explicit claim to be a person of a particular kind', he observed, 'he [sic] automatically exerts a moral demand upon the others, obliging them to value and treat him in the manner that persons of his kind have a right to expect. He also implicitly forgoes all claims to be things he does not appear to be'.[28] But this, in turn, set up a tense situation and prospect, for 'when individuals witness a show that was not meant for them, they may, then, become disillusioned about this show as well as about the show that was meant for them'.[29] This, we think, is what Gourou was driving at when he invoked the 'stormy debates' at IPR conferences. Goffman did not (as far as we know) have the IPR in mind when he wrote these words, but their timbre can be heard in its conference proceedings.

One of the problems in thinking that the IPR was able to stage rationalist deliberation was that different IPR National Councils and conference delegates defined rationality in different ways. For the Japanese, for instance, it meant the rational calculation of national interests opposed to Western imperialism, whereas the Americans saw nationalism as irrational because they thought it culminated in authoritarianism. The IPR also struggled with questions of focus. For some, the Pacific was an object of study and debate, with dedicated teams of regional experts pouring over different aspects of it. For others, and not least Carter and Holland, it was a more relational entity. During the 1930 and 1940s, Carter and Holland undertook grand tours of the IPR's domains (from Moscow to Honolulu – see Figure 10.1) and 'the Pacific' in their minds was a looser and changing mix of Asian and Western influences, and imperial, communist and democratic forces.[30]

Hot Springs 1945

The Hot Springs conference took place a month before the Yalta Conference, where Churchill, Roosevelt and Stalin met to plan the post-war reorganization of Germany and Europe, and seven months before the nuclear bombing of Hiroshima and Nagasaki. This IPR gathering sought to address the defeat and future of Japan, and the desire for what one American delegate, William Johnstone, described as 'a world collective security organisation'.[31] Over 150 delegates from twelve countries and nine national councils attended. That the British and French delegates made the hazardous journey across the Atlantic, dodging German U boats, attests to the importance attached to the meeting; and that they were hosted in the swanky Homestead Hotel, set in 200 acres of scenic Virginia landscape and a favourite of US presidents since the time of Thomas Jefferson, was deemed an exceedingly welcome release from the privations and horrors of war.[32] US undersecretary of state and former ambassador to Japan Joseph Grew opened the proceedings, hosting a cocktail reception at the hotel.[33]

The IPR's research secretary at the time, Horace Belshaw (like Condliffe, from New Zealand), noted that the sparse published proceedings of the event were 'based on the rapporteurs' summaries of these discussions and on addresses and statements made in plenary sessions'.[34] As Yukata Sasaki attests, 'no verbatim records' of the discussions were kept, supposedly because of security concerns.[35] 'The rapporteurs' statements were accepted by the Round Tables (although in some cases after being amended)', Belshaw continued, although 'it should not be taken that every member of a round table approved of every opinion in a report'.[36]

The round table and plenary sessions focused on four topics: the future of Japan; the future of dependent (colonial) territories; economic recovery in the Pacific region; and questions of collective security. Japan came first and was discussed in the absence of any Japanese representation. Going by Belshaw's and Johnstone's reports, it was represented through a dictatorial language of 'needs' and 'musts'.[37] The manner in which Japan would be defeated was still 'unpredictable,' it was divulged, but defeated it would be, and there was apparently 'unanimous agreement' that 'total defeat' needed to be accompanied by 'total disarmament' and hefty 'reparations in kind'. However, further agreement that 'Japan could gain [re]admission to the comity of nations only when a government which showed promise of representing the wishes of the people and a desire to cooperate in the maintenance of peace' pointed to another eventuality: that the large American delegation at Hot Springs saw itself as the natural leader of this agenda and arbiter of conference resolutions.

Gourou reflected on his astonishment at how this American position was evidently assumed rather than up for debate on the conference floor. Indeed, the focus on Japan soon spiralled into something else altogether. In his paper, Gourou addressed the 1944–5 famine in Indochina and pondered the ways and extent to which it had been precipitated or worsened by Japanese occupation.[38] But as he confided, and Holland also noted in his memoirs, the round-table discussions became very boisterous because of the way the American delegation, and particularly its spokesman, William Waymack (a Pulitzer Prize–winning journalist in Roosevelt's inner circle), touted a stridently American vision of a Pacific and world future without colonial empires. Holland observed that there were 'sharp exchanges' over the matter, and Gourou recorded that British, French and Dutch delegates stormed out of the meeting 'visibly upset' about American criticism of their nations' colonial records.[39] Gourou spurned the American 'platitude' that colonialism was 'chiefly responsible for the backwardness of the dominated countries', and while he did not directly draw parallels between the American delegation, uniformed, he remarked, in double-breasted pin-striped suits, and the zealous contingent of German geographers in Nazi regalia he had encountered at the 1938 International Geographical Congress meeting in Amsterdam, he deemed both strident and dictatorial in the way they comported themselves.[40]

Out of the hazy record of the Hot Springs conference, and with the likes of Gourou helping us to fill in some of the blanks, comes an image of a less-than-egalitarian conference space and with its 'front regions' and 'back regions' blurred. Goffman observed:

> the private office of an executive is certainly the front region where his status in the organization is intensively expressed by means of the quality of his office furnishings. And yet it is here that he can take his jacket off, loosen his tie, keep a bottle of liquor handy, and act in a chummy and even boisterous way with fellow executives of his own rank.[41]

Akin to this scenario, Gourou and others felt affronted by the way American delegates 'loosened their ties' among fellow participants in this international office and treated Hot Springs as a backyard for the expression of a decidedly American vision of the post-war world.

Stratford-upon-Avon 1947

A similar thing happened at the Stratford-upon-Avon conference, in September 1947, which was hosted by the British National Council. The conference began at Chatham House in central London, with Lord and Lady Astor providing a welcoming reception at Cliveden, their luxuriant country estate in Buckinghamshire, but was held largely in the quaint Shakespeare Hotel in Stratford-upon-Avon. This time Gourou led the show and did so by taking a leaf out of the Americans' 'internationalist' book. 'The economic reconstruction in the Far East' and question of Japanese reparations were placed centre stage, and Belshaw set the tone with a paper on 'Agricultural reconstruction in Asia'. But the round-table discussions quickly veered off into the escalating imperial crisis and military situation in French Indochina, and principally thanks to Gourou, who delivered a plenary address entitled 'The future of Indochina' in which he endeavoured to impress upon delegates from Western councils the need to back France and Britain in the Far East.[42] Gourou sought to cut through the strong emotions surrounding the status of 'dependent territories' and 'colonial trusteeship' by claiming that Indochina was a 'rational creation of France' and that its loss to communist revolutionaries would bring instability and chaos to the wider Pacific region.[43] He hoped that his appeal to rationality would have some truck among IPR delegates, and Indochina subsequently dominated the round-table discussions and apparently put the Americans on the back foot. At the same time, Lattimore (with the American contingent) bemoaned that the conference was largely bereft of Asian delegates and deplored the fact that the French and Dutch councils had refused to allow Indochinese and Indonesian representatives to attend.[44]

Lucknow 1950

The reconstituted Japanese Institute of Pacific Relations had been petitioning Holland to be readmitted to the IPR since 1948, and its request was met at the organization's Eleventh International Conference in Lucknow in October 1950, 'where the eyes of the world fixed anxiously on that disturbed continent' of Asia, as a Canadian rapporteur, Edgar McInnis, saw things.[45] Japan sent a skeletal entourage of four representatives, to test the waters, its secretary, Matsuhei Matsuo, implied.[46] Carter agitated for the conference to be held in Lucknow because he deemed it neutral territory for Japan's readmission. But as Conrado Benitez of the Philippine IPR pointed out to Holland before the meeting, prospective delegates from Southeast Asian councils still harboured 'disgust' and 'deep resentment' towards Japan.[47] The small Japanese contingent presented their papers on the country's domestic economy, Pacific trade, post-war nationalism and security, quietly and without fuss, it was reported.[48] They also conversed at length with Gourou, who presented a wide-ranging paper entitled 'The economic problems of Monsoon Asia and the example of Japan', in which he queried the global (and to his mind imperial) sway of the 1947 Truman Doctrine and 1948 Marshall Plan, which, by 1950, were deemed templates for Pacific reconstruction.[49] Gourou held Japan's own unique and disciplined fusion of modern and traditional, and industrial and agricultural, ways up as a model for the development of the rest of Monsoon Asia.

Over the following ten days delegates met first, and as before, in discussion groups that focused on pre-selected topics and in round tables that were organized according to region (South Asia, Southeast Asia and East Asia). The rapporteurs then produced their reports, which the delegates were asked to approve before carefully chosen headlines from them were released to the press. The second half of the conference was organized differently. The delegates were divided between three sessions, one of which was devoted to political issues and two of which were devoted to social and economic issues. Here discussion took place in two distinct registers. There was the presentation and discussion of a wide variety of specialist research, including Gourou's on Japan and the Far East, which was characteristic of so much of the IPR's work. But there was also a more intractable form of politicking that was driven less by a desire for discussion over problems of reconstruction and development than by a sense of geopolitical opportunism. Debate about the nature and future of communism in Asia became a potent, if unofficial, theme of the conference and was fronted quite forcefully by the American delegation. Similarly, the Kashmir issue (unresolved by Partition) ended up on the agenda, fomenting heated debate between Indian and Pakistani delegates.

In short, despite the insistence by many that the myriad issues surrounding Japan were central to the conference's agenda, the concerns of the United States, and new tensions between the Indian and Pakistani delegations (with eleven and six delegates respectively), prevailed. East Asian issues got a very limited airing at Lucknow. The conference was hosted by the Indian Council of World Affairs and came not long after the momentous 1947 Asian Relations Conference, which had been modelled on the IPR format.[50] Lucknow was the second largest IPR gathering in its history after Hot Springs, but a smaller number of delegates from Western IPR councils attended (Gourou was in a party of just five from France). However, with the Korean War not long underway the American Council sent sixteen delegates and was keen to learn about the 'position' India would adopt with respect to 'Soviet expansion', 'Chinese communism' and 'Western imperialism'.[51]

Lucknow is of special interest, too, because it was the first IPR meeting involving delegations from a number of newly independent nations (not just India and Pakistan but also Burma, Ceylon, Indonesia and the Philippines) as well as ones still within the imperial fold (South Vietnam and Malaya), although Communist China declined to send a delegation and its absence was keenly felt, as its post-revolutionary position on Asian and Pacific affairs was of interest to India and Pakistan, and the United States.

Attention once more switched away from Japan and East Asia – this time towards South Asia. The British commentator C. J. Chancellor observed that while 'Under the management of Mr Holland and his efficient staff the Lucknow Conference, like its predecessors, ran smoothly and according to a pre-arranged programme', the host nation had an overwhelming bearing on the event. '[A]ll discussions', about East Asia, and especially China and Japan, 'had an air of unreality about them' and while 'There is no party line and no unanimity rule' pertaining to the round-table discussions, they were quickly and vociferously skewed towards India.[52] Indian prime minister Jawaharlal Nehru opened the event with a stirring speech about India's unique place in world affairs that reverberated through the conference exchanges. One of the Pakistani delegates, K. Sarwar Hasan (a law professor and founder of the Pakistan Institute of International Affairs), concurred with Chancellor, albeit from his own partisan perspective, noting that 'For a scientific conference, the discussions were, in some respects, unreal'.[53] The Soviet Union had not sent a delegation either, and Hasan characterized the two Vietnamese delegates as 'fanatically pro-French and anti-Viet Minh'.[54] In a more ecumenical spirit, McInnis thought that while 'It was probably inevitable, given the setting of the Conference, and size of the host delegation, that consideration of Asian problems should lead. . . . The Indian Council, whose arrangements throughout the Conference deserve the most sincere admiration, acted in complete accord with the spirit of the I.P.R. in seeking delegates from different groups with different points of view.'[55]

Commentators, including Holland, found the accommodation, in the city's redoubtable (if by 1950 slightly down at heel) Carlton Hotel (built in 1890 for British colonial officialdom and recently fitted with electric ceiling fans), and the general atmosphere of the conference, to be 'highly satisfactory'.[56] The sessions themselves were held at the University of Lucknow, where students assisted in the day-to-day running of events and the hosting of delegates. The usual conference format was followed, with the sessions taking place away from the eyes and ears of the press and rapporteurs briefing the media. Until Lucknow, this process had worked reasonably well. However, in the context of the post-partition subcontinent, it became a politically charged bone of contention. As Holland himself later acknowledged, feeling short-changed by the tight-lipped IPR rapporteurs, parts of the Indian press began to feed off the Soviet propaganda machine in imagining that the conference was geared foremost to opening India to American capital and trade.[57]

The ostensible theme of the Lucknow conference was 'Nationalism in the Far East and Its International Consequences', but it was belied by its ostensibly South Asian focus, and this was exemplified by Nehru.[58] Arguing that the problems arising from nationalist tensions across Asia needed to be solved by Asians themselves, and not by outside interlopers, Nehru's speech brushed against the internationalist grain of the IPR and was seen by some within IPR ranks as a warning. As Hasan noted, 'Sometimes it seemed that the Conference was really only between India and the United States.'[59] Communism was, of course, the issue at hand, and holding forth from a stage adjacent to the conference venue, Nehru observed, 'I am often asked by people coming from abroad: what is your reaction to Communism? Well, the answer is a complicated one. . . . No argument in any country of Asia is going to have weight, if it goes counter to the national spirit of that country – Communism or no Communism.'[60]

Kyoto 1954

Finally, by the time Japan eventually held the spotlight in round-table discussions, at the Kyoto conference of September 1954 (just a few months after France's colonial capitulation at Dien Bien Phu and a year before the Bandung conference), the American National Council was under investigation by Joseph McCarthy and sent a small delegation of just six, and British support for the IPR was waning.[61] Holland confided in his close Australian IPR colleague, William Macmahon Ball, that the sparse American turnout was 'one more reflection of the current genius of the U.S. for isolating itself from the rest of the world'.[62]

The conference was chaired by McInnis, but the agenda was set by the Asian councils, including a re-energized Korean National Council that was eager to reflect on the recent war, and Indonesian and Philippine delegates still keen to highlight and lambast the effects of wartime Japanese occupation. Also high on the agenda was

Gourou's paper from 1950, which, the Japanese hosts opined, had received short shrift at Lucknow.⁶³ Gourou did not attend the conference (he was working for the Belgian government in the Congo) but Asian delegates were keen to return to what he had surveyed – questions of poverty, living standards and overpopulation – and did so with a clearer sense of 'the Far East' as a cultural unit than before, thanks to Gourou's lauded surveys *La terre et l'homme en Extrême-Orient* (1940) and *L'Asie* (1953), which stressed the common geographical and cultural ties between Asian countries.⁶⁴

Michael Anderson suggests that if Asian voices were finally able to come to the fore at Kyoto it had more to do with 'the division among the Western delegates' than it did with the assertion of a new pan-Asian consciousness or an overcoming of differences between the IPR's Chinese, Japanese and Korean councils.⁶⁵ But as correspondence in the IPR's American fonds reveal, this Asian focus did not stop American delegates from politicking behind the scenes through an American diplomat in Kyoto, Gregory Henderson. The Americans sought to get motions on the conference agenda forbidding Communist China and the Soviet Union readmission to the IPR, which the Asian councils favoured in an internationalist spirit of peaceful coexistence. Meanwhile, as Anderson relates, 'the British as well as the Americans [were] more aware of the value of private Asian-West contact facilitated by the IPR; without this connection, Asian elites might very well go their own way and form an all-Asian group'.⁶⁶

Conclusion

To be sure, drivers of the IPR such as Carter, Condliffe and Holland had noble internationalist intentions. But as we have shown, and Glenda Sluga reflects, 'The IPR stood for an internationalism built out of regions', and one that got in the way of the importance the organization placed on 'cultural information and exchange', and 'social experiments in racial equality'.⁶⁷ Similarly, Priscilla Roberts reflects that 'the IPR's checkered experience also suggested that conflicting national interests dividing member states had great potential to undercut attempts to establish broader transnational groupings'.⁶⁸ More specifically, in this chapter we have sought to point to the role that the space in which this internationalism was promulgated – the IPR's lavishly hosted and intricately organized international conferences – played in how this internationalism worked. By most accounts, IPR discussions were open and frank, and with a diverse exchange of views in structured paper presentation sessions and more free-wheeling round-table discussions, which sometimes lasted for days and were kept away from a prying media spotlight. This putatively egalitarian and non-partisan mode of international conferencing was expedited by the conference template fashioned by Condliffe (and subsequently emulated by other international organizations) and by the International Secretariat and National Council apparatus forged by Carter and Holland.

However, there were fissures in this project and set-up, and the many gaps in the IPR conference record preclude us from giving a full assessment of the influence of this conference space on the internationalism espoused by this organization. However, as Goffman helps us to see, the IPR was not able to 'prepare in advance for all possible expressive contingencies'.[69] Such contingencies – which, as Tawney related, were in fact world historical forces compressed into a few decades – along with the sanctity that Carter and Holland cherished for IPR conference delegates, made this space opaque. The IPR's best laid plans were sent off kilter by factors, agendas and eventualities that were both within its control (such as where to host a conference) and beyond it.

Even so, understanding of how and why this mode and moment of internationalism took the forms it did, and went awry, in the space in which it was convened takes on a vibrant hue when tracked from the vantage point of things that the IPR sought yet struggled to spotlight and structure. One of these was Japan, traced here from the perspective of conference participants who had an off-centre (neither central nor completely marginal) stake in this process, in the present case Gourou. When the conference stage-managing of collaboration and dialogue fostered by IPR figureheads such as Carter, Condliffe and Holland is traced via such lateral means and figures, the regional, national and international scales of internationalism that were bolted together at the IPR's transitory international meetings become scales (meaning measures and gauges) of dispersion in efforts to internationalize the Pacific. This dispersion of argument, expression and influence took place around the conference table, issuing from 'expert' papers and rapporteurs summaries and briefings, and stretching across 'front' and 'back' regions of interaction. In vital respects, the collaborative settings – international conferences – in which the IPR operated, and its principled intentions were forged, constituted its internationalism, and as Sean Phillips observes, many subsequent 'semi-official' organizations 'drew influence from the IPR's constitution, research and conference method'.[70] The nature and functioning of such settings – what made them effectual connectors of people and interests, but also what made them vulnerable to more divisive politicking – warrants close investigation.

Notes

1. For this earlier period, see Tomoko Akami, *Internationalizing the Pacific: The United States, Japan and the Institute of Pacific Relations, 1919–1945* (London & New York: Routledge, 2002).
2. Pierre Gourou, *L'utilisation du sol en Indochine française* (New York & Paris: Institute of Pacific Relations; Centre d'études de politique étrangère, 1940). For a fuller reading of Gourou's connections to the IPR, see Gavin Bowd & Daniel Clayton, *Impure and Worldly Geography: Pierre Gourou and Tropicality* (Abingdon: Routledge, 2019), 194–7, 222–40.
3. Erving Goffman, *The Presentation of Self in Everyday Life* (Edinburgh: University of Edinburgh Social Sciences Research Centre, 1956), 6, 82, 112.
4. Goffman, *Presentation of Self*, 66, 112.
5. Anthony Giddens, 'On Rereading *The Presentation of Self*: Some Reflections', *Social Psychology Quarterly* 72, no. 4 (2009): 290–5, 291.
6. Pierre Gourou, 'La géographie comme divertissement? Entretiens de Pierre Gourou avec Jean Malaurie, Paul Pélissier, Gilles Sautter, Yves Lacoste', *Hérodote* 33 (1984): 66–79.
7. Goffman, *Presentation of Self*, 159–60 and passim.

8 This phrasing comes from Peter K. Manning, 'Goffman on Organizations', *Organization Studies* 29 (2008): 677–99, 678. On the spectre of 'the authoritarian personality' and the post-war feeling that it was innate to, rather than just a deformation of, or blip in, modernity, see Theodor Adorno et al., *The Authoritarian Personality*, orig. pub. 1950 (London: Verso, 2019); and Hannah Arendt, 'Authority in the Twentieth Century,' *The Review of Politics* 18 (1956): 403–17. For a more general survey, see Oona Hathaway & Scott Shapiro, *The Internationalists: And Their Plan to Outlaw War* (London: Allen Lane, 2017).
9 There are holdings of IPR records – organized chiefly around conference, correspondence, Pacific (executive) and national council, publication and secretariat (administrative and financial) series – at the University of Hawai'i, Mānoa (Honolulu), Columbia University (New York) and the University of British Columbia (Vancouver).
10 Akami, *Internationalizing the Pacific*, 13. Most work on the IPR focuses either on the pre-war era or on the 1950s demise of organization.
11 Paul F. Hooper, *Elusive Destiny: The Internationalist Movement in Modern Hawaii* (Honolulu: University of Hawai'i Press, 1980), vii. Also see Paul F. Hooper, 'The Institute of Pacific Relations and the Origins of Asian and Pacific Studies', *Pacific Affairs* 61 (1988): 98–121.
12 Lawrence T. Woods, 'Letters in Support of the Institute of Pacific Relations: Defending a Nongovernmental Organization', *Pacific Affairs* 76 (2003): 611–21.
13 Carter and other leading IPR figures were investigated by the US Senate Internal Security Subcommittee, chaired by Patrick McCarran, which fed into Senator Joseph McCarthy's wider investigation of communist subversion and espionage in American society, presaging the organization's demise and eventual closure in 1960. The Senate testimony of Alfred Kohlberg, a powerful American businessman in Washington's so-called China-lobby, played a key role behind the scenes in the arraignment of Carter and Lattimore for supposedly betraying China to the communists. US Senate, 82nd Congress, *Report of Committee on the Judiciary, on the Institute of Pacific Relations* (Washington, DC: US Government Printing Office, 1952). Also see Warren I. Cohen, 'Who's Afraid of Alfred Kohlberg', *Reviews in American History* 3 (1975): 118–23; David Harvey, 'Owen Lattimore: A Memoire,' *Antipode* 15, no. 3 (1983): 3–11; and on the wider webs of Cold War espionage and spying within which the IPR was deemed to be implicated, Robert D. Johnson, *Congress and the Cold War* (Cambridge: Cambridge University Press, 2005), 52 and passim.
14 See, for example, Inderjeet S. Parmar, *Think Tanks and Power in Foreign Policy: A Comparative Study of the Role and Influence of the Council on Foreign Relations and the Royal Institute of International Affairs, 1939-1945* (Basingstoke UK: Palgrave Macmillan, 2004), 89–107.
15 Roger Lévy, *Relations de la Chine et du Japon* (Paris: Centre d'études de politiques étrangère/Institute of Pacific Relations, 1938); Roger Lévy, *L'Indochine et ses traites* (Paris: Centre d'études de politiques étrangère/Institute of Pacific Relations, 1947).
16 Paul F. Hooper (ed.), *Remembering the Institute of Pacific Relations: The Memoirs of William L. Holland* (Tokyo: Ryukei, 1995), 26.
17 Goffman, *Presentation of Self*, 63.
18 See the final chapter of R. H. Tawney's *Land and Labour in China* (London: G. Allen & Unwin, 1932), which was commissioned by the IPR and stemmed from his participation in the 1931 Conference. On Tawney's association with the Nankai Institute, see Yung-chien Chiang, *Social Engineering and the Social Sciences in China, 1919-1949* (Cambridge: Cambridge University Press, 2001), 102–8.

19 Goffman, *Presentation of Self*, 145.
20 Pierre Gourou, *Terres de bonne espérance, le monde tropical* (Paris: Plon, 1982), 345; Pierre Gourou, 'Le souvenir de Roger Lévy', *Politique étrangère* 43 (1978): 347–53, 352–3; Roger Lévy, 'Review of Pierre Gourou Pour une géographie humaine', *Politique étrangère* 38 (1973): 647–8. All translations from French are by the authors.
21 Mike Heffernan, Personal communication. Also see, Appendix 3 – 'John B. Condliffe's Reminiscences', in Hooper, *Reminiscences of the Institute of Pacific Relations*; J. B. Condliffe (ed.), *Problems of the Pacific, 1929: Proceedings of the Third Conference of the Institute of Pacific Relations, Nara and Kyoto, Japan, October 23 to November 9, 1929* (Chicago: University of Chicago Press, 1930); and Jo-Anne Pemberton, *The Story of International Relations, Part One: Cold-Bloodied Idealists* (London: Palgrave Macmillan, 2020), ch. 5.
22 Source provided by Mike Heffernan, from UNESCO Archives (Paris), Archives of the International Institute of Intellectual Co-operation (IIIC), file K.I.3, Conférence permanente des hautes études internationales: généralités.
23 William L. Holland (ed.), *Asian Nationalism and the West: A Symposium Based on Documents and Reports of the Eleventh IPR Conference, Lucknow, 1950* (New York: IPR, 1951), Preface (William L. Holland), iv; William L. Holland, 'Research Program, Institute of Pacific Relations, 1949-50', *Pacific Affairs* 22 (1949): 398–413, 398–400.
24 Holland, 'Research Program', 400.
25 Holland, 'Research Program', 399.
26 Holland, *Asian Nationalism and the West*, iv.
27 Jon Thares Davidann, '"Colossal Illusions": U.S.-Japanese Relations in the Institute of Pacific Relations, 1919-1938', *Journal of World History* 12, no. 1 (2001): 155–82, 155.
28 Goffman, *Presentation of Self*, 6, 14, 151.
29 Goffman, *Presentation of Self*, 151.
30 See Hooper, *Remembering the Institute of Pacific Relations*, for Holland's chronicles.
31 What is known about the conference has been pieced together from conference agendas, published summaries and delegate submissions: *Security of the Pacific: Preliminary Report on the Ninth Conference of the Institute of Pacific Relations, Hot Springs, Virginia, 6-17 January 1945* (New York: IPR, 1945); and the American position is summarized in William C. Johnstone, 'The Hot Springs Conference', *Far Eastern Review* 14 (1945): 16–22; also see UBCA Institute of Pacific Relations Fonds, 54-4: draft memoranda.
32 This expensive resort hotel was used frequently by an array of US government departments and international organizations during the 1930s and 1940s.
33 For more on the American side of the conference, see Dayna L. Barnes, *Architects of Occupation: American Experts and Planning for Postwar Japan* (Ithaca, NY: Cornell University Press, 2017), ch. 3.
34 Belshaw, *Security of the Pacific*, 8.
35 Yutaka Sasaki, 'Foreign Policy Experts as Service Intellectuals: The American Institute of Pacific Relations, the Council of Foreign Relations, and Planning the Occupation of Japan during World War II', in *The United States and the Second World War: New Perspectives on Diplomacy, War, and the Home Front*, eds. G. Kurt Piehler & Sidney Pash (New York: Fordham University Press, 2010), 293–332.
36 *Security in the Pacific*, [Belshaw], 2.
37 *Security in the Pacific*, 2, 5–7, 16–18; Johnstone, 'Hot Springs'.
38 UBCA: Institute of Pacific Relations Fonds, 54-54: Gourou.

39 UBCA: Institute of Pacific Relations Fonds, 51-59: Hot Springs; Gourou, *Terres de bonne espèrance*, 368-9; Holland, *Remembering the Institute of Pacific Relations*, 39.
40 Gourou, *Terres de bonne espèrance*, 345.
41 Goffman, *Presentation of Self*, 77.
42 Pierre Gourou, *L'avenir de l'Indochine* (Paris: Centre d'études de politique étrangère/Institute of Pacific Relations, 1947). Resisting the idea that this was 'the future', and to stress the partiality of Gourou's position, the paper was translated with the title 'For a French Indo-Chinese Federation', *Pacific Affairs* 20 (1947): 18-29. And see *Problems of Economic Reconstruction in the Far East: Report of the Tenth Annual Conference of the Institute of Pacific Relations, Stratford-upon-Avon, England, 7-20 September 1947* (New York: IPR International Secretariat, 1947).
43 Gourou, *L'avenir de l'Indochine*, 8. The Australian National Council also presented a lengthy disquisition on the subject: *Dependencies and Trusteeship in the Pacific Area* (New York: IPR, 1947, mimeo).
44 Lattimore's private reflections, discussed in Robert F. Newman, *Owen Lattimore and the 'Loss' of China* (Berkeley: University of California Press, 1992), 171.
45 Edgar McInnis, 'The Lucknow Conference', *International Journal* 6 (1951): 1-6, 1.
46 See Michael R. Anderson, 'Pacific Dreams: The Institute of Pacific Relations and the Struggle for the Mind of Asia', PhD dissertation, University of Austin at Texas, 2009, 133.
47 Cited in Anderson, 'Pacific Dreams', 138.
48 Holland, *Asian Nationalism and the West*, 7-11.
49 UBCA: Institute of Pacific Relations Fonds, 84-3: Report on the organization and activities of the Japanese Institute of Pacific Relations, 1949-1950 (May 1950); UBCA: Institute of Pacific Relations Fonds 86-11: Pierre Gourou, 'The Economic Problems of Monsoon Asia and the Example of Japan'.
50 Vineet Thakur, 'An Asian Drama: The Asian Relations Conference, 1947', *The International History Review* 41, no. 3 (2019): 673-95.
51 UBCA: Institute of Pacific Relations Fonds 86-5: Rapporteur's report, 11th IPR Conference, Round Table C – East Asia (4-7 October 1950). Delegate lists and conference membership in *Asian Nationalism and the West*, 65-77.
52 C. J. Chancellor, 'Nationalism in Asia: The Eleventh Conference of the Institute of Pacific Relations', *International Affairs* 27 (1951): 184-91, 185.
53 K. Sarwar Hasan, 'The Lucknow Conference', *Pakistan Horizon* 3 (1950): 202-7, 206.
54 Hasan, 'Lucknow Conference', 206.
55 McInnis, 'Lucknow Conference', 2-3.
56 Hooper, *Remembering the Institute of Pacific Relations*, 57.
57 US Senate, Institute of Pacific Relations, 1226-8; William L. Holland, *Truth and Fancy about the Institute of Pacific Relations* (New York: American Institute of Pacific Relations, 1953).
58 Reprinted in Holland, *Asian Nationalism and the West*, 1-8.
59 Hasan, 'Lucknow Conference', 207.
60 Holland, *Asian Nationalism and the West*, 7.
61 *Proceedings of the Twelfth Institute of Pacific Relations Conference, Kyoto, 27 September to 8 October 1954* (New York: IPR, 1955), 2-5, 17-28. And see Anderson, 'Pacific Dreams', 138-55.
62 UBCA: Institute of Pacific Relations Fonds 41-2: Holland to Ball, 25 August 1954. Also cited in Anderson, 'Pacific Dreams', 199, fn. 50.
63 The papers and correspondence pertaining to Gourou are collated in UBCA Institute of Pacific Relations Fonds, 51-10/14 Kyoto Conference 1954.

64 Published by Armand Colin and Hachette, respectively.
65 Anderson, 'Pacific Dreams', 198.
66 Anderson, 'Pacific Dreams', 192.
67 Glenda Sluga, *Internationalism in the Age of Nationalism* (Philadelphia, PA: University of Pennsylvania Press, 1963), 63.
68 Roberts, 'Institute of Pacific Relations', 836.
69 Goffman, *Presentation of Self*, 145.
70 Sean Phillips, 'A Pacific Precedent: The Institute of Pacific Relations in the Emergence of Asia-Pacific Studies', *The Asia Dialogue* (27 June 2018), https://theasiadialogue.com/2018/06/27/a-pacific-precedent-the-institute-of-pacific-relations-in-the-emergence-of-asia-pacific-studies/.

Part IV

Political networks

11

Alternative internationalisms in East Asia

The Conferences of the Asian Peoples, Japanese–Chinese rivalry and Japanese imperialism, 1924–43

Torsten Weber

Introduction

The August 1926 issue of the *League of Nations News*, a pro-internationalist monthly published by the New York-based League of Nations Non-Partisan Association, carried a map of the world with North America at its centre (see Figure 11.1). Compiled by Charles Hodges (1895–1964), a professor of international politics at New York University, it showed 'World Affairs at a Glance' (July 1926), categorized as 'international, colonial, or civil wars', 'international crisis', 'principal events', and 'league or related activity'.[1] Among others, the map listed several League of Nations meetings, including on disarmament, health and intellectual cooperation, as well as other 'world meetings' on drug traffic (Philadelphia), water power (Basle), by League Societies (Wales), the women's peace congress (Dublin) and the Pan-Slav Congress (Prague). As such, the map testified to the diversity and quantity of international meetings in that one month alone. The map also marked one 'principal event' in Japan, namely the 'Pan-Asiatic Congress in Tokyo', which was 'frowned upon by the Japanese government as trouble-maker'. In the magazine's news section, Hodges explained that the sponsors of the Congress followed the principle 'that race is more important than nationality as a basis for world stability'. However, he continued, 'Japanese politicians of all parties are disavowing any activity in connection with the conference [. . .] and the Japanese Government very apparently is placing every difficulty in the way of any trouble developing'.[2] The fact that the *League of Nations News* took notice of this Pan-Asian Congress attests to the relevance pro-League internationalists attributed to this gathering, most likely not because it was seen as representing an idea of internationalism compatible to League internationalism in a relatively remote part of the world but rather because it appeared to be a threat to that very kind of internationalism. After all, the pan-Asianists not only criticized the Western-centrism of the Geneva-based League but also proposed to create an alternative, Asian League of Nations to enable Asians to deal with Asian affairs. This undertaking, however,

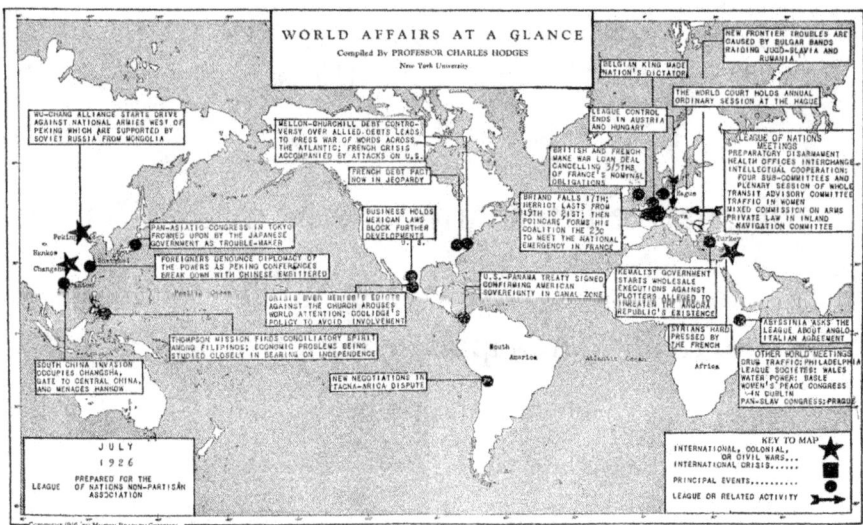

Figure 11.1 'World Affairs at a Glance', 1926, compiled by Charles Hodges. From *League of Nations News* 3, no. 56 (1926), 14.

ended in a failure, mainly because there was little consensus among pan-Asianists apart from their rejection of the 'Whites' and the 'West'. The conflicting voices within this movement with their antagonistic agendas eventually proved stronger than the shared sense of Asian internationalism.

This chapter examines the activities of a group of pan-Asian-minded politicians, writers and activists mainly from China and Japan who convened two Pan-Asian Congresses, also known as the Conferences of the Asian Peoples.[3] They took place in Nagasaki in 1926 and in Shanghai in 1927. Although the assemblies failed to create the envisioned Asian League of Nations and their direct impact remained limited, the conferences made important contributions to the spread of alternative ideas of international cooperation, in particular as they sought to reconcile internationalist and anti-imperialist aspirations with nationalist and imperialist realities in many parts of Asia. In the final sections of this chapter, their transnational interwar activities are compared with two state-centred Asian internationalist conferences during Japan's war against China and in the Asia Pacific (1931–45).

'Asia' against the 'West'?

The idea of a joint Asian enterprise against 'White' and 'Euro-American' imperialism enjoyed its heyday in the first half of the twentieth century. After Japan's surprise victory over Russia in the Russo-Japanese War (1904/5), for the first time an Asian counterattack on the Western imperial powers appeared feasible.[4] As the strongest country in terms of military and political power and the most modern nation in Asia was believed to be Japan, many Japanese saw themselves as the natural leaders of such a project. However, pan-Asian ideas contradicted Japan's pursuit of Westernization which had dominated the country's modernization paradigm since the Meiji Restoration of 1868.[5] The idea of pan-Asian unity which underlay this anti-Western rhetoric was further challenged by Chinese claims for leadership (as the largest and most populous, albeit divided and partly colonized country in Asia) and by growing anti-Japanese sentiments in parts of East Asia, in particular after Japan's annexation of Korea (1910) and its increasing interference in Chinese domestic politics (Twenty-One Demands, 1915).[6] The First World War and the subsequent Paris Peace Conference could potentially have solved the issue of Asian–Western antagonisms had it ended the age of colonialism and liberated the Asian (and other) peoples.[7] Despite proclamations of self-determination, liberty and equality, however, the Powers assembled at Versailles in 1919 did not seek to implement these ideals in all parts of the world. In East and Southeast Asia, for example, France, Britain, the Netherlands, the United States and Portugal retained most of their political, economic and territorial privileges after 1919 through mandates, protectorates and colonies, for example in India, Laos, Cambodia, Vietnam, Indonesia, Malaysia, Singapore, the Philippines and parts of China, including Hong Kong and Macao. As a direct result of the First World War, Japan too was not only able to keep its colonial and quasi-colonial possessions in Taiwan (since 1895), Korea (since 1905) and Manchuria (since 1905) but could even expand its empire and spheres of influence as it seized the German possessions in China (Qingdao, Shandong peninsula) and in the South Pacific (Mariana, Caroline, and Marshall islands). Therefore, a collaborative Asianist project had become less, not more likely between 1905 and 1919.

However, the disappointment over the results of the Paris Peace Conference and the plans for the League of Nations reinvigorated Asian-minded thinkers and activists in the first half of the 1920s, in particular in Japan and China.[8] While Japanese Asianists felt insulted by the rejection of the racial non-discrimination clause its government had (together with the Chinese delegation) proposed,[9] the Chinese rejected the outcome of the Paris Peace Conference altogether because it did not immediately return foreign possessions to China. For this reason, China never signed the peace treaty and its delegation left France prematurely. As a consequence, the League and its internationalism quickly became discredited among Japanese and Chinese, and alternative ideas grew in popularity: an Asian League of Nations as an implementation of Asianism, a kind of exclusively Asian internationalism. Asianism (Japanese *Ajiashugi*, Chinese *Yazhou zhuyi*)[10] as a political neologism had first started to penetrate public discourse in Japan and China during the early 1910s and most generally represented the claim that Asia mattered as a significant and positive geographical and civilizational unit (however defined) and that Asians themselves should be put in charge of Asian affairs. Importantly, this claim to regional self-government did not necessarily denote national self-determination or a general rejection of imperialism. On the contrary, 'Asia for the Asians' – imitating 'America for the Americans' – could also represent the opposite, namely hegemony of one country over others in the region. This geopolitical and regionalist conception of Asianism was also called Asian Monroe Doctrine, in allusion to the American Monroe Doctrine.[11] The tension between (quasi-)imperialist and anti-imperialist conceptions of Asianism[12] would overshadow the Pan-Asian

Conferences in 1926 and 1927 as it separated the Japanese delegation from the other participants, most notably from the Chinese.

In its fundamentals, however, Asianism as a sentiment of resistance against the West had the potential to unify Japanese, Chinese, Indians and other Asians. In 1924, this sentiment peaked. In May, the United States had practically closed the door to Asian immigrants which had caused an upsurge in Asianist publications in Japan (as the last Asian country that was added to the list of countries banned) that argued for the unification of Asia and resistance against the oppression of Asia by 'Whites'[13]; in June, the Bengali Nobel laureate Rabindranath Tagore (1861–1941) visited Japan and added a spiritual dimension to the virulent Asianist mood that focused on the assumed civilizational superiority of Asia. In a speech in Tokyo, Tagore argued that 'the materialistic civilization of the West, working hand in hand with its strong nationalism, has reached the height of unreasonableness. But the West will suffocate after a short time and will bow to the great and natural thought of the East';[14] and in November, Sun Yat-sen (1866–1925), the founder of modern China, visited Japan and similarly argued for the superiority of Asian civilization, based on virtue and benevolence as opposed to Western despotic rule by force. Sun's famous Kobe speech, advocating 'Greater Asianism', was later exploited by Japanese imperialist and Chinese collaborationist propaganda, but in 1924 and the following decade it became widely cited as the most prominent call for a joint Asian revolt against the West.[15]

Transnational pan-Asianist activities and the first Conference of the Asian Peoples (1926)

In this mixed mood of humiliation and enthusiasm, Japanese politicians, entrepreneurs, academics and writers founded the All Asia Association in Tokyo in July 1924 to promote 'the development of freedom based on the equality of all human beings' and 'to work towards the establishment of a new global civilization'.[16] While its broader outlook was universal, the association was centrally concerned with Asia itself. It defined its most immediate aim as the 'awakening of the Asians of our generation who are the grandchildren of the Asian race that possessed a high civilization already some thousand years ago and which constitutes the basis of modern culture'. In other words, it sought to raise an awareness of being Asian among Asians and to define this Asian identity positively by reminding Asians of their alleged glorious past. Nevertheless, the association's founding manifesto was neither outspokenly anti-Western nor radically anti-colonial. Instead, it emphasized reconciliation and harmony rather than confrontation. Its main spokesman was Imazato Juntarō,[17] a minor political figure from the centre-right *Rikken Seiyūkai* (Friends of Constitutional Government) party and a member of the Japanese Lower House from 1924 to 1928. Imazato was a pro-Chinese politician who frequently criticized the China policies of the Japanese government which, despite the termination of the Anglo-Japanese Alliance in 1922 and the notably pro-Asianist shift in published opinion, continued to take a pro-Western and accomodationist stance.

In order to seek cooperation with existing Asianist groups and activists outside of Japan, the association sent Imazato to Beijing where a Great Alliance of Asian Peoples (Yaxiya Minzu Da Tongmeng) had been established in August 1925.[18] Led by low-ranking officials[19] of the Chinese Nationalist Party (Guomindang) of Sun Yat-sen, who had died in March, its membership included academics, journalists and entrepreneurs from China, Japan, Korea and India. It was a truly transnational Asianist organization and defined its main purpose as 'to resist the countries that practice imperialism in Asia and to attain the aim of freedom and equality of all peoples'.[20] The fact alone that the organization was founded with this transnational membership proves the urgency to act jointly felt by many Asians from different countries, including Japan. Acknowledging the complications of being nationals of an imperialist country but members of an anti-imperialist Asianist organization, the Japanese members of the alliance made a statement in which they distanced themselves from the Japanese government and its imperialist policies.[21] The government's opposition to these Asianist activities, as noted in the *League of Nations News* previously quoted, is therefore self-explanatory. After several meetings in China and Japan, the Japanese Association and the Chinese Alliance decided to convene an international conference of Asian peoples in order to constitute an Asian League of Nations and to promote 'freedom and happiness by abolishing class, racial, and religious discrimination'.[22] The founding conference was originally scheduled to be held in Shanghai or Tokyo in the spring of 1926.

Various Japanese government agencies, including the Home Ministry and diplomatic missions of Japan abroad, closely watched the activities of the association and the preparations for the Congress.[23] As a result of this surveillance by the authorities, the originally planned locations of Shanghai or Tokyo were abandoned and replaced by Nagasaki, a port city in southern Japan and close to Imazato's home. The Japanese government was not only 'placing every difficulty in the way of any trouble developing', as Hodges noticed, but even tried to prevent the conference from taking place, for example by delaying the issuing of visa for participants. Mehandra Pratap, an Indian nationalist representing Afghanistan, was refused entry into Japan until after the conference[24] and the Home Ministry sent surveillance staff to Nagasaki that reported in detail about the assembly.

The delegates for the conference were recruited through the Japanese and Chinese host organizations. Fifteen Japanese, eleven Chinese, four Indians, four Filipinos, three Koreans,[25] one Afghani, one Vietnamese participated as delegates in the Nagasaki conference, in addition to an unspecified number of observers and guests.[26] The conference opened on 1 August 1926, and the choice of its venue reflected the pragmatic and internationalist character of this meeting: it took place in Nagasaki's YMCA meeting hall. For an undertaking that was supposedly (or potentially) anti-Western in nature, it may have been an unusual venue, but it also symbolized the non-essentialist and open approach of the delegates to their understanding of 'Asia' (Figure 11.2).

On the first day, several delegates gave speeches on their views and ambitions for the conference and the Asianist project in general. Imazato, as the host and leader of the Japanese Association, delivered the opening speech in which he emphasized 'love, righteousness, freedom, equality, prosperity, and happiness' as universal values which

Figure 11.2 'Scenes from the site of the Conference of Asian Peoples. Standing on the podium is the Indian delegate Mr. Bose (at the Nagasaki YMCA)'. From *Tokyo Asahi*, 4 August 1926, 2. Courtesy of *Asahi* newspaper.

must be extended to the peoples of Asia.[27] Huang Gongsu, a member of Parliament and leader of the Chinese Alliance, stressed that the conference did not aim at 'uniting the coloured people of Asia in order to expel the Whites but to resist against the invasion of Asia by the Whites to realize freedom and equality of the humankind'. Huang also demanded a complete abolition of the unequal treaties between Japan and China so that both countries could fully cooperate in the global arena. After Pratap's telegram from the port in Osaka, where he was waiting for the permission to enter Japan, had been read out, the Indian revolutionary Rash Bihari Bose explained the differences between the League of Nations and the Asian League that the conference aspired to found.[28] Bose had lived in exile in Japan for more than a decade and throughout the conference played an important role as mediator between Japanese and Chinese participants.

> Some people may ask why we should create an Asian League as there already is an International League [of Nations]. But those two differ profoundly. The League of Nations was created for 500 million people, however, the Asian League will be made for 1500 million coloured people. [...] We must not only unite to give birth

to a new Asian civilization but also to give birth to a new civilization. Eventually, this is not only for the good of the Asian peoples but to save the unfortunate human race globally.[29]

Bose criticized the existing instruments of internationalism as serving the interests of the Euro-American 'Whites' only. The internationalism of the League therefore was perceived as Western internationalism whereas the envisioned new internationalism was Asian with a global perspective. At the same time, Bose principally agreed to the organization of an International League as an adequate instrument of international politics. How much the Congress was inspired and indebted to the League of Nations becomes obvious in the Provisional Constitution (see below) adopted by the delegates in Nagasaki. Article One defined the object of the proposed Asian League as bringing 'permanent peace to the world, based on the principle of equality and justice, eliminating all discrimination, whether social, religious or racial, and thus to assure liberty and happiness to all the races of the world'.[30] In other words, the Asian League was to accomplish more or less the same goals as the League of Nations. Of course, this included rather prominently the abolition of racial discrimination, the demand that the Japanese and Chinese government delegations had first proposed at Versailles but had failed to have implemented.[31] Despite its critique of the League, the assembly recommended that Asians should neither ignore the League of Nations nor lobby for Japan's withdrawal.

On the second day, the delegates discussed practical issues to foster inter-Asian connectivity and exchange. The eleven proposals made included the construction of a trans-Asian railway from either the Manchurian city of Fengtian (Mukden) or the East Chinese province of Shandong all the way to Turkey and the establishment of Asian Cultural and Study Centres, of an Asian Bank and of an institute for the promotion of trans-Asian business and industry. As all of these plans were proposed by Japanese delegates, they were met with immediate suspicion by Chinese delegates who criticized them as means of further Japanese economic penetration and subjugation of China; a trans-Asian railway could facilitate cheaper and easier travel, but it could potentially also serve economic and military penetration; an Asian Bank could provide money without relying on the Western powers, but it could potentially also enforce financial and therefore political dependency on Japan; the encouragement to use goods produced in Asia could promote indigenous industry but potentially it could also undermine anti-Japanese boycotts. Eventually, only less controversial proposals such as the establishment of a joint inter-Asian publication and of an Asian college were passed, while others such as the railway and monetary projects issues were deferred on Chinese demand.[32] In addition to tensions between China and Japan regarding Japan's infamous Twenty-One Demands on China which led to the first controversy between Japanese and Chinese delegates before the Congress had even convened, the question of Indian independence caused controversy. Huang had proposed to actively work towards the independence of India as the first step of Asia's liberation from the 'White Powers'. Imazato warned that such far-reaching claims may lead to the forced dissolving of the conference by the Japanese authorities. He offered to have this proposal discussed on the third day in a closed meeting, but it was eventually withdrawn due to 'improper terminology'. The convention was closed at quarter past two in the afternoon and officially ended with a banquet given by the mayor of Nagasaki in the evening on 3 August.

Before the assembly was dissolved, on the third day, the provisional statutes of the Asian League were adopted as follows:

Art.1 We establish the Asian League with the objective of bringing permanent peace to the world, based on the principle of equality and justice, eliminating all discrimination, whether social, religious or racial, and thus to assure liberty and happiness to all the races of the world.

Art. 2 In order to accomplish these objectives, the League will strive to realize the following points:

- the reconstruction of Asia's spiritual and material culture
- the improvement of the conditions in which Asian peoples live under foreign rule
- the abolition of the existing unequal treaties between Asian countries
- the cooperation of Asian peoples in the fields of culture, economy, and politics
- the promotion of the use and of the production of Asian products

Art. 3 The League shall set up its headquarters in Tokyo and establish branch offices where necessary.

Art. 4 The highest organ of the League is the Executive Board and it shall consist of 25 members.

Art. 5 The Board shall decide a place and convene a General Assembly once a year to discuss important issues pertaining to the League.

Art. 6 The Board shall give official recognition to groups from Asian countries that share the aims of the League and shall invite their delegates to participate in the general Assembly.

Art. 7 The Board shall invite individuals who make outstanding contributions to [the cause of] Asia to participate in the General Assembly.[33]

These statutes reveal the ambition of the delegates to create an international organization of lasting relevance and impact. Simultaneously, the phrasing of the aims appears rather moderate compared to the issues at stake. After all, the proposals made by the delegates meant nothing less than the complete revision of the status quo in most parts of Asia, affecting not only the Asian peoples but also the vested interests of the Powers, including Japan. Neither international media nor the Japanese authorities took this plan very seriously.[34] This was partly because of the limited prominence and limited representativeness of the participants. Although the Japanese Association could list a number of prominent Japanese as supporters of their enterprise,[35] the fact that none of them actually travelled to Nagasaki to participate in the conference showed the lack of commitment by these people towards the implementation of their – real or professed – Asianist ideals. A more important reason for the denigrating comments on the conference, however, may have been the obvious disunity of the participants on the project of Asian unity.

The split between the moderates and radicals was best demonstrated in the difficulties between the Chinese and Japanese delegates. Although the conference adopted a resolution to appoint a special committee to undertake research into the problems between the two countries, there was little common ground in both countries for a joint Asianist project. Chinese observers of the conference openly questioned the Japanese understanding of Asianism as the underlying principle of the conference; to them, Asianism was a positive and useful idea but one could not trust any Japanese Asianist proposal. Even moderate liberals in China found it hard to distinguish official Japanese state policy on the one hand and transnational civil society activities that included Japanese participation on the other hand. A lead article, published in the Chinese liberal journal *Xiandai Pinglun* just one week after the conference, praised the Asianist ideal of 'Asia is the Asia of the Asians' and 'Greater Asianism' as 'a very good instrument for the Asians to oppose to the Euro-American invasion'. It warned, however, that 'as long as the Japanese do not abandon their imperialist thinking they cannot gain the consent of other Asian peoples. [. . .] Towards China, Japan as ever pursues the principle and policy of invasion and to Korea it refuses to grant independence'. The article concluded, therefore, that 'as for now, Greater Asianism is Japan's Greater Asianism, not the Greater Asianism of the peoples of Asia'.[36]

While this contemporary comment tackled the question of which kind of Asianist policy should be pursued and by whom, it skipped the more fundamental question of who the peoples of Asia were anyway and who could rightfully speak on their behalf and how. At the conference, which aimed at providing answers to these questions, the language problem reflected well the artificial and forced character of the concept of 'Asia' in general. By the mid-1920s Chinese was no longer a common language for most Asians and certainly not for those assembled in Nagasaki. Refugees from British- and French-colonized countries were usually Japanophiles and had a better command of Japanese than of Chinese. Understandably, however, the Chinese were suspicious of Japanese as the official language since Japan was the only imperialist among Asian countries represented. Logically, Japanese was not an option as the language of choice to discuss the Asianist cause. But English, perceived as the main language of the imperialist 'West', of course, was not acceptable either. Esperanto as an alternative was briefly discussed but likewise rejected as a language originating in the 'West'. Since no solution to the language problem was found, communication during the sessions at the Congress was mainly conducted in Japanese, Chinese and English. As a future task, the Congress decided to undertake research into the invention of an Asian version of Esperanto as a neutral language.[37] After the official closing of the conference on 3 August, some delegates travelled to Osaka to meet the delegate for Afghanistan, Mahendra Pratap, who had been permitted to enter Japan in the meantime and continued their gathering informally.

The second Pan-Asian Conference in Shanghai

The Nagasaki conference could be characterized as a success in so far as it facilitated a controversial political debate about the future of Asia in a global context. Its concrete results, however, were slim and few. Nevertheless, both co-hosting organizations and many of the delegates were keen on pushing their dialogue and projects forward and decided to reconvene for a second Pan-Asian Conference.[38]

Originally, the second Pan-Asian Conference had been announced to take place in Beijing from 1 to 3 November 1927. Against the background of China's national unification process under General Chiang Kai-shek (Jiang Jieshi) from 1926 onwards and the establishment of a new central government in Nanjing, Huang Gongsu proposed to move the meeting further south, to Shanghai. Shanghai may be seen as a particularly fitting location since its foreign concessions were a constant reminder of the presence of Western (and Japanese) imperialism in China – an issue the Congress sought to tackle. Again, the conference almost failed before its opening which was delayed several times because of tensions between the Japanese and Chinese. In their preparatory meeting, the Chinese delegates demanded Japanese support for the abolition of extraterritorial rights, of all unequal treaties between Asian countries, and the termination of Japan's invasion of Manchuria and Mongolia.[39] Eventually, Pratap, who had arrived in Shanghai by boat via Qingdao on 3 November, managed to convince the Chinese to alter their proposals so that they did not offend Japanese interests too blatantly.[40] In exchange, the Japanese dropped their plans for an Asian Central Monetary Institution and the inter-Asian railway project which had both caused much suspicion on the Chinese side. While these examples may serve as proof of the difficulties of any practical joint Asian enterprise beyond Asianist rhetoric, they also demonstrate the possibilities of inter-Asian – and more specifically Chinese– Japanese – dialogue and compromise at a time of fierce nationalist agitation within both countries.

With a delay of six days, the actual conference opened on 7 November 1927 in Southern Shanghai's Bansong Garden, which had become a popular spot for recreation and gatherings since its opening in 1918. In May 1920, a meeting of the progressive New Citizen Study Society, in which Mao Zedong also participated, had taken place at the same venue. The second Pan-Asian Conference was attended by an audience of fifty-two people and eleven official delegates. Continuity regarding participants testifies to the significance attributed to the joint Asianist undertaking. As in the previous year, the Chinese Alliance, led by Huang Gongsu, co-hosted the conference together with the Japanese Association, led by Imazato. Other returning delegates included Bose (India) and Pratap (Afghanistan). The Japanese delegates' proposals included rather general and uncontroversial demands for the abolition of racial discrimination, the reform of the League of Nations, the withdrawal of US and British naval bases in Hawaii and Singapore, and the fight against communism in Asia. The Chinese side repeated its proposal to support Asian peoples in securing self-determination and specifically demanded a revision of Japan's policies towards China.[41]

On its opening day, the conference received orders by the municipal authorities to close down. All gatherings in Shanghai had been forbidden for fear of political instigation on the anniversary of the Russian October Revolution on 7 November. The assembly hurriedly adopted a ten-point 'common proposal' including the desire to 'help China by a sincere cooperation with Japan'. The delegates elected a standing executive committee, including Huang, Imazato, Bose, and Pratap, and departed for

Nanjing to continue informally as a private gathering but did not produce any notable results.⁴² Upon Pratap's suggestion, a third Pan-Asian Conference was announced for the following year in Kabul but historians have been unable to uncover any proof for its actual convention.⁴³ Similarly little is known about the host organisations after 1927.

The second Pan-Asian Conference remained unnoticed not only by the *League of Nations News*. There was much less international press coverage in general and the *Manchester Guardian* speculated that 'the delegates were trying to avoid the American and British newspaper correspondents'.⁴⁴ Given the negative press reports and level of official surveillance the first conference had received, the organizers made only limited efforts to publicize their second meeting. Also Chinese and Japanese news coverage was much smaller compared to the first conference and the surveillance activities were downscaled considerably. Apparently the Japanese authorities were less concerned because the conference took place in China and because the first assembly in Nagasaki had turned out much less radical than initially feared.

State-sponsored Pan-Asian Conferences in Dalian (1934) and Tokyo (1943)

Against the background of the political situation in East Asia during the mid-1920s, the failure of the Pan-Asian Conferences of Nagasaki and Shanghai to achieve any practical results and to continue its activities in the following years are not very surprising. The political circumstances, above all the fierce rivalry and tensions between China and Japan but also the domestic turmoil within China, made joint civil society-driven enterprises extremely difficult. The two co-hosting organizations themselves were far from representing any sort of Asian unity and consequently also failed to properly address Asian concerns that transcended the scope of East Asia. Pan-Asian internationalism did not cease to exist after 1927 but it changed in character, particularly after Japan formalized its occupation of Manchuria.⁴⁵ After the so-called Manchurian Incident of 1931, the Japanese Army occupied vast parts of Northeast China and founded the puppet regime of Manchukuo in 1932. Asianism, which the Japanese government had hitherto rejected, now became a welcome tool to justify Japanese rule in this multi-ethnic part of China. Gradually, it adopted Asianist rhetoric, such as *gozoku kyōwa* ('harmonious cooperation of the five races') and *ōdō rakudo* ('paradise of the Kingly Way'), that it had rejected just a few years earlier when the Chinese and Japanese Asianist organizations had first joined hands to convene the Nagasaki conference.

This shifting place of Asianism in public discourse also left its mark on pan-Asian internationalist activities during the 1930 and 1940s. A very different kind of Pan-Asian Conference, convened in February 1934 in the Chinese city of Dalian (Port Arthur), was part of the official Manchukuo propaganda of harmonious coexistence of the Asian races. As opposed to the Nagasaki and Shanghai conferences, it was not co-organized by pan-Asianists from different countries but convened by several nationalist groups from Japan. Chinese were excluded from the committee. The Japan-centred character of the enterprise was also obvious in the choice of its opening day as 11 February, Japan's mythical national founding day. The conference even cooperated with the Japanese military[46] and Pratap, one of the few participants who had also attended the Pan-Asian Conferences in the 1920s and received a last-minute invitation to Dalian, criticized that 'the Japanese language was adopted as the only official language of the meeting'.[47] Pan-Asian internationalism had changed from a transnational and civil society project to a state-sponsored and Japan-centred project.

As Japan's war in East and Southeast Asia as well as the Pacific intensified from the late 1930s onwards, Asianist rhetoric became a central part of Japanese war propaganda. In 1938, Prime Minister Konoe Fumimaro declared the aim to erect a 'New Order in East Asia' in order to realize the so-called Greater East Asia Co-Prosperity Sphere.[48] After the Japanese attack on Pearl Harbor in December 1941, the war was officially called 'Greater East Asia War', in an attempt to pretend that Japan fought the war on behalf of its fellow Asian peoples. In reality, it monopolized Asian resources for Japan and replaced 'White' with Japanese imperialism. Pro-Japanese regimes in occupied areas also made extensive use of Asianist rhetoric which served as justification for collaboration but also ensured some leeway for these regimes. The most prominent example is Wang Jingwei's pro-Japanese collaborationist regime in Nanjing (1940–5) which rhetorically tried to merge Sun Yat-sen's Asianism with Asianist war propaganda from Japan.[49]

This Japan-centred, imperialist appropriation of pan-Asian internationalism reached its climax in November 1943 when the Japanese government convened the 'Greater East Asia Conference' in Tokyo.[50] At a time when Japan's empire had begun to shrink and defeat looked more likely than a Japanese victory in the war, its leaders staged a conference in order 'to strengthen solidarity among Asians [. . .] in the fight against Western powers'.[51] Some scholarship stresses that the conference was a sincere and friendly attempt by Japan to redefine its relations with its Asian allies in 'a new Asian spirit of amity, independence, equality, prosperity, and cooperation'.[52] Indeed, Japan had made some concessions to China (abolition of extraterritoriality and acknowledgement of China's unity), to Burma and to the Philippines (acknowledgment of independence). However, Japan retained its de facto control and neither granted self-government nor equality. Therefore, as Jessamyn Abel emphasizes, 'this could not be called a gathering of equal and independent nations'[53]. The imperialist context and Japan-centred character of the conference also meant that fewer nations were represented in Tokyo than at the Nagasaki conference in 1926; in addition to Japan as host, only China (represented by Wang Jingwei's collaborationist Nanjing government), Japan's puppet-state of Manchukuo, Burma, the Philippines and Thailand were represented. Subhas Chandra Bose participated as observer for Free India.

Like the tensions between the Japanese and Chinese at the Nagasaki and Shanghai conferences, in Tokyo in 1943 there was also considerable dispute about Japan's unwillingness to abandon its empire and the desire of Asian nations for real autonomy. In his opening address, the Japanese prime minister Tōjō Hideki emphasized the need for collaboration in order 'to bring the war to a successful conclusion'. Other delegates, however, were much less interested in fighting Japan's war than in finally attaining complete independence and improving the economic and social conditions of their country. President José P. Laurel of the Philippines therefore demanded the 'recognition of political independence and territorial integrity' and warned against 'any particular member monopolizing the resulting prosperity of any given country or nation'.[54] The Joint Declaration, adopted unanimously by the assembly, included 'sovereignty and independence' as its principles but exclusively focused on the British Empire and the United States as countries that 'have in seeking their own prosperity oppressed other nations and countries.'[55] Anti-Westernism, again, was the lowest common denominator of this pan-Asian internationalist undertaking. For the delegates assembled in the empire's capital it was probably also the only way to frame their criticism of Japan, namely in terms of a rejection of the materialistic nature and aggressive character of 'Western civilization', regardless of whether the aggressor was Western or Asian imperialism.

Conclusion

The idea of internationalism and international cooperation enjoyed great popularity in many parts of Asia, particularly after the founding of the League of Nations in 1920. At the same time, its perceived neglect of non-Western affairs and its unwillingness to extend rights and sovereignty to non-Western peoples inspired an Asian version of internationalism: Asianism. Asianism enjoyed its greatest popularity during the 1920s and 1930s. It inspired hundreds of essays, speeches, dozens of books and the founding of political or cultural organizations. In an attempt to decentre the League of Nations' internationalism, the Japanese and Chinese Asianist organizations studied earlier successfully convened two conferences in Nagasaki in 1926 and in Shanghai in 1927 which, however, remained without lasting direct impact. At the time they were 'ridiculed by official and liberal circles in Japan'[56] (and elsewhere). However, the fact that seventeen years later the Japanese government picked up the very same idea and hosted its own 'Greater East Asia Conference' in Tokyo testifies at least to the indirect impact and lasting legacy of the 1920s conferences and their internationalist ideas.

Cemil Aydin has drawn attention to the similarity of the Asian internationalist projects and their 'Western' models. He writes that '[a]s the declarations of the 1926 Nagasaki pan-Asiatic conference had looked similar to the principles of the League of Nations, so the Greater East Asia Conference declaration also looked like a modification of the Atlantic Charter, with slight alterations affording sensitivity to the cultural traditions of non-Western societies'.[57] It should not be forgotten, however, that the precise policies and issues debated at those assemblies differed profoundly. An even more noteworthy characteristic of the Pan-Asian Conferences lay in the origins of their participants. The Nagasaki conference pioneered an approach made famous at Bandung three decades later, in which Asians assembled to speak not only on Asian affairs but with a global outlook. The real problem the 'trouble-makers' at Nagasaki had caused was less their assumed racism than their insistence on being entitled to the same rights as their counterparts in Europe and America.

Notes

1 Charles Hodges, 'World Affairs at a Glance', *League of Nation News* 3, no. 56 (August 1926): 14.
2 Charles Hodges, 'Monthly Digest of World Affairs', *League of Nation News* 3, no. 56 (August 1926): 18.
3 The two conferences have not attracted much attention in English-language scholarship. In addition to Torsten Weber, *Embracing Asia in China and Japan: Asianism Discourse and the Contest for Hegemony, 1912–1933* (Cham: Palgrave, 2018), and Torsten Weber, 'From Versailles to Shanghai: Pan-Asianist Legacies of the Paris Peace Conference and the Failure of Asianism from Below', in *Asia After Versailles: Asian Perspectives on the Paris Peace Conference and the Interwar Order 1919-1933*, ed. Urs Matthias Zachmann (Edinburgh: Edinburgh University Press, 2017), 77–97, see Cemil Aydin, *The Politics of Anti-Westernism in Asia: Visions of World Order in Pan-Islamic and Pan-Asian Thought* (New York: Columbia University Press, 2007) and Sven Saaler, 'The Pan-Asiatic Society and the Conference of Asian Peoples in Nagasaki, 1926', in *Pan-Asianism: A Documentary History 1860–2010*, Vol. 2, eds. Sven Saaler & Christopher W. A. Szpilman (Boulder, CO: Rowman & Littlefield, 2011), 97–105; in Chinese, Zhou Bin, 'Yaxiya Minzu Huiyi yu Zhongguo de fandui yundong' [The Asian Peoples' Congress and the Chinese Opposition Movement], *Kang-Ri Zhanzheng Yanjiu* [Studies of China's War of Resistance against Japan] 3 (2006): 128–59 and in Japanese, Mizuno Naoki, '1920 nendai Nihon, Chōsen, Chūgoku ni okeru Ajia ninshiki no ichidanmen: Ajia minzoku kaigi o meguru sangoku no ronchō' [One Section of Asia Consciousness in Japan, Korea, and China in the 1920s: Debates Concerning the Pan-Asian Conferences], in *Kindai Nihon no Ajia Ninshiki* [Modern Japanese Asia Consciousness], ed. Furuya Tetsuo (Tokyo: Ryokuin Shobō, 1996), 509–48; Matsuura Masataka, *Daitōa sensō wa naze okitanoka: han Ajiashugi no seiji keizaishi* [Why Did the 'Greater East Asian War' Happen? A Political and Economic History of Pan-Asianism] (Nagoya: Nagoya Daigaku Shuppankai, 2010), and Hirobe Izumi, *Jinshu sensō to iu gūwa: Kōkaron to ajia shugi* [A Fable Called Race War: Yellow Peril and Asianism] (Nagoya: Nagoya Daigaku Shuppankai, 2017), ch. 3.
4 On the impact of the Russo-Japanese War, see *The Impact of the Russo-Japanese War*, ed. Rotem Kowner (London: Routledge, 2007).
5 See William G. Beasley, *The Rise of Modern Japan* (New York: St. Martin's Press, 2000).
6 On anti-Japanese sentiments in China, see Rana Mitter, *A Bitter Revolution: China's struggle with the Modern World* (Oxford: Oxford University Press, 2004).
7 See Erez Manela, *The Wilsonian Moment: Self-Determination and the International Origins of Anticolonial Nationalism* (Oxford: Oxford University Press, 2007).
8 See Weber, 'From Versailles to Shanghai'.
9 See Naoko Shimazu, *Japan, Race, and Equality: The Racial Equality Proposal of 1919* (New York: Routledge, 1998).
10 Asianism was also referred to as Pan-Asianism in the English-language literature but both in Japan and in China the most widespread term was 'Asianism' or 'Greater Asianism'.
11 On the Monroe Doctrine, see Stephen Legg & Alexander Vasudevan, 'Introduction: Geographies of the Nomos'. in *Spatiality, Sovereignty and Carl Schmitt: Geographies of the Nomos*, ed. Stephen Legg (London: Routledge, 2011), 1–23.

12 On the tensions between imperialist and anti-imperialist conceptions of Asianism, see Torsten Weber, 'Pan-Asianism', in *The Palgrave Encyclopedia of Imperialism and Anti-Imperialism*, eds. Immanuel Ness & Zak Cope (Cham: Palgrave Macmillan, 2021), 2164–74.
13 On the impact of the 1924 Immigration Act, see Nancy Stalker, 'Suicide, Boycotts and Embracing Tagore: The Japanese Popular Response to the 1924 US Immigration Exclusion Law', *Japanese Studies* 26, no. 2 (September 2006): 153–70 and Izumi Hirobe, *Japanese Pride, American Prejudice: Modifying the Exclusion Clause of the 1924 Immigration Act* (Stanford: Stanford University Press, 2001).
14 Tagore quoted after Stephen N. Hay, *Asian Ideas of East and West: Tagore and His Critics in Japan, China, and India* (Cambridge, MA: Harvard University Press, 1970), 316.
15 On Sun's Kobe speech and its reception in Japan and China, see Weber, *Embracing 'Asia'*, ch. 5.
16 'Zen Ajia Kyōkai setsuritsu shushi' [Purpose for the Establishment of the All Asia Association], *Zen Ajia Kyōkai Kaihō* [Bulletin of the All Asia Association], April 1926, 1.
17 Imazato originates from Ōmura, a city in Nagasaki prefecture and graduated from the politics and economy department of Tokyo's Waseda University. He became a member of parliament in May 1924 when the debate over racial discrimination and pan-Asian solidarity in the context of the US immigration law reached its climax in Japan.
18 On the alliance's origins, see Huang Gongsu, *Yaxiya Minzu di yici Dahui shimo ji* [Complete Record of the First Conference of the Asian Peoples] (Yaxiya Minzu Datongmeng, 1926), 3–4 and Zhou, 'Yaxiya Minzu Huiyi'.
19 For details on the participants, see Zhou, 'Yaxiya Minzu Huiyi', 129–33. The leading initiators were Huang Gongsu and Li Zhaofu (1887-1950), both members of the dissolved parliament of the Chinese Republic.
20 Quoted after Zhou, 'Yaxiya Minzu Huiyi', 130.
21 Quoted after Zhou, 'Yaxiya Minzu Huiyi', 130.
22 'Zen Ajia Kyōkai setsuritsu shushi' [Purpose for the Establishment of the All Asia Association], *Zen Ajia Kyōkai Kaihō* [Bulletin of the All Asia Association], April 1926, 2–3.
23 A large collection of official reports on the host organizations and the Nagasaki conference, comprising several hundreds of pages, is available online via the Japan Center for Asian Historical Records (http://www.jacar.go.jp/). These detailed reports suggest that the Japanese government was extremely concerned about the potential damage the association's activities and the conference may inflict on Japan's image as a cooperationist partner of the West. Both Japan's Home and Foreign Offices also closely watched foreign press reporting on the conference. See *Zen Ajia Minzoku Kaigi tenmatsu* [Details of the All Asian Peoples Conference], ed. Naimushō Keihōkyoku Hoan Ka [Home Ministry, Special Observation Office, Public Security Division], October 1926.
24 Aydin, *Anti-Westernism in Asia*, 156, and Carolien Stolte, 'Enough of the Great Napoleons! Raja Mahendra Pratap's Pan-Asian Projects (1929–1939)', *Modern Asian Studies* 46, no. 2 (2012): 403–23, 412.
25 Since Korea had been a part of Japan since 1905 (officially annexed in 1910), technically the Korean delegates were Japanese too.
26 Primary and secondary sources give conflicting numbers of participants, probably resulting from a conflation of delegates, participants and observers and caused by

shifting numbers of attendees during different sessions of the conference. Based on accounts by the Japanese Home Ministry, Zhou and Saaler give the number of thirty-four delegates but contemporary Japanese media reports state participant numbers in the range of fifty-one to seventy (see 'Minzoku no kyōei o kakuho suru Zen Ajia Renmei no undō' [The Movement for an All Asian League to Secure the Peoples' Mutual Prosperity'], *Osaka Mainichi*, 24 July 1926, and 'Ajia Minzoku Taikai' [Asian Peoples Conference], *Osaka Asahi*, 1 August 1926).

27 The speeches are reprinted in Japanese in *Zen Ajia Minzoku Kaigi tenmatsu*.
28 On Bose, see Eri Hotta, 'Rash Behari Bose: The Indian Independence Movement and Japan', in *Pan-Asianism: A Documentary History 1860-2010*, Vol. 1, eds. Sven Saaler & Christopher W. A. Szpilman (Boulder, CO: Rowman & Littlefield, 2011), 231–40.
29 'Imazato Juntarō o gichō ni kaigi hajimaru' [The Conference Starts with Imazato as Chairman], *Osaka Mainichi*, 2 August 1926, and 'Ajia Minzoku Taikai' [Asian Peoples Conference], *Osaka Asahi*, 1 August 1926.
30 'Ajia Minzoku Taikai'.
31 See 'Ajia Minzoku Taikai'.
32 See 'Ajia Minzoku Taikai'.
33 See 'Zen Ajia Renmei zantei kiyaku' [Provisional Statutes of the All Asia League], *Tokyo Nichi Nichi*, 3 August 1926. Articles 8 and 9 on the procedures of elections of the Board and Chairman are omitted.
34 An excellent account of reactions in Western media can be found in Hirobe, *Jinshu sensō*, ch. 3.
35 See Saaler, 'The Pan-Asiatic Society', 98. They included former home and foreign minister Gotō Shinpei, members of Parliament, as well as the prominent writer Ōkawa Shūmei.
36 'Da Yazhou Minzu Huiyi' [Greater Asian Peoples Conference], *Xiandai Pinglun* [Contemporary Review], 14 August 1926; quoted after Zhou, 'Yaxiya Minzu Huiyi', 147–8. The *Xiandai Pinglun* was a moderate journal of Northern Chinese liberals.
37 On the language problem, see Asada Hajime, 'Ajia minzoku kaigi ni nan kokugo o tsukau ka' [What Language to be Used at the Asian Peoples Conference?], *Osaka Asahi*, 29–30 July 1926, 'Ajia Minzoku Taikai' [Asian Peoples' Conference], *Osaka Asahi*, 1 August 1926, and 'Pan-Asiatic Congress', *Japan Weekly Chronicle*, 12 August 1926, 191.
38 See Zhou, 'Yaxiya Minzu Huiyi', 152.
39 See Mizuno, '1920 nendai', 515.
40 Zhou, 'Yaxiya Minzu Huiyi', 151–2.
41 See Mizuno, '1920 nendai', 514–15.
42 See Zhou, 'Yaxiya Minzu Huiyi', 152, and Mizuno, '1920 nendai', 515.
43 See Mizuno, '1920 nendai', 515, and Hirobe, *Jinshu sensō*, 117. It appears likely that the conference was cancelled due to continuing Sino-Japanese disputes, official opposition from both countries and in the light of the unstable domestic situation in Afghanistan in the late 1920s. Saaler claims that the Kabul conference took place in 1928 but does not provide any details or evidence. Matsuura links the state-sponsored Pan-Asian Conference, held in 1934 in Japanese-occupied Dalian (discussed later), to the Nagasaki and Shanghai conferences.
44 'Second Pan-Asian Conference', *Manchester Guardian*, 22 December 1927, 5.
45 On the Japanese occupation of Manchuria, see Shinichi Yamamuro, *Manchuria under Japanese Dominion*, trans. Joshua A. Fogel (Philadelphia, PA: University of Pennsylvania Press, 2006).

46 Matsuura, *Daitōa sensō*, 181.
47 Mahendra Pratap, *My Life Story of Fifty-five Years* (Delhi: World Federation, 1947), 269.
48 On this project, see Jeremy Yellen, *The Greater East Asia Co-Prosperity Sphere: When Total Empire Met Total War* (Ithaca, NY: Cornell University Press, 2019).
49 See Torsten Weber, 'Finding China's "Asia" in Japanese Asianism', in *Translating the Occupation: The Japanese Invasion of China, 1931–45*, eds. Jonathan Henshaw, Craig A. Smith & Norman Smith (Vancouver: University of British Columbia Press, 2021), 209–22.
50 On this conference, see Li Narangoa, 'The Assembly of the Greater East Asiatic Nations, 1943', in *Pan-Asianism: A Documentary History 1860–2010*, Vol. 2, eds. Sven Saaler & Christopher W. A. Szpilman (Boulder, CO: Rowman & Littlefield, 2011), 243–53; Jessamyn R. Abel, *The International Minimum: Creativity and Contradiction in Japan's Global Engagement, 1933-1964* (Honolulu: University of Hawai'i Press, 2015), ch. 7, and Yellen, *Greater East Asia*, ch. 5.
51 Narangoa, 'The Assembly', 243.
52 Yellen, *Greater East Asia*, 141.
53 Abel, *International Minimum*, 195.
54 Quoted after Narangoa, 'The Assembly', 246.
55 'Joint Declaration of Greater East-Asiatic Nations', in *The Assembly of Greater East Asiatic Nations* (Tokyo: Nippon Times, 1943), without page numbers.
56 Aydin, *Anti-Westernism in Asia*, 161.
57 Aydin, *Anti-Westernism in Asia*, 186.

12

Partnership in/against empire

Pan-African and imperial conferencing after the Second World War

Marc Matera

Six months after the historic Pan-African Congress in Manchester between 15 and 21 October 1945, a number of the same Caribbean and African intellectuals participated in the 'Conference on the Relationship between the British and Colonial Peoples', organized by the Fabian Colonial Bureau (FCB) and held in Clacton-on-Sea on 12–14 April 1946. These conferences represented two competing visions of international organization and partnership – one dedicated to dismantling the structures of colonialism and global white supremacy, the other rooted in a vision of a reformed British Empire as a modernizing force of social progress. 'Partnership' emerged as the new buzzword for imperial relations during the urgent wartime rebranding effort. While the British socialists who organized the Clacton conference and the post-war Labour Government envisioned partnership between Britons and colonial peoples in colonial economic development and, eventually, devolution of political power within the British Commonwealth, the African, Afro-Caribbean and African-American organizers and attendees of the Pan-African Congress articulated a vision of internationalist partnership in the struggle against empire. Both claimed to be socialist in their essentials, called for cooperation across colonial divisions and presented colonial freedom as the final goal, but they defined colonial freedom – and the best route to it – differently.

Conferencing could be and was used as a strategy for maintaining as well as for challenging empire and racism. Beginning at least with the Berlin Conferences of 1884 and 1885 through the Round Table Conferences of 1930–2 and African Conference of Governors in 1947–8, conferences lent a veneer of diplomatic legitimacy to the pursuit and maintenance of empire. They formed part of the 'stalling strategy' of successive British governments on the question of political reform from the interwar period onwards.[1] Conferencing was also an important facet of anti-colonial agitation. African, Afro-diasporan, Asian and Arab activists and intellectuals held shadow gatherings alongside or intervened directly in imperial and diplomatic conferences, exhibitions and commissions between 1919 and 1945. From the 1900 Pan-African Conference in London to the 1955 Asian-African Conference in Bandung and the 1958 All-African People's Conference in Accra, conferencing remained a mainstay of transregional political networking among anti-colonial intellectuals, liberation movements and, after decolonization, representatives of post-colonial states. The relationship between the Pan-African Congresses and the larger history of pan-Africanism and Black internationalism remains a subject of research and debate, but the practice of conferencing was central to efforts to link and amplify struggles across Africa and the African diaspora.[2] Certain conferences, such as the Manchester Pan-African Congress and Bandung, have become symbols of the 'moment' or 'era' of decolonization and the emergence of post-colonial nation states.

The 1945 Pan-African Congress was an outgrowth of networks of Black anti-colonialists across Britain, the British Empire and the anglophone Atlantic world, the reach of which it in turn extended. Emboldened by the recent Pan-African Congress, the African and Afro-Caribbean attendees of the 1946 FCB conference used it as a platform from which to advance the case for colonial self-determination, reiterating the congress's core demands and critiquing the Labour government's attempt to build social democracy in Britain on imperialism and colonial exploitation. The FCB conference provides an opportunity to explore Black internationalist visions of colonial liberation and federation in relation to the contradictions of post-war Labour Party's imperial socialist internationalism.

Historians have critiqued the methodological nationalism of histories of decolonization from a variety of perspectives.[3] While Europeanists have explored the neocolonial impulses behind federalist schemes in the late Dutch, Portuguese and French empires and even European integration, the recent work of scholars such as Frederick Cooper, Gary Wilder and Adom Getachew 'expands the range of projects that constituted the mid-twentieth-century "federal moment" to include efforts that were supranational but expressly postcolonial'.[4] Cooper and Wilder have returned to the attempts of francophone West African and Antillean intellectuals to transform the French Empire into an egalitarian, multiracial federation. By contrast, within the British Empire, African and Afro-Caribbean anti-colonialists' calls for internal self-government turned rather quickly into demands for complete independence during the late 1940s and 1950s. Seizing upon the language of the Atlantic Charter outlining the Allies' war aims in 1942, the delegates at the 1945 Pan-African Congress demanded the right to 'self-determination'. A number of those who participated in it subsequently led anti-colonial liberation movements that resulted in new independent nation states. However, national and regional ambitions did not exhaust the political identifications of anglophone African and Afro-Caribbean anti-colonialists. The 'combination of nationalism and internationalism that [Kwame] Nkrumah and others articulated' might be described, as Getachew suggests, as 'internationalism of the nation-state'.[5] Many continued to articulate their goals in terms of regional units and envisioned them as building blocks of either a reconstituted British Commonwealth of Nations or a global confederation of self-governing post-colonial states. West African intellectuals saw the creation of a united, federal state in British West Africa as the first step towards continental political integration.

Black activist-intellectuals used 'federation' in two complementary senses, both of which presupposed difference within a functional unity. As a form of organizing in associational life, federation implied an elective assembly of formally independent organizations representing distinct but related constituencies and struggles. For many, federation also represented the preferred political form for the attainment of colonial freedom. The organizers of the 1945 Pan-African Congress employed international conferencing as a means towards the networking and coordination of localized liberation struggles, and at the same time, articulated the ultimate goals of those struggles in terms of federal political structures.

Towards Pan-African Federation

Planning for the Fifth Pan-African Congress in Manchester began in earnest in 1944, but in many ways, preparations for another Pan-African conference of some sort started much earlier. Unlike the previous congresses, which had been organized by W. E. B. Du Bois from the United States, the organizers were based mainly in London. The Pan-African Federation (PAF), an umbrella group representing several Black organizations in Britain and the colonies and led by a group of Africans and Afro-Caribbeans around the Trinidadian radical George Padmore, formed a secretariat to lead the planning effort. This group included the Kenyan Jomo Kenyatta, the South African writer Peter Abrahams and the Guyanese T. Ras Makonnen (born Thomas Griffiths). Makonnen, who had moved to Manchester at the start of the war and ran several businesses, and the physician and president of the PAF Dr Peter Milliard, who also lived in the city, provided crucial connections and on-the-ground support.

Nevertheless, the 1945 Pan-African Congress was a product of transcolonial networking beyond the contacts and capacities of any individual or organization. As John Munro observes, 'In bringing together a geographically dispersed group of scholars and activists to orchestrate a common project designed to further the cause of freedom from colonialism, the efforts that preceded conferences such as the 1945 Pan-African Congress were often as important as the event itself.'[6] The idea for another international gathering of people of African descent had been circulating among interconnected circles of Black intellectuals and activists on both sides of the Atlantic since the mid-1930s. Before settling in London, Padmore collaborated with Tiemoko Garan Kouyaté and a 'politically diverse collection of the black intellectual luminaries on the Paris scene' in abortive effort to organize a Congress of the Negro Peoples of the World in Paris, London, or Geneva in July 1935.[7] In 1938, Dr Harold Moody, the Jamaican founder-president of the League of Coloured People (LCP), announced that the group was planning a World Conference of Africans and people of African descent to be held in 1940.[8]

The end of the war and the United Nations Conference on International Organization, which met in San Francisco through the spring of 1945 and produced the United Nations Charter, gave renewed urgency to Black anti-colonial organizing and to plans for a Pan-African conference while also providing new opportunities for agitation. Black intellectuals and activists called on the imperial powers to extend the right of self-determination promulgated in the Atlantic Charter to their colonies. Moody of the LCP contacted Du Bois in early 1944 regarding organizing a Pan-African conference. Participants in a LCP conference in late July adopted a 'Charter for Coloured Peoples' demanding 'full self-government'.[9] Du Bois also corresponded with Amy Jacques Garvey in Kingston about holding a Pan-African Congress in London or somewhere in Africa and approached the National Association for the Advancement of Colored People (NAACP), which he had recently rejoined, and the New York-based Council on African Affairs (CAA) for assistance. Led by Max Yergan, Paul and Eslanda Robeson, and William Alphaeus Hunton, Jr, the CAA held a conference, 'Africa – New Perspectives', in New York on 14 April 1944. Du Bois took part in the conference, which demanded the application of the principles of the Atlantic Charter to European colonies in Africa. In February 1945, Du Bois wrote to Moody proposing Dakar, Freetown and Monrovia as possible sites for a NAACP-sponsored Pan-African Congress. In April, Du Bois organized a preliminary workshop of prominent African-American, Afro-Caribbean and African intellectuals at the Schomburg Library in Harlem that produced resolutions citing colonialism as the cause of the war and demanding independence of European and US colonies – major themes of the book Du Bois was completing, *Color and Democracy: Colonies and Peace* (1945). Soon afterwards, he travelled to San Francisco for part of the United Nations conference.[10]

In the end, George Padmore and the representatives of the various groups that made up the expanded PAF took the initiative first. The immediate impetus for the Pan-African Congress came from the conferences of the World Federation of Trade Unions (WFTU) in London and Paris in 1945.[11] Representatives of trade union movements in the Caribbean and West Africa attended the World Trade Unions Conference in London in February. Some had been released recently from imprisonment or extended internments, including Ken Hill from Jamaica, I. T. A. Wallace-Johnson from Sierra Leone and Hubert Critchlow from Guyana. The African and Caribbean trade unionists who had attended the London conference were joined by colleagues from Trinidad and Tobago, Nigeria and British Guiana at the first official World Trade Unions Congress in Paris. All but one participated in the Pan-African Congress.

The PAF invited the delegates from West Africa and the Caribbean to a meeting in Manchester on February 24 during which Padmore proposed holding a Pan-African Congress in Paris in September, following the World Trade Union Congress. This led to the formation of an organizing committee and was followed by a larger public meeting, reportedly attended by 300 people. The organizing committee crafted a 'Manifesto on Africa in the Post-War World', signed by African and Caribbean trade unionists and representatives of the West African Students' Union (WASU), LCP and PAF, and sent it to the United Nations Conference in San Francisco.[12] The same organizations along with the Federation of Indian Associations in Britain, Ceylon Students Association and Burma Association, constituting themselves as a 'Provisional Committee of United Colonial Peoples Federation', held an All Colonial Peoples' Conference (or Subject Peoples' Conference) at Holborn Town Hall in London on 10 June 1945. In pieces published in the *Pittsburgh Courier* in the United States and the *Daily Gleaner* in Jamaica, Padmore heralded the 'historic' event as the first step towards 'a sort of "Colonial International"'. In content and form, as Hakim Adi points out, 'the conference proved to be something of a dress rehearsal for the Manchester Pan-African Congress', but one gesturing towards wider transcolonial solidarities.[13]

Kwame Nkrumah's arrival in London in early 1945 also proved to be fortuitous. Nkrumah had been in the United States for a decade, studying at Lincoln University and the University of Pennsylvania and spending his summers in Harlem. There, he first encountered Marcus Garvey's writings and participated in local branches of the Universal Negro Improvement Association and African student organizations.[14] Nkrumah spoke at the CAA's 'Africa – New Perspectives' conference in 1944 and Du Bois's Harlem Workshop in 1945. In London, the energetic young firebrand immediately became active in the PAF and WASU. Peter Abrahams recalled that Nkrumah 'had quickly become part of our African colony in London and . . . our protests against colonialism'.[15] He formed a West African secretariat, which functioned semi-autonomously in the months leading up to the Pan-African Congress. Nkrumah's prominent position as a co-convener and keynote speaker at the conference alongside W. E. B. Du Bois elevated his standing in the eyes of African and Caribbean students, activists and trade unionists as well as British politicians and colonial officials.

Representatives of the PAF, LCP and WASU met in Manchester on July 17, the day after the opening of the Potsdam Conference, to hammer out a provisional agenda but did not finalize a date or a location for the Pan-African Congress. After the same organizations came together for a two-day conference in Manchester in early August, Padmore wrote to Du Bois to inform him that the Pan-African Congress would begin on October 15, six days after the World Trade Unions Congress but that the location had been changed to Britain, citing among other reasons a more hospitable environment after the Labour Party's recent electoral victory.[16] In the days between the congress and the opening of the Pan-African Congress in Manchester, there was a second Subject Peoples' Conference at Memorial Hall in London. Though the discussion focused largely on anti-colonial movements in South and Southeast Asia, Wallace-Johnson expressed hope that the 'unity among the coloured races the vast majority of whom are workers and peasants may yet lay the foundation for the wider unity among all workers and exploited and oppressed'. Peter Abrahams once again called for the creation of a 'colonial federation' dedicated to supporting anti-colonial movements everywhere.[17]

The choice of Manchester as the location of the Pan-African Congress was a pragmatic one reflecting the entrepreneurial talents of Ras Makonnen. It was functionally the headquarters of the PAF and the site of many of the planning events. Makonnen owned two businesses – the Ethiopian Teashop and The Cosmopolitan – in the city, and he was a member of the local branch of the Labour Party and an acquaintance of the party secretary and the Lord Mayor of Manchester through whom he secured the use of Chorlton-on-Medlock Town Hall as a venue for the congress. His restaurant, The Cosmopolitan, which Kenyatta managed for a time in the early 1940s, provided financial support for the congress and doubled as a meeting space for the PAF in Manchester. Located on Oxford Road, the restaurant's menu catered to its diverse clientele of Afro-Caribbean coalminers, African university students and African-American soldiers stationed in Manchester. Its staff, which included Indian servers and two Chinese chefs from Cardiff, was equally international.[18] The African-American sociologist St. Clair Drake 'was told that one of the reasons they had the conference in Manchester instead of down in London in 1945 was because they could eat out of Makonnen's restaurant'.[19] Makonnen and Milliard also used their connections to the local Black community to find accommodations for delegates in the city.[20]

Ninety delegates and roughly 200 people in total attended the Pan-African Congress. Du Bois presided over the conference. The Jamaican Amy Ashwood Garvey, who had participated in the CAA's 'Africa – New Perspectives' conference in New York, chaired the opening session. A number of future post-colonial leaders in Africa – Kenyatta, Nkrumah, Nnamdi Azikiwe, Obafemi Awolowo and Hastings Banda – were present. Wallace-Johnson represented the Sierra Leonean affiliates of the Trade Union Congress and West African Youth League. Black organizations across Britain took part, as did representatives of political parties, such as the People's National Party in Jamaica and the National Council of Nigeria and the Cameroons. Unlike the previous Pan-Africanist Congresses, Black trade unionists from Africa, the Caribbean and Britain were well represented, reflecting the opportunity provided by the World Trade Unions Congress and the organizers' wishes. The participation of organizations in Africa, including the Sierra Youth League, Kikuyu Central Association and Friends of African Freedom, also distinguished the Manchester conference from the earlier congresses. The gathering was overwhelmingly one of people of African descent within the British Empire, but at least two Black Americans besides Du Bois took part – Henry Lee Moon, a representative of the NAACP and Congress of Industrial Unions, and Aaron Mozelle, an African-American émigré representing the Colonial and Coloured People's Association of Cardiff.[21] Representatives of the Independent Labour Party, Women's International League, Ceylon Lanka Sama Samaj and the Federation of Indian Associations of Great Britain attended as 'fraternal delegates' or outside 'observers'. *Picture Post* dispatched photographer John Deakin to Manchester to cover the event. Deakin's images show a large, partially filled hall of predominately dark-skinned men in well-worn European-style suits with a scattering of Black women (many still wearing their outerwear), a few white men and a trio of white women taking notes in front of the stage (see Figure 12.1). Posters bearing slogans such as 'Africa Arise!' 'Oppressed People of the World Unite!' 'Freedom for Subject Peoples!' 'Down with Colour Bar!' 'Down with Anti-Semitism!' and 'Arabs and Jews Unite Against British Imperialism!' adorned the walls and podium. In one photograph, John McNair, the general secretary of the Independent Labour Party, addresses the audience as the chair, Amy Ashwood Garvey, looks on.[22]

Over the course of a week, the congress heard talks on a wide range of issues and places and unanimously adopted some twelve pages of resolutions covering the United Nations Organization, the Caribbean and Africa. One notable addition to the provisional agenda for the conference was 'The Colour Problem in Britain', the topic of the first day's session which Ashwood Garvey chaired. In his address, Du Bois declared, 'We demand for Black Africa autonomy and independence, so far and no further than it is possible in this "ONE WORLD" for groups and peoples to rule themselves subject to inevitable world unity and federation.' Nkrumah argued that 'the struggle for political power by colonial and subject peoples is the first step towards, and the necessary prerequisite to, complete social, economic and political emancipation', and called upon 'Colonial and Subject Peoples of the World' to 'Unite'. Representing the Federation of

Figure 12.1 The audience listening to speakers at the Pan-African Congress in Manchester. Photograph by John Deakin for the *Picture Post*, October 1945. Source: John Deakin / Picture Post / Getty Images.

Indian Associations of Great Britain, Surat Ali appealed for Africans and Indians to come together in 'common struggle . . . so that coloured people would no longer be oppressed'. Ashwood Garvey injected a feminist perspective into the male-dominated conversation on 19 October: 'Very much has been written and spoken of the Negro, but for some reason very little has been said about the black woman. She has been shunted into the social background to be a child-bearer. This has been principally her lot.'[23]

Led by Nkrumah, the West African National Secretariat drafted a separate set of resolutions on the region. 'The claims "partnership", "trusteeship", "guardianship", and the "mandate system"', the delegates maintained, 'do not serve the political wishes of the people of West Africa.' They insisted that 'the artificial divisions and territorial boundaries created by the imperialist powers are deliberate steps to obstruct the political unity of the West African people' and 'THAT COMPLETE AND ABSOLUTE INDEPENDENCE FOR THE PEOPLES OF WEST AFRICA IS THE ONLY SOLUTION TO THE EXISTING PROBLEMS!!'[24]

The PAF worked to circulate the conference resolutions widely. The British press largely ignored the Pan-African Congress, aside from brief coverage in the *Manchester Guardian* and *Daily Herald* and a feature, accompanied by Deakin's photographs, in *Picture Post*. The Independent Labour Party publication, *The New Leader*, and its successor, *Socialist Leader*, featured contributions from PAF members before and after the Pan-African Congress, including a piece by Abrahams on the event.[25] Before returning to the United States, Du Bois held a press conference in London, and the PAF held demonstration in London's Trafalgar Square on 9 December 1945 to further publicize the resolutions adopted at the congress. On the other side of the Atlantic, the African-American newspaper, the *Pittsburgh Courier*, reported on the event, and Padmore summarized some of the speeches in the *Chicago Defender*. Nnamdi Azikiwe, who had contributed financially to the congress, published several articles in the *West African Pilot*. After the conference, Makonnen opened a bookstore and press in Manchester and, for two years, edited the PAF's *Pan-Africa: Journal of African Life and Thought*, while advocating and arranging legal support for Black residents in Manchester and Liverpool. *Pan-Africa*, the cover of which featured a map of the African diaspora around the Atlantic with the words 'United States of Africa' emblazoned on the African continent, published the resolutions adopted at the Pan-African Congress.[26] Padmore edited and self-published 2,000 copies of the conference proceedings as *Colonial and . . . Coloured Unity – A Programme of Action – History of the Pan-African Congress* in 1947.

Though Nkrumah remained a member of the PAF's executive committee, Abrahams remembered that he 'drifted away from us (the PAF)' and increasingly devoted his energies to 'his own West African group', the West African National Secretariat (WANS).[27] The group was a direct outgrowth of the Pan-African Congress.[28] However, it drew on regional West African political imaginaries and the legacy of the National Congress of British West Africa, as much as the tradition of the earlier congresses. The WANS's main goals mirrored those of the WASU or represented an escalation of the latter's demands, and most of the WANS's members were active in both groups. At a meeting in December 1945, the founding members agreed that the WANS's purpose was to support and coordinate with 'progressive organizations in West Africa with a view to realising a West African Front for a United West African National Independence'.[29] The WANS and WASU organized a conference of West Africans, including representatives of two French colonies, in London at the end of August 1946 with the goal of forming an All-West African Congress. Despite nagging financial problems, the WANS produced a journal, *The New African*, and published several pamphlets, most notably Bankole Awoonor-Renner's *West African Soviet Union* (1946) and Nkrumah's *Towards Colonial Freedom* (1947). The WANS's journal *The New African* and Awooner-Renner's *West African Soviet Union* reprinted the resolutions of the West African delegates. In the preface to *West African Soviet Union*, Awoonor-Renner writes, 'It is only a united and independent West Africa, free from every vestige of foreign control, that could ensure security, happiness and prosperity'; 'help us . . . to create a free, united, strong and independent West African Federated Nation.' 'The freedom of the continent of Africa', he asserts, 'lies in the bosom of West Africa.'[30] For Nkrumah and Awoonor-Renner, this expansive conception of united West Africa would be a stepping stone towards – and a regional component of – a continent-wide federation.

Padmore, Makonnen and Abrahams objected both to the WANS's exclusive focus on West Africa and its ties to the Communist Party.[31] To the former charge, Nkrumah insisted, 'West African nationalism does not preclude African nationalism . . . a united free and independent West Africa is the political condition for Africa's redemption and emancipation ... [and] for the emancipation of the Africans and peoples of African Descent throughout the world.'[32] Despite their disagreements, the tactics and goals of Nkrumah and Awoonor-Renner remained similar to those of Abrahams and the Caribbean pan-Africanists Padmore and Makonnen, and relations among them, if strained at times, were never broken. Both the PAF and WANS made it clear that their ultimate goal was not merely independence along existing territorial lines but a union of socialist African states. When St. Clair Drake came to Britain in 1947, Padmore and others told him that they agreed 'that what they ought to do, now that the conference was over, was to get home as soon as possible and put themselves at the head of the mass movements that were already brewing'. Kenyatta returned to Kenya in 1946. At about the same time, the WANS began preparing for Nkrumah's return to the Gold Coast, and he left the following year. During the 1950s, he and Padmore remained close, with Padmore eventually serving as one of Nkrumah's advisers in Ghana. They organized the 1958 All-African Peoples Conference in Accra soon after Ghanaian independence. 'The perspective at this Pan-African conference and its aftermath was not fifty African states, it was continental government of the continent.'[33]

The Manchester conference and the frenzy of activity preceding and following it forged new links between Black internationalist intellectuals and emerging labour and political movements in the Caribbean and Africa and helped to propel Nkrumah and Kenyatta to the forefront of growing anti-colonial movements after they returned to Africa. In hindsight, the congress assumed the proportions of a major turning point for many who attended it. At Manchester, many later suggested, the pan-Africanist movement of educated Afro-American intellectuals became one of and for the African masses. Nkrumah claimed that it 'brought about the awakening of African political consciousness. It became in fact, a mass movement of Africa for the Africans.'[34] For Abrahams, 'The Fifth Pan-African Congress was the first truly representative one.'[35] Such statements testify to the long symbolic afterlife of the conference. This version of Manchester has been deployed often in the service of teleological narratives of the triumph of anti-colonial nationalism. At shorter remove, in 'The Congress in Perspective', Abrahams situated the event alongside the Subject Peoples' Conference that preceded it as signs of rising 'Colonial and Coloured unity' and linked it to a federalist political project: '*FORWARD TO THE SOCIALIST UNITED STATES OF AFRICA! LONG LIVE PAN-AFRICANISM!*' [36]

Imperialism divides – Socialism unites

De sun was bright, de day was fair,
Me heart was full wid glee,
As bans a wee jump off a train,
At Clacton pon de sea.

Black and wite an some wee-droppers
From near and far dem come

Fe spen week en' have conference
An murder up dem gum.

Dem lick dem gum 'gains' politics
Dem beat it up pon war
Dem batter it wid colour prejudice
An colour bar!

Dem jam teet eena Exploitation
Bite hypocrisy
Dem naw pon Complete Freedom an
Pon Race Equality...

Louise Bennett, 'Po' Gum'[37]

The 'Conference on the Relationship between the British and Colonial Peoples', organized by the FCB and held in Clacton-on-Sea in April 1946, staged a conversation among an impressive collection of Black intellectuals, British socialists and social scientists who worked on the colonies. Rita Hinden and J. F. Horrabin, cofounders and the secretary and chairperson of the FCB respectively, presided over the conference. The social anthropologist Kenneth Little delivered a talk based on his recent fieldwork in Sierra Leone. The sociologist Thomas S. Simey, who had served as the social welfare adviser to the Comptroller of Development in Jamaica since 1941, chaired the conference. Little went on to publish his revised doctoral thesis, *Negroes in Britain* (1948), and books on Sierra Leone, while Simey published *Welfare and Planning in the West Indies* in 1946 and became 'a key proponent of the "modern sociology" and of the burgeoning field of social policy'.[38] Roughly sixty people from the colonies, mainly Afro-Caribbeans and Africans, attended the Clacton conference. Nkrumah, Saint Lucian economist W. Arthur Lewis and Trinidadian sociologist Lloyd Braithwaite delivered speeches at the Clacton conference. Padmore, Kenyatta, Abrahams and the Jamaican historian Elsa Goveia intervened critically in the discussions. Though largely forgotten today, the conference was immortalized in Black literature, inspiring the Jamaican poet Louise Bennett's satirical dialect verse 'Po' Gum' and a pivotal moment in Abrahams's pan-Africanist novel, *A Wreath for Udomo* (1956).

Founded in 1940 ostensibly as an independent think tank, the FCB functioned as an advisory body and, as the WASU put it, and 'unofficial mouthpiece' of the Labour Party.[39] The Labour MP and future colonial secretary Arthur Creech Jones served as the bureau's first chair, succeeded by J. F. Horrabin, but the executive secretary Dr Rita Hinden, a Jewish South African economist, directed its activities. A lifelong socialist, Horrabin was a cartoonist, illustrator, editor and cartographer. He edited multiple socialist periodicals, including the FCB's journal, *Empire*, and applied a critical socialist approach to geography, producing atlases that graphically displayed imperial rivals and hierarchies and global networks of economic interdependence and exploitation. Hinden had spent much of the 1930s in Palestine, where she and her husband were active in the Labour Zionist movement, before settling in London in 1938. Though she claimed to know little about Britain's colonial empire prior to working for the FCB, she produced the majority of the bureau's pamphlets, articles, work-in-progress reports and news briefs for Members of Parliament as well as books such as *Plan for Africa* (1941).[40] As the end of the war approached and movements for colonial liberation gained momentum, the FCB's attention focused increasingly on colonial Africa, and the bureau took a leading role in articulating a new rationale for colonial rule. Writing in the WASU's journal, Hinden dismissed the possibility of 'a complete dissolution of the association between Britain and the colonial empire', and instead proposed a 'partnership . . . between progressives forces of Britain and their counterparts in the colonies', arguing that the best way forward for Britain's African colonies was 'to remain inside some form of commonwealth or empire, but bearing a new status'. The word 'partnership' and the closely related goal of colonial economic development were intended to signal a new orientation for the post-war empire, especially in Africa.[41]

African and Afro-Caribbean intellectuals in Britain expressed scepticism regarding the attempted rebranding of imperial relations, but like their counterparts in the French Empire, some appropriated the notion of partnership to argue for a radical transformation of the British Empire into an egalitarian Commonwealth. In *Colour Bar* (1944), Moody wrote, 'The spirit of trusteeship, which emerged with the last war, must give way to the idea of partnership', and colonial 'peoples . . . must . . . play their full part in the great enterprise of the British Commonwealth of Nations'.[42] Throughout the war years, Padmore called on British workers to transform the British Empire into a socialist federation of self-governing states, arguing that their peace and prosperity was bound up with the issue of colonial freedom. In a 1942 interview with Nancy Cunard, Padmore explained, 'we would like to see the collaboration and co-operation of all the lands which now comprise the British Empire put on a federal basis, evolving towards a socialist commonwealth'. Moreover, 'the islands [of the Caribbean] should then be federated to form the United West Indies', and 'the four units – Sierra Leone, Gambia, the Gold Coast, Nigeria, which now constitute West Africa – should be federated along the lines suggested for the West Indies'.[43] Written in fits and starts during the war years with his partner and collaborator Dorothy Pizer and completed hastily at war's end, *How Russia Transformed Her Colonial Empire: A Challenge to the Imperialist Powers* (1946) denounces both 'Tory' and 'Fabian imperialism', and as Leslie James notes, 'essentially provides a blueprint to British workers for how to transform their own empire'.[44]

In late July 1945, as plans for the Pan-African Congress were coming together, the Labour Party won a historic victory in the first general election in Britain for a decade. Africans and Afro-Caribbeans in the metropole supported Labour Party candidates, delivering speeches and canvassing door to door. 'From W.A.S.U. our general headquarters', Joseph Appiah recalled, 'went the war cry to every member: "The Tories must be destroyed wherever they are!"'[45] Once the results became official, H. O. Davies drafted a letter of congratulations on behalf of the WASU to his former professor and one of the primary architects of Labour's victory, Harold Laski.[46] The *League of Coloured Peoples Newsletter* congratulated the LCP's 'good friends for many years – Mr. A. Creech Jones and Mr. Reginald Sorensen'.[47] Such outpourings of goodwill were also statements of expectations for radical change. Only weeks prior to the Manchester Pan-African Congress, the PAF and WASU produced an 'Open Letter to the Prime Minister' which insisted upon 'the immediate right to self-determination' for colonial peoples: 'We wish to welcome Labour's great victory, for which we, as colonials, have hoped and worked alongside Britain's workers. . . . It is the challenge of our time that you, Mr. Attlee, and your Government should give the Socialist answer to the Tory imperialism of Mr. Churchill's "what we have we hold". What will your answer be?'[48]

The post-war Labour government insisted that political reform in the colonies was subordinate to – indeed, depended upon – progress in economic development and social welfare. Though successive Labour colonial secretaries, George Hall and Creech Jones, and multiple white papers and platform statements reaffirmed that 'responsible self-government' was the ultimate goal of colonial policy, the government rebuffed demands for national self-determination as contrary to socialist internationalism, geopolitical realities and even the best interest of colonial populations under existing circumstances.

With the turn to colonial development, the need to enlist the support of young educated Africans was greater than ever before. Two prominent, well-respected Black intellectuals, Lewis and the Sierra Leonean Dr Robert Wellesley Cole, served on the FCB's advisory committee during the mid-1940s, and Lewis and the Guyanese actor Robert Adams contributed to the FCB's *Freedom for Colonial Peoples* (1942). At the same time, Hinden and other authorities on colonial affairs with whom she corresponded expressed cynicism regarding the prospects for cooperation with intellectuals and activists from the colonies – the educated African 'elite' – whom they viewed as single-mindedly and self-servingly focused on political reform and self-determination. Such views surfaced during both the planning process and the proceedings of the FCB conference at Clacton-on-Sea. Hinden hoped the event would foster greater understanding and cooperation between British socialists and Black intellectuals, especially students, from the colonies. However, her draft schedule buried the topic of political self-government at the end of the conference, and her initial list of proposed participants excluded Black radicals in London. Ultimately, at Lewis's urging, Hinden invited Padmore, Nkrumah, Kenyatta and Abrahams as well as representatives of the LCP, WASU and West Indian Students' Union to attend a preliminary meeting on 8 February 1946 and to take part in the conference itself.[49]

Roughly one hundred and twenty people attended the weekend conference in Clacton-on-Sea (see Figure 12.2). Approximately half of them hailed from the colonies. As Louise Bennett puts it in the dialect poem that she wrote for the occasion, 'de sun was bright, de day was fair' as attendees, travelling mainly from London, arrived by train on 12 April. They stayed at a Workers' Travel Association hostel in the seaside resort town popular with working- and lower-middle-class Londoners. According to the FCB's pamphlet with selections from the conference proceedings, 'It was a beautiful sunny weekend, and the talks took place in the friendliest and most comfortable of surroundings.' The preface suggests that the location and favourable weather 'enabled the candour of the speakers to be unsullied by personal animosities, and for good comradeship to overlay even the sharpest criticisms'. This characterization minimizes the level of disagreement at the conference. The organizers had hoped the conference

Figure 12.2 Oulton Hall, Clacton-on-Sea. Source: Aero Pictorial, Air Photograph No. 4765 / Historic England, AP/121452.

would help to break 'the vicious circle of misunderstandings and recriminations' and to 'win the colonial people's confidence', but afterwards, Hinden privately acknowledged that it was a failure.[50]

From the beginning of the conference, the Afro-Caribbean and African participants criticized the Labour government's inaction on racial discrimination and political reform. Lloyd Braithwaite, then a postgraduate student at the London School of Economics, and Nkrumah spoke during the opening session on Friday evening on 'Reasons for Distrust on the Part of the Colonial Peoples'. Braithwaite highlighted the inherently racist nature of colonialism and challenged the Labour Party's socialist credentials: 'Any country possessing an empire must to some extent hold the theory of a master race.' If the Labour Party 'does not pay attention to colonial problems', he added, 'it is in a sense a nationalist, not a truly Socialist, party'.[51] Nkrumah reiterated the demand for 'COMPLETE AND ABSOLUTE INDEPENDENCE' and read the long list of resolutions adopted by the West African delegates at the Pan-African Congress. During the ensuing discussion, others railed against the self-interest and racial paternalism underlining British socialists' emphasis social and economic development and their ceaseless invocations of partnership. Abrahams interjected, 'Who are these Englishmen to say "you are not fit for self-government – you should first develop along certain lines.". . . . If we are human beings, we have the right to self-determination.' Kenyatta insisted, 'Racial discrimination is the worst factor – the Labour Government should make a declaration abolishing racial discrimination in all British colonies.' Padmore, on the other hand, emphasized the lack of political rights in the colonies: 'Race is not the primary factor – distrust exists because there was domination.'[52]

During the discussion in second session on Saturday morning, Hinden presented the differences between anti-colonialists such as Nkrumah and British socialists like herself as ones of 'approach' and 'focus' in pursuit of the same goals of 'independence and social justice'. She explained, 'When Mr. Nkrumah said "We want absolute independence" it left me absolutely cool. Why? . . . colonial peoples today want self-government and independence. British socialists are not so concerned with ideals like independence and self-government, but with the idea of social justice.' Kenyatta objected, 'Why is there a difference of approach on the part of us colonial people?. . . . The freedom which we claim can never be given by the Fabian Colonial Bureau, and whether or not you are sympathetic to our claim, we shall get that freedom.' The tension within the room mounted as the day went on. During the evening session, Padmore brought up the PAF's open letter to Prime Minister Attlee, crafted amid preparations for the Manchester conference, as an example of the government's unresponsiveness. A few minutes later, Kenyatta exclaimed, 'To the question of partnership: I am tired of talking about this. We are not asking the Labour Government to be revolutionary but to do certain things which it has promised to do. . . . If we are to cooperate at all, it must be on an equal basis. . . . We must have the opportunity to put our own point of view.' Like Padmore, Kenyatta referenced the work of the PAF, citing the Manchester Pan-African Congress: 'English socialists say that the Pan African Federation does not represent anything. Yet we are able to call a conference of our people from all the territories. Unless you change your attitude we cannot cooperate.'[53]

The FCB subsequently published excerpts of the speeches delivered at the Clacton conference as *Domination or Co-operation?* – the first pamphlet in a new 'Colonial Controversy Series'. It includes a portion of Nkrumah's remarks, the bulk of which consist of the resolutions adopted by the West African Secretariat at the Manchester Pan-African Congress.[54] Ironically, this text appeared more than a year before Padmore's edition of the proceedings of the Pan-African Congress. Though the organizers sought to contain the conversation and define the nature of colonial freedom, during the conference and in print, Black intellectuals at Clacton continued to insist that imperialism, whether directed by a socialist or Tory government, was incompatible with democracy and justice. They converted the Clacton conference into a platform for the causes of self-determination and pan-African unity.

Conclusion

'When passion comes to conferences, reason goes out. Let it not be said that our conference was without reason.' With these words, the young peer Lord Rosslee attempts to quiet the crowded hall during Peter Abrahams's fictionalized version of the FCB conference in *A Wreath for Udomo*. The 'uproar' broke out after Thomas Lanwood, a fictionalized Padmore, denounced the 'vulgar chauvinism' of a Progressive Party MP 'recognized as an expert on colonial affairs'.[55] Moments earlier, Mhendi 'wearily' uttered, 'I am a little tired of all you people . . . I'm tired of all your talk about multi-racial commonwealths and freedom and protecting our so-called backward brethren from us. I'm tired of the whole lot of it because I've heard it so often' – remarks strikingly similar to Kenyatta's at the Clacton conference.[56] The trouble started when the conference chairperson interrupted another member of the African Freedom Group on procedural grounds. The chapter and first part of the novel ends with a conversation between Mhendi and the eponymous Udomo, modelled on Nkrumah, on the night between the first and second days of the conference. The pair resolve to assist each other in the liberation of their respective homelands, Panafrica and Pluralia. Mhendi implores, 'You'd have to win freedom first . . . It is my only hope.'[57] Udomo's fiery remarks during the day's session sparked Mhendi's revelation that the success of his struggle in Pluralia was linked to, perhaps even depended upon, that of Udomo's in Panafrica.

The 1945 Manchester Pan-African Congress is by far the better known of these conferences today. The Clacton conference, by comparison, is largely forgotten. The two events and their legacies were connected in a number of ways. The Pan-African Congress, staged opportunistically as a counterpoint to the World Trade Union Congress, was only one expression of black anti-colonial and antiracist activity after the Second World War that led Hinden to organize in the FCB conference in the weeks after it. The Pan-African Congress informed the discussion at the Clacton conference and Black intellectuals' critiques of their self-appointed friends within the Labour Party and FCB. The latter's failure, in turn, led Hinden to convince Creech Jones of the need for a larger official conference, and in 1948, he presided over the Africa conference at Lancaster House, which was attended by sixty-six delegates, including thirty-three Africans, representing the legislative councils of African territories.[58]

These quite different gatherings highlight the centrality of the practice of conferencing in anti-colonial agitation and its perceived affinity with organizing across differences and extra-national political formations such as federations. At the same time, conferences were arenas for competing visions and multiple agendas, for talking past as much as talking with others, and they beget nothing so much as more conferences. African and Afro-Caribbean anti-colonialists understood that, like federalism, conferencing could be employed to silence, to manage and to maintain as well as to challenge colonialism.

Notes

The author would like to thank the Estate of Louise Bennett Coverley for permission to reproduce an excerpt from Louise Bennett Coverley's poem, 'Po' Gum'.

1. Fitzroy Baptiste, 'The African Conference of Governors and Indigenous Collaborators, 1947-1948: Strategy to Blunt the 1945 Manchester Pan African Congress', in *George Padmore: Pan African Revolutionary*, eds. Fitzroy Baptiste & Rupert Lewis (Kingston, Jamaica: Ian Randle, 2009), 37–65 [41].
2. See George Shepperson, 'Pan-Africanism and "Pan-Africanism": Some Historical Notes', *Phylon* 23 (Winter 1962): 346–58; Hakim Adi & Marika Sherwood, *The 1945 Manchester Pan-African Congress Revisited* (London: New Beacon Books, 1995).
3. See Todd Shepard, *Invention of Decolonization: The Algerian War and the Remaking of France* (Ithaca, NY: Cornell University Press, 2006); Michael Collins, 'Decolonisation and the "Federal Moment"', *Diplomacy and Statecraft*, 24 (2013): 21–40; Frederick Cooper, *Citizenship Between Empire and Nation: Remaking France and French Africa, 1945-1960* (Princeton, NJ: Princeton University Press, 2014); Gary Wilder, *Freedom Time: Negritude, Decolonization, and the Future of the World* (Durham, NC: Duke University Press, 2015); Adom Getachew, *Worldmaking after Empire: The Rise and Fall of Self-Determination* (Princeton, NJ: Princeton University Press, 2019).
4. Adom Getachew, 'Securing Postcolonial Independence: Kwame Nkrumah and the Federal Idea in the Age of Decolonization', *Ab Imperio* 3 (2018): 92.
5. Getachew, *Worldmaking after Empire*, 25.
6. John Munro, *The Anticolonial Front: The African American Freedom Struggle and Global Decolonisation, 1945-1960* (Cambridge: Cambridge University Press, 2017), 48.
7. Brent Hayes Edwards, *The Practice of Diaspora: Literature, Translation, and the Rise of Black Internationalism* (Cambridge, MA: Harvard University Press, 2003), 277.
8. Harold Moody, 'President's Message', *The Keys* 5, no. 4 (April–June 1938): 79.
9. The National Archives, Kew, United Kingdom, CO 968/159/9 (1944).
10. Adi, 'George Padmore and the 1945 Manchester Pan-African Congress', 71, 75–6; Munro, *The Anticolonial Front*, 44–6.
11. See George Padmore (ed.), *The Voice of Coloured Labour* (Manchester: PanAf Service Ltd., 1945).
12. Hakim Adi, 'Pan-Africanism in Britain: Background to the 1945 Manchester Congress', in Adi and Sherwood, *The 1945 Manchester Pan-African Congress Revisited*, 17.
13. Padmore quoted in Adi, 'George Padmore and the 1945 Manchester Pan-African Congress', 78–9.
14. Getachew, *Worldmaking after Empire*, 7–8.
15. Peter Abrahams, 'Nkrumah, Kenyatta and the Old Order', in *African Heritage*, ed. Jacob Drachler (New York: Crowell-Collier, 1963), 138. See also Marika Sherwood, 'Kwame Nkrumah: The London Years, 1945-1947', in *Africans in Britain*, ed. David Killingray (London: Frank Cass, 1994), 164–95.
16. Adi, 'George Padmore and the 1945 Manchester Pan-African Congress', 77.
17. Abrahams quoted in Adi, 'Pan-Africanism in Britain', 25.
18. Ras Makonnen, *Pan-Africanism from Within*, ed. Kenneth King (London: Oxford University Press, 1973), 137–8. See also C. L. R. James, *Nkrumah and the Ghana Revolution* (Westport, CT: L. Hill, 1977), 76; John McLeod, 'A Night at

"the Cosmopolitan": Axes of Transnational Encounter in the 1930s and 1940s', *Interventions: International Journal of Postcolonial Studies* 4, no. 1 (2002): 53–67.
19 George Shepperson & St. Clair Drake, 'The Fifth Pan-African Conference, 1945 and the All African Peoples Congress, 1958', *Contributions in Black Studies* 8, Article 5 (September 2008): 43.
20 Makonnen, *Pan-Africanism from Within*, 163.
21 Munro, *The Anticolonial Front*, 54–5, 71; Shepperson & Drake, 'The Fifth Pan-African Conference', 41–2.
22 Hilde Marchant, 'Africa Speaks in Manchester', *Picture Post* (10 November 1945): 19–20.
23 George Padmore (ed.), *Colonial and . . . Coloured Unity: History of the Pan-African Congress* (London: Hammersmith Bookshop Ltd., 1947), 69.
24 Reprinted in Bankole Awooner-Renner, *West African Soviet Union* (London: Wans Press, 1946), 14–16.
25 Marchant, 'Africa Speaks in Manchester', 19–20; W. O. Maloba, *Kenyatta and Britain: An Account of Political Transformation, 1929-1963* (Cham, Switzerland: Palgrave Macmillan, 2018), 88–91; Munro, *The Anticolonial Front*, 63–6.
26 *Pan-Africa* 1, no. 1 (January 1947); Shepperson & Drake, 'The Fifth Pan-African Conference', 40.
27 Abrahams, 'Nkrumah, Kenyatta and the Old Order', 138.
28 Adi, *West Africans in Britain*, 128–9. For a list of WANS members, see Sherwood, 'Kwame Nkrumah', 192, fn. 33.
29 Library of Congress, Washington, DC, National Association for the Advancement of Colored People Papers, Group 2, Box 44, 'Aims and Objectives', 8–9.
30 Awooner-Renner, *West African Soviet Union*, 16.
31 Makonnen, *Pan-Africanism from Within*, 262–3.
32 TNA, CO 964/24, Letter from Nkrumah to J. B. Danquah (April 21, 1947).
33 Shepperson & Drake, 'The Fifth Pan-African Conference', 42, 50.
34 Quoted in J. Ayodele Langley, *Pan-Africanism and Nationalism in West Africa, 1900-1945: A Study of Ideology and Social Classes* (Oxford: Oxford University Press, 1973), 355–6.
35 Peter Abrahams, *The Coyoba Chronicles: Reflections on the Black Experience in the 20th Century* (Kingston, Jamaica: Ian Randle, 2000), 46.
36 Adi & Sherwood, *The 1945 Manchester Pan-African Congress Revisited*, 60–1.
37 'Po'Gum' is an original poem by Louise Bennett Coverley and is reproduced with the permission of the Louise Bennett Coverley Estate. Bodleian Library, Oxford University, Fabian Colonial Bureau Papers, MSS Brit. Emp. s. 365, Box 69, File 2, Louise Bennett, 'Po' Gum.'
38 Mary Chamberlain, 'Small Worlds: Childhood and Empire', *Journal of Family History* 27, no. 2 (2002): 189.
39 'Produce and Politics', *Wāsù* 12, no. 3 (Summer 1947): 5.
40 See Patricia Pugh, *Educate, Agitate, Organize: 100 Years of Fabian Socialism* (New York: Routledge, 2010 [1984]), 188–93; Gilles Palsky, 'Maps Against Imperialism: Frank Horrabin and Alexander Radó's Atlases in the Interwar Period', in *Mapping Empires: Colonial Cartographies of Land and Sea*, eds. Alexander James Kent, Soetkin Vervust, Imre Josef Demhardt & Nick Millea (Cham: Springer, 2020), 159–76.
41 Rita Hinden, 'Partnership and What It Means', *Wāsù* 12, no. 1 (March 1945): 9–10.
42 Harold A. Moody, *Colour Bar* (London: New Mildmay Press, 1944), 22.

43 Nancy Cunard with George Padmore, 'The White Man's Duty: An Analysis of the Colonial Question in Light of the Atlantic Charter', in Nancy Cunard, *Essays on Race and Empire*, ed. Maureen Moynagh (Peterborough, Canada: Broadview, 2002), 145–6.
44 Leslie James, *George Padmore and Decolonization from Below: Pan-Africanism, Cold War, and the End of Empire* (New York: Palgrave Macmillan, 2015), 108.
45 Joseph Appiah, *Joe Appiah: The Autobiography of an African Patriot* (New York: Praeger, 1990), 163.
46 *Wāsù* 12, no. 2 (March 1946): 32.
47 *League of Coloured Peoples Newsletter* 12, no. 72 (September 1945): 127.
48 Quoted in Adi, 'Pan-Africanism in Britain', 23–4.
49 Letter from W. Arthur Lewis to Rita Hinden (17 January 1946), FCB Papers, Box 69, File 3 – Conference on the Relationship between the British and Colonial Peoples, Clacton-on-Sea, 12–14 April 1946.
50 Fabian Colonial Bureau, *Domination or Co-operation? Report on a Conference Between the British and Colonial Peoples* (London: Fabian Publications and Victor Gollancz, 1946), 1–2; John D. Hargreaves, *Decolonization in Africa*, 2nd ed. (London: Routledge, 2014), 105–6.
51 Fabian Colonial Bureau, *Domination or Co-operation?* 3.
52 FCB Papers, Box 69, File 3.
53 FCB Papers, Box 69, File 3.
54 Fabian Colonial Bureau, *Domination or Co-operation?* 4–5.
55 Peter Abrahams, *A Wreath for Udomo* (New York: Knopf, 1956), 75.
56 Abrahams, *A Wreath for Udomo*, 72.
57 Abrahams, *A Wreath for Udomo*, 80.
58 Hargreaves, *Decolonization in Africa*, 106.

13

Skies that bind

Air travel in the Bandung era

Su Lin Lewis

In the 1950s, conferences helped forge bonds of solidarity and collective purpose among Asians and Africans across the decolonizing world. The famed 1955 Asian-African Conference in Bandung is often seen as an inaugural moment for the Third World and the Non-Aligned Movement amid the escalation of the Cold War.[1] Beyond the high diplomacy of Bandung, a broader arc of conferences involved the participation of activists, women, writers and other non-state actors in a range of gatherings that promoted Afro-Asian solidarity.[2] Many of the participants at the 1955 Afro-Asian Conference in Bandung first met in the 1947 Asian Relations Conference in Delhi. The 1953 Asian Socialist Conference in Rangoon laid out many of the early principles of the Bandung conference, from neutralism to Afro-Asian cooperation to a commitment to human rights.[3] After Bandung, the Afro-Asian People's Conference followed in Cairo in 1957, while 1958 saw the Afro-Asian Writers' Conference in Tashkent, the All-African People's Conference in Accra and the first Afro-Asian Women's Conference in Colombo.

Such gatherings were facilitated by air travel, which brought together – at an unprecedented speed – Asian and African political leaders, as well as intellectuals, activists and trade unionists sponsored by various national and international organizations. These pan-Asian, Afro-Asian and pan-African conferences took place on an expanding network of international air routes. While the ability of delegates and observers to travel was essential to the workings and prestige of international conferences, little has been written about the way mobility shaped their dynamics.[4] When examining their material environment, scholars have focused on the conference itself, as in Naoko Shimazu's exploration of Bandung as a site of diplomatic performativity and Sukarno's use of the city's built environment as a theatrical stage for the 'coming out' of the Third World.[5] But as Stephen Legg argues in his study of the Indian Round Table conference and the steamship journeys that Indian delegates took to travel there, journeys to and from conferences also form part of the much wider environment of the event itself beyond the conference hall.[6] These journeys constituted part of the informal world of the Bandung-era conference, shaping delegates' perceptions and experiences of not only the conference but the post-imperial world that they collectively sought to shape.

Air travel was intimately linked to the process of decolonization. In the interwar era, transcontinental air routes had begun to criss-cross Asia and Africa, but high costs made them inaccessible to anti-colonial nationalists, activists and intellectuals. Air travel in the interwar age thus literally constituted what Dipesh Chakrabarty has called the 'waiting room of history': an as-yet unattainable future.[7] Imperial air routes ferried high-level government officials and business elites across imperial spaces, as with the British Overseas Airways Corporation (BOAC) or Royal Dutch Airlines (KLM), which boasted the world's longest air route from Amsterdam to Batavia in the 1930s. Famous European and American aviators stopped in Asian and African cities on round-the-world tours. The only Asians and Africans likely to experience flight in the 1920s were a small group of wealthy elites who could afford their own aeroplanes, including Egyptian and Siamese princes or Indian and Malayan-Chinese tycoons.[8] Increasingly, by the late 1930s, a handful of other air travel enthusiasts acquired aviators' licences, joined flying clubs and took to the skies. As Yoav Di-Capua argues, aviation became a site of class struggle in 1930s Egypt; where the upper class sought to make the skies an exclusive and cosmopolitan space, the *effendiya* (educated middle-class men, often in the civil service) of the late 1930s sought to 'purge local aviation of its foreign elements and forge an authentic aeronautical culture which emphasized equal participation and accessibility to all classes'.[9] After the Second World War, air travel became newly accessible to a wider range of passengers in Asia and Africa. New post-colonial governments and political parties in Asia justified the expense of air travel through the demands of international diplomacy. Bolstered by wartime advances in aviation technology, the late 1940s and 1950s heralded the advent of the jet age, which allowed aeroplanes to travel further, altering the geography of flight paths. Old imperial airlines expanded their routes but faced heavy competition from emerging Asian and African airlines. Indian business mogul J. R. D. Tata created India's first domestic and unsubsidized airline in the 1930s; this became Air India in 1946, nationalized along with other domestic airlines in 1953. Misr Airwork, Egypt's first domestic carrier and an offshoot of the British company Airwork, was acquired by the Egyptian government in 1949.[10] Decolonization resulted in the handover of the Indonesian branch of KLM; at the end of 1949, Sukarno renamed the airline Garuda Indonesia Airways, after the mythical Hindu bird which became the national emblem of the country.

In the 1950s, the gleam of modern aircraft was visible in airports and skies around the Global South and served as a tool of Cold War competition.[11] The most common vessel taken by Asian and African conference delegates was the Douglas DC-3, the world's first successful commercial airliner, pioneered by American industrialists in the mid-1930s. The plane revolutionized commercial aviation in the interwar era and was relatively affordable for new post-colonial governments.[12] Later in the decade, due to closer relations between the Soviet Union and the Afro-Asian world, activists and writers travelled to conferences such as the Tashkent Afro-Asian Writers' Conference in 1958 on Soviet aircraft. The Indonesian writer Pramoedya Ananta Toer remarked that the Illyushin jet on which he travelled from Delhi to Tashkent was twice the size of any aeroplane he had ever taken, fostering a sense of a wonder at the technological progress and potential of the Soviet Union.¹³ Air India's Delhi to Moscow (via Tashkent) route was inaugurated in August 1958, two months prior to the Tashkent conference, with the Soviet Union's Aeroflot airways (see Figure 13.1).

Scholars have shown how US, Soviet and Chinese governments funded the crisscrossing journeys of political leaders, activists, intellectuals, labour leaders, women, sports teams, jazz musicians and dancers to win hearts and minds.¹⁴ By contrast, a focus on the journeys to conferences in Asian and African metropoles highlights the interactions of Asians and Africans with each other, and shows how these journeys contributed to the imagining of the 'Third World' as an alternative pathway to the warring sides of an escalating Cold War. The experiences of journeying to such conferences, often with layovers in Asian cities, provided participants with a sense of comparison and connection between their native countries and societies across the Global South. As we will see, the contrast between air travel and layover stays in hotels and diplomatic residences, alongside on-the-ground experiences of extreme poverty, led delegates to assess the inequalities of the global economic order well before conference sessions on development in the Third World.¹⁵

Air travel, then, was the site of a new politics of decolonization and a contest over the meanings of modernity. It enabled multiple pilgrimages to new destinations across Asia and Africa to collectively imagine a post-imperial future. For post-colonial elites

Figure 13.1 Air India route map, October 1958, Detail of Asia-Africa-Europe route. Courtesy of www.airindiacollector.com/www.indianairmails.com.

who often travelled by chartered plane, arrival on the tarmac served as a spectacular moment of diplomatic performativity. For all those able to take to the skies, travel was exhilarating, illuminating and altered the geography of the imagination, but it could also be dangerous, tiring and lonely, at times leaving one stranded in unfamiliar settings. But most importantly, air travel in the Bandung era offered the possibility of real, face-to-face connections between Asians and Africans, many of whom were travelling outside the bounds of their new countries for the first time. Through air travel, they experienced the contours of solidarity – and its limits – both on and off the ground.

Journeys in the making of Third World diplomacy

In the immediate aftermath of the Second World War, post-colonial governments sought to establish themselves as new diplomatic actors. Conferences allowed post-colonial leaders to meet face-to-face through the spectacle of a 'summit', in place of as-yet-lacking formal diplomatic infrastructure.[16] Flight served to sever imperial ties and forge new links across Afro-Asia, even as some post-colonial governments continued to fight wars of decolonization. Indonesian attempts to get to the 1947 Asian Relations Conference in Delhi, in the waning days of the Indonesian Revolution, faced the obstacle of a Dutch blockade. The story is recounted in the memoirs of Ali Sastroamijoyo, then secretary of Indonesia's National Defence Council, who would later host the 1955 Bandung conference. The Indonesian delegation to Delhi consisted of representatives of different political parties, as well as workers', women's and youth organizations. Serendipitously, in the run-up to the event, a DC-3 landed at Maguwo Airport in Jogjakarta, the seat of the Republican government, carrying a sole Egyptian diplomat sent by King Farouk to transmit a letter recognizing the Republic's sovereignty. The diplomat agreed to allow the delegation of thirty to accompany him on the plane to Singapore. Although the size of the delegation exceeded the passenger capacity of the plane, the delegation leader argued that the Indonesians 'consisted of very thin and light men' because the toils of the revolution had left them 'lacking in nutritious food'.[17] They were duly let on, the plane barely able to lift off the runway. Post-colonial solidarity among new political elites could gloss over the usual hassles of air travel and border-crossings. The speed with which the Indonesian delegation had to arrange their travel to Delhi meant that proper passports could not be arranged; instead, a representative from the Department of Foreign Affairs hurriedly furnished them with paper affidavits. Sastroamijoyo recalled his nervousness at travelling overseas with 'such a "primitive" document'. Arrival in Rangoon, however, was apparently not a problem; delegates were treated as official representatives of the Republic of Indonesia despite their lack of formal diplomatic status. The 'passport' was well received, and Sastroamijoyo speculated that 'probably the Burmese officials were influenced by the words Republic of Indonesia, as they knew that the Indonesian people were fighting against Dutch colonialism'.[18]

One vital member of the Indonesian delegation arrived late to the Delhi conference. Indonesian prime minister and head of Indonesia's Socialist Party, Sutan Sjahrir, was in the midst of finalizing negotiations for Indonesia's formal independence with the Dutch, when he offered to ship 500,000 tonnes of Javanese rice to India towards famine relief, signalling Indonesia's intention to prioritize new pan-Asian relationships. Amid rumors that Sjahrir might travel to Delhi on a British plane, the Dutch government offered a special KLM plane.[19] In a declaration of aeronautical non-alignment, Indian prime minister Jawaharlal Nehru sent his friend Biju Patnaik, a Bengali businessman and aviation mogul, to fly to Java and pick up Sjahrir, an act for which Patnaik was given honorary Indonesian citizenship. On Sjahrir's arrival, Nehru gave him a grand welcome on the airport tarmac, along with his daughter Indira and Sjahrir's estranged Dutch wife Mies du Chateau, who had flown from Holland to surprise him (unbeknown to her, Sjahrir was travelling with a young Indonesian woman, Poppy Saleh, who would become his second wife). Despite the awkwardness of meeting, with Sjahrir hurried into a private car, the press attention surrounding Sjahrir's dramatic arrival across the Dutch blockade contributed to his status as one of the most popular and charismatic figures at the conference. The short hops of long-distance air travel in the 1950s necessitated frequent stopovers to refuel. This allowed participants to work their way to a conference through multiple stops, allowing them to get to know the territory in between, connect with diaspora populations and build personal relationships. For many of the delegates of these conferences, journeys there provided them with the first opportunity to travel and see the region. When the Indonesian delegation travelled to Delhi via Singapore, they were greeted by an Indonesian community waving red and white flags, moving many of the delegates who saw their flag for the first time in a foreign country.[20] On the diplomatic side, the necessity of a layover gave political leaders the opportunity to connect on a one-to-one basis before and after the conference, and pave the way for more gatherings. On Sjahrir's return to Indonesia, he stopped in Rangoon, meeting with the Burmese prime minister U Nu and other socialist leaders, as well as in Singapore, meeting with the United Malay National Organiation. These meetings with Asian leaders, enabled by the need for a layover, helped prepare the groundwork for the Asian Socialist Conference, held in Rangoon in 1953.[21]

The 1955 Bandung conference necessitated many journeys by new political elites and freedom fighters from across the Afro-Asian world. Egypt's Gamal Abdel Nasser travelled to Bandung from Cairo via Karachi and Delhi on a chartered Air India plane, intending to stop in Delhi for a three-day visit to the Indian capital.[22] Carolien Stolte has noted that a number of delegates on their way to Bandung stopped in Delhi to attend a 'People's Conference', a grassroots event compared to the highly orchestrated affair at Bandung.[23] Rameshwari Nehru, the chairman of the Indian reception committee, convinced Nehru to issue visas to foreign delegates, despite his claims that a 'rival conference' in Delhi was embarrassing to the hosts at Bandung.[24] Nasser nonetheless attended the event and was pictured sitting with Nehru, combining his visit with bilateral talks with the Indian prime minister.[25] As Stolte argues, this was not simply an Indian diplomatic event but was convened by actors from a range of backgrounds and nationalities involved in the World Peace Movement.[26] Nasser then agreed to host the 1957 Afro-Asian People's Solidarity Conference in Cairo, a bottom-up event convened by a range of non-state actors similarly branded as a 'People's Bandung'.²⁷ After Delhi, both Nehru and Nasser then travelled together to Rangoon on the way to Bandung, where they met U Nu to participate in Burma's New Year Water Festival (*Thingyan*) celebrations, donning traditional Burmese *longyi* and *gaung baung* (Figure 13.2). This episode is absent in the Bandung literature, yet was crucial in forging a sense of en-route solidarity between the conference's key players. Young Burmese men and women doused the leading lights of the decolonizing world with water. That year's dousing, a Burmese newspaper noted, was 'symbolic and auspicious, since they were on the eve of an international assembly at Bandung, where cool heads and tempers would be required'.²⁸ Zhou Enlai had also arrived in Rangoon a day earlier before Nehru and Nasser, donning Burmese dress to accompany U Nu to a Burmese play and participate in water-throwing festivities across the city.

The 'atmosphere' of Bandung, then, was already formulated in the journeys undertaken by these leaders to the conference.²⁹ As they met in Delhi and Rangoon en route to Bandung, informal conversations between Nehru, Nasser and U Nu – as well as other officials and delegates in their entourage – must have sparked conversations about shared visions for the Afro-Asian world days before Sukarno welcomed them at the Merdeka Palace in Jakarta. The four then all embarked for Bandung by plane together, circumventing civil strife in the Darul Islam rebellion on the roads of Central Java. Though we know little about what was discussed on these journeys, by the time the four leaders arrived at Bandung, the camaraderie between these figures, and their shared commitment to non-alignment, was central to the spirit of the conference.

Figure 13.2 Nasser, U Nu, Nehru and Egyptian minister Salah Salem celebrating the Water Festival in Rangoon en route to the 1955 Bandung conference. Source: Getty Images.

Despite the media-chronicled gaiety of his Rangoon stopover, Zhou's travels to Bandung constituted an international drama in itself. One week before the Bandung conference, the 'Kashmir Princess', an Air India Constellation passenger airliner chartered by the Chinese government, was due to carry Zhou and the Chinese delegation out of Hong Kong to Bandung. Five hours into the flight and 18,000 feet over the South China Sea, an explosion went off, killing all of the plane's eleven passengers.[30] Rumours spread among other delegates making their way to Bandung, including C. S. Jha, Nehru's secretary of external affairs, during his layover in Singapore.[31] But Zhou, it emerged, had never boarded the plane, having been warned of the plot beforehand. The act of sabotage looked to be the work of Kuomintang Intelligence officers in Hong Kong, under the order of Chiang Kai-shek, amid the backdrop of the Taiwan Straits Crisis and the perceived need to prevent the PRC from joining the United Nations, an issue that Zhou was sure to discuss both formally and informally with Bandung delegates.[32] The incident only added to the charm offensive that Zhou cultivated at Bandung. Many have speculated why Zhou never recalled the delegation of young party cadres and journalists who boarded the Kashmir Princess. As Steve Tsang has argued, the incident was followed by the Chinese delegation's exploitation of the propaganda value of the incident.[33] The Chinese Foreign Ministry blamed both the Kuomintang and the United States, claiming that CIA agents had worked with Chiang to sabotage the chartered plane and to subvert the aims of the Bandung conference. The suspected (yet unfounded) involvement of American agents fed into China's attempt to style itself as a 'fellow underdog' of the 'proletariat world' of coloured peoples, rather than a threat to the smaller nations of the region.[34] At Bandung, Zhou was amicable and conciliatory; he won friends among the delegates, aided by the image of being an early victim of airline sabotage cultivated even before Sukarno's opening speech.

While the United States was not officially invited to the conference (nor was the Soviet Union), African-American politicians, intellectuals and journalists sought to join the decolonizing world's struggle against the global colour bar and to participate in what Sukarno heralded as 'the first intercontinental conference of coloured peoples in the history of mankind'.[35] The ways in which they travelled (or didn't) signalled their own departure from US government policies. Harlem congressman Adam Clayton Powell travelled to Bandung via Honolulu and Manila on US military aircraft, where he was met by American diplomatic representatives and officials; his trip from Manila to Bandung, however, was to be considered 'unofficial'. Powell travelled on a Garuda Airways plane and was not met by US Embassy representatives in Jakarta, but only to be given the type of assistance accorded to American journalists.[36]

Richard Wright's *Colour Curtain* has become a canonical account of the conference.[37] Much of the first part of the text constitute interviews with Asians and their views on nationalism, some gathered on Wright's flight to Bandung. After reading about the conference in a café in Paris, where Wright was in self-imposed exile, Wright paid for his airline ticket with a publisher's advance to write a book on the event. He barely slept on the forty-eight-hour flight via Madrid, Rome, Cairo, Baghdad, Karachi, Calcutta, Bangkok and Jakarta. After boarding a KLM Constellation for Cairo, seen from the air as a 'far-flung lake of shimmering lights', he met a group of French journalists en route to the conference 'with the latest news as well as red-fezzed North Africans from Morocco, Algeria, and Tunisia climbing aboard: revolutionaries and nationalists from the turbulent areas of French rule along the life line of Western European imperialism'.[38] He overheard excited discussions of Palestine and plans to raise the 'question of Jewish aggression' (Nasser and other Arab delegations indeed pressed this at the conference, and a declaration of full support for the rights of the Arab people of Palestine appeared in the final communiqué).[39] One of the delegates passed around photos of Arab refugees, which Wright found 'authentic' and 'grim', prompting a reflection on the power and 'irrational' passions of religion in the non-Western world, which continued as he saw turban-clad Sikhs boarding the plane at Karachi and saffron-robed Buddhists at Bangkok. Approaching Baghdad, Wright spoke to a young Indonesian student returning from Leiden who expressed animosity to the West as well as towards Indonesian Chinese (the question of powerful Asian diaspora communities also emerged at Bandung). He also met a Japanese newspaperman en route to the conference from Calcutta to Jakarta, who lamented the Japanese lack of knowledge about Africa, and confessed that Japan's position at the conference would be 'very delicate'.[40] These were essentialist and often inaccurate 'surface' impressions, but nonetheless shed light on the ways in which positions taken at the conference were established, shared and felt among participants even before the event, contributing to their wider emotional history.[41]

The Bandung conference also highlighted significant absences. French and British governments dissuaded leaders from African colonies from participating, including Kwame Nkrumah, who nonetheless negotiated to send a three-man delegation from the Gold Coast.[42] Two of the most famous African Americans in the world at the time were restricted from travelling as a result of America's war against communism. Since 1951, W. E. B. Du Bois and Paul Robeson had had their passports revoked by the US State Department for their sympathies with the Soviet Union and suspected membership of America's Communist Party. They were unable to travel not only to Bandung but to the Asia-Pacific Peace Conference in Beijing in 1952, where both were invited as members of the World Peace Movement. As Stolte has argued, public outrage across Asia and Africa at Robeson's 'grounding' became a rallying point for Afro-Asian solidarity, one particularly pronounced in India, where Robeson had many friends.[43]

The United States was not the only national government to police travel to conferences. Socialist solidarity among Asians and Africans was also hampered by the hardening of national borders and restricted from the very governments that convened at Bandung. The Asian Socialist Conference (ASC), which had initially met in Rangoon in 1953, became a permanent organizational body – retaining 'Conference' in its name – and served as a hub for socialist and decolonizing movements throughout Asia and Africa. Apart from in Burma, most socialist parties in Asia were in political opposition to larger and more powerful nationalist parties. Later bureau meetings of the ASC took place in Hyderabad and Tokyo to discuss economic cooperation and further links with Africa. Indonesian socialists had hoped to host the ASC's third meeting in 1954 in Bandung, but due to the Indonesian government's refusal to allow entry to socialist leaders from Israel, the meeting was moved to Kalaw, Burma. Indonesian socialists speculated that the Sukarno government did not want to grant its political opposition the publicity that such a gathering would entail, one year before the Bandung conference.⁴⁴ Pakistan's government refused visas to members of India's Praja Socialist Party for the meeting of the Pakistan Socialist Party's National Conference in 1954. Efforts to organize international gatherings were thus undermined by barriers created by new national governments.⁴⁵

Major political upheavals also prevented travel and opportunities for Afro-Asian solidarity. Delegates travelled to the Second Asian Socialist Conference, held in Bombay in early November 1956, in the immediate aftermath of the Suez Crisis. The American scholar-activist Alijah Gordon, who was researching Arab nationalism, attended as a member of Lebanon's Socialist Party.⁴⁶ Then also writing articles for the German daily *Die Welt*, she managed with help from the publication to pay for a student ticket, leaving Beirut on Iranian Airways to travel to Bombay via Isfahan, Yazd, Kerman, Zahedan, Kandahar and Karachi. She heard of the Israeli attack on Egypt when she reached Karachi airport and learned upon arrival in Bombay that she was the only one from the Arab world who had arrived; the Lebanese delegation

Figure 13.3 Hamid Algadri's personal photo album, featuring his arrival into Tunis in 1958. Courtesy of the Algadri family.

never boarded their Pan-Am flight with airports in Beirut shut down in the midst of bombardment. The lack of Arab representation at a conference where Israeli socialists were present made, she felt, for a 'rotten atmosphere in which the conference swam'.[47] Facing political opposition at home and ideological rifts among delegates, the ASC fell apart shortly after the Bombay conference. Asian socialists, however, such as Hamid Algadri (brother of Ali Algadri, featured in Figure 13.3), continued to pursue Afro-Asian connections. Algadri led the Indonesian government's support for Tunisian independence, and his personal photo album contains multiple images of his arrival by plane into Tunisia the year after the country's independence, greeted by an official delegation.

In the 1950s, the layover meeting and the tarmac greeting heralded a new age of Afro-Asian diplomacy. The tragedy of the Kashmir Princess flight to Bandung constituted one of the first internationally significant acts of airline sabotage in the commercial era. The new nationalized airlines of post-colonial governments, including Air India and Garuda Airways, ferried conference participants across Asia in the run-up to Bandung. But with the high cost of air travel, powerful patronage networks served as gatekeepers for who could travel and interact. Air travel knitted the world together, but also introduced a new kind of post-colonial politics: the advent of civil aviation had turned borders, visas and passports into the hallmarks of national identity and created new technologies of surveillance. The ideas of solidarity that characterized the Bandung era were both propped up and undermined by national interests and the ability of new national governments to control who flowed in and out of its borders.

'Progress' and 'solidarity' in the literati's layover

Other international conferences attended by Asians and Africans came before and after Bandung, encompassing a broader range of actors from trade union leaders to writers and social workers. The different kinds of journeys participants took to get there show that air travel was still not always accessible or easy for those outside the political elite. Air travel was expensive, and so sea and ground travel continued to be an alternative means of travel for those who could not afford the high cost of a flight. In 1952, members of the Burma Workers and Peasants Party travelled by steamship to Beijing to take part in the Asia-Pacific Peace Conference, a global call to arms by the PRC against the Korean War. They then travelled by rail through Mongolia, Siberia, Moscow, Hungary and Budapest, arriving in Vienna in December 1952 for the World Congress of People for Peace, where they met workers, farmers, doctors, athletes, musicians, and intelligentsia from 85 different countries; the conference opened with a speech by Jean-Paul Sartre. The entire journey – there and back – took four months, breaking friendships among comrades and brothers, and constitute a different kind of travel from that of the post-colonial leaders who leaped through, with few hurdles, the balmy, cosmopolitan ports of the Indian Ocean.[48] Others flew to the Beijing Peace Conference. Latin American delegations took Pan-American Airways routes that hopped through Lima, Mexico City, Honolulu and Tokyo. Panama's delegation were tracked by US intelligence services along the way. Some Latin American delegations, such as the Colombian delegation, journeyed through the Soviet Union, presumably taking the Trans-Siberian railway from Europe. As Rachel Leow argues, such communist peace conferences came under scrutiny precisely 'because of the mobilities they seemed to foster'.[49] Some had difficulties in getting visas and travel papers or risked not being allowed to re-enter their home countries.

Both steamship and air travel affected the way in which delegates thought about the world they sought to stitch together, imprinting the diverse landscapes of the two continents in the imagination of delegates. Because of the nature of the steamship journey or the long-haul flight, with its multiple stops between origin and destination, delegates could see, document and reflect on the territory in between, and witness the stark contrasts between one location and another. In his exploration of modernization in the Arab world, Nathan Citino has shown how air travel was intimately linked with ideas of modernization. The speed of air travel, he argues, not only opened up the world but created a compression of experience that 'altered the politics of intercultural encounters'.[50] As delegates made their way to conferences where development and the inequities of the global economic order were high on the agenda, they compared the locales through which they transited in terms of social progress. On their way to Bandung, Arab leaders stayed in Calcutta at the governor's palace but encountered widespread poverty on city streets. Drawing on the memoirs of Syrian leader Khalid al-Azm, Citino recounts how the experiences of travelling through Asian cities to and after Bandung brought him 'face to face with poverty outside of the Arab world' and led him to provide visceral descriptions of the naked, 'emaciated, and sunburned bodies' of Calcutta's poor and the 'foul-smelling rice paddies' of Bangkok, alongside the potential of farming techniques in Taiwan. As Citino argues, these observations shaped the meaning of 'underdevelopment' for Arab elites and their views of modernization in Afro-Asia.[51]

Asian cities were sites of multiple stopovers for delegates travelling to Afro-Asian conferences, from Bandung to later conferences in Cairo in 1957 and the 1958 Afro-Asian Writers' Conference in Tashkent. Like al-Azm, other Asian writers left vivid descriptions of their journeys to Tashkent, and particularly their stopovers in Delhi, Calcutta, Rangoon and Bangkok, comparing them to Europe, the Soviet Union, as well as their home countries in terms of social progress. For the Japanese writer Katō Shūichi, the bureaucratic hassles of travel through India affected his views of Asia and Afro-Asian solidarity. Upon arrival in Calcutta, he was scheduled to change planes and go on to New Delhi, then to Tashkent. While a Tokyo travel agency assured him he would not need a visa, an airport official told him he could not get into India. As Katō recounts:

> Around that time I got a feeling I had finally embarked on my journey into 'Asia.' Officials in full uniform, half-naked men standing or sitting everywhere, curious American tourists looking over their surroundings, the killing heat, the languid ceiling fans, and the questioning that went on for over an hour with frequent interruptions.[52]

The use of tropes of 'half-naked men', 'languid ceiling fans' and endless questioning echoed colonial-era Orientalist stereotypes of Southern Asians as poor and inefficient, pointing to perceived hierarchies among Asian participants.

The next morning, as Katō embarked for Tashkent, overwhelmed by a 'sense of emancipation', he watched the arid, sparsely populated landscapes of Central Asia unfold before his eyes. 'And', he noted, 'at the end of this unforgiving Central Asian landscape where nomads roamed in antiquity, and indeed at this very extremity of history itself, the modern city of Tashkent suddenly loomed before my eyes'.[53] The descent into Tashkent unveiled a modern socialist city dotted with hospitals, schools and an airport lined with passenger jets, leading Shuichi to compare the city to Tokyo and Europe. Meanwhile, the Indian poet and playwright Krishnalal Shridharani found in Tashkent a 'familiar Easterness' despite 'the world's biggest textile factory and asphalt roads', where 'faces, beards, and suits' were reminiscent of 'Kashmir, Darjeeling, and Bombay'.[54] As Rossen Djagalov notes, despite the intentions of the hosts to showcase Soviet achievements, the real benefit of the conference as observed by Afro-Asian writers was its ability to forge, in the words of Ngũgĩ wa Thiong'o, 'links that bind us': Afro-Asian literary networks, consolidated, in part, by face-to-face connections.[55] These extended beyond the conference site to return journeys. On his return, Katō stayed in India in the company of an Indian friend he had met at the Tashkent conference and was thus able to see the country, 'from the inside':

> Nearly every issue facing underdeveloped regions reached dramatic intensity in India, and I suppose nearly every question facing India also applied to other underdeveloped regions in general. . . . Later on, whenever I heard such phrases as 'underdeveloped countries', 'the 'Third World', or 'Asia, African, and Latin America', what invariably came to mind was the overwhelming site of mass starvation and pervasive poverty among people everywhere – at the roadside of bustling amusement quarters, inside the entrances to government buildings, and in villages in faraway mountains. . . . It is foolish to preach the abstract idea of freedom to someone with an empty stomach. But it is even more foolish to think one can make a hungry man happy simply by throwing crumbs of bread at his feet.[56]

On-the-ground experiences of poverty and comparative 'underdevelopment' across Asia – which weighed heavily in the minds of post-colonial writers – were thus shaped by these encounters, with the 'Afro-Asian conference' providing an excuse to travel and witness the shared, seemingly insurmountable challenges of making a post-imperial world.

The Indonesian writer Pramoedya Ananta Toer, on a layover in Delhi to Tashkent, was also struck by the stark contrasts between rich and poor. Rows of people were crowded together, 'close together as fish drying from the sun', sleeping on mats of the sidewalk, while Indian women emerged from nightclubs, lifting luxurious saris to avoid the dirt on their way to expensive cars. 'The differences', he observed 'between the haves and the have-nots was both obvious and extreme. In that respect, at least, Indonesia was far better off than India was at the time.'[57] Pramoedya's impressions dismantled the myth of Indian superiority, cultivated in the schoolbooks of his childhood, and of Nehru's aim to position India at the vanguard of the decolonising world. The journey caused him to reflect on what he had learned about India during the revolution: 'poverty, caste oppression, periods of mass starvation and death surprised me. How could this mother country, the source of two of the world's great religions and reputedly the mother culture of Southeast Asia, be so incapable of taking care of itself? Even in the midst of the revolution Indonesia managed to send to India rice, shirting, and calico cloth.'[58]

Air travel connected the dots across the imaginative geography of Afro-Asian writers. The importance of geography was evident in a chapter of Pramoedya's memoirs, simply titled 'Geography'. Pramoedya wrote of the journey to his daughter Yudi, inquiring about her progress in the subject; he advised her to take her school atlas, open it to Asia, and to follow his journey and to trace the countries, rivers, mountains, and cities over which he flew. He travelled from Jakarta on a Qantas flight for Singapore and a Cathay Pacific flight to overnight in Bangkok, before leaving for Delhi on Air India. W. E. B. Du Bois similarly wrote to his daughter Yolande, describing his flight to Tashkent. The conference took place the year that Du Bois' passport was reinstated following a US Supreme Court ruling. At the age of 90, the indefatigable Du Bois treated his wife Shirley Graham Du Bois to a first-class steamship journey from New York to Europe, feeling 'like a released prisoner'.[59] While in Europe, he received an urgent telegram requiring his presence at the Tashkent conference, 'expenses paid'.[60] Du Bois excitedly described his flight to Tashkent to Yolande: 'We flew by jet plane and found Tashkent not only hundreds of miles south but also as far east of Moscow as Los Angeles is of New York! We were in central Asia, near Xanadu, "Where Kublai Khan, a stately palace built!"'.

Personal experiences in new surroundings and intercultural encounters could alter or enforce ideas about Afro-Asian solidarity amid the miseries of travel. As Katō traveled through India to Tashkent, having had his passport confiscated, he arrived late at his Delhi hotel and was told he could not pay for the room in travelers' cheques without the passport. The myth of the Bandung spirit was shattered, at least momentarily:

> Totally exhausted and not knowing what to do, I found myself cursing 'Asia-Africa' and myself. My wretchedness must have been written all over my face. When a group of high-spirited, young Indonesian officers marched into the hotel, one of them approached me and asked sympathetically, 'What's the matter?' I briefly explained to him my circumstances, and he was kind enough to pay for my room for the night in Indian currency, saying, 'We should help one another in times of trouble.' That was how I was rescued from my helpless predicament by an officer of Sukarno's army.[61]

Pramoedya, travelling back from Tashkent, found himself stranded in Rangoon without an onward ticket home to Jakarta. He had paid for his own ticket to Tashkent, and though he officially represented Indonesia he received little by way of government support: 'All we got form the government was its blessing, an exit permit, an official government passport, and a suit.'[62] With no funds left in Rangoon, it was a Burmese bus driver who took him into town, free of charge, and waited while Pramoedya tried to get help from the Indonesian Embassy. Embassy staff proved resolutely unhelpful until he threatened to go to the Burmese press, upon which they checked him into a hotel by the railway station without clean water. After three days, during which Pramoedya fell ill with dysentery, the embassy arranged a trip on a KLM flight back to Jakarta via Bangkok (and would later send him an extortionate hotel bill). Pramoedya lamented the lost opportunity to engage with Burmese history or culture and reflected: 'the only thing I got from that visit was ill treatment at the hands of Indonesian government officials who, no different from their colleagues at home, seemed unaware that I was giving twenty percent of every cent I earned to the state. This thought made me bitter, as if my trip had no meaning or mission whatsoever.'[63] Two months after his return, Pramoedya met President Sukarno, providing him with a set of resolutions from the Tashkent conference. He appealed to the president to send, along with formal invitations to other countries for state visits, invitations to writers of those countries to 'present a broader picture of Indonesia to his fellow countrymen'.[64] Sukarno hastily agreed and put Pramoedya in charge of any visiting writers to the country. The journey to Tashkent would be one of Pramoedya's last chances to travel the world for almost a half a century – with the events of 1965 and the overthrow of Sukarno in a military coup, amid the persecution, arrest and killing of half a million communist sympathizers, Pramoedya was exiled to a prison colony in the remote island of Buru; his books were banned, and he would not travel abroad again until 1999.

As Tsitsi Jaji has noted of travellers to Pan-African conferences of the 1960s, few of the participants came from beyond the ranks of intellectuals, politicians or prominent writers and artists.[65] But the experiences of left-leaning intellectuals and writers who attended the peace conferences and writers' conferences of the 1950s differed from that of the high-flying diplomats and political elites who easily travelled through Asia's port-cities. Writers spoke to the gaps between high expectations of Afro-Asian solidarity, development and the all-embracing domain of post-colonial nationalism, and realities on the ground. As they made their way to conferences dedicated to building a better, post-imperial world, the grittiness of travel across Asia reflected the challenges of the task – from the striking inequalities between rich and poor to the corruption and insensitivity of government officials to those in need. It also showed that solidarity and kindness could come from the unlikeliest of heroes: an Indonesian soldier far from home, a sympathetic Burmese bus driver – decent people on the ground, rather than charismatic politicians at lofty heights.

Conclusion

If Bandung, and other forgotten conferences of the era, acted as nodes within the new networks of post-colonial internationalism, then we must take seriously the way in which new kinds of mobility shaped those networks. Sukarno's speech at the opening of the Bandung conference referred to the 'terrific dynamism' of the past fifty years, and the way that man had 'learned to consume distance', while also stressing the new-found proximity between Asian and African nations who no longer had to meet on foreign continents.[66] Air travel brought together participants at an unprecedented speed, creating a visual spectacle of post-colonial freedom and solidarity that displaced links between metropole and colony. Tracing participants' journeys across Afro-Asian conferences in the 1950s expands our notion of the conference site as a place of performativity, interaction and worldmaking. Our methodology for examining such conferences should include sources about and produced at conference sites but also experiences to and from events. These collective testimonies sharpen the contradictions between reality and rhetoric felt by the participants, and highlight the performative, material and multisensory nature of the conference at both the macro and micro scale. But as others have shown, if mobility was a central process in shaping the history of globalization, we must also be aware of the way in which such processes were increasingly regulated and exclusionary.[67] Air travel was still inaccessible to most, and as political leaders travelled differently from struggling writers and activists, we might remember how this affected the experience of the conference – and its wider aims – both on and off the ground. This was particularly true of the Afro-Asian conference, which had at its heart a goal of building cross-cultural solidarity and a better, more peaceful, less unequal world. Moreover, the ability to travel to conferences was affected by the rise of visa regimes put in place by the Cold War and new postcolonial governments keen to restrict movement of certain people and nationalities across their borders. Just as travel expenses and visa regimes have often hindered the in-person participation of scholars from the Global South in conferences in the Global North, such barriers have highlighted the unevenness and bitter-sweet nature of global connection.

Notes

1. Scholarship on Bandung is extensive. See, for example, Vijay Prashad, *The Darker Nations: A People's History of the Third World* (New York: New Press People's History, 2007); Christopher J. Lee (ed.), *Making a World After Empire: The Bandung Moment and Its Political Afterlives* (Athens, OH: Ohio University Press, 2010); Antonia Finnane & Derek McDougall (eds), *Bandung 1955: Little Histories* (Caulfield: Monash University Press, 2010); Luis Eslava, Michael Fakhri & Vasuki Nesiah (eds), *Bandung, Global History, and International Law: Critical Pasts and Pending Futures* (Cambridge: Cambridge University Press, 2017).
2. Su Lin Lewis & Carolien Stolte, 'Other Bandungs: Afro-Asian Internationalisms in the Early Cold War', *Journal of World History* 30, no. 2 (2019): 1–19; Afro-Asian Networks Research Collective, 'Manifesto: Networks of Decolonisation in Asia and Africa', *Radical History Review* 131 (May 2018): 176–82. For a data visualization of these conferences and their attendees, see https://afroasiannetworks.com/visualisation/
3. Kyaw Zaw Win, 'The 1953 Asian Socialist Conference in Rangoon: Precursor to the Bandung Conference', in *Bandung 1955: Little Histories,* ed. Antonia Finnane & Derek McDougall (Caulfield: Monash University Press, 2010).
4. Exceptions include Tobias Wofford, 'Diasporic Returns in the Jet Age: The First World Festival of Negro Arts and the Promise of Air Travel', *Interventions* 20, no. 7 (2018): 952–94 and Martin Mahony's chapter in this volume.
5. Naoko Shimazu, 'Diplomacy as Theatre: Staging the Bandung Conference of 1955', *Modern Asian Studies* 48, no. 1 (2014): 225–52.

6   Stephen Legg, 'Political Lives at Sea: Working and Socialising to and from the India Round Table Conference in London, 1930–1932', *Journal of Historical Geography* 68 (April 2020), 21–32.
7   Dipesh Chakrabarty, *Provincializing Europe: Postcolonial Thought and Historical Difference* (Princeton, NJ: Princeton University Press, 2008), 8.
8   Su Lin Lewis, *Cities in Motion: Urban Life and Cosmopolitanism in Southeast Asia* (Cambridge: Cambridge University Press, 2016), 45.
9   Yoav Di-Capua, 'Common Skies Divided Horizons: Aviation, Class and Modernity in Early Twentieth Century Egypt', *Journal of Social History* 41, no. 4 (2008): 917–42, 918.
10 Ben R. Guttery, *Encyclopedia of African Airlines* (Jefferson: McFarland & Co., 1998), 52.
11 On technological competition in the post-war period, see Marc Dierikx, *Clipping the Clouds: How Air Travel Changed the World* (Westport: Praeger, 2008), 35–71, and Jenifer van Vleck, *Empire of the Air: Aviation and the American Ascendency* (Cambridge, MA: Harvard University Press, 2013).
12 T. A. Heppenheimer, *Turbulent Skies: The History of Commercial Aviation* (New York: Wiley, 1995).
13 Pramoedya Ananta Toer, *The Mute's Soliloquy: A Memoir*, trans. Willem Samuels (New York: Penguin, 1999), 263. According to the itinerary of this route, this would have been a Tupolev Tu-104, one of the world's first twinjet airliners, which replaced Ilyushin aircraft.
14 See Penny M. von Eschen, *Race Against Empire: Black Americans and Anticolonialism 1937-1957* (Ithaca, NY: Cornell University Press, 1997); Naima Prevots, *Dance for Export: Cultural Diplomacy and the Cold War* (Middletown, CT: Wesleyan University Press, 2012); Odd Arne Westad, *The Global Cold War: Third World Interventions and the Making of Our Times* (Cambridge: Cambridge University Press, 2005); Hugh Wilford, *The Mighty Wurlitzer: How the CIA Played America* (Cambridge, MA: Harvard University Press, 2009); Penny M. von Eschen, *Satchmo Blows Up the World: Jazz Ambassadors Play the Cold War* (Cambridge, MA: Harvard University Press, 2009); Jeremy Friedman, *Shadow Cold War: The Sino-Soviet Competition for the Third World* (Chapel Hill, NC: University of North Carolina Press, 2015); Jason C. Parker, *Hearts, Minds, Voices: US Cold War Public Diplomacy and the Formation of the Third World* (Oxford: Oxford University Press, 2016); Gregg A. Brazinsky, *Winning the Third World: Sino-American Rivalry during the Cold War* (Chapel Hill, NC: The University of North Carolina Press, 2017).
15 On Bandung as a development project, see Frank Gerits, 'Bandung as the Call for a Better Development Project: US, British, French and Gold Coast Perceptions of the Afro-Asian Conference (1955)', *Cold War History* 16, no. 3 (2016): 255–72.
16 On summits, see David Reynolds, *Summits: Six Meetings that Shaped the Twentieth Century* (London: Allen Lane, 2010) and Chris Tudda, *Cold War Summits: A History, From Potsdam to Malta* (London: Bloomsbury, 2015). I thank the editors for contributing this point.
17 Ali Sastroamidjojo, *Milestones on My Journey: The Memoirs of Ali Sastroamijoyo, Indonesian Patriot and Political Leader*, ed. C. L. M. Penders (St. Lucia: University of Queensland Press, 1979), 134–5.
18 Sastroamidjojo, *Milestones on My Journey*, 134–5.
19 Rudolf Mrázek, *Sjahrir: Politics and Exile in Indonesia* (Ithaca, NY: SEAP Publications, 1994), 335.

20 Sastroamidjojo, *Milestones on My Journey*, 135.
21 On the ASC, see Kyaw Zaw Win, 'The 1953 Asian Socialist Conference in Rangoon'; Su Lin Lewis, 'Asian Socialism and the Forgotten Architects of Post-Colonial Freedom, 1952–1956', *Journal of World History* 30, nos 1–2 (2019): 55–88.
22 'Bandung Talks: Col. Nasser Will Fly with Premier', *Times of India*, 20 March 1955.
23 Carolien Stolte, '"The People's Bandung": Local Anti-imperialists on an Afro-Asian Stage', *Journal of World History* 30, nos 1–2 (2019): 125–56.
24 Om Prakash Paliwal, *Rameshwari Nehru: Patriot and Internationalist* (New Delhi: National Book Trust, 1986).
25 Stolte features this photo in her post 'The "Other" Bandung', *Afro-Asian Visions*, 25 May 2016 < https://medium.com/afro-asian-visions/the-other-bandung-6b3dcc8e6762>.
26 Stolte, 'The People's Bandung', 128.
27 Stolte, 'The People's Bandung', 153.
28 'Rangoon Celebrates Premiers' Thingyan', *The Burman*, 19 April 1955.
29 Stephen Legg, '"Political Atmospherics": The India Round Table Conference's Atmospheric Environments, Bodies and Representations, London 1930-1932', *Annals of the American Association of Geographers* 110, no. 3 (2020): 774–92.
30 See Steve Tsang, 'Target Zhou Enlai: The "Kashmir Princess" Incident of 1955', *The China Quarterly* 139 (1994): 766–82; A. K. Mitra, *Disaster in the Air: The Crash of the Kashmir Princess, 1955* (New Delhi: Reliance Publishing House, 2001).
31 C. S. Jha, *From Bandung to Tashkent: Glimpses of India's Foreign Policy* (London: Sangam, 1983), 64.
32 Tsang, 'Target Zhou Enlai'.
33 Tsang, 'Target Zhou Enlai'.
34 See David Kimche, *The Afro-Asian Movement: Ideology and Foreign Policy of the Third World* (Jerusalem: Israel Universities Press, 1973), 18; Sally Percival Wood, '"Chou Gags Critics in Bandoeng" or How the Media Framed Premier Zhou Enlai at the Bandung Conference, 1955', *Modern Asian Studies* 44, no. 5 (2010): 1001–27.
35 George McTurnan Kahin, *The Asian-African Conference, Bandung, Indonesia, April 1955* (Port Washington: Kennikat, 1972), 39.
36 'CODEL Powell – Trip of Representative Adam Clayton Powell', 1 April 1955, RG 84 US Embassy Indonesia 1950-1955 Box 74, NARA.
37 For a deconstruction of Wright's text and Indonesian responses, see Brian Russell Roberts & Keith Foulcher (eds), *Indonesian Notebook: A Sourcebook on Richard Wright and the Bandung Conference* (Durham, NC: Duke University Press, 2016).
38 Richard Wright, *The Colour Curtain: A Report on the Bandung Conference* (London: Dobson, 1956).
39 Wright, *Colour Curtain*, 488; Kahin, 12, 82. G. H. Jansen explores the way the Palestine question was discussed at Bandung and the friction between Asian and Arab delegates in more detail in *Afro-Asian and Non-Alignment* (London: Faber, 1966), 200–1.
40 Wright, *Colour Curtain*, 492. On Japan's role at Bandung, see Kweku Ampiah, *The Political and Moral Imperatives of the Bandung Conference of 1955: The Reactions of the US, UK and Japan* (Folkestone: Global Oriental, 2007).
41 See Roland Burke, 'Emotional Diplomacy and Human Rights at the United Nations', *Human Rights Quarterly* 39, no. 2 (2017): 273–95; Rachel Leow, 'A Missing Peace: The Asia-Pacific Peace Conference in 1952 and the Emotional Making of Third World Internationalism', *Journal of World History* 30, nos 1–2 (2019): 21–53, 51.

42 See Gerits, 'Bandung as the Call for a Better Development Project', 262.
43 Carolien Stolte, 'Grounded: On Not Traveling in the Afro-Asian Era', *Afro-Asian Visions*, 26 March 2019 <https://medium.com/afro-asian-visions/grounded-on-not-travelling-in-the-bandung-era-83b3031ed809>.
44 'Statement of Partai Sosialis Indonesia: On the Failure to Convene the Conference Bureau Asian Socialists in Indonesia', in FO 371/11928 Reports on Meetings of the Asian Socialist Conference, TNA.
45 Lewis, 'Asian Socialism', 80.
46 Alijah Gordon, *On Becoming Alijah* (Kuala Lumpur: Alijah Gordon, 2003), 265.
47 Gordon, *On Becoming Alijah*, 267.
48 Siman'gèin hnín Bandāyèi Wungyì Htānā/ Naingngainlòun hsain'yā kawmiti gabá nyèin'gyàn'yèi kun'garet (bamā naingngan) hnín pat'thet'thàw sāywet-sādàn-myà [Ministry of Planning and Accounts, Documents related to the World Peace Congress (Nation-wide committee, Burma)], National Archives, Yangon 11/8 (27).
49 See Leow, 'A Missing Peace', 51.
50 Nathan J. Citino, *Envisioning the Arab Future: Modernization in US-Arab Relations, 1945–1967* (Cambridge: Cambridge University Press, 2017), 20.
51 Citino, *Envisioning the Arab Future*, 29.
52 Katō Shūichi, *A Sheep's Song: A Writer's Reminiscences of Japan and the World* (Berkeley: University of California Press, 1999), 380.
53 Katō, *Sheep's Song*, 381.
54 Shridharani, 'Pisateli stran Azii I Afriki v Tashkente', quoted in Rossen Djagalov, *From Internationalism to Postcolonialism: Literature and Cinema between the Second and the Third World*, (Montreal: McGill-Queens University Press, 2020), 70.
55 Djagalov, *From Internationalism to Postcolonialism*, 72.
56 Katō, *Sheep's Song*, 388.
57 Pramoedya, *Mute's Soliloquy*, 260.
58 Pramoedya, *Mute's Soliloquy*, 262.
59 Shirley Graham Du Bois, *His Day Is Marching On: A Memoir of W. E. B. Du Bois* (Philadelphia: Lippincott, 1971), 239.
60 Mark D. Higbee, 'A Letter from W. E. B. Du Bois to His Daughter Yolande, Dated "Moscow, December 10, 1958" Introduction and Footnotes', *The Journal of Negro History* 78, no. 3 (1993): 188–95, 190.
61 Katō, *Sheep's Song*, 380–1.
62 Pramoedya, *Mute's Soliloquy*, 267.
63 Pramoedya, *Mute's Soliloquy*, 269.
64 Pramoedya, *Mute's Soliloquy*, 270.
65 Tsitsi Jaji, '"The Next Best Thing to Being There": Covering the 1966 Dakar Festival and Its Legacy in Black Popular Magazines', in *The First World Festival of Negro Arts, Dakar 1966*, ed. David Murphy (Liverpool: Liverpool University Press, 2016), 113–29.
66 'Opening address given by Sukarno (Bandung, 18 April 1955)', *Asia-Africa Speak from Bandung* (Djakarta: The Ministry of Foreign Affairs, Republic of Indonesia, 1955), 19–29.
67 Adam M. McKeown, *Melancholy Order: Asian Migration and the Globalization of Borders* (New York: Columbia University Press, 2008); Valeska Huber, *Channelling Mobilities: Migration and Globalisation in the Suez Canal Region and Beyond, 1869-1914* (Cambridge: Cambridge University Press, 2013).

Index

A Wreath for Udomo (Abrahams) 225, 230
Aachen, Germany
    Congress of (1818) 45
abolition of the slave trade and
    slavery 40, 42–6
Abrahams, Peter (1919-2017) 8, 218,
    220, 223–5, 227, 229–30, *see also*
    A Wreath for Udomo
Ab'Saber, Aziz (1924-2012) 120
Accra, Ghana
    All-African People's Congress
    (1958) 217, 224, 234
Adams, Robert (1902-1965) 227
Adi, Hakim 25, 219
Aeroflot 236
Afghanistan 203, 207–8, 214 n.43
Africa 3, 43, 70–4, 78–80, 150–2,
    217–26, 235–41
    East 98
    North 42
    West 217, 219, 222–3, 226, 229
Afro-Asian cooperation 29, 234, 241–8
Ahlmann, Hans Wilhelmsson
    (1889-1974) 127–8
Ahmad, Nafis (1912-1982) 128
Air India 235–6, 238, 240, 243, 246
airships 5, 7, 87–100
airspace 88–9
air travel 234–51
al-Azm, Khalid (1903-1965) 244
Algadri, Hamid (1912-1998) 242–3
Algiers 22
Ali, Surat (aka Alley, Surat) 222
All Asia Association (Tokyo) 202–3, 206, 208
Alpert, Leo (1915-1998) 125
ambassadorial conferences 41–3, 50
Anglo-Japanese Alliance 202
anti-colonialism 13, 19, 25–9, 137,
    151–4, 178, 202, 216–24, 229–30
anti-Semitism 50, 111, 165, 221
Appiah, Joseph (1918-1990) 226

art, and conferences 7–8, 57, 105, 147
Ashwood Garvey, Amy (1897-1969)
    221–2
Asia 3, 6, 26–7, 97, 150, 178–80, 188–90,
    235–6, 241, 243–7
    Central 245–6
    East 199–211
    Southeast 220
Asian internationalism 6, 29, 200–1,
    203, 205, 209–11
Asianism 6, 201–3, 207, 209–12 n.10
Asian League (of Nations) 199–201,
    203–6
Asian Monroe Doctrine 201
Asian Relations Conference 26
Atlantic Charter 211, 217, 219
atmospheres, at conference 88–99, 112,
    118, 121–9, 145–9, 162–71, 190,
    239, 243
Attlee, Clement (1883-1967) 227, 229
Atwood, Wallace W. Jnr. (1907-1992) 128
Australia 90, 93
Austria 40
aviation 87–91, 93, 96, 235, 238, 243
Awolowo, Obafemi (1909-1987) 221
Awooner-Renner, Bankole
    (1898-1970) 223–4
Azikiwe, Nnamdi (1904-1996) 221, 223

Baghdad, Iraq 240–1
Balfour Declaration (1917) 23, 90, 98
Banda, Hastings (c1898-1997) 73–4,
    76–7, 79, 221
Bandung
    Afro-Asia Conference (1955) 6–7,
    26–30, 73, 190, 211, 217, 235–48
    spirit 28, 246
Bangkok, Thailand 20, 240–1, 244, 246–7
Beijing, China 26–7, 203, 208, 241, 243
    Asia-Pacific Peace Conference
    (1952) 27, 241, 243
Belgium 43, 47, 138, 142

Bennett(-Coverley), Louise
(1919-2006)   8, 224–5, 227
Berlin, Germany   14, 17
   Congress of (1884)   17, 216
   East (DDR)   80
   Preussische Staatsbibliothek   109
Black internationalism   217, 224
Bloch, Adolpho (1908-1995)   122
Bocanegra, Gertrudis (1765-1817)   58
Bolivia   55
Bombay (Mumbai), India
   Asian Socialist Conference
   (1956)   27–8, 242–3, 245
Bonnet, Henri (1888-1978)   106, 111
Bose, Rash Bihari (1886-1945)   204–5, 208
Bose, Subhas Chandra (1897-1945)   210
Braithwaite, Lloyd (1919–1995)   225, 228
Brazil   119–24, 129
   Bahia   119
Bretton Woods, NH, USA
   United Nations Monetary and
   Financial Conference (1944)   6–7, 154, 161–73
Britain   43–7, 72, 88–9, 92, 95–6, 170–1, 188, 224–6
British Commonwealth, *see*
   Commonwealth of Nations
British Empire   5, 22–3, 71, 80, 90–1, 211, 216–21, 226
   dominions   5, 23–4, 89–90, 93–4, 96, 98, 99, 201
   Statute of Westminster   98
British imperialism   221
British Overseas Airways Corporation
   (BOAC)   235
Bruce, Stanley (1883-1967)   93–5
Brussels, Belgium   20, 46, 178
Burma (Myanmar)   189, 210, 219, 237–9, 241, 246–7, *see also* Rangoon
   Workers and Peasants Party   243
Burney, Charles Dennistoun
   (1875-1930)   89, 95
Busch, German (1903-1939)   56

Cailleux, Andre (1907-1986)   124
Cairo, Egypt   26, 234, 238, 240, 244
   Afro-Asian People's Conference
   (1957)   234, 238–9, 244

Calcutta, India   240–1, 244
Câmara, Jaime de Barros (1894-1971)   124
camaraderie   5, 8, 118, 125, 130–1, 239
Cambridge, University of   80, 172
Canada   23, 46, 89–90, 98, 180–1
Cárdenas, Lázaro (1895-1970)   56–61
Cardington, UK   89, 92, 94–6, 99
Carter, Edward (1878-1954)   179–83, 185–6, 188
Castlereagh, Robert Stewart
   (1769-1822)   40, 42–3
Catholic Church   13, 62, 154, 163
Catholicism   111, 146–9
Central African Federation   72–3
Cerda, Pedro Aguirre (1879-1941)   60–1
Chiang Kai-shek (1887-1975)   208, 240
Chile   60–5
China   25–7, 80, 118, 130, 170–8, 181–91, 200–10, 235–6, 240
   Chinese-Japanese relations   208–10
   Chinese Nationalist Party
   (Guomindang)   203
Churchill, Winston Spencer
   (1874-1965)   186, 227
CIA, *see* United States of America, Central
   Intelligence Agency (CIA)
civil society   39, 42, 44, 49–50, 105, 207–10
Clacton-on-Sea, UK
   Fabian Colonial Bureau Conference
   (1946)   6, 8, 216, 224–5, 227–30
Cobham, Alan (1894-1973)   90
Cold War   5–6, 27–9, 118, 123–8, 130–1, 178, 234–6, 248
Cole, Monica (1922-1994)   124
Colima, César   56–64
collective security   139, 141, 147, 154, 186
Colmore, R. B. (1887-1930)   99
Colombia   61
Colombo
   Afro-Asian Women's Conference
   (1958)   26, 234
Colombo, Sri Lanka   26, 234
Colonial and Coloured People's
   Association of Cardiff   221
colonial and imperial conferences   23–4
colonial development   216, 227

Commonwealth Heads of Government
    Meetings 24, 27
Commonwealth of Nations 23–4, 77, 87,
    89, 95, 216–17, 226, 230
communist
    Cold War blocs 27, 178
    delegates at conference 127, 129–30,
        191, 244
    internationalism 25, 147, 188
    rhetoric 142–4
Communist Party
    of Great Britain 80, 223
    of USA 241
Concert of Europe 16, 41, 43
Condliffe, John (1891-1981) 182, 186,
    191
conference staff (secretaries, typists,
        etc) 21, 96, 106, 160–6, 171, 181,
        189, 220
Congo 50, 191
Congress of Industrial Unions 221
Coñuepán, Venancio (1905-1968) 56–64
Corrêa Filho, Virgílio (1887-1973) 125
Council on African Affairs (CAA)
    219–20
    Africa-New Perspectives (*see*
        New York, Conference on Africa-
        New Perspectives (1944))
Creech Jones, Arthur (1891-1964)
    225–7, 230
Critchlow, Hubert (1884-1958) 219–20
Croydon, UK 96
Cuba 129
Cunard, Nancy (1896-1965) 226
Curie, Marie (1867-1934) 111
Czechoslovakia 138

Dalian, China (Port Arthur)
    Pan-Asian Conference (1934)
        209–10
Davies, Hezekiah Oladipo
    (1905-1989) 226
Davitaia, Feofan (1911-1979) 125
Deakin, John (1912-1972) 8, 221–2
decolonization 3, 5–7, 25–8, 70–81, 217,
    234–7, 239–41, 246
Delhi, India 3, 26–7, 235–7, 244–6
    Asian Relations Conference
        (1947) 26, 189, 234, 237

Denmark 47
Deutsche Kongress-Zentrale 108
Di-Capua, Yoav 235
Djagalov, Rossen 245
Douglas DC-3 airliner 235, 237
Drake, St Clair (1911-1990) 220–1, 224
Drummond, Eric (1876-1951) 4, 21,
    137
Du Bois, William Edward Burghardt
    (1868-1963) 218–21, 223, 241,
    246
du Chateau, Mies 238

Edinburgh, UK 123
Egypt 27, 47, 98–9, 118, 171, 235, 237–9,
    242
    Misr Airwork 235
Einstein, Albert (1879-1955) 109, 111
emotions 8, 169, 188
entomology 95
Escalante, José Angel (1883-1965) 57
Esperanto 207
espionage 71–2, 75–6, 80, 193 n.13
Ethiopia 126
Euro-America 205, 207

Fabian Colonial Bureau (FCB) 6, 216,
    225, 227, 229
    Conference on the Relationship
        between the British and Colonial
        Peoples, Clacton-on-Sea (1946)
fatigue and exhaustion 169, 229–30,
    246
federalism 23, 72–3, 98, 180, 217–21,
    223–4, 226, 229–30
Federation of Indian Associations of Great
    Britain 219, 221–2
First World War 2–3, 18, 25, 41, 72, 105,
    151, 201
food and drink 4, 8, 13, 99, 129, 161,
    165, 172, 206, 220–1
forestry 95
Forster, Edward Morgan (1879-
    1970) 112
France 42–50, 71–2, 108, 144, 188–9
    overseas empire 201
Francis I, of France (1494-1547) 13
Frankfurt, Germany 46
Friends of African Freedom 221

Gandhi, Indira (1917-1984)   238
Garuda Indonesia Airways   235, 240, 243
Garvey, Amy Ashwood, *see* Ashwood
  Garvey, Amy
Garvey, Amy Jacques (1895-1973)   219
Garvey, Marcus (1887-1940)   25, 220
Geneva, Switzerland   20–2, 87, 138, 218
geopolitics   118–31
Germany   11, 22, 50, 110–11, 186
  Federal Republic of Germany
    (FDR)   130
  German Democratic Republic
    (DDR)   126–7
  Greater   47
  Nazi   5, 108, 150
Getachew, Adom   217
Ghana, *see* Gold Coast
Global South   26–9, 61, 235–6, 248
Goffman, Erving (1922-1982)
  front and back regions   182, 187
  presentation of self   179, 187
Gold Coast (Ghana)   224, 226, 241
Gordon, Alijah   242
Gourou, Pierre (1900-1999)   178–85,
  187–9, 191–2
Goveia, Elsa (1925-1980)   225
Great Alliance of Asian Peoples (Beijing)
  203–4, 208
Greater East Asia Co-Prosperity
  Sphere   210
Griffiths, Thomas, *see* Makonnen, T. Ras
Guatemala   55
Gundermann, Hans   63

Haber, Fritz (1868-1934)   109
Habsburg, Empire   47
Hague Peace Conferences   18
Hall, George (1881-1965)   227
Hawai'i, USA   167, 180, 208
Heidelberg, University of   46
Henri II (of France) (1519-1559)   126
Herriot, Edouard (1872-1957)   112
Hidalgo, Manuel (1878-1967)   60
Hill, Ken (1909-1979)   219
Hinden, Rita (1909-1971)   225–30
Hoare, Samuel (1880-1959)   90–3, 99, 100
Hodges, Charles (1895-1964)   199–200, 203
Holland, William (1907-2008)   179–81,
  183–92

Honolulu, Hawai'i   180–1, 186, 240, 243
Horrabin, J. F. (1884-1962)   225
hotels   60, 75–6, 106, 161–71, 173, 181,
  184, 186, 188, 190, 236, 246–7
Hot Springs, VA, USA
  Institute of Pacific Relations
    Conference (1945)   178, 183–7,
    189
Howden, UK   89
Huang Gongsu   204–5, 208
Huizinga, Johan (1872-1945)   104, 107,
  112–13
Humanitarianism   50, 111, 147, 153
Hungary   47, 126, 243
Hunton Jr, William Alphaeus
  (1903-1970)   219
Hyderabad, India   241

Ibáñez del Campo, Carlos (1877-1960)   63
Iceland   126
Illyushin   235, 249 n.13
Imazato Juntarō   202–3, 205, 208
imperial internationalism   23, 87, 91
imperialism   7, 19, 22–4, 88–90, 224,
  226–9
  and the future   100
  anti-   6, 25–9
  Western   186, 189, 241
  'Yankee'   64
Independent Labour Party (UK)   221–2
  see also Labour Party
India   21–2, 89–90, 98–100, 142, 170–2,
  180–1, 189–90, 201–4, 208–10, 219,
  235–8, 243–6
  British   15
  Government of   23
  and Imperial Conferences   24–5
  Praja Socialist Party   242
  'Sepoy Mutiny', 1857   23
indigeneity   55–65
Indonesia   73, 181, 188–90, 201, 235,
  237–8, 241, 243, 245–7
Institute of Pacific Relations
  International Secretariat   181–2
  national councils   185, 187, 190–1
International Geographical Union   118
International Organisations and NGOs
  General   15, 21–2, 50, 109, 137,
    180–5, 234

Index 257

international relations 1, 12–14, 19–21, 39–46, 182
Israel 241–3
Italy 47, 90, 111
  Fascist 109, 150
  Renaissance 13

Jaji, Tsitsi 247
Jakarta, Indonesia 239–41, 246–7
Japan 6, 22, 124, 151, 178–92, 199–211, 241
  imperialism 199–212
  Japanese-Chinese relations, see China, Chinese-Japanese relations
Java, Indonesia 238–9
Jewish
  discrimination against, see anti-Semitism
Jha, Chandra Shekhar 240
Jiang Jieshi, see Chiang Kai-shek
Jiraudo, Laura 56
Jogjakarta, Indonesia 237
Jolly, Jennifer 56, 59, 61
Jones, Arthur Creech, see Creech Jones, Arthur

Kabul, Afghanistan 209, 214 n.43
Karachi, Pakistan 238, 240–2
Kashmir Princess, air disaster 240, 243
Katō Shūichi (1919-2008) 244–6
Kaunda, Kenneth (1924-2021) 24, 79
Kenya 71–2, 74, 76–7, 80, 224
Kenyatta, Jomo (c.1897-1978) 79–80, 218, 220–1, 224–5, 227, 229–30
Kessler, Hans Graf (1868-1937) 109
Keynes, John Maynard (1883-1946) 163–4, 167–8, 172
Kiddle, Amelia Marie 60–1
Kikuyu Central Association 221
KLM, see Royal Dutch Airlines
Konoe Fumimaro (1891-1945) 210
Korean War 189, 243
Kouyaté, Tiemoko Garan (1902-1942) 218
Kruss, Hugo Andres (1879-1945) 109–12

Kubitschek, Juscelino (1902-1976) 121–2, 124, 129
Kyoto, Japan 3
  Institute of Pacific Relations Conference (1954) 178, 183, 190–1

Labbé, Edmond (1868-1944) 106–7, 138, 217, 220, 225–9
Labour Party (UK) 89, 217, 220, 225–30, see also Independent Labour Party
Lacerda, Carlos (1914-1977) 122
language 15, 21, 62, 119, 129–30, 152, 170–1, 207–10
La Paz, Bolivia 56
Laski, Harold (1893-1950) 226
Lattimore, Owen (1900-1989) 180, 188, 193 n.13
Laurel, José P. (1891-1959) 211
League Against Imperialism 25
League of Coloured People (LCP) 218–19, 226–7
League of Nations 2–6, 12, 18–19, 21–3, 25, 87, 95, 104–13, 137–55, 180–2, 199–201, 203–5, 208–11
  imperialism of 151–3
  International Committee on Intellectual Co-operation 55, 104–13
  International Labour Office 55
  League of Nations Non-Partisan Association 199
Lebanon 242–3
Legg, Stephen 234
Leow, Rachel 27, 244
Lévy, Roger (1914-2006) 181–2
Lewis, W. Arthur 225, 227
Lima, Peru 243
  International Conference of American States (1938) 55
Little, Kenneth (1908-1991) 225
Li Zhaofu (1887-1950) 213 n.19
Lloyd, Geoffrey (1902-1984) 91
London, UK 7, 14, 20, 23–4, 41–7, 70–81, 90, 94–5, 218–21, 223, 225, 227–8
  African Conference, Lancaster House (1948) 230
  African Conference of Governors (1947–8) 216

Index

All Colonial People's Conferences (1945) (Subject Peoples' Conferences) 219–20, 224
Chatham House (RIIA) 181, 187
Colonial Conference (1887) 23
Conference of Empire Meteorologists (1929) 5, 96–8
Downing Street (Prime Minister's residence) 90, 98
First Pan-African Congress (1900) 50, 217
Great Exhibition (1851) 22, 50
Imperial Conference (1926) 5, 90–6
Imperial Conference (1930) 5, 23, 87, 98–100
Kingsway (Air Ministry) 89, 91–6, 99
Lancaster House 70–81, 230
Round Table Conferences (1930-2) 24, 71, 216, 234
School of Economics (LSE) 172
World Trade Unions Congress, London & Paris (1945) 219–21, 230
Lucknow, India
Institute of Pacific Relations Conference (1950) 3, 178–9, 183–5, 188–91

Macleod, Iain (1913-1970) 71–4, 77–8
MacLeod, Roy 96
Macmillan, Harold (1894-1986) 71, 73–4
McNair, John (1887-1968) 221
Madrid, Spain 109, 240
Makonnen, T. Ras (1909-1983) 218, 220–1, 223–4
Malaya 71, 77, 97, 189, 235
Manchester, UK 3, 6, 8, 25, 216–24, 227, 229–30, 243
Chorlton-on-Medlock Town Hall 8, 220
The Cosmopolitan 220
Ethiopian Teashop 220
Fifth Pan-African Congress (1945) 6, 8, 25, 216–24, 227, 229–30
Manchuria/Manchukuo 137, 151, 178, 201, 208–10
mandates 151–3, 201
Mann, Thomas (1875-1955) 108
Mao Zedong (1893-1976) 208
map 26–7, 56, 140, 151, 199, 223, 236

Mapuche 56–64
Araucanian Corporation 56
media management 167–8
Meiji Restoration (1868) 201
Mendes-France, Pierre (1907-1982) 170
methodology
methodological nationalism 217
Metternich, Klemens von (1773-1859) 40, 42
Mexico 5, 25, 55–65
1910–20 Revolution 56
Hidalgo 58
Michoacán 57
Mexico City, Mexico 57, 61, 65
Milliard, Peter (1882-c.1953) 218, 221
Millward, Liz 88
Monbeig, Pierre (1908-1987) 123–4
Moody, Harold (1882-1947) 218–19, 226
Moon, Henry Lee (1901-1985) 221
Morelos, Jose Maria (1765-1815) 57
Morgenthau, Henry (1891-1967) 163, 165, 167–9, 171–2
Moscow, Russia 171, 186, 236, 243, 246
Mozelle, Aaron (aka Moselle, Aaron) 221
Munro, John 218
Murray, Gilbert (1866-1957) 106, 112
mycology 95

Nagasaki, Japan 3, 186, 200, 203–7, 209
First Conference of the Asian Peoples (1926) 6, 199–200, 209–11
Nanjing, China 208–10
Nasser, Gamal Abdel (1918-1970) 238–9, 241
National Association for the Advancement of Coloured People (NAACP) 219, 221
nationalism 16
Nazi Party 108, 110, 139, 150, 187
Nehru, Jawaharlal (1889-1964) 25, 27, 189–90, 238–9, 245–6
Nehru, Rameshwari (1886-1966) 238
neutralism 234
New Delhi, *see* Delhi
Newspapers/Magazines 11, 56, 60, 64, 91, 94–5, 121–9, 204–9, 223, 239
Chicago Defender (USA) 223
Daily Herald (UK) 222

Diário Carioca (Brazil)   122
Diário de Notícias (Brazil)   122
Die Welt (Germany)   242
El Comercio (Bolivia)   57, 60
Empire (UK)   225
The Guardian (UK)   209, 222
Imprensa Popular (Brazil)   122
Jornal do Brasil (Brazil)   122
League of Nations News (Switzerland)   199–200, 203, 209
Manchete (Brazil)   119, 125, 127
O Correio da Manhã (Brazil)   122, 129
O Globo (Brazil)   122, 129
O Jornal (Brazil)   122
The New African (UK)   223
The New Leader (USA)   222
The New York Times (USA)   59, 112, 171
A Noite (Brazil)   122, 128
Pan-Africa: Journal of African Life and Thought (UK)   223
Picture Post (UK)   221–2
Pittsburgh Courier (USA)   219, 223
Revista da Semana (Brazil)   122
Socialist Leader (UK)   222–3
The Spectator (UK)   92
The Times (UK)   73, 92
Tribuna da Imprensa (Brazil)   122, 129
West African Pilot (Nigeria)   223
Xiandai Pinglun (China)   207
New Year Water Festival (Burma), *see* Thingyan
New York, NY, USA   3, 167, 181, 246
   Conference on Africa-New Perspectives (1944)   219–21
   Council on Foreign Relations   181
   League of Nations Non-Partisan Association   199
   World's Fair (1939)   6, 138, 144–54
New Zealand   23, 93, 182, 186
Ngũgĩ wa Thiong'o   245
Nicolson, Harold (1886-1968)   1, 11, 13
Nigeria   71, 219, 221, 226
Nkrumah, Kwame (1909-1972)   75, 217, 220–5, 227–30, 241
non-aligned movement   25, 27–8, 234, 239

Northern Rhodesia   72, 75, 78–9
Nyasaland   71–4, 76–9
Nyerere, Julius (1922-1999)   68 n.38, 77–8

Odinga, Oginga (1911-1994)   76, 80
Ottawa, Canada   90
Oxford, University of   170, 172

Padmore, George (1903-1959)   218–20, 223–7, 229–30
Painemal, Martin   63
Pakistan   24, 128, 181, 189, 242
Pan-African Conferences, *see* London, First Pan-African Congress (1900); Manchester, Fifth Pan-African Congress (1945)
Pan-African Federation (PAF)   6, 218–20, 222–4, 227, 229
pan-Africanism   224
   Pan-Africa: Journal of African Life and Thought   223
Pan American Airways   243
pan-Asianism, *see* Asianism
Paris, France   20, 25, 42, 45–50, 72, 90, 178, 218–19, 240
   Bois de Vincennes   22
   Centre d'études de politique etrangere   181
   Conference permanente des Hautes Etudes internationales   105–6
   Eiffel Tower   104
   Hotel de Ville   110
   International Institute of Intellectual Cooperation   106–8
   Louvre   106
   Month of Intellectual Cooperation (1937)   5–6, 104–13, 137–55
   Musee d'Art Contemporain   105
   Palais Royal   106
   Paris Peace Conferences (1919–20) (Versailles)   1–4, 11–12, 14, 17–19, 28, 30, 151, 160, 201
   Peace of (1856)   43
   World Congress of Universal Documentation   105, 111
   World Exposition (1889)   50
   World Exposition (1931)   22–3

World Exposition (1937)   104, 138–44
World Trade Unions Congress, London & Paris (1945)   219–21, 230
partnership, colonial   6, 216, 222, 226, 229
Patnaik, Biju (1916-1997)   238
Pátzcuaro, Mexico   55–65
   Caltzontzin Theatre   57
   First Inter-American Indigenista Congress (1940)   55–65
   Tanganxuan II Monument   58
peace movement   27, 46, 48–50, 142, 144, 238
Peru   55, 60–1
Philippines   181, 188–90, 201, 210–11
Pizer, Dorothy (c.1906-1964)   226
Port Arthur, *see* Dalian
Powell, Adam Clayton, Jr (1908-1972)   240
Prague, Czechia   47, 199
Pramoedya Ananta Toer (1925-2006)   235, 245–7
Pratap, Mehandra (1886-1979)   203–4, 207–10
proletarian internationalism   19, 25, 142, 144

Qantas   246
Quetelet, Adolphe (1796-1874)   47, 49
Quiroga, Vasco de (1470-1565)   57

race   25, 42, 62–5, 118, 153, 199–202, 205, 209, 220, 225, 228–9
   racial difference   23, 46, 58, 64
   racial discrimination   153, 201, 203, 205–6, 208, 228–30
   'whites'   62, 200, 202, 204–5, 210
Rangoon (Yangon), Myanmar   237–40, 244, 246–7
   First Asian Socialist Conference (1953)   27, 234, 238, 241, 243
Reynold, Gonzague de (1880-1970)   109–11
Ribeiro, Orlando (1911-1997)   123
Rio de Janeiro, Brazil   118–31
   Brazilian Equestrian Society   129–30
   Brazilian Hippodrome   129
   Brazilian Institute of Geography and Statistics   123
   Brazilian Naval School (Villegaignon Island)   118, 126
   Guanabara Bay   126
   International Geographical Congress (1956)   118–31
   Nossa Senhora do Monte do Carmo Church   124
   Paqueta Island   129
Robeson, Eslanda (1895-1965)   219
Robeson, Paul (1898-1976)   219, 241
Rocco, Alfredo (1875-1935)   109
Rome, Italy   43, 240
Roosevelt, Franklin Delano (1882-1945)   58, 63, 163–4, 167, 169
Royal Air Force (RAF)   89
Royal Dutch Airlines (KLM)   235, 238, 240, 247
Russo-Japanese War (1904/05)   200

Sakamoto Masaka   124
Saleh, Poppy   238
San Francisco, CA, USA
   United Nations Conference on International Organization (1945)   154, 218–19
San Juan Teotihuacán, Mexico   58
Santiago, Chile   60
   Library of National Congress   62
Santos, Milton (1926-2001)   119
Sartre, Jean-Paul (1905-1980)   243
Sastroamijoyo, Ali (1903-1975)   237
Satow, Ernest (1843-1929)   1, 18, 22
Schoelvinck, Auguste (1909-1979)   104
self-determination   104, 153, 201, 208, 217, 219, 227, 229
Shanghai, China   3, 181, 203, 207–11
   Second Conference of the Asian Peoples (1927)   6, 200–2, 207–11
Shenandoah, USS   91, 95
Shotwell, James T (1874-1965)   112
Shridharani, Krishnalal (1911-1960)   245
Shute, Nevil (1899-1960)   99
Sierra Youth League   221
Simey, Thomas S. (1906-1969)   218–20, 223–5, 240–1
Simm, Thomas   99–100

Singapore   24, 201, 208, 237–8, 240, 246
Sjahrir, Sutan (1909-1966)   238
Sluga, Glenda   112
socialism   57, 111, 142–4, 146, 216–17, 223–9, 238, 241–3, 245
  socialist conferences   6, 27–8, 216, 224–9, 234, 238, 241–2
  socialist internationalism   13, 25, 217, 227
  socialist realism (art)   138–40, 142–3
Solé-Sabarís, Luis (1908-1985)   124
solidarity   4, 6, 25, 63, 141, 147, 210, 234, 237–9, 241–4, 246–8
Sorensen, Reginald (1891-1971)   226
South Africa   23–4, 97
Soviet Union, *see* Union of Soviet Socialist Republics
Spanner, Edward F. (1888-1953)   93–4
spectacle   93, 129, 139, 237, 247
Speer, Alfred (1905-1981)   104, 108
Stalin, Joseph (1878-1953)   144, 186
Stamp, Dudley (1898-1966)   126–8
Stein, Gertrude (1874-1946)   112
Stockholm, Sweden   124, 127–8
  Royal Swedish Academy of Sciences   128
Stolte, Carolien   28–9, 238, 241
Strasbourg, France   120
Stratford-upon-Avon, UK
  Institute of Pacific Relations Conference (1947)   178, 183, 187–8
subalternity   7, 56, 61, 64
Suez Crisis   118, 242
Sukarno (1901-1970)   234–5, 239–41, 246–7
Sun Yat-sen (1866-1925)   202–3, 210
Swanson, Heather Anne   89
Switzerland   47, 124

Tagore, Rabindranath (1861-1941)   202
Taiwan Straits Crisis   240
Talleyrand, Charles-Maurice de (1754-1838)   40, 43
Tanganyika (Tanzania)   74, 77–8
Tashkent, Uzbekistan   234–6, 244–7
  Afro-Asian Writers' Conference (1958)   234–5, 244, 247
Tata, Jehangir Ratanji Dadabhoy (1904-1993)   235

technology   4, 8, 15, 77–9, 92–3, 98, 100, 138
  telegraph   14, 20, 88
theatricality   7–8, 27, 29, 78
Thingyan (Burmese New Year Water Festival)   239
Thomson, Christopher (Lord) (1875-1930)   89, 99–100
Tilley, Helen   98
Tōjō Hideki (1884-1948)   210
Tokyo, Japan   199, 202–3, 206, 210–11, 241, 243–5
  Greater East Asia Conference (1943)   3, 6, 210–11
Tricart, Jean (1920-2003)   120
Troll, Carl (1899-1975)   124
Tsang, Steve   240

Uganda   72, 77–8, 80
Union of Soviet Socialist Republics   27, 104, 108, 124–9, 139–40, 143–4, 163, 170–1, 189–91, 235–6, 240–1, 243–5
  October Revolution   208
  Russia   16–17, 47, 127–8, 130, 139, 200, 226
U Nu (1907-1995)   238–9
United Kingdom, *see* Britain
United Malay National Organiation   238
United Nations   3, 6, 19, 154, 167–8, 218–19, 221, 240
  Monetary and Financial Conference, Bretton Woods (1944), *see* Bretton Woods
United States of America   121, 124–5, 127–9, 138, 144–51, 160, 164–7, 170–1, 189, 201–2, 211
  abolitionism   44–6
  Central Intelligence Agency (CIA)   240, 243
  hegemony   89, 160, 167
  imperialism   56, 64
  Indian New Deal   58, 63–4
  and the League of Nations   22, 145, 154, 180
  Supreme Court   246
Universal Negro Improvement Association   220

Valery, Paul (1871-1945)   107
Vargas, Getúlio (1882-1954)   121–2
Vergara, Jorge Iván   63
Verne, Jules (1828-1905)   95
Verona, Congress of (1822), Italy   41, 45
Versailles, France   110
  Treaty of   89
Vickers, UK company   89
Vicks, Brian   59
Vienna, Austria   123, 243
  Congress of Vienna (1815)   1, 16, 39–54
  International Telegraph Conference (1868)   15
  World Congress of People for Peace (1952)   243
Villegaignon, Nicolas Durand de (1510-1571)   126

Wallace-Johnson, Isaac Theophilus Akunna (1894-1965)   219–21
Wang Jingwei (1883-1944)   210
Warsaw, Poland   20
Washington DC, USA
  International Geographical Congress (1952)   123
Wellesley Cole, Robert (1907-1995)   227
Wells, Herbert George (1866-1946)   95
West Africa, *see* Africa, West
West African National Secretariat (WANS)   220, 222–4, 229
  The New African   223
West African Students' Union (WASU)   219–20, 223, 225–7
West African Youth League   221
West Indian Students' Union   227
Westphalia, Congress of   14
Wilder, Gary   217
Wilder, Thornton (1897-1975)   112
Wilson, Woodrow (1856-1924)   2, 105, 145
women
  campaigners   44, 46
  conference attendees   125, 221, 234, 236
  conference delegates   24, 45, 59
  conferences of   24, 26–7, 199, 234
  diplomatic staff   21
  exclusion from diplomatic meetings   44, 46
  groups   19
  organisations   22, 27, 221, 237
  traffic in   20
Women's International League   221
World Expositions
  New York (1939)   138, 144–50
  Paris (1889)   50
  Paris (1931)   22–3
  Paris (1937)   104, 138–44
World Federation of Trade Unions (WFTU)   219
Wright, Richard (1908-1960)   28, 240–1

Yalta Conference (1945)   154, 186
Yergan, Max (1892-1975)   219

Zhou Enlai (1898-1976)   239–40

www.ingramcontent.com/pod-product-compliance
Lightning Source LLC
Chambersburg PA
CBHW062123300426
44115CB00012BA/1791